MARTIN BUBER'S THE

NEW JEWISH PHILOSOPHY AND THOUGHT

Zachary J. Braiterman

MARTIN BUBER'S THEOPOLITICS

Samuel Hayim Brody

Indiana University Press

This book is a publication of

Indiana University Press
Office of Scholarly Publishing
Herman B Wells Library 350
1320 East 10th Street
Bloomington, Indiana 47405 USA

iupress.indiana.edu

The paper used in this publication meets the minimum
requirements of the American National Standard for Information
Sciences—Permanence of Paper for Printed Library Materials,
ANSI Z39.48-1992.

Manufactured in the United States of America

Library of Congress Cataloging-in-Publication Data

Names: Brody, Samuel Hayim, author.
Title: Martin Buber's theopolitics / Samuel Hayim Brody.
Description: Bloomington, Indiana : Indiana University Press,
    [2018] | Series: New Jewish philosophy and thought | Includes
    bibliographical references and index.
Identifiers: LCCN 2017054186 (print) | LCCN 2017054647 (e-book) |
    ISBN 9780253030221 (e-book) | ISBN 9780253029751 (cloth :
    alk. paper) | ISBN 9780253030030 (pbk. : alk. paper)
Subjects: LCSH: Buber, Martin, 1878–1965. | Judaism and politics. |
    Politics in the Bible. | Arab-Israeli conflict. | Zionism and
    Judaism. | Palestine—In Judaism.
Classification: LCC B3213.B84 (e-book) | LCC B3213.B84 B76 2018
    (print) | DDC 296.3/82092—dc23
LC record available at https://lccn.loc.gov/2017054186

1 2 3 4 5   23 22 21 20 19 18

To my parents

אהב את-המלאכה, ושנא את-הרבנות, ואל תתודע לרשות.

Love work. Hate positions of domination. Do not make yourself known to the authorities.

—Shemayah, *Pirkei Avot* 1:10 (translation of *Siddur Sim Shalom*)

Contents

Preface

THIS BOOK IS about what it might be like to think about religion and politics together in a liberating rather than an oppressive way. It explores the topic primarily through the lens of one thinker, the Jewish author Martin Buber (1878–1965).

Buber was born and raised in Habsburg Galicia and Vienna, and educated in Germany. He lived through World War I, the end of the Kaiser's reign, the rise and fall of the Weimar Republic, and five years of the Nazi Reich. In 1938 he fled to Palestine, which was itself in the midst of the Arab Revolt against the Zionists and the British. There he witnessed the declaration of the State of Israel and the first decades of its existence. And throughout this whole period, he was writing.

So, this book is about the kingship of God. It is about anarchists and Zionists, ancient Israelites and modern Israelis, German liberals and Nazis. It is about the conflict between Zionism and the Palestinian struggle, and how one man tried to reconcile the two. It is about how modern Jews have read and continue to read the Bible for answers to their questions.

The book is intended to be read as one long story, but each chapter can stand on its own for readers with a special interest in a particular topic. Readers who are primarily interested in anarchism and revolution should start with chapter 1. Readers interested in German politics and theology in the Weimar era can turn to chapter 2. Those concerned with Zionism, its conflict with the Palestinians, and the special role that Buber plays in arguments on these topics may skip to chapter 7, although I hope they then go back to read the other chapters. Finally, chapter 8 will be of most interest to readers who follow contemporary trends in philosophy and political theory.

Chapters 3–6 are the heart of the book. Chapter 3 focuses intensely on Buber's 1932 work *Kingship of God*, to lay out his idea of theopolitics as fully as possible. Chapters 4–6 then show how the ideas of *Kingship of God* are elaborated in Buber's other, later biblical writings: *Moses* (chapter 4), *The Anointed* (the unfinished, still-untranslated sequel to *Kingship of God*, presented in chapter 5), and *The Prophetic Faith* (chapter 6). These chapters are the living center that radiate outward to the rest of the book, orienting everything from anarchism to Zionism.

Caption for Cover Art

This work appeared on the frontispiece to the issue of *Masken*, the Düsseldorf theater journal, in which appeared Martin Buber's eulogy "Landauer und die Revolution." Signed by H. Petermann (possibly Hedwig Petermann, a Düsseldorf artist with whom Landauer corresponded), it seems intended to evoke the Brescia church mural described by Buber at the end of his eulogy (see chapter 1). In this context, however, it evokes not only the ten thousand martyrs of medieval Christian art but also the crucified of the Spartacus revolts, both ancient and modern, among whom Buber saw Landauer hanging. *Masken: Halbmonatschrift des Düsseldorfer Schauspielhauses* 14.18–19 (1919).

Acknowledgments

PAUL MENDES-FLOHR, my *Doktorvater*, and the University of Chicago Divinity School provided a warm and challenging atmosphere for my graduate study. In particular, I'd like to thank Michael Fishbane, Bruce Lincoln, Margaret Mitchell, David Nirenberg, Lucy Pick, Jim Robinson, Richard Rosengarten, and Eric Santner. And finally, the late Jean Bethke Elshtain, with whom I disagreed about much in theology and politics but who was a giving and thoughtful teacher.

The administration and faculty of the Graduate School of the Jewish Theological Seminary generously funded my master's degree. I owe a great deal to the many wonderful teachers I had there, especially Alan Mittleman, whose dry wit and reasoned disagreements sharpened my thinking.

The University of Cincinnati Department of Judaic Studies and the Department of Religious Studies at the University of Kansas gave me welcoming institutional homes to teach, research, and finish my work on this book. I'd especially like to thank my colleagues at KU: Jackie Brinton, Bill Lindsey, Joshua Lollar, Tim Miller, Paul Mirecki, Hamsa Stainton, Dan Stevenson, Molly Zahn, and Michael Zogry.

Sections of this book were presented as papers over the years at the conferences of the American Academy of Religion, the Association of Jewish Studies, and the Society for Jewish Ethics, as well as at the Yale Modern Jewish History Colloquium, the Harvard Jewish Studies Workshop, and the Israel-Palestine Graduate Group at Boston College. I am grateful to all of them for their invitations and critical feedback.

Thanks to Dee Mortensen and Paige Rasmussen of Indiana University Press for taking on this project, and for being so easy to work with. And thanks to Asher Biemann and Michael Morgan, the manuscript's outside readers, for their critical and constructive feedback.

The Borrowing Unit Staff at the Interlibrary Loan department of the Van Pelt Library, at the University of Pennsylvania, assisted me in an extensive search for the image that appears on this book's cover. The ILL office of the library of Washington University in St. Louis was finally able to supply it. Both have my gratitude. Heba Mostafa and Mary Channen Caldwell generously assisted me in tracing the image's lineage.

Thanks to the Klau Library, Hebrew Union College–Jewish Institute of Religion, Cincinnati, for permission to publish the appendix. The original letter can be found there in the Hans Kohn Collection, box 1, I: Correspondence: 1939, 1.

Thanks to Walter de Gruyter in Berlin for permission to republish material from Samuel Hayim Brody, "Is Theopolitics an Antipolitics?" in *Dialogue as a Trans-Disciplinary Concept: Martin Buber's Philosophy of Dialogue and Its Contemporary Reception*, edited by Paul Mendes-Flohr, 61–88 (Berlin: Walter de Gruyter, 2015).

Many colleagues make my fields quite simply decent places to be—or as decent as possible in the face of unrelenting political and economic indecency. Martin Kavka and Randi Rashkover above all, and others too many to name. They know who they are.

Carrie Caine is most likely the only person besides my parents to have read this book in all its forms. She did drudge work on the footnotes to chapter 6 and provided crucial editorial suggestions in the crunch. She truly does whatever a Carrie Caine.

This book is dedicated to my parents, Ruth Sussman and Jules Brody, who taught me to love learning, and whose love and support have always shaped my life.

Note on Translation
and Transliteration

T<small>RANSLATIONS</small> <small>FROM</small> <small>THE</small> Tanakh are usually drawn from the old Jewish Publication Society (1917) version, though I have frequently tweaked the translation to bring it closer to the new JPS. New Testament translations are from the New Revised Standard Version.

I have not employed any standardized transliteration schemes, such as that of the Society of Biblical Literature, preferring to employ less specialized transliterations more accessible to general readers. When I cite German biblical scholarship, I leave their conventions the way they are (e.g., JHWH for the Tetragrammaton, *Nabi* for prophet). But when I write for myself, I choose approximations closer to English usage (e.g., YHVH for the Tetragrammaton, *Navi* for prophet).

List of Abbreviations

Works of Martin Buber

KG   *Kingship of God*, trans. Richard Scheimann (Amherst, NY: Humanity Books, 1990)

LMB   *The Letters of Martin Buber: A Life of Dialogue*, ed. Nahum N. Glatzer and Paul Mendes-Flohr, trans. Richard and Clara Winston and Harry Zohn (Syracuse, NY: Syracuse University Press, 1996)

LTP   *A Land of Two Peoples: Martin Buber on Jews and Arabs*, ed. Paul Mendes-Flohr (Chicago: University of Chicago Press, 2005)

MRC   *Moses: The Revelation and the Covenant* (Amherst, NY: Humanity Books, 1998)

PF   *The Prophetic Faith*, trans. Carlyle Witton-Davies (Princeton, NJ: Princeton University Press, 2015)

PU   *Paths in Utopia*, trans. R. F. C. Hull (Boston: Beacon Press, 1958)

PW   *Pointing the Way: Collected Essays*, ed. and trans. Maurice Friedman (New York: Schocken Books, 1974)

SM   *Martin Buber Werkausgabe. Band 15: Schriften zum Messianismus*, ed. Samuel Hayim Brody (Gütersloh: Gütersloher Verlaghaus, 2014)

ST   *Scripture and Translation*, trans. Lawrence Rosenwald, with Everett Fox (Bloomington: Indiana University Press, 1994)

WZB   *Werke. Zweiter Band: Schriften zur Bibel* (Heidelberg: Lambert Schneider, 1964)

Other Works

FMD   Paul Mendes-Flohr, *From Mysticism to Dialogue: Martin Buber's Transformation of German Social Thought* (Detroit: Wayne State University Press, 1989)

GLPU   Ruth Link-Salinger (Hyman), *Gustav Landauer: Philosopher of Utopia* (Indianapolis: Hackett, 1977)

MBCP   Paul Mendes-Flohr, ed., *Martin Buber: A Contemporary Perspective* (Syracuse, NY: Syracuse University Press, 2002)

MBEY   Maurice Friedman, *Martin Buber's Life and Work: The Early Years, 1878–1923* (Detroit: Wayne State University Press, 1988)

MBLY   Maurice Friedman, *Martin Buber's Life and Work: The Later Years, 1945–1965* (Detroit: Wayne State University Press, 1988)

MBMY   Maurice Friedman, *Martin Buber's Life and Work: The Middle Years, 1923–1945* (Detroit: Wayne State University Press, 1988)

NPMB   Michael Zank, ed., *New Perspectives on Martin Buber.* Religion in Philosophy and Theology 22. (Tübingen: Mohr Siebeck, 2006)

PC   Eugene Lunn, *Prophet of Community: The Romantic Socialism of Gustav Landauer* (Berkeley: University of California Press, 1973)

MARTIN BUBER'S THEOPOLITICS

Introduction

What Is Theopolitics?

The human being is an *animal which*, when it lives among others of its species, *has need of a master*. . . . But where will he get this master? Nowhere else but from the human species. But then this master is exactly as much an animal who has need of a master. Try as he may, therefore, there is no seeing how he can procure a supreme power for public right that is itself just. . . . This problem is therefore the most difficult of all; indeed, its perfect solution is even impossible; out of such crooked wood as the human being is made, nothing entirely straight can be fabricated.

—Immanuel Kant, *Idea for a Universal History with a Cosmopolitan Aim*

The covenant at Sinai signifies, according to its positive content, that the wandering tribes accept JHWH "for ever and ever" as their King. According to its negative content it signifies that no man is to be called king of the sons of Israel.

—Martin Buber, *Kingship of God*

Locating Theopolitics

"Antipolitics," writes Michael Walzer, "is a kind of politics." This puzzling statement occurs in Walzer's recent work on the Bible, which he calls "a political book," though it is one that has "no political theory" in it; its writers are "engaged with politics" but are "not very interested in politics," though he admits that "writers who are uninterested in politics nonetheless have a lot to say that is politically interesting."[1] Walzer is a clear writer, so if these statements seem convoluted, this may be due to the subject matter itself. Close examination of the relationship of religion and politics can call into question our very understanding of the nature of both "religion" and "politics" as distinct and separate spheres that can each be described according to its own special set of characteristics. This is an inconvenient situation for university departments like political science and religion, which would like to assume that the objects of their study do in fact exist.

Martin Buber (1878–1965) encountered this problem when he attempted to secure a position at the Hebrew University of Jerusalem, founded on a European, and particularly a German, model of higher education. Judah Magnes, the first chancellor of the university, was eager to bring Buber, already well known as a writer, editor, and speaker, to Palestine. However, as Paul Mendes-Flohr has written, pertinent academic committees blocked Magnes's recommendation because Buber lacked a clear scholarly profile. "Was he a philosopher, a biblical scholar, a historian of Jewish mysticism and Hasidism? Or was he perhaps a scholar of comparative religion (*Religionswissenschaft*)?"[2] At the University of Frankfurt, where he taught from 1923 until 1933, when he was "vacationed" by the Nazis, Buber was first an adjunct lecturer in Jewish science of religion and ethics, before his promotion in 1930 to honorary professor of comparative religion. Nowhere among these titles is Buber considered a specialist in the field of political thought. And yet Hans Kohn's 1929 biography of him carried the subtitle *Ein Versuch über Religion und Politik* [*An Essay on Religion and Politics*].[3] Kohn understood Buber's position, articulated three years later in his biblical study *Königtum Gottes* [*Kingship of God*] (1932), that the Sinai covenant, the central event in Jewish history, must be understood as "a theo-political act"—that for Israel "*there is no political sphere outside the theo-political.*"[4] In 1939, just one year after he fled Nazi Germany for Palestine, Buber raised with Kohn the possibility of publishing his upcoming works in English. The proposed projects included the following:

> 6. Religion and Politics. For this book there is only a pile of schemes and sketches. It shall contain 3 parts: a history of the relation between religion and politics, from ancient China up to our time; a systematic disquisition with examples; and practical conclusions for the main problems of actual society, state and civilization. . . . [C]ertainly this will be the most voluminous of all my books—and perhaps the most important too.[5]

This work never came to fruition, but Buber's expectation that it might become his most important book shows how seriously he took the theme of religion and politics.

Few scholars have focused on Buber's politics, and those who do often complain about their lack of company. Robert Weltsch, for example, writes of the "fallacy" of seeing Buber solely as a "religious thinker" and "social philosopher" rather than "a man of politics."[6] Twenty years later, Steven Schwarzschild reports the "striking exception" of politics from general scholarly interest in Buber. "In at least some instances," Schwarzschild claims, "this exception is made tendentiously: Buber's reputation is to be used for institutional and political self-advancement, but the nature of his political thought and programme would resist such purposes."[7] Whether scholars simply do not *see* Buber as a political writer, or whether they find the topic dangerous, no definitive treatment of Buber's politics exists.

Weltsch is correct that scholars have simply been more interested in other aspects of Buber's work. His fame is due primarily to *Ich und Du* [*I and Thou*] (1923), a short but powerful book widely read as an existentialist manifesto, as well as to his collections of Hasidic tales and his commentaries on them, which introduced a hitherto-unknown religious phenomenon to Western readers. Even when Buber is recognized as having a politics, it is usually characterized as a subdivision of his philosophy: the political utopia Buber sought logically ensues from his existential meditations on the I-Thou relation.[8] This stance makes sense if we treat ontology (the study of Being) as the most fundamental branch of philosophy, and if we also read Buber's "philosophy of dialogue" as his version of an ontology. From the perspective of the philosophy of dialogue, utopia is that configuration of society with the fewest possible obstacles to the fundamental human desire for a community based on recognition and mutual concern. Social structures that discourage such regard, and demand subservience to laws of instrumentality, such as the state and the market, obstruct I-Thou encounters. Such social structures would be transformed in utopia, constituting a direct connection between Buber's philosophy and his politics. Bernard Susser sums up this approach: "Federalism as Buber understands it is the principle of dialogue writ large and socialized."[9]

In this book, however, I "bracket" ontology and Hasidism, the most familiar aspects of Buber's thought, to focus on Buber's biblical writings as a key source of his political thought. By "bracket," I do not mean to downplay the importance of Buber's philosophical anthropology or the inspiration he took from his interpretation of the Hasidic movement. I simply mean to set them to the side for the moment, as if in parentheses, to focus on more neglected aspects of his work. My bracketing of Buber's most famous writings thus should not be read as an argument for replacing them with the biblical and political writings. I simply choose to turn the prism one more time, to look at Buber through different lenses, and to reveal other colors.[10]

The past few decades have seen a resurgence of interest in the idea of political theology, usually in the sense given to that term by the German Catholic jurist and erstwhile Nazi Party member Carl Schmitt (1888–1985).[11] For Schmitt, "political theology" meant that no matter how modern and secular a political concept might seem, if we analyze its intellectual history and trajectory, we will discover that it is a transformed version of a theological concept. Schmitt thought this was especially true of concepts related to the legitimation of authority. He further characterized "the political" as defined by the decision between friend and enemy, and he derided liberalism as an attempt to evade politics and decision making by indulging in endless, indecisive discussion. Buber rarely uses the term "political theology," but he frequently uses the term *Theopolitik* (theopolitics), a word that seems at first as though it might mean the same thing. However, I follow Christoph Schmidt's belief that for Buber, the term "theopolitics" is intended to function as a deep *inversion* of "political theology," a conceptual attack on Schmitt and what he stands for.[12] There are many potential angles from which to oppose Schmitt. The German-Jewish historian and intellectual Leo Strauss counterposed his own concept of political philosophy to Schmitt's political theology, thereby indicating the legitimacy of a political thought (liberal or otherwise) that was not traceable to revelation. Yet Buber does not seem to fall into either camp. To be sure, his valorization of "dialogue" has tempted many to classify him among the liberals. This judgment, however, is hasty and mistaken. In many ways, theopolitics can seem just as illiberal and "decisionist" as political theology; it reflects the same era of crisis and uses a similar vocabulary.[13] At the same time, it invokes the divine in a way that seems to disqualify it from being political philosophy. I propose that Buber's theopolitics constitutes a different type of answer, then, to political theology: an anarchist one. Where political theology deploys the power of the divine in the service of the authoritarian state, theopolitics denies any possibility of truly legitimizing institutional human power. If political theology borders on the fascistic, theopolitics is its anarchistic antipode.

My suggestion to link theopolitics with anarchism may seem counterintuitive. Anarchism, also known as libertarian socialism, is usually understood as a current of nineteenth-century European radicalism. Anarchists declared war on every oppressive social structure, chief among them the state, capitalism, and organized religion. This uncompromising stance put them at odds with communists (who wanted a workers' state to overcome capitalism) and liberals (who saw the unfettered operations of capitalist markets as "free" and did not consider private concentrations of power to be as threatening as government), as well as conservatives (who wanted to defend all the great pillars of law and order, from the family to the church to the state). There have always been strong streams of religious anarchism, however, running alongside the antireligious mainstream; Leo Tolstoy and Mahatma Gandhi, at various times, exemplified the trend. Religious anarchists typically distinguish between the essential truths to be found in their traditions and the oppressive attempts by human beings to institutionalize those truths.

Buber's mentor in anarchism was his closest friend of twenty years, the activist, writer, and critic Gustav Landauer (1870–1919), to whom the Prussian secret police in 1893 gave the title "most significant agitator of the radical-revolutionary movement in all of Germany."[14] Despite this accolade, and despite Landauer's prominent role in the November Revolution (the wave of leftist revolt that swept Germany in 1918 and 1919), he has often been treated as apolitically as Buber. He has been called "impractical" and "excessively romantic" even by proponents of revolutionary change, and "saintly, unpolitical, and inept" by its opponents.[15] Landauer's comrade during the uprising of the Bavarian Council Republic, Erich Mühsam, defended him against such charges, calling him "a strong, fearless spirit, always ready to act" who could not be absorbed "in a sweet brew of bourgeois-ethical love for everyone and everything" (an anticipation of Schwarzschild's description of Buber's own political fate).[16] Of course, as an anarchist, Mühsam was himself subject to the same criticisms as all those involved in what the Communist Party of the time sneeringly called the "Bavarian Coffeehouse Republic."[17] This is symptomatic of how anarchism and theopolitics are intertwined, since both question the borders of the political. The shadow of the failed revolution fell on the new German polity that emerged after the world war: intellectual life was obsessed with the nature and limits of politics. But the revolution itself was hidden by that very shadow.

Historical and Intellectual Contexts of Theopolitics

The Weimar Republic survived for barely fourteen years. When scholars refer to "Weimar" cultural, intellectual, religious, or political trends, they are talking about a "Weimar moment" in the lives of people who also lived during the Wilhelmine and Nazi periods.[18] The focus on Weimar today is driven by intense interest in the way religion, politics, philosophy, and law played out amid an emergent modernity and a doomed democracy, with special attention to political theology in all its varied connotations. Many of the remarkable Central European figures of the time continue to sustain cottage industries in various humanistic fields, from philosophy and theology to cultural studies, from sociology to legal and political theory.[19]

Buber, however, has not usually been given a prominent place in the most recent discussions of the Weimar problematic.[20] Perhaps Buber's age and fame during the Weimar period (he was forty in 1918) create a perception that he was really a last-generation Wilhelmine thinker, like Hermann Cohen and Max Weber. There were certainly some at the time who already saw Buber as an authority against whom to rebel.[21] However, Buber's best-known work, *I and Thou*, was published in 1923 and is generally agreed to have signaled the "dialogical turn" that inaugurated his "mature" status as a thinker.[22] Furthermore, Buber's religious writing from this period forward has more in common with his friend Rosenzweig and even with Protestant crisis theology (launched by Karl Barth's 1918 *Epistle to the Romans*) than with any theology of the nineteenth century.[23] Perhaps, then, what accounts for Buber's absence from current discussions is the apparent distance of I and Thou from what Leo Strauss calls "the theologico-political predicament."[24] Buber seems to belong to a different, more apolitical discussion, known from the 1950s through the 1970s as religious existentialism. The waning of this trend dimmed Buber's star, and he settled into the niche he occupies today: an important figure in Jewish ethics, whose works on Hasidism spurred the renewal of Jewish youth movements in Europe in the early twentieth century, who is still read in Protestant seminaries and liberal rabbinical schools as an exemplar of modern Jewish thought outside the strictures of *halakha*, and as a voice of conscience in Israeli politics. I intend to place Buber into the context of Weimar political theology. This approach entails a different view of his intellectual trajectory and a shift in emphasis and angle, and part 1 of the book (chapters 1–3) is devoted to this project.

As noted already, for Schmitt political theology went hand in hand with a critique of liberalism. Parliamentary representation allegedly fractures society into interest groups, removing questions of ultimate significance from public debate and thus transforming political contestation into technocratic management.[25] Such a critique formed a crucial component of the "conservative revolution" against the new republic, which charged that such a party-state could never deliver general justice. The Lutheran theologian Emanuel Hirsch wrote in 1919 that "the more democratic a state is today, the more dependent it tends to become on large economic monetary powers, and the less social justice can be expected from it."[26] It is important to remember, however, that the Weimar Republic was born not just of Germany's defeat in the Great War but also through the suppression of the November Revolution. The specter of leftist radicalism haunted both the supporters of the short-lived republic and its reactionary opponents. This fact has less impact than it should on discussions of Weimar intellectual life, and very little on questions of political theology. The communist and anarchist critiques of liberalism and capitalism seem to lie on the opposite end of the spectrum from the conservative bent of political theology—all political, and not at all theological. Efforts to link them have focused on a few logical points of intersection, such as the relationship between revolution and messianic hope in thinkers like Walter Benjamin and Ernst Bloch.[27] Moreover, historians were more inclined to focus on the left while the Soviet Union still existed and Marxism remained a global force. The fact that liberalism is still with us, while communism is a memory, may partially explain why the conservative critique of liberalism by thinkers like Schmitt seems relevant again, even to contemporary scholars who identify as leftists.[28] But the last word has not been said on the theological-political problem and the left, especially if one takes into account the intellectual-cultural environment of the Weimar period in which both right and left concerned themselves with such issues as *Gemeinschaft* (community) versus *Gesellschaft* (society), organism versus mechanism, the nature of the *Volk*, and the role of religious authority in political life.[29]

My attempt to situate Buber's theopolitics simultaneously in these two Weimar contexts, the left and political theology, begins in chapter 1 by examining his relationship to Landauer, who was murdered by counterrevolutionary troops at the very start of the period, and then moves on to Buber's place in the currents of Weimar, in chapter 2. Thus I begin in the Wilhelmine era, focusing on the Buber-Landauer friendship. This relationship is well known, and usually characterized as fruitful for both. I examine this friendship both to recontextualize some of Buber's early "nonpolitical" work and to determine where Buber and Landauer agreed and disagreed politically. Their careers followed similar trajectories: an initial burst of political activity (anarchism for Landauer, Zionism for Buber), followed by withdrawal from active life and a focus on mystical-philosophical concerns, followed in turn by renewed political activity after a prolonged period of study.[30] I stress the simultaneity of their varied endeavors, which are often treated separately. Buber edited *Die Gesellschaft*, his series of social-psychological monographs, at the same time that he labored on his first anthologies of Hasidic writings, while Landauer edited Fritz Mauthner's *Sprachkritik* [Critique of Language] and translated Meister Eckhart into modern German while he was in prison for publishing his radical newspaper, *Der Sozialist*. Neither man saw his life as compartmentalized into political and aesthetic spheres.

This approach avoids the temptation to view the 1916 disagreement between Buber and Landauer over the First World War in terms of aestheticism or mysticism on the one hand (Buber) and a keen sense of the political on the other (Landauer). Although Landauer did in fact shock Buber by accusing him of aestheticism, both men combined these elements in their thought. The disagreement between them reflects not any strict separation between aesthetics and politics, but rather different ways of conceiving the mutual involvement of these categories, in both theory and practice. In this view, Buber's new intellectual trajectory, under Landauer's inspiration, does not climax in 1923 with *I and Thou*; rather, it runs from *Der Heilige Weg* [*The Holy Way*] of 1919 through the collaboration with Rosenzweig on the Bible translation and the Frankfurt *Lehrhaus* in the 1920s (which also saw his editorship of the interfaith journal *Die Kreatur*) and culminates in *Kingship of God* (the subject of chapter 3). Martin Kavka recently expressed the hope that a philosophical critique of *I and Thou* might "contribute to the claim that *I and Thou* should not be taken as the mature expression of Buber's thought."[31] My own brief is not philosophical but historical; I seek to show what might result from decentering *I and Thou* as the keystone of Buber's work, rather than treating everything that comes before it as an anticipation and everything that comes after it as an elaboration.[32] I seek to enable a new conversation, not to replace *I and Thou* with *Kingship of God* in yet another deterministic narrative.

Buber and Bible Scholarship, Buber and the Bible

Buber reveals his ambivalence toward the ivory tower of his time in the preface to the first edition of *Kingship of God*. Acknowledging a significant debt to the great sociologist Max Weber, both to his written work and to "conversation with the extraordinary man," Buber relates this anecdote:

> I shall never forget—it was about 1910—after a lecture on Jewish piety which I had delivered before Heidelberg students, Max Weber, requested by the young people to open the discussion, stepped up to me and asked me whether it were agreeable to me if he spoke now; he could, to be sure, offer "only science about religion and not religion." Also my book here is not intended to express faith, but a knowledge about it; *it asserts admittedly that one can possess a knowledge*

about faith legitimately only then when the eye remains directed upon the cosmic margin, never given as object, at which faith is given a habitation.[33]

The fascinating caveat of the italicized words is left unexplained here, but Buber clearly suspects that prevailing methods in the study of religion will miss the mark as long as they lack a transcendent orientation (to a "margin . . . never given as object"). That this criticism appears in *Kingship of God* is itself remarkable, given that in this work Buber intended to demonstrate his scholarly credentials, with a belated *Habilitationsschrift* meant to secure him a position at the Hebrew University.[34] It is a testament to the distance between Buber and what he called "official scholarship."[35]

Nonetheless, in *Kingship of God*, Buber represents himself as a biblical scholar, hewing to scholarly conventions as viewed from an informed outsider's perspective. This gives the work a sense of performance; Buber is playing at scholarship, although with his own livelihood at stake.[36] But the performance is so effective that scholars have been moved to argue for a stronger appreciation of Buber's status as a *Religionswissenschaftler*. They emphasize that *I and Thou* was originally intended to lay the groundwork for a multipart work in comparative religion and had its origins in Buber's 1922 Frankfurt lectures, "Religion as Presence."[37] Among the notes from these lectures are plans for a larger book series, in which *I and Thou* was to be a first installment.[38] Stroumsa remarks that "very few of its readers . . . have read it as an introduction to the study of religious phenomena, and Buber, quite wisely, never bothered to enlighten them on the book's original meaning in the mind of its author."[39] This implies that Buber was happy to be seen the way the readers of *I and Thou* preferred to see him, as an existentialist sage and spiritual guide. Stroumsa thinks nevertheless that these plans show that "the comparative study of religious phenomena stood at the very centre of Buber's intellectual life, from his early years on." Zank agrees, arguing that Buber's abandonment of his systematic plans in comparative religion indicates not a turning away from the field but "an increasingly sophisticated awareness of problems related to the study of religion."[40] Zank goes further than Stroumsa in his ultimate judgment on Buber's contribution. Where Stroumsa concludes that "Buber never approached scholarship with the demanding exclusiveness that it requires,"[41] Zank thinks that attention to his scholarly endeavors can clarify "the taxonomic difficulty of classifying the author and his multifarious work."[42] For Zank, it makes more sense to call Buber a scholar of religious studies than anything else—even a philosopher. I would add that in Buber's unrealized plans of research in comparative religion, the final volume would often be the same: "The Religious Power and Our Time (The Power and the Kingdom)." The telos of Buber's scholarship was theopolitics.

Whether or not Buber is currently respected as a serious biblical scholar, he was a renowned teacher of Bible.[43] Buber's position in this respect was close to that of traditional Jewish religious leaders, with a modern twist: instead of at a yeshiva, Buber taught in the Frankfurt Lehrhaus established by his friend and colleague, Franz Rosenzweig.[44] It was Rosenzweig who in 1923 convinced Buber to advance his candidacy for the university lecturer position, arguing as one man "free of silly academicism" to another that the position might serve as a launching pad to transform university religious studies from within: "Your presence and your indubitably *apikoros* personality will give that faculty its character and direction during the process of formation. This can be done only by one who is wholly free of any deference for the existing university, and who, at the same time, brings to the job the kind of personal reputation which will forbid the university's interfering with him."[45] And together with Rosenzweig, in 1925 Buber embarked on his most extended engagement with the Hebrew Bible, a new translation into German that their joint religious philosophies and hermeneutic approaches would inform.[46]

It would be the first major German translation of the Tanakh by Jewish philosophers, and aimed at a primarily Jewish readership, since Moses Mendelssohn's version in the eighteenth century. As Hannah Arendt pointed out, however, the linguistic purposes of the two translations were precisely inverse: "A hundred and fifty years ago, at the beginning of the emancipation, Moses Mendelssohn's German translation of the Bible in Hebrew letters enabled the Jewish youth of the ghetto to learn German and to enter, by this oddly circuitous path, into the German and European life of the period. Similarly, in our own day, Buber's marvelous undertaking is but a circuitous way of bringing the Jews back to Hebrew, the language of the Bible; a way of bringing them back to the Jewish past, its values and requirements."[47]

Wilhelm Stapel, a friend of Carl Schmitt and the editor of the conservative, Protestant *Deutsches Volkstum*, well known for his antisemitic views, accused Buber and Rosenzweig of having produced a "half-jargon," a "Hebraic German" that was "the strangest German that was ever written."[48] Buber not only takes this view of Stapel's to be ignorant on the linguistic merits; he also sees Stapel's opposition as motivated by a sense of political threat: "He had seen clearly what danger to his conception of a 'Christian statesman'—i.e., a sham Christian offering religious sanction to all the violences of the state—would be entailed among the German people by the dissemination of the actual Scriptures, which demand the shaping of society on the basis of belief."[49] This is why Buber calls Stapel "the most perceptive of our antagonists." Whether or not he is correct about Stapel's motivations, what matters is that Buber finds that "the dissemination of the actual Scriptures" works politically, against efforts to offer "religious sanction to all the violences of the state." Thus theopolitics is Buber's telos not just as a biblical scholar but as a popular teacher as well.[50]

Much scholarship focuses on Buber's interpretive approaches to the Bible. This focus can be so strong that it excludes the possibility that Buber actually came to conclusions because of these approaches. Scholars take Buber's own refrain, "Ich habe keine Lehre," or "I have no teaching," too seriously when they treat his approach to the Bible as nothing more than a tool available to any generation in order to "make the Bible relevant to our time." While Buber was certainly interested in making the Bible relevant, he does have a teaching as well as a method, and part 2 of this book is dedicated to elaborating it. From the beginnings of his work in *Kingship of God* and its unfinished sequel, *Der Gesalbte* [*The Anointed*] (the subject of chapter 4), in Germany, to its continuation in *Moshe* (1946) (chapter 5) and *Torat Ha-Nevi'im* [*Torah of the Prophets*, translated into English as *The Prophetic Faith*] (1944) (chapter 6) after moving to Palestine, Buber's biblical writings sketch out a theopolitical history of Israel, from exodus to exile. They emerge from the context of Weimar political theology and address themselves to the political project with which Buber was most concerned, Zionism. Part 3 of the book (chapters 7–8) thus deals with applications of theopolitics, both in Buber's own time and in ours.

Theopolitics and Zionism

Buber wrote about migrations of Jewish people to the Land of Israel, and their construction of polities there, in many registers. One of these was in his Zionist writing; another was in his biblical scholarship. Buber's argument was that the Jews had been elected by God, freed from bondage, and brought to the land, but not to create a state that resembled those around it, with their political theologies of kingship (in the ancient world) and their unequal distribution of life outcomes based on nation or race (in the modern one). Rather, Buber believed that in the ancient world as in the modern, "the creation of a genuine and just community on a voluntary basis . . . will show the world the possibility of basing social justice on voluntary action."[51] Buber's Zionism is the subject of chapter 7, which presents it as an anarchistic modern translation of biblical prophecy, in which Jewish life has a necessarily political component, albeit defined against the prevailing understandings of politics. The typical adjectives for Buber's Zionism, whether cultural, or spiritual, or binationalist, fail to capture this essential element. Buber never called his own Zionism "theopolitical" (he preferred the even more unwieldy *Wirklichkeitzionismus*, or "Zionism of reality"), but reading his Zionism through the concept of theopolitics makes the best sense of it.

The famous term "binationalism" attempts to capture the most famous public aspect of Buber's Zionism, his insistent call for Jews and Arabs to share power in the land between the Jordan River and the Mediterranean Sea. "Binationalism" coheres with the usual picture of Buber as a philosopher—of course the thinker of "dialogue" believed in negotiations with Arabs!—and as such is rarely investigated closely for its political content. The sociologist and historian Gershon Shafir has argued, following Baruch Kimmerling, that "whereas Israelis tend to focus on the non-colonialist reasons and motivations for their immigration to Palestine, Arabs direct their attention to its results. Until the former learn about results and the latter about intentions, neither is likely to gain access to new knowledge."[52] The question of how to relate intentions to results becomes even more complicated when dealing with a minority position like Buber's, which failed to have its desired effect on the movement to which it belonged. I argue that Buber's theopolitics, as elaborated in his biblical works, casts him in the role of prophet with respect to Zionism: having failed to achieve the anarcho-theocracy that he considered the ultimate and only purpose of Jewish election, Buber accepts the Jewish state as a fait accompli while simultaneously adopting an oppositional stance toward it, attempting to recall it to the service of God by arguing that true Judaism is impossible in Palestine as long as Jewish sovereignty oppresses and excludes Palestinians. Failure in this mission, Buber fears, would entail devastating consequences, not just for the Jewish people, who risk a third exile, but for the idea they had been called upon to embody.

Theopolitics in Contemporary Thought

Buber's theopolitics provides a missing coordinate in the contemporary constellation of conversations about political theology, the return of religion, and the clash of civilizations. Chapter 8 introduces theopolitics to the contemporary theoretical landscape. Buber's prophetic politics contests the prevailing versions of secularized apocalyptic messianism; his anarchism challenges the reigning neoliberal ideology of the West while engaging the aporias of the postcommunist left; his Zionism attacks the deadlock between those who can understand Jewish power only as domination (whether right-wing settlers or left-wing Diasporist thinkers) as well as those who argue that Jewish power in its current form deviates only slightly from its true, enlightened, and tolerant incarnation (liberal Zionists). This is not to say that Buber can easily be inserted into contemporary circumstances, as though nothing has changed since his death in 1965. But it does mean that his theopolitics—long overshadowed by the popularity of his other work, invisible to those for whom any unconventional politics is an antipolitics, scrambled through its presentation between the lines of obscure works of biblical scholarship—may now emerge to speak to this pathless hour.

Notes

1. Michael Walzer, *In God's Shadow: Politics in the Hebrew Bible* (New Haven, CT: Yale University Press, 2012), xiii.

2. Paul Mendes-Flohr, "The Kingdom of God: Martin Buber's Critique of Messianic Politics," *Behemoth: A Journal on Civilization* 1.2 (2008): 27n5. Cf. Mendes-Flohr, "Martin Buber's Rhetoric," in MBCP 1–24.

3. The second edition of 1961 changed the subtitle to *Ein Beitrag zur Geistesgeschichte Mitteleuropas, 1880-1930.*

4. KG 136.

5. Buber to Kohn, October 4, 1939, Talbiyeh, Jerusalem. I discovered this letter, composed in Buber's hand and in English, in Kohn's papers at the Klau Library of Hebrew Union College in Cincinnati. A version of the letter found in the Adolph Oko papers of the American Jewish Archives was previously published in Frederic Krome, "Correspondence between Martin Buber, Hans Kohn, Abraham Joshua Heschel and Adolph Oko, 1939–44," *Jewish Culture and History* 5.1 (Summer 2002): 121–134. Krome consulted Oko's copy of the letter, which was transcribed and likely "cleaned up" by Kohn before forwarding, removing text Buber had crossed out and omitting personal references to his relationship with Kohn. Buber also wrote a very similar letter to Oko himself, two weeks later, in which he intriguingly refers to his religion and politics manuscript as "drafted"; I thank Dr. Krome for making that letter available to me. See the appendix for the full text of the original letter to Kohn, including crossed-out portions represented in strikethrough.

6. Robert Weltsch, ""Buber's Political Philosophy," in *The Philosophy of Martin Buber*, ed. Paul Arthur Schilpp and Maurice Friedman (La Salle, IL: Open Court Press, 1967), 435–449.

7. Steven Schwarzschild, "A Critique of Martin Buber's Political Philosophy: An Affectionate Reappraisal," in *The Pursuit of the Ideal: Jewish Writings of Steven Schwarzschild*, ed. Menachem Kellner (Albany, NY: SUNY Press, 1990), 185–207.

8. Mendes-Flohr, "The Desert within and Social Renewal—Martin Buber's Vision of Utopia," in NPMB 219–230.

9. Bernard Susser, "The Anarcho-Federalism of Martin Buber," *Publius* 9.4 (Autumn 1979): 103–116.

10. This method assumes that much can be said on Buber's politics without having recourse to his "philosophy," not ruling out the prospect of reintroducing the philosophy later.

11. Vincent W. Lloyd has delineated three uses of the term "political theology": (1) a narrow sense, referring to Schmitt's account of the role of religious concepts in political theory; (2) a broad sense, interchangeable with almost any form of the conjunction "religion and politics"; (3) a "sectarian" sense, indicating a branch of theology (usually Christian) that deals with politics. I deal with the first sense, the context in which it emerged and was originally received. Lloyd, introduction to *Race and Political Theology*, ed. Vincent W. Lloyd (Stanford, CA: Stanford University Press, 2012), 1–21.

12. Christoph Schmidt, "Die theopolitische Stunde: Martin Bubers Begriff der Theopolitik, seine prophetischen Ursprünge, seine Aktualität und Bedeutung für die Definition Zionistischer Politik," in *Die theopolitische Stunde: Zwölf Perspektiven auf das eschatologische Problem der Moderne* (Munich: Wilhelm Fink, 2009), 205–225; cf. Schmidt, "The Theopolitical Hour," trans. Samuel Hayim Brody, in *Makers of Jewish Modernity: Thinkers, Artists, Leaders, and the World They Made*, ed. Jacques Picard et al. (Princeton, NJ: Princeton University Press, 2016), 187–203. Besides Buber's own use of the term, Schmidt's article is the primary source of my choice of the term "theopolitical" to describe Buber's attitude toward the nexus of religion and politics.

13. This is still a source of liberal criticism of Buber; Uri Ram, *The Return of Martin Buber: National and Social Thought in Israel from Buber to Neo-Buberism* (Tel Aviv: Resling, 2015) (in Hebrew).

14. Potsdam State Archives Pr. Br. Rep. 30, Berlin C Polizei Präs. 16346 Der Schriftsteller Gustav Landauer 1892-1902: "Landauer ist in ganz Deutschland der bedeutendest Agitator der radical-revolutionären Bewegung." Cited in Ruth Link-Salinger (Hyman), *Gustav Landauer: Philosopher of Utopia* (Indianapolis, IN: Hackett, 1977), 46.

15. "Impractical romantic anarchism," James Joll, *The Second International, 1899–1914* (New York: Harper & Row, 1966), 64; "excessively romantic," George Woodcock, *Anarchism:*

A History of Libertarian Ideas and Movements (Toronto: University of Toronto Press, 2009), 363; "saintly, unpolitical, and inept," Amos Elon, *The Pity of It All: A Portrait of the German-Jewish Epoch, 1743–1933* (New York: Picador, 2002), 351.

16. Cited in Gabriel Kuhn and Siegbert Wolf, introduction to Gustav Landauer, *Revolution and Other Writings: A Political Reader*, ed. and trans. Gabriel Kuhn (Oakland, CA: PM Press, 2010), 29. Mühsam also defends Landauer from strains of "proletarian" anarchism that derided Landauer's poetic and spiritual preoccupations as bourgeois; Ulrich Linse, "'Poetic Anarchism' versus 'Party Anarchism': Gustav Landauer and the Anarchist Movement in Wilhelmian Germany," in *Gustav Landauer: Anarchist and Jew*, ed. Paul Mendes-Flohr and Anya Mali, with Hanna Delf von Wolzogen (Berlin: Walter De Gruyter, 2014), 62–63.

17. Elon, *Pity of It All*, targets Mühsam as well. For "coffeehouse republic," see Gabriel Kuhn, introduction to Erich Mühsam, *Liberating Society from the State and Other Writings: A Political Reader*, ed. and trans. Gabriel Kuhn (Oakland, CA: PM Press, 2011), 20n60.

18. Leonard Kaplan and Rudy Koshar, eds., *The Weimar Moment: Liberalism, Political Theology, and Law* (Lanham, MD: Lexington Books, 2012).

19. "Weimar" serves as a synecdoche for the whole German-speaking world of the interwar period.

20. Two important recent exceptions: Gregory Kaplan, "Power and Israel in Martin Buber's Critique of Carl Schmitt's Political Theology," in *Judaism, Liberalism, and Political Theology*, ed. Randi Rashkover and Martin Kavka (Bloomington: Indiana University Press, 2014), 155–177; and Nitzan Lebovic, "The Jerusalem School: The Theopolitical Hour," *New German Critique* 105, 35.3 (Fall 2008): 97–120.

21. Critical references to Buber are scattered throughout Gershom Scholem's recollections of the prewar and early Weimar periods. For example, he uses the term *Bubertät* ("Buberty") to denote "the effusive imitations of Buber by the great master's disciples," implying that affinity for Buber needed to be overcome to reach maturity; Scholem, *From Berlin to Jerusalem: Memoirs of My Youth*, trans. Harry Zohn (New York: Schocken, 1980), 60. Herzl himself had supposedly once made a similar play on the *Bub* (lad) in Buber's name, claiming that "Buber is not a surname but a comparative."

22. The locus classicus for this view of Buber's career remains FMD. Recently, Israel Koren, *Mystery of the Earth: Mysticism and Hasidism in the thought of Martin Buber* (Boston: Brill, 2010), denies any "turn" and argues that Buber's work as a whole belongs to the Jewish mystical tradition. Michael Zank already disagreed with an earlier expression of this position. See Koren, "Between Buber's *Daniel* and His *I and Thou*: A New Examination," *Modern Judaism* 22 (2002): 169–198. Zank also acknowledges that Mendes-Flohr's position remains the view of most scholars but disagrees with its view of *I and Thou* as "the end-point of a development rather than a point of departure"; Zank, "Buber and *Religionswissenschaft*: The Case of His Studies on Biblical Faith," in NPMB 61–82. With Guy Stroumsa, Zank reads *I and Thou* as a work of *Religionswissenschaft*, academic study of religion, rather than as a philosophical magnum opus; Guy Stroumsa, "Presence, Not Gnosis: Buber as a Historian of Religion," in MBCP 25–47.

23. Buber's earlier thought came under harsh attack by Rosenzweig in 1914 for its "atheistic" and liberal tendencies, although Buber probably did not see the critique until many years later. Franz Rosenzweig, "Atheistic Theology," in *Philosophical and Theological Writings*, trans. and ed. Paul W. Franks and Michael L. Morgan (Indianapolis, IN: Hackett, 2000), 10–24.

24. Leo Strauss, "Preface to *Spinoza's Critique of Religion*," in *Jewish Philosophy and the Crisis of Modernity: Essays and Lectures in Modern Jewish Thought*, ed. Kenneth H. Green (New York: SUNY Press, 1997), 137.

25. Carl Schmitt, *The Crisis of Parliamentary Democracy*, trans. Ellen Kennedy (Cambridge, MA: MIT Press, 1988).

26. Emanuel Hirsch, "Demokratie und Christentum," *Der Geisteskampf der Gegenwart* 54 (1918): 57–60, cited in Klaus Tanner, "Protestant Revolt against Modernity," in *The Weimar Moment*, 8.

27. Anson Rabinbach, "Between Apocalypse and Enlightenment: Benjamin, Bloch, and Modern German-Jewish Messianism," *In the Shadow of Catastrophe: German Intellectuals between Apocalypse and Enlightenment* (Berkeley: University of California Press, 1997), 27–65; Michael Jennings, "Walter Benjamin, Religion, and a Theological Politics, ca. 1922," in *The Weimar Moment*, 109–121.

28. A "left-Schmittianism" existed already in the 1960s and bore some responsibility for rehabilitating Schmitt's reputation as a thinker after he refused denazification. More recently: Gopal Balakrishnan, *The Enemy: An Intellectual Portrait of Carl Schmitt* (London: Verso, 2000); Chantal Mouffe, ed., *The Challenge of Carl Schmitt* (London: Verso, 1999).

29. Scholars have noted the prevalence of "romantic" orientation across political lines. Paul Breines, "A Völkisch Left?," *Reviews in European History* 1.1 (June 1974): 133–138; George Mosse, "The Influence of the *Völkisch* Idea on German Jewry," *Studies of the Leo Baeck Institute*, ed. Max Kreutzberger (New York: Frederick Ungar, 1967), 81–114.

30. Yossef Schwartz, "The Politicization of the Mystical in Buber and His Contemporaries," in NPMB 205–218.

31. Kavka cites Zank, "Buber and *Religionswissenschaft*," as a previous iteration of the claim. Martin Kavka, "Verification (*Bewährung*) in Martin Buber," *Journal of Jewish Thought and Philosophy* 20.1 (2012): 71–98.

32. Paradigmatic is the prolific Buber scholar Maurice Friedman, whose three-volume biography of Buber is replete with expressions such as "however long it would take Buber to reach the life of dialogue in its fullness, here is already one of the important milestones on the way." MBEY 114.

33. KG 19–20. My emphasis.

34. Or at least, it "seems to have been intended as a *Habilitationsschrift*." Mendes-Flohr, "Buber's Rhetoric," 2. Mendes-Flohr also describes Buber's eventual symbolic acceptance by the Israeli academy on February 28, 1960, when he was unanimously named president of the Israel Academy of Sciences and Humanities. Such acceptance did not guarantee subsequent scholarly reputation. Scholem's major attack on Buber's interpretation of Hasidism was published the same year, as if to place Buber's new status in question as soon as it was granted. (Thanks to Moshe Idel for this point.)

35. Letter to S. H. Bergmann, September 1929, cited in Mendes-Flohr, "Kingdom of God," 27. The context relates to KG as Buber states that he "has no idea" whether or when that work will be "recognized by official [*sic*] scholarship despite its ideas and methods." Mendes-Flohr cites another letter to Bergmann, in which Buber flatly states: "Ich bin kein Universitätsmensch."

36. Buber's interest in the topics and approaches of the science of religion was genuine. He kept a notebook listing the more than six thousand volumes in his library that touched on "Religionskunde, Religionsphilosophie und verwandte Gebiete." Furthermore, he constructed his lectures at the University of Frankfurt around such topics as "Wie ist Religionswissenschaft möglich?" (1924) and "Probleme der Religionssoziologie" (1933); Stroumsa, "Presence, Not Gnosis," 27, 31.

37. Rivka Horwitz, *Buber's Way to* I and Thou: *The Development of Martin Buber's Thought and His "Religion as Presence" Lectures* (New York: Jewish Publication Society, 1988).

38. Ibid. Stroumsa provides two of these plans. In both, *I and Thou* appears as the first volume, followed by entries on such topics as "Primary Forms of Religious Life" and "Magic," and concluding with "Religious Power and Our Time (The Power and the Kingdom)."

39. Ibid., 30.

40. Zank, "Buber and *Religionswissenschaft*," 64–65. Zank argues on the basis of Buber's lecture topics in the years following the publication of *Ich und Du*, as well as the "'Schematic sketch of the university-based study of religion' . . . which Buber presumably submitted to Gershom Scholem in 1933 when he applied for a professorship at the Hebrew University." This document increases the five sections of Buber's previous plans to seven.

41. Stroumsa, "Presence, Not Gnosis," 43. He qualifies this verdict with the judgment that "Buber is still sorely needed in the Israeli academe—so sorely that few understand what is missing," 47.

42. Zank, "Buber and *Religionswissenschaft*," 63.

43. One estimate is that Buber's writings on the Bible constitute "more than a quarter of his literary output." Karl-Johan Illman, "Buber and the Bible: Guiding Principles and the Legacy of His Interpretation," in MBCP 87.

44. Michael Brenner, *The Renaissance of Jewish Culture in Weimar Germany* (New Haven, CT: Yale University Press, 1996), 69–99; Nahum N. Glatzer, "The Frankfort Lehrhaus," *Leo Baeck Institute Yearbook I*, ed. Robert Weltsch (London: East and West Library, 1956), 105–122.

45. Rosenzweig to Buber, January 12, 1923, cited in Mendes-Flohr, "Buber's Rhetoric," 4. *Apikoros* is a rabbinic term for a kind of heretic.

46. Buber, "The How and Why of Our Bible Translation," in ST 212.

47. Hannah Arendt, "A Guide for Youth: Martin Buber," in *The Jewish Writings*, by Hannah Arendt, ed. Jerome Kohn and Ron H. Feldman (New York: Schocken Books, 2007), 32–33.

48. Donald L. Niewyk, *The Jews in Weimar Germany* (New Brunswick, NJ: Transaction Publishers, 2001), 58. On Stapel, see Schmidt, "'The Politicization of Heaven': Wilhelm Stapel's Political Theology of Nationalist Sovereignty," in *Race and Political Theology*, 54–82.

49. Ibid; cf. Buber, "From a Letter to Hermann Gerson," January 1929, in ST 200–202.

50. Siegfried Kracauer criticized the Buber-Rosenzweig translation as reactionary, since its individualistic conception of divine-human dialogue allegedly inhibited social solidarity; Martin Jay, "Politics of Translation: Siegfried Kracauer and Walter Benjamin on the Buber-Rosenzweig Bible," *Leo Baeck Institute Year Book XXI* (London: Secker & Warburg, 1976), 3–24.

51. Martin Buber, Judah Magnes, and Moshe Smilansky, *Palestine a Bi-National State* (New York: Ihud, 1946), 32–36.

52. Cited in Gershon Shafir, *Land, Labor and the Origins of the Israeli-Palestinian Conflict, 1882–1914* (Cambridge: Cambridge University Press, 1989), xxiv.

PART I

From Anarchism to Anarcho-Theocracy: The Birth of Theopolitics

O, personality of man! Can it be that for sixty centuries you have groveled in this abjection? You call yourself holy and sacred, but you are only the prostitute, the unwearied and unpaid prostitute, of your servants, of your monks, and of your soldiers. You know it, and you permit it. To be GOVERNED is to be kept in sight, inspected, spied upon, directed, law-driven, numbered, enrolled, indoctrinated, preached at, controlled, estimated, valued, censured, commanded, by creatures who have neither the right, nor the wisdom, nor the virtue to do so. . . . To be GOVERNED is to be at every operation, at every transaction, noted, registered, enrolled, taxed, stamped, measured, numbered, assessed, licensed, authorized, admonished, forbidden, reformed, corrected, punished. It is, under the pretext of public utility, and in the name of the general interest, to be placed under contribution, trained, ransomed, exploited, monopolized, extorted, squeezed, mystified, robbed; then, at the slightest resistance, the first word of complaint, to be repressed, fined, despised, harassed, tracked, abused, clubbed, disarmed, choked, imprisoned, judged, condemned, shot, deported, sacrificed, sold, betrayed; and, to crown all, mocked, ridiculed, outraged, dishonored. That is government; that is its justice; that is its morality.

—Pierre-Joseph Proudhon, *The General Idea of the Revolution in the Nineteenth Century*

Socialism is the attempt to lead man's common life to a bond of common spirit in freedom, that is, to religion.

—Gustav Landauer

1 The True Front

Buber and Landauer on Anarchism and Revolution

Me? I'm the king of the twentieth century. I'm the boogeyman. The villain . . .
The black sheep of the family.

    —V to Evey, *V for Vendetta*

These anarchists are not anarchic enough for me.

    —Gustav Landauer, "Anarchic Thoughts on Anarchism"

Introduction: Anarchism by Any Other Name

Martin Buber and Gustav Landauer met in Berlin circa 1900 at a gathering of the Neue Gemeinschaft (New Community), a mystical society that Landauer would shortly quit. The two men maintained a mutually beneficial intellectual and personal relationship for many years, often seeing each other nearly daily. They had a falling out during the Great War, when Landauer pilloried Buber's naïve exaltation of the supposedly noble spirit of sacrifice prevailing in Europe. This criticism led to an about-face in which Buber reexamined his previous philosophical commitments, beginning the process that would eventually lead to the publication of *Ich und Du* (*I and Thou*) in 1923. Before that happened, however, Landauer was murdered in May 1919 by the Freikorps (Free Corps) paramilitary troops sent from Berlin to put down the short-lived Bavarian Council Republic, and Buber honored his memory as the literary executor of his estate.

This narrative of friendship, told most definitively by Paul Mendes-Flohr, has been adopted by nearly every scholar since.[1] Ordinarily, however, this story is invoked to say something about the origins of Buber's dialogic philosophy. Here, I attend more to the political implications of Buber's friendship with Landauer than to the gradual changes in his philosophical vocabulary, and I ask different questions: What does it mean that Buber spent nearly two decades as the close confidante of perhaps the most important German anarchist of the century? How should we understand the fact that, with the exception of Buber's interest in Palestine as a site for the realization of their shared ideals, and in the "Jewish movement" (of which Zionism was one part) as a potential vehicle for this realization, there is little to no daylight between the two men's political outlooks? This was especially true after 1916, when in the wake of Landauer's denunciation of Buber's war politics, Buber began to stress the dangers of nationalism and imperialism attendant on the Zionist effort.

It is not that Mendes-Flohr plays down these affinities. For example, he shows that Buber's 1918 essay *Der Heilige Weg* (*The Holy Way*) "indicates a considerable debt to Landauer, in particular to his political anarchism," and he notes that "the very first essays that mark this volte-face focus on the problem of the state."[2] Nonetheless, later scholars have hesitated to fully develop these indications, and politics is underplayed in the secondary literature. Not only do scholars hesitate to describe Buber as an anarchist; some find it difficult to even admit that he has a politics at all.[3] Maurice Friedman, for example, bases his claim that Buber was "neither a pacifist nor an anarchist like Gustav Landauer" on an exchange in August 1963 between Buber and a young student of the kibbutz movement, Hermann Meier-Cronemeyer.[4] Having read Buber's work *Paths in Utopia* (1947), and his essay "Society and the State" (1951), Meier-Cronemeyer wrote to ask Buber why he did not refer to his politics of "the social principle" as "anarchism." Was it fear of the dubious reputation of the term? Buber responded that the term "anarchism" did not speak to him because "it means an overcoming of relations of power—which is impossible as long as the nature of man is what it is."[5]

One could argue that this is ample evidence to justify Friedman's claim that Buber is not an anarchist, since he never explicitly avows anarchism, and on at least this one occasion he disavows it.[6] One historian of anarchism, Peter Marshall, agrees: "Buber ultimately parted company with the anarchists by arguing that the State can in some circumstances have a legitimate role."[7] However, as another historian of anarchism, George Woodcock, has shown, there has been an increasing tendency over the years for anarchists to embrace the view "that human beings are improvable but not . . . perfectible. We must accept the probability of imperfection and limit anti-sociality where it impinges on the lives of others. . . . The more we build and strengthen an alternative society, the more the state is weakened."[8] By these lights, the precise view in the name of which Buber disavowed anarchism is declared to be anarchism.[9] Acceptance of this wider understanding of anarchism, developed partially under the influence of renewed readings of Landauer himself, explains why other scholars since the 1970s have felt little need to justify calling Buber an anarchist.[10] In uncritically accepting Buber's distinction between his own politics and anarchism, however, Friedman continuously describes Buber's political orientation using awkward euphemisms and neologisms, such as "the politics of the social principle."[11]

Yet Buber himself set the precedent for these vague, cumbersome labels. He knew well, for example, that Landauer understood his own anarchism not to entail any kind of final, idyllic "overcoming of power-relations." On the contrary, Landauer argued in a work commissioned and published by Buber himself that "no revolution will ever achieve its goals."[12] In his 1947 work *Paths in Utopia*, Buber praises Landauer for declining to formulate "the absolute goal," for understanding that "all true socialism is relative," and for his insight that "socialism is not the invention of anything new but the discovery of something actually present, of something that has grown."[13] As Buber explains, *Paths in Utopia* is structured progressively, unfolding a core idea from its beginnings: "In the history of utopian socialism three pairs of active thinkers emerge, each pair being bound together in a peculiar way and also to its generation: Saint-Simon and Fourier, Owen and Proudhon, Kropotkin and Gustav Landauer."[14] Buber here places Landauer at the end of an intellectual lineage that includes the classical anarchist theorists Pierre-Joseph Proudhon (1809–1865) and Peter Kropotkin (1842–1921), arguing that he makes essential improvements on this line of thought, *from within it*.[15] He also, however, designates this line of thought as "socialism" or "utopian socialism." Buber is aware that "socialism" is a term that, like "democracy," allows for variants, and the purpose of *Paths in Utopia* is to discern a particular line within that term. Despite the fact, however, that those whom he treats in the book's central chapters all referred to themselves as anarchists, and used "anarchism" and "socialism" interchangeably (from Proudhon on this is a defining trait of "utopian socialism" as against its "scientific" cousin, Marxism), he declines to use this term himself but alternates between assorted alternatives. This sets the precedent for all the vagaries in the secondary literature, which reference Buber's "social philosophy" rather than his political thought, or his "decentralized federalism" or espousal of "anocracy" rather than his relationship to anarchism.[16] Meier-Cronemeyer may have been right to suggest that Buber was afraid to be tarred with the anarchist brush, hoping to have more success with utopian socialism.[17]

If, however, there is little to no difference between Buber and Landauer on the plane of political and social theory, then this deserves greater recognition. In the end, such recognition might lead one to remove Landauer from the list of anarchist authors rather than add Buber to it. Yet for scholars to argue that Buber has no politics, or to take him at his word in distinguishing his politics from anarchism, without investigating his relationship to Landauer and other anarchist thinkers, is to take sides unwittingly in a dispute among socialists. Moreover, there is a sense in which terminology is destiny. There is an anarchist "canon," in which William Godwin (1756–1836), Proudhon, Mikhail Bakunin (1814–1876), and Kropotkin, along with Alexander Berkman (1870–1936), Rudolf Rocker (1873–1958), and Emma Goldman (1869–1940), number among the classics. For the most part, this canon receives little academic attention as compared to its Marxist "big brother," and it is studied today primarily by those personally attracted to anarchism.[18] Buber demonstrates in *Paths in Utopia* that he knows this literature well, often thanks to Landauer's translations, but Buber scholars have shown little interest in contextualizing their understanding of Buber through independent exploration of anarchist thought. Consequently, the general perception of his politics follows the nebulous lines that Friedman, following Buber himself, laid down.

Landauer before Buber: Anarchist Activism, 1890–1899

When he met Buber, Landauer already had a long record of radical agitation behind him. In fact, at that very moment he was embroiled in a highly politicized libel case, which would result in a six-month prison sentence.[19] Moritz von Egidy, a former lieutenant colonel who became a Christian anarchist and pacifist, had asked Landauer's help in securing a retrial for Albert Ziethen, a prisoner whom von Egidy believed to have been railroaded. In February 1898, Landauer published an article in his newspaper, *Der Sozialist*, accusing a Berlin police official of manufacturing evidence in the case, and he repeated the charges in a letter to members of the Reichstag and the state's attorney's office.[20] But von Egidy died before the trial, and Landauer dedicated the entire January 1899 issue of *Der Sozialist* to his memory.[21] In that issue Landauer quotes this passage by von Egidy, which he could have easily written himself: "Unthinking men connect the idea of 'Anarchy' with the idea of disorder; that, however, is contained neither in the word nor in the strivings of those who call themselves anarchists. On the contrary: a more complete order, an order that rests upon self-discipline and self-rule; an order without force."[22] A month later, still in mourning for his friend, Landauer attended the meeting of the Neue Gemeinschaft at which he met his second wife, Hedwig Lachmann, and other future collaborators, possibly including Buber.

Commenting on the early years of Buber and Landauer's friendship, Mendes-Flohr contends that "Buber's earlier intellectual relationship with Landauer was found[ed] on common aesthetic and metaphysical concerns; political and social questions were almost entirely absent from their prewar relationship."[23] I would qualify this judgment in two ways: first, at the moment that Landauer and Buber first met, the former was on the cusp of a withdrawal from his stormy public political career, which would persist for the first eight years of their acquaintance. Second, I emphasize different elements of Buber's 1904 essay on Landauer's thought. These steps will help us determine the extent to which Buber and Landauer agreed politically before the outbreak of the Great War, in order to contextualize their subsequent relationship. However, we have to consider Landauer's life and career before his encounter with Buber, in order to avoid defining their initial interest in each other according to their later accomplishments.

Landauer was born in Karlsruhe in 1870, nearly twins with Otto von Bismarck's united Germany. In 1875, the Sozialistische Arbeiterpartei Deutschlands (SAPD) was established through the fusion of the two previously dominant left-wing factions: Ferdinand Lassalle's Allgemeiner Deutscher Arbeiterverein (General German Workers' Association) and the Sozialdemokratische Arbeiterpartei Deutschlands (Social Democratic Workers' Party of Germany) of Wilhelm Liebknecht and August Bebel.[24] The Sozialistengesetze (Socialist Laws) of 1878 attempted to outlaw socialist organizing but failed, and when Bismarck retired in 1890, the Reichstag declined to renew them. Now allowed to organize openly once again, the SAPD renamed itself the Sozialdemokratische Partei Deutschlands (SPD), the Social Democratic Party of Germany. Between 1891 and 1914, the SPD expanded continually until it became the single largest party in the country.

The lapse of the antisocialist laws occurred when Landauer was twenty years old, a student of German classicism and romanticism at University of Berlin.[25] At that point, however, he was more interested in his studies than in new opportunities for activism, and he soon left Berlin for a term at University of Strasbourg (1890–1891), during which he read Nietzsche's *Birth of Tragedy* and *Thus Spoke Zarathustra*. He was profoundly influenced by Nietzsche's passionate advocacy of free, individual creativity, and he would eventually strive to integrate his politics with Nietzsche's philosophy, despite the latter's virulent antipathy to socialism and anarchism.[26] Upon his return to Berlin in April 1891, Landauer became involved with the Freie Volksbühne (Free People's Theater), an institution established by the socialist Bruno Wille for the cultural education of the working class through cheap access to theatrical performances. It was through Wille and his theater that Landauer met the group that would introduce him to anarchism.[27]

Funding for the Freie Volksbühne was provided by the SPD, which had grown from a mere political party into a mass cultural institution.[28] However, the SPD's growth was not without its casualties. At a party convention in Erfurt in 1891, the newly legalized SPD adopted the program of Karl Kautsky, both recommitting itself to the seizure of the means of production from capitalists and endorsing the moderate and legally available means of parliamentary activity. Kautsky reasoned that revolution was inevitable according to the Marxist understanding of history, such that the socialist task was the amelioration of workers' living conditions until the final battle in the class struggle. In the course of the debate over the Erfurt Program, a group of radical youth who had been members of the SAPD and who advocated boycotting electoral politics were expelled from the congress, and as a result they excluded themselves from the newly formed SPD.[29] Known as the Verein der unabhängigen Sozialisten (Association of Independent Socialists), or simply the Jungen (Young Ones), this was the group with whom Landauer chose to affiliate upon his entrance into political activism. As a result, he could later say, "I was an anarchist before I was a socialist, and one of the few who had not taken a detour via social democracy."[30] For Landauer, the conflict with the Jungen marked the SPD as rotten from the beginning, and in 1919, only weeks before he would die at the hands of its contracted militiamen, he declared, "In the entire natural history I know of no more disgusting creature than the Social Democratic Party."[31]

The split of the Jungen led rapidly to the founding of two projects that heavily involved Landauer. The first was the newspaper *Der Sozialist*, the official organ of the dissenters; Landauer soon became one of its primary editors. In its opening statement of purpose, the newspaper charged the SPD executive with opportunism, reformism, and authoritarianism: "We are opponents of legislative-parliamentary activity; experience has shown that it leads unavoidably to corruption and possibilism. We must stress the fact that parliament is an institution through which the bourgeoisie exercises its rule over the proletariat."[32] Landauer's early articles focused on the antistatist socialism of figures like Eugen Dühring (1833–1921) and Benedikt Friedländer (1866–1908), a friend and neighbor who introduced Landauer to the work of Max Stirner.[33] The title *Der Sozialist* was retained as a polemical thrust that anarchism was the only true socialism; in 1895 Landauer changed the subtitle of the paper to *Organ für Anarchismus-Sozialismus*, arguing that "anyone who is not blinded by the dogmas of the political parties will recognize that anarchism and socialism are not opposed but co-dependent. True cooperative labor and true community can only exist where individuals are free, and free individuals can only exist where our needs are met by brotherly solidarity."[34] In the fall of 1892 the second project was born when Wille and others accused the SPD of attempting to turn the Freie Volksbühne into an arm of the party, forming the Neue Freie Volksbühne in response. Landauer served on the board of the new theater for several years.[35]

The content of Landauer's anarchism evolved over the years 1893–1898, moving from an urban-focused industrial syndicalism (promoting the consolidation of democratically organized unions of factory workers) toward a rurally based valorization of agricultural work and village life that seemed to share more with *völkisch* romanticism than with modern socialist ideology.[36] The move was partially rooted in an effort to appeal to constituencies neglected by the SPD, which adhered closely to the Marxist line that the industrial proletariat was the only real revolutionary subject and that the *lumpenproletariat* and the peasantry were irrelevant. Landauer was consistent, however, in his insistence that anarchism stood for the free development of individuality in the context of a democratically organized socialist community, and that steps could be taken toward the immediate achievement of socialism, without having to wait for the forces of history to reach a predetermined juncture. His 1895 pamphlet, *A Way to the Liberation of the Working Class*, was written to support a producer cooperative launched by Wilhelm Weise, an anarchist construction worker who worked for the *Sozialist*.

In it he argued that active participation in mutual-aid projects was a necessary sentimental education as well as a revolutionary activity; workers would learn self-reliance and cooperation and unlearn bad habits of deference to authority while also building institutions that would bypass the state and capitalism by providing for the needs of their members. Not only would such a method of revolution be nonviolent; it was also the *only* way to realize socialism, since even if socialist revolutionaries were somehow to storm the halls of power and defeat the army, a people uneducated in cooperative ventures would simply restore the state the very next day.[37]

At this point we should note that anarchism was a minority movement within socialism throughout Europe and was especially weak in Germany, where *Der Sozialist* was the only anarchist paper at the time of its first run.[38] The SPD never faced any real competition for the loyalty of the urban, industrial workers, and it never acknowledged anarchism as a legitimate type of socialism. The expulsion of the Jungen from the SPD congress, which echoed the expulsion of Bakunin and the anarchists from the First International, would soon be followed by yet another (physical, forcible) expulsion of Landauer and his compatriots from the 1893 Zurich meeting of the Second International.[39] At the 1896 meeting in London another attempt was made, but the outcome was the same, except this time Landauer was able to give his speech in favor of anarchist admission before the expulsion vote came.[40] Landauer's entry into political life was thus marked by a tension: he quickly became a big fish in a very small pond.

Despite its numerical weakness, however, anarchism assumed outsized importance in the eyes of the state and the public because of its association with spectacular acts of terrorism, including bombings and political assassinations worldwide, which were then known as "propaganda by the deed." These in turn led to repressive state measures against anarchists, even in countries like Germany with very little violent anarchist agitation. Landauer himself was arrested for the first time in October 1893 merely for advocating disobedience of the law; his sentence was extended to a total of eleven months through the further charges that he had called for violent overthrow of the government; sixteen other writers for *Der Sozialist* were arrested and imprisoned on similar grounds by the end of 1894, and in January 1895 the paper was forced to close, reopening only six months later.[41]

The police campaign against *Der Sozialist* was ironic, as the paper always opposed violence, not merely because it would lead to state reprisals but also on principle. Anarchism desires a society free from coercion, whereas violence is the ultimate form of coercion. The society that anarchists want therefore cannot be built by violent means, which is contrary to the practice of voluntary association: "The anarchist idea is a peaceful idea, opposed to aggressiveness and violence," Landauer wrote in 1897.[42] He never swerved from this position, which also entails the rejection of class war on Marxist lines, the rejection of the idea of a vanguard political party, and the rejection of the dictatorship of the proletariat: "Whoever believes it is in order to demand the imposition of 'his Truth' along with the violent suppression of those with a divergent belief, may wish to wander down that road. The anarchists will walk down theirs."[43] And in 1901, in the essay "Anarchic Thoughts on Anarchism," he went on to accuse those radicals who saw themselves as the purest revolutionaries of being no better than the states they opposed:

> The anarchist politics of assassination only stems from the intention of a small group among them that wants to follow the example of the big political parties. What drives them is vanity—a craving for recognition. What they are trying to say is: "We are also doing politics. We are not idle. We are a force to be reckoned with!"
>
> These anarchists are not anarchic enough for me. They still act like a political party. Their politics are akin to simple-minded reform politics.[44]

Landauer invoked Tolstoy in support of his claim that "any kind of violence is dictatorial . . . a goal can only be reached if it is already reflected in its means." The claim that violence was needed to bring freedom to the world, Landauer argued, proved the dictatorial tendencies of its advocates: "This is yet another crucial fallacy: that one can—or must—bring anarchism to the world; that anarchy is an affair of all of humanity; that there will indeed be a day of judgment followed by a millennial era. Those who want 'to bring freedom to the world'—which will always be *their* idea of freedom—are tyrants, not anarchists."[45]

Although Landauer was far from alone among anarchists in his criticism of propaganda by the deed, it distanced him from the movement, insofar as praise of it disgusted him. Landauer thought that *Der Sozialist* had a pedagogical function of encouraging workers to think for themselves. He therefore published articles on theoretical-philosophical questions, eschewing the clear question-and-answer format of the propaganda broadsheet. In May 1897, a rival paper, *Neues Leben*, was established, which soon drew away at least half of Landauer's readership as well as much of his funding. The slow death of *Der Sozialist* over the course of 1898 discouraged and demoralized Landauer, and it coincided with an economic upswing that meant a general decline in labor agitation, thus making activism more difficult. By the time he was jailed in 1899 for the Ziethen affair, he was ready to spend time away from active engagement in politics, and to renew his focus on aesthetic and philosophical questions. This phase of his career, which scholars often refer to as his period of "isolation" or "withdrawal," lasted nearly ten years.[46]

It was at this point that Landauer attended the first meeting of the Neue Gemeinschaft, a Berlin group led by the brothers Heinrich and Julius Hart. The Hart brothers, inspired by Nietzsche's Dionysian exaltation of becoming, billed the Neue Gemeinschaft as "a community of knowledge and life."[47] The group held public lectures and discussions, published a journal called *Das Reich der Erfüllung* (The Kingdom of Fulfillment), and planned the purchase of land for communal settlement, all in the name of a mystical worldview in which suffering is caused primarily by the illusion of individuation (the separateness of phenomena).[48] Landauer was intrigued by these ideas and returned to the Neue Gemeinschaft after his release from prison in 1900, when he gave a lecture there that was to underlie much of his future thought. This may even have been the occasion of his first meeting with Buber. Before dealing with the contents of this lecture, however, we turn to Buber's youthful experiences up to the turn of the century.

Between Politics and Mysticism: Buber and Landauer, 1900–1907

Born in 1878 in Vienna, Buber lived from age three to fourteen at the house of his grandfather, Solomon Buber, a great scholar of the Haskalah, or Jewish Enlightenment, in Lemberg/Lviv (in Galicia, today Ukraine). In 1897, after four more years in Lemberg at the farm of his father, Carl, Buber enrolled at the University of Vienna and came into contact with the "superficial salon culture of bourgeoisie who despised everything Jewish from the bottom of their hearts" and who defined *Kultur* for affluent Viennese youth.[49] He was educated in both of these worlds, speaking German at home, Polish at school, and Yiddish and Hebrew at synagogue. He could read Greek, Latin, Spanish, and Dutch, and also speak English and French.[50] In his adolescence he was drawn to the poetry of Schiller and the philosophy of Kant, although Nietzsche was by far the most powerful influence on him at this time; when he was seventeen he embarked on a translation of *Thus Spoke Zarathustra* into Polish.[51] After spending the fall semester of 1897 in Vienna, he continued his education at the universities of Leipzig (winter 1897–spring 1899), Zurich (fall 1899), and Berlin (winter 1899–1900). In 1900, a few months after the death of Nietzsche, Buber wrote an essay that shows how thoroughly he then considered himself Nietzsche's disciple (although he later characterized himself as having struggled against this influence). According to this essay, Nietzsche "uncovered the feeble lies of our values and our truths . . . from dead cultures he wrested elements for new formation. In the confused and barren turmoil of the present, he collected the authentic and the productive." Here Nietzsche is read in the light of *Birth of Tragedy*, offering a project for reviving a desiccated present through the return to sources of ancient cultural power. Buber's discussion of Nietzsche marks a beginning point for his lifelong fascination with the idea of the unclassifiable:

> Is he a philosopher? He did not create a unified edifice of thought. Is he an artist? He did not create any objects. Is he a psychologist? His deepest knowledge deals with the future of the soul. Is he a poet? Only if we think of poets as they once existed: "Visionaries who tell us what might be," who give us "a foretaste

of future virtues." Is he the founder of a new *Gemeinschaft*? Many rise up in his name, but they do not unite, for each . . . owes him not thanks for general knowledge of a kind that can unite people, but the release of his own innermost powers.[52]

This idealization of Nietzsche as a founder who sought only to empower would resonate in much of Buber's later work, from his theory of pedagogy to his theopolitics.

Scholars have justifiably considered much of Buber's early work, from his anthologies of Hasidic tales to his youthful Zionist poetry, as a species of *Kulturpolitik* or *Kulturkritik*.[53] *Kultur* had an exalted sense in fin-de-siècle thought, at which the English word "culture" only gestures; *Kulturpolitik* viewed *Kultur* as the primary medium of political and social change. To be sure, Buber had a youthful interest in Lassalle, and some connections to Polish socialist student groups (his uncle Rafael Buber was a prominent Polish socialist). His early interest in Zionism was more active; in August 1899 he traveled from Leipzig, where he had founded the first Zionist student chapter, to attend the Third Zionist Congress in Basel, where he spoke as a member of the Agitations Committee.[54] But his *Kulturpolitik* meant that he saw both socialism and Zionism as in need of elevation by cultural elites, a Nietzschean *Geistesaristokratie* (aristocracy of the spirit).[55] These movements could not remain "merely" political but had to aim at achieving cultural renaissance.[56] In 1901, at age twenty-three, Buber brought this attitude to the position of editor at Theodor Herzl's Zionist newspaper *Die Welt*, and to his leadership in the "cultural Zionist" Democratic Fraction at the Fifth Zionist Congress, which stood with Ahad Ha'am against Herzl's purely "political" Zionism.[57]

When the twenty-two-year-old Buber had heard the thirty-year-old Landauer speak at the Neue Gemeinschaft in June 1900, the younger man was a middle-class student Nietzschean and the older man in the early stages of a transition, embracing the opportunity to address a new audience. Landauer's lecture was entitled "Durch Absonderung zur Gemeinschaft" (Through Separation to Community), and it was soon published in *Das Reich der Erfüllung*. Although Landauer left the Neue Gemeinschaft less than a year later, perceiving that neither its endless conversations about mystical unity nor its tentative establishment of a small commune (really a shared kitchen) would lead to meaningful social action, he did not disavow this work; it was substantially incorporated in 1903 into his first major philosophical statement, *Skepsis und Mystik: Versuche im Anschluss an Mauthners Sprachkritik* (Skepticism and Mysticism: Essays following Mauthner's Critique of Language).[58] Because *Skepsis und Mystik* also includes a critique of Julius Hart's mysticism from the standpoint of politics and ethics, we can infer that Landauer did not see his own mysticism as subject to a similar critique.[59]

In one sense, "Through Separation to Community" would have appealed to the young Buber's *geistesaristokratisch* sensibilities, as it addresses itself to an imagined vanguard or spiritual elite. However, this vanguard is different; belonging to it "is not a matter of knowledge or ability, but of perspective and orientation."[60] Only those who overcome traditional ties to authority, custom, class, faith, and profession belong to the vanguard. Landauer portrays himself as a failed preacher who had descended to the masses hoping to pull them up but had not been equal to the task. It was time for a new strategy: "We must cease descending to the masses. Instead we must precede them."[61] This meant first separating from the world of the masses, and then forming a new world, a community unto itself. This community would be a free association of men and women who were deeply in touch with the ultimate community, the relationship of the human being to the universe itself.

Landauer argued that modern modes of reasoning, which privileged abstract concepts and placed the individual subject at the center, were a political problem and not merely a philosophical error. Combining Kant and Nietzsche, Landauer reasoned that because one could prove neither that individual subjectivity formed the basis of all truth and reality, nor that it did not, he was authorized to simply assert the truth he desired: "My inner feeling that I am an isolated unit can be wrong—and I declare it so, because I do not want to be isolated. . . . I reject the certainty of my I so that I can bear life. . . . The I kills itself so that the World-I can live." Drawing on his readings of the Christian mystic Meister Eckhart, Landauer asserted that we can understand the universe through intensive study of the individual organism, our own selves.[62] Thus "the way to create a community that encompasses the entire world leads not outward, but inward. We must realize that we do not just perceive the world, but that we *are* the world." The purpose of this introspection, however, was not the idealism of Berkeley, in which the world is a reflection of our individual mind, but the recognition that we ourselves are "part-souls of the world-soul." The mystical form of this statement is paired to a more philosophical version: "'The individual' is a rigid and absolute expression for something that is very mobile and relative."[63] In both time, in which individuals carry within themselves the genetic and social presence of their ancestors, and in space, in which they can be marked out discretely only on the particular and arbitrary level visible to the human eye, Landauer found that the concept of the individual needed redescription. In its current form, the concept only validated the arbitrary faux communities into which people are born and in which they are held captive by authority; eliminating this concept would give rise to both "true" individuality, "deep, ancient, and everlasting," and to true fellowship, in place of sham communities like the state.[64]

We can only speculate as to the immediate impact of Landauer's lecture on Buber.[65] A year later, however, he quoted it in his own talk to the Neue

Gemeinschaft, on the topic "Alte und Neue Gemeinschaft" (Old and New Community).[66] Here Buber claims, in the vein of what Mendes-Flohr has called his "*Erlebnis*-mysticism," that there are fleeting, ecstatic moments in which we experience the unity of everything, and that our goal should be to extend such moments to encompass the existential particulars of the day-to-day.[67] Landauer, however, had not dwelled on the experience of unity as much as on the recognition of it. Buber's interpretation (he in fact identifies the *Erlebnis* of which he speaks with Landauer's words) thus represents his own interest in intense, heightened experience.[68] Buber waxed rhapsodic, proclaiming that "our community does not *want* revolution; it *is* revolution." If the subject of this battle cry is the Neue Gemeinschaft, which Buber would soon follow Landauer in deserting, it must be read as the naïve enthusiasm of youth. If, however, we take note of the idea of revolution as a present state of being rather than an anticipated future event, we find the core of a commitment that would endure throughout the years. It is unlikely, at any rate, that Buber interpreted Landauer's retreat from the public political scene as an endorsement of quietism, given his own subsequent Zionist activism and Landauer's "Anarchic Thoughts on Anarchism." More likely, he took Landauer to be referring to a kind of nonpolitical, cultural activism, through the ringing call: "Let us create our communal life, let us form centers of a new kind of being, let us free ourselves from the commonness of our contemporaries!"[69]

Given that the form of Buber's cultural activism in 1900–1903 was Zionism, and that he returned to Zionism at the end of the decade in his "Speeches on Judaism," it is worth inspecting another passage of "Through Separation to Community," one we find echoed in those speeches:

> The more firmly an individual stands on its own ground, the deeper it retreats into itself . . . the more it will find itself united with the past, with what it originally is. What man originally is, what his most intimate and hidden is, what his inviolable own is, is the large community of the living in himself, his blood and his kin. Blood is thicker than water; the community, as which the individual finds itself, is more powerful and more noble and more ancient than the weak influences of state and society. Our most individual is our most universal. The more deeply I go into myself, the more I become part of the world.[70]

Despite his invocation of blood, however, Landauer nowhere mentions the nation as the exemplar of the community he means, let alone the race. Although Landauer does mean that one bears one's ancestry and social customs within oneself as a powerful influence, this sense does not carry with it any kind of hierarchy of ancestries; there is no pseudoscientific racialism here and no injunction against unnatural mixing of heritages. Landauer has not departed from anarchism to embrace *völkisch* racialism; he has attempted to deepen his anarchism by rooting it in a richer conception of subjectivity. Buber, however, meeting Landauer at a moment of transition from active politics to philosophical contemplation, may not have recognized the particular relationship that Landauer saw between his mysticism and his anarchism. In his attempt to apply Landauer's insights in the speeches on Judaism, he would skirt the line of racialism, as in his outlandish claims that the Jew's motor functions differ from those of the Gentile, or that the Jew experiences time more keenly than space.[71] This suggests that as late as 1916, when the second *Drei Reden* were published as *Vom Geist des Judentums*, Buber failed to appreciate significant elements of Landauer's thought, and he would continue to do so until their clash over the Great War.

Buber left Berlin for Leipzig in 1901 with a missionary zeal for social action, which he realized during highly productive yet tempestuous years of service to official Zionism. He attended the Fifth and Sixth Zionist Congresses, first as a favored protégé of Herzl and then as an ideological opponent. Landauer, meanwhile, left for England with Hedwig Lachmann, moving first to London, where he came to know Rudolf Rocker, and then to Bromley, where he was a neighbor of Peter Kropotkin.[72] Although he was withdrawn from activism, 1903 was a banner year for Landauer's profile as a writer: his renderings of Eckhart were finally published, as was *Macht und Mächte*, a collection of novellas; finally, and most important, he released *Skepsis und Mystik*, which included "Through Separation to Community," largely unchanged, as the first section.[73] In 1904, the same year that he withdrew from high-profile Zionist activity following Herzl's death, Buber submitted his dissertation on the problem of individuation in Nicholas of Cusa and Jakob Böhme, prepared to move to Florence to begin his research on Hasidism, and wrote a review of Landauer's recent work for the Vienna journal *Die Zeit*.[74]

In this essay, entitled "Gustav Landauer," Buber reveals a wide knowledge of Landauer's work. It is nearly a literary biography; it opens with an epigraph taken from Landauer's Eckhart translation, followed by a comparison of two articles on anarchism published six years apart in *Zukunft*, before moving on to cover *Skepsis und Mystik*, then working its way back to Landauer's Nietzschean novellas: *Der Todesprediger* (*Preacher of Death*), *Arnold Himmelheber*, and *Lebendig Tot* (*Living Dead*).[75] Buber accords Landauer his highest praise: he sees him as developing, growing both as an artist and as a thinker. In particular, he claims that the two articles on anarchism, one from 1895 and one from 1901, reveal "one of the most beautiful documents of human self-liberation."[76] The earlier essay taught a dogma, anarchism, which, though held by many to be the purest expression of freedom, and taught by Landauer in as undogmatic a way as possible, remained dogma. The later essay achieves what Buber considers a magnificent psychological insight: that even the desire to bring freedom to others can indicate a despotic personality, especially if one intends to employ "free violence" as a means. Buber is highly impressed with Landauer's claim that such a person "is a despot, not an anarchist," and inspired by his vision of a new society in the midst of the old. Paraphrasing Landauer, Buber claims that "anarchy is in truth a basic disposition of every man."[77]

However, Buber also argues that although Landauer had fully developed as an activist and a thinker, he had yet to form fully as an artist.[78] The final lines of his essay read, "Only when this will have happened, will we, when we single out the representative men of this time, be able to stamp the superscription: Gustav Landauer, or, the anarchist."[79] This conclusion implies that one becomes an anarchist by becoming free, by developing one's individuality and deepest self. Thus, says Buber, by Landauer's own definition, he will not truly be an anarchist until he perfects his art, since this is what will make him a man in full. Once again, as with the 1901 lecture, there is great similarity between Buber and Landauer but also a significant difference. Buber seems to agree with Landauer that nonstate socialism is the only politics for free people, and he also takes with him the further step that one must criticize anarchism as a dogma in order to become truly anarchistic. The Buber of 1904, however, emphasizes the necessity of aesthetic creation to the process of liberation to a much greater degree than does Landauer.

The year 1905 was quiet for both men, but plans were set in motion that would lead to both of them "emerging from seclusion."[80] While working as a consulting editor for the publishing firm Rütten & Loening, Buber conceived of the idea of a series of monographs that would increase the presence of the fledgling discipline of sociology in German public intellectual life: *Die Gesellschaft* (Society). He first approached Georg Simmel, who had been his teacher at the University of Berlin and sparked his interest in sociology, with the proposal to edit the series, but he took on the job himself when Simmel declined.[81] Each monograph would be devoted to a particular topic, for which Buber sought out the writer he considered most appropriate; these titles ranged widely, from *Sport* to *Dilettantism* to *The Erotic* to *The Department Store*. There were also a number of entries addressing clearly "political" topics. The first seven volumes of the forty-volume series were published in 1906, the same year that Buber's studies of Hasidism bore their first fruit with the release of *Die Geschichten des Rabbi Nachman* (*Tales of Rabbi Nachman*). This first crop included *Das Proletariat*, by Werner Sombart; *Die Religion*, by Georg Simmel; *Die Politik*, by Alexander Ular; and *Der Streik*, by Eduard Bernstein.[82] The series, aimed at the educated but nonspecialist upper middle class, was well received.[83]

The political orientation of *Die Gesellschaft* was carefully curated to appeal to its core audience, which meant that the views represented began at liberalism and moved left from there, excluding conservative nationalists as well as orthodox Marxists.[84] The 1906 group of titles set the tone: non-Marxist socialism was well represented in depth and variety through the presence of Sombart and Bernstein (the latter already famous as a critic of historical materialism).[85] The group of 1907 titles followed suit, including such works as *Das Parlament*, by Hellmut von Gerlach; *Der Staat*, by Franz Oppenheimer; and *Die Revolution*, by Gustav Landauer.[86]

Our Revolution, 1907–1914

Buber wrote to Landauer on July 26, 1906, to solicit his involvement in *Die Gesellschaft*: "The publisher is understandably interested in a volume on the current and interesting theme 'revolution,' and *I* cannot think of anyone better than you. Do you think I am wrong in this, and can you with a clear conscience mention even *one* other name to me?"[87] Buber expressed confidence that Landauer had the experience and the "*absolute* honesty" necessary for the proper treatment of the subject. Landauer responded favorably, and a year later *Die Revolution* appeared.[88]

Revolution is an idiosyncratic work, but this is probably what makes it the book that Buber wanted. It scrupulously avoids discussing revolutionary strategy, arguing for the anarchist rather than the Marxist method of revolution, debating whether revolution is preferable to reform, or carrying out comparative analysis of specific historical revolutions. In fact, it begins with a mockery of such a project, on the assumption that "the best way to prove that something cannot be treated in a certain form is to do this with honesty and sincerity until we cannot carry on any longer."[89] It does not even make clear, for much of the book, what revolution is or whether Landauer thinks it is a good thing. He can seem very ambivalent:

> The era from the year 1500 until now (and beyond) is an era without a common spirit. It is an era where spirit is present only in certain individuals; an era of individualism, and hence of atomized individuals as well as uprooted and dissolved masses; an era of personalism, and hence individual melancholic and ingenious spirits; an era without truth (like any era without spirit) . . . an era of human beings without any heart, without integrity, without courage, without tolerance. However, because of all this, it is also an era of experimentation, audacity, boldness, bravery, and rebellion. This is the complexity in which we find ourselves, this is our transition, our disorientation, our search—*our revolution*.[90]

This attitude toward the period commonly labeled "modernity" (although Landauer critiques labels like "antiquity" and "the Middle Ages" as biased terminology reflecting Renaissance prejudices), especially compared to his praise of the communal life of the preceding thousand years, has led many to consider *Revolution* a work of romanticism. Landauer, however, reports that he takes much of his information and many of his quotations concerning "the Christian era" directly from Kropotkin's *Mutual Aid*.[91] The two men make similar use of the medieval period. What they prize in the years 500–1500 is not the church and the monarchy playing their "proper" roles in society but instead what Landauer calls the "principle of ordered multiplicity": "multiple mutually exclusive social institutions existed side by side, were permeated by a unifying spirit, and constituted a union of many sovereign elements that came together in liberty."[92] No single institution—the church, the state, the lords, the village organization, the guilds, the various local or regional political assemblies—could claim to define communal life. Each person could belong simultaneously to any or many of these institutions, which overlapped so that the totality of society formed a *Gesellschaft der Gesellschaften*, a society of societies. Of course, "there was also feudalism, clericalism, inquisition, and oppression. To those I can only say: I know, but . . ."[93] Rather than a reactionary will to restoration, both Kropotkin and Landauer wish to infuse contemporary struggles with a vision of something achievable, because it once existed.

Much of *Revolution* addresses the questions and problems of writing history. Landauer tends to assume that writing history is inevitably activist; he is skeptical of claims to objectivity and thinks that when we call up the past, we also intervene in it, in the service of our contemporary interests. Leaning on Fritz Mauthner's critique of language, Landauer becomes a sophisticated critic of historical categories, which he sees as literary in nature and beholden to the arbitrary narratives he rejects. Landauer takes the longest possible view of human history, from which vantage point the history we "know about"—recorded history—seems very short indeed: "Since humanity is many thousands of years old . . . how can we not regard those who have shared the last few millennia with us as contemporaries?"[94]

Thus Landauer treats historical figures as though they were currently living allies and enemies, fighting in (or against) the one revolution that has stretched out over the past few centuries. The "obnoxious . . . sinister . . . terrible" Martin Luther comes in for special condemnation, as the man who fought Rome (the church) only to revive Rome (the society). The Reformation sought to end scholasticism, clericalism, and narrow-mindedness, but it only "laid the foundation for the acceptance of the absolute power of the princes, and hence for the original forms of the modern state. . . . [Luther] radically separated life from faith and substituted organized violence for spirit [in his fight against the Peasants' War]."[95] Yet it turns out that the revolutionaries too are contaminated by this privatization of spirit. They come to see goodwill toward their enemies as powerlessness, forgetting that "*there is no creation without community, spirit, and love.*"[96] Hence the succession of merely political revolutions, seeking to change only who holds which power-positions, while abandoning the effort to revolutionize *all* of life— what Landauer considers the true revolution.[97]

No single individual has an outsized role in the millennia-spanning story of Landauer's *Revolution*. But if, for the sake of drama, Martin Luther can be said to be the villain of the piece, then Étienne de La Boétie (1530–1563) is without a doubt the hero. La Boétie was a judge, poet, and author of *Discours sur la servitude volontaire* (*Discourse on Voluntary Servitude*), which, according to his great friend Michel de Montaigne, he wrote when he was only sixteen years old.[98] La Boétie's question, as Landauer sees it, is how "an entire people, consisting of countless individuals, [can] allow a single person to torture them, abuse them, and rule over them against their interests and against their will." Landauer summarizes La Boétie's view of how humanity lost its natural freedom: "At some point—caused by outside attack or internal corruption—human beings lost their freedom. They were followed by individuals who never knew freedom and had no idea how sweet it tasted. It became a habit to be complacent in servitude; and habit is stronger than nature."[99] Add to that the bread and circuses that tyrants provide, the co-optation of the priesthood, and a class of people close to the king who profit from the tyranny, and we can understand how servitude becomes possible. It is at this point that La Boétie makes what Landauer considers his ultimate contribution. According to La Boétie:

> We need nothing . . . but the desire and the will to be free. We suffer a servitude that is voluntary. It almost seems as if we humans reject the beautiful gift of freedom because it is too easy to attain: "Be determined to no longer be servants and you will be free. I do not encourage you to chase away the tyrant or to throw him off his throne. All you need to do is stop supporting him—you will see how he will consequently, like a huge colossus deprived of its base, tumble and disappear."[100]

Landauer compares tyranny in this picture to a fire that cannot be put out by water but will die if the people who are feeding it cease to do so. As the first to provide us with this image, and for replacing a negative and critical revolutionary stance by a positive one, Landauer puts La Boétie at the head of his own most precious canon, the anarchist one: "[He] already said what others would later say in various languages: Godwin, Stirner, Proudhon, Bakunin, Tolstoy. . . . The message is: It is *in you*! It is not on the outside. It *is you*. Humans shall not be united by domination, but as brothers *without domination: an-archy*. Today, however, we still lack the consciousness for such a positive motto, so for now the motto must remain: *without domination*: _____."[101]

The simultaneity of *Revolution* and Buber's early Hasidic anthologies is striking and not usually noted. *Revolution* is bracketed by them, with *The Tales of Rabbi Nachman* (1906) on one side and *Die Legende des Baalschem* (*The Legend of the Baal-Shem*) (1908) on the other. Buber's presentation of Hasidism in these works attracted attention and wide renown, eventually leading to an invitation to address the Bar Kochba Society of young Zionists in Prague. The "Speeches on Judaism" he delivered there, beginning in 1909, made Buber a leader of Central European Jewish youth; their influence is often described as electrifying.[102] The mission of the Hasidic anthologies and the "Speeches," taken together, according to Buber, is the renewal (*Erneuerung*) of Judaism—a word specifically chosen to augment and supplement "renaissance," perhaps in acknowledgment of Landauer's critique of the European Renaissance.[103] At the very beginning of his work on Rabbi Nachman, echoing Landauer's statements on the function of history, Buber disavows a "philological" purpose, proclaiming instead that his goal is to recover the essence of the tales, to make them available for contemporary use.[104] By presenting Hasidic sources as part of a broader effort to renew Judaism, Buber avoids the destructive effects of a purely negative revolutionary attitude. He is seeking to create a new community of positive alliances, "through life" and not through contemplation. Landauer recognized this fact in his glowing review of *Legend of the Baal Shem* in 1910, which marked a turning point for him in terms of a positive view of his own Judaism.[105] The effects of this renewed interest in Judaism could be seen nearly immediately, in the 1911 work *Aufruf zum Sozialismus*, wherein Landauer interprets the Mosaic institution of the Jubilee as a command for permanent revolution: "Revolt as constitution; transformation and revolution as a rule established once and for all; order through the spirit as intention; that was the great and sacred heart of the Mosaic social order. We need that again: a new rule and transformation by the spirit, which will not establish things and institutions in a final form, but will declare itself as permanently at work in them."[106] This is not to say that he moved closer to religious Judaism, only that he came to a more favorable understanding of Judaism as something he could claim as his own tradition. Whereas other religions feature gods helping their nation and protecting its heroes, in Judaism "God is *eternally opposed* to servility; he is, therefore, the insurrectionary [*Aufrührer*], the arouser [*Aufrüttler*], the admonisher [*Mahner*]."[107] As Michael Löwy has noted, for Landauer the Jewish religion became a manifestation of "the people's holy dissatisfaction with itself."[108]

Revolution marked Landauer's return to public political activity. He announced this intention at the end of the work: "Our aim is that all those who understand the conditions we live in and who feel incapable of supporting them any longer unite in alliances and work for their own, immediate consumption: in settlements, in cooperatives, and so forth."[109] In May and June 1908 he gave the lectures that would become the *Aufruf*; it was at those meetings that he collected the first signatures for the founding of the Sozialist Bund, an effort to realize at last his own vision of anarchism through a network of independent groups committed to "replacing" rather than overthrowing capitalism and the state. He supported this vision through the revival of *Der Sozialist* in 1909, this time truly as his own paper, for propagating the views of the Bund; in other venues he published essays such as "Thirty Socialist Theses" and "The Twelve Articles of the Socialist Bund."[110] Bund groups formed throughout Germany and in other countries, reaching a total of about eight hundred members. Buber joined, as did Erich Mühsam, a young anarchist bohemian Landauer had met at the Neue Gemeinschaft who would later be Landauer's closest collaborator in the Bavarian Revolution.[111] For several years, Landauer relished the project of helping the Sozialist Bund to grow, as well as the opportunity to develop and debate his ideas in conversation with the wider socialist and anarchist movements. By September 1911, however, he was filled with foreboding over an imminent European war and worked over the following few years to prevent such a war from becoming reality.[112]

The Clarifying Fire: World War I

Although Buber and Landauer maintained their strong friendship during the years leading up to World War I, this may have been the period when their work diverged most broadly. While Landauer organized and agitated, Buber continued to publish his mystical texts, including *Ekstatische Confessionen* (*Ecstatic Confessions*, 1909), a collection of reports from mystics across the world's traditions, as well as two anthologies of Chinese texts in translation. He worked on his set of mystical dialogues, *Daniel* (1913), and his edition of the Finnish epic *Kalevala* (1914). Landauer did, however, write an appreciation of Buber in 1913 for an issue of *Neue Blätter* dedicated to him, in which he declared him "the apostle of Judaism to humanity."[113] Shortly thereafter, they finally collaborated on a political project (Buber belonged to the Sozialist Bund, but there is little evidence that he exerted himself greatly on its behalf), when they worked together to prevent the breakout of the war.[114] The so-called Forte-Kreis, which met in Potsdam in June 1914, attempted to enlist intellectuals from across Europe in an international statement in favor of peace.[115] However, some Forte-Kreis members proved recalcitrant in their nationalism, and others preferred epistolary exchanges to in-person meetings. Buber and Landauer cosigned a letter in November 1914 demanding a meeting of the whole group, but Buber's heart was perhaps not in the endeavor, as he had already expressed his enthusiasm for the new spirit he felt the war to be awakening in Europe and among Europe's Jews.[116]

Buber's succumbing to *Kriegserlebnis*, a kind of intense enthusiasm for war, disgusted Landauer and strained their relationship.[117] The *Kriegserlebnis* swept Germany, and consistent antimilitarism was rare—so rare that the few who continued to oppose the war were often shocked at how isolated they had become from their former friends and associates. Karl Liebknecht, for example, broke from the Social Democratic Party (SPD), cofounded by his own father, over its support for the war in 1917; in response to it he created first the Independent Social-Democratic Party (USPD), then the Spartacist League and the German Communist Party (KPD).[118] Meanwhile, far from the halls of party politics, Karl Barth, a Swiss Reformed theologian, was dismayed by the lockstep support on the part of his German mentors in liberal theology for the war and blamed nineteenth-century theology for their political failures.[119] His *Epistle to the Romans* (1918) launched the revolution of "crisis theology" in response. This Christian story has a Jewish parallel, in Gershom Scholem's rage against Hermann Cohen's Germanic patriotism. And when Martin Buber began to write in support of the war, and Landauer called him the *Kriegsbuber* (War-Buber), he too found himself named a traitor.

In the heyday of his "cultural Zionist" activism, Buber had briefly considered, along with Berthold Feiwel and Chaim Weizmann, starting a journal called *Der Jude*, but that project did not come to fruition until more than ten years later. In the first issue, in April 1916, Buber argued in an editorial entitled "Die Losung" (The Watchword) that the war would unite even those Jews on opposite sides of the battlefield in a transcendental community of feeling.[120] This was Buber's most public statement so far of views he had already expressed privately as early as September 1914.[121] Although Buber's support for the war exalted an all-encompassing, quasi-mystical *Erlebnis*, rather than a nationalistic assertion of Germany's right to rule Europe, he remained just as tolerant of the carnage.[122] Both Landauer and Walter Benjamin refused to publish in *Der Jude* as long as Buber supported the war.[123]

Landauer's fierce condemnation of his friend, in a letter of May 12, 1916, is credited by Mendes-Flohr with effecting a "volte-face" in Buber's career. This position remains the consensus view of scholars.[124] The letter attacks not only Buber's "Watchword" essay but also the fourth of his "Speeches on Judaism," entitled "Der Geist des Orients und das Judentum" (The Spirit of the Orient and Judaism), which Landauer describes as "repugnant, border[ing] on incomprehensibility."[125] Landauer accuses Buber of "aestheticism and formalism," claiming that he "had no right . . . to publicly take a stand on the political events of the present day." He prophesies that his friend will one day come to his senses: "In the future you will not take part in the German war against the other peoples of Europe, nor in the war of Europe against itself, as you do now in your profound confusion and bewilderment." Until then, Landauer could not work with Buber: "I do not want to collaborate with you any further for the duration of the war. . . . [A] journal that publishes . . . what the Hapsburgs, the Hohenzollerns, and the interests allied with them want to hear, but does not publish the contrary, cannot be my journal." We have no response from Buber to this letter, but there is evidence that Buber immediately traveled to see Landauer to discuss it.[126] In Buber's first published statements following this interchange, he no longer addresses the war's transcendental significance or its relationship to the Absolute. We find only a moral critic who warns against excessive nationalism and patriotism.

Buber's conduct during the war has embarrassed his acolytes; those who know him from the popular *I and Thou* often seem to share Landauer's shock that the sage of "dialogue" could ever have been labeled the *Kriegsbuber*. Maurice Friedman, for one, protests that Buber "was never a German superpatriot, like Hermann Cohen," that he never "signed any document supporting the Kaiser," yet "he was neither a pacifist nor an anarchist like Gustav Landauer" and was therefore "unable to maintain Landauer's almost fanatic clarity of opposition."[127] Even Friedman, however, admits that "[Buber's] own philosophy helped to seduce him into an enthusiasm in which even his faithfulness to that philosophy became questionable."[128] Marking 1916 as a turning point in Buber's career thus seems justified, inasmuch as he directed his literary executor to prohibit the publication of anything written prior to that date (if not already published before his death).[129] Of the writings from this period that were later republished, many omitted the very passages Landauer had condemned.[130] Arthur Cohen has opined, "It is surprising, given the intensity of their friendship and the presumable breadth of their intellectual itinerary, that Landauer and Buber had not, until the outbreak of war, articulated their disagreement over the question of violence and pacifism, German imperialism and German humanism."[131] Perhaps, but we should not overlook Landauer's possible reasons for believing that he and Buber agreed: namely, Buber's endorsement in 1904 of Landauer's statement in "Anarchic Thoughts on Anarchism" that "one never comes through violence to non-violence." Thus Buber's war politics did not merely express a hitherto latent attitude; they belied his previous praise of his friend's work. He was presumably embarrassed and ashamed of himself.[132]

Buber's new philosophical direction in the wake of his turnabout also entailed the appropriation, or reappropriation, as the case may be, of some of Landauer's ideas. As we have seen, in Buber's various appreciations of Landauer, some element was always lacking. This is consistent with the "*Erlebnis*-mysticism" that Mendes-Flohr describes. In his 1901 lecture, Buber focused more than Landauer on intensity of experience as the locus of mystical unity. In the 1904 essay, he suggested that Landauer could not be a complete anarchist until he was a complete artist. Buber's closeness to Landauer from 1900 to 1916 was far from complete; there was a significant difference in their understandings of the relationship between aesthetics and mysticism on the one hand and politics on the other. After 1916, however, this gap began to narrow. Buber did not adopt all of Landauer's positions; they would continue to differ, for example, on the nature of the relationship between their German and Jewish identities, and eventually on the matter of Landauer's role in the Bavarian Council Republic. However, this latter disagreement stemmed not from Buber's resistance to Landauer's basic *Weltanschauung* but from his conviction that *Landauer* was the one who had become untrue to his own principles.

From *Kulturpolitik* to *Der Heilige Weg*: A Theopolitical Turn at Reich's End?

In the summer of 1916, Buber engaged in a heated debate with Hermann Cohen over Zionism.[133] Cohen argued that "it is only through the state, by virtue of a pure act of political morality, that the nation is constituted." Buber replied that, for him, "just as the state in general is not the determining goal of mankind, so the 'Jewish state' is not the determining goal for the Jews."[134] For all its passion, the debate is not a true meeting of the minds. One wishes that Buber had better appreciated Cohen's method of idealization, in which "the ideal of the state" refers not to the existing state but rather to an ideal by which to critique the existing state.[135] Buber may have been eager to demonstrate his about-face through a rapid public commitment to a Landauerian position. In response to a comment of Cohen's on "the viable ethnic group's need for power," Buber wrote, "I have seen and heard too much of the results of empty needs for power."[136] In his early cultural-Zionist work Buber had dismissed the diplomatic route to the achievement of a state in favor of work in the present, *Gegenwartsarbeit*. We find him now dismissing the *goal* of political Zionism: "[Our argument] . . . does not concern the Jewish state, that, yes, were it to be founded today would be built upon the same principles as any other modern state. It does not concern the addition of one more trifling power structure. . . . Zion restored will become the house of the Lord for all peoples and the center of the new world . . . in which 'the blood-stained garment of war is burned' and 'the swords are turned into plowshares.'"

This political shift toward Landauer is accompanied by a theological shift, also already in the 1916 debate with Cohen. For example, in his prewar writings, Buber frequently mentioned the idea of "realizing God," a provocative claim that implies that God depends on human beings to become fully actual.[137] In his reply to Cohen, however, Buber speaks more often of "realizing *Judaism*." God, then, is served, not realized: "Not to acknowledge God with our words while betraying God with our lives, but to serve God faithfully through the establishment of a human community according to his will." The still-transitional nature of this moment is made clear from his conclusion, that when we live a true human life, we show "how God lives in us[;] . . . we realize both ourselves and God within us."[138]

The theme of service to God comes with a traditional, conservative-sounding corollary: rebellion is negative. Buber's lecture *Der Heilige Weg: Ein Wort an die Juden und an die Völker (The Holy Way: A Word to the Jews and to the Nations,* May 1918) explored this theme more fully.[139] Here Buber announced, "We Jews are all renegades [*Abtrünnige*]."[140] Buber means by this that rebellion against God manifests itself through service to the nations and their states, and so service to God becomes rebellion against such powers—not through civil war and strife in each nation, however, but by leaving the Exile to form a new divine community in Palestine. Buber gave this lecture, originally entitled "Das Judentum und die wahre Gemeinschaft" (Judaism and True Community), at least three times in 1918: in May, in Vienna; in October, in Berlin; and in December, in Munich.[141] In December 1918, however, Munich was not just one more city in which to give a lecture. It was undergoing revolutionary upheaval. Kurt Eisner had declared Bavaria a republic on November 7, two days before the general proclamation of the German Republic in Berlin, and on November 14 he had invited Landauer to Munich "to advance the transformation of souls as a speaker."[142] The following day, Landauer wrote to Buber: "You should come too; there is enough work to do. I will write once I have found a suitable task for you. . . . I wish I might be sent to

Berlin as a representative from Bavaria, and would like to see you working in the same capacity in Vienna."[143] He reiterated the invitation a week later:

> The situation in Munich is very serious: it will almost be a miracle if the revolution can survive the economic problems left by the war. The worst danger is that the Entente demands a central government, elected by the people through a national assembly, in order to engage in peace negotiations. Otherwise, the autonomous republics would manage despite all difficulties . . .
>
> In any case—and this I can promise—Bavaria will not abdicate its autonomy. You should write down your thoughts on people's education, on publishing, etc., and send them to me; or even better: you should come with them to Munich soon! . . . The collaboration with Eisner functions very well. I am sure you have seen from his proclamations how "anarchist" his understanding of democracy is: he favors the active participation of the people in all social bodies, not bleak parliamentarism.[144]

Clearly, Landauer thought at the time that Buber might heed his call to take part in the revolution in Munich, and it appears that Buber did indeed visit in December when he delivered *The Holy Way*.[145]

The Holy Way lecture Buber delivered in Munich is by far his most Landauerian work to that point. Summarizing the words of La Boétie, Landauer had said: "It is *in you*! It is not on the outside. It *is you*. Humans shall not be united by domination, but as brothers *without domination: an-archy*."[146] In *The Holy Way*, Buber encapsulates the principles of the "Jewish will to realization" as follows: "All these principles can be summed up in the watchword: from within! Nothing new can be established by stripping an autocratic constitution off a country and superimposing on it a communist one instead when life between man and man remains unchanged, and so too the methods of government."[147] Landauer had said that after the first wave of cooperative settlements, the revolution would confront the state-imposed obstacle of the lack of land and would then "enter a new phase that we can say nothing about. The same goes for social regeneration; we can proclaim it, but we can say nothing about how it will develop. It will depend on the following generations and their judgment."[148] Buber concludes *The Holy Way* with a similar warning:

> It is not my task today to speak of the establishment of a true community in Zion beyond the general. . . . Nor is it up to us to impose structural schemes upon future developments. . . . [W]e do not know how far we shall succeed in keeping [the masses] out of the land where they will probably smell an opportunity for exploitation and profit. But far more profoundly, beyond all past and future disappointment, we are certain of Israel, and expectantly ready for God.[149]

Buber has transposed Landauer's ideals and values from Germany to Zion. He strengthens that shift by politicizing the binary distinction of the productive elite and the masses. The "resistant" masses are no longer merely artistically uncreative; they are capitalistically driven. Zionism is therefore not a matter of mass immigration and colonization, but a project for a small core interested in realizing Judaism.[150]

At first, the Judaism of *The Holy Way* seems to closely resemble the Judaism of the first six "Speeches on Judaism," with their interest in unconditionality and realization. As Mendes-Flohr has pointed out, however, there is now a new emphasis on the category of the Between (*das Zwischenmenschliche*), an important indicator of the way that Buber's conception of human existence is undergoing a shift at this time, concurrently with the developments described here.[151] Also noteworthy is the way Buber retains the idea of "European dualism," which "sanctions the splitting of man's being into two realms, each existing in its own right and independent of the other—the truth of the spirit and the reality of life," but drops the contrast to an "Oriental" or "Asiatic" opposite.[152] Instead, "Judaism" operates alone here, not as the expression of a general Eastern spirit but as the specific revelatory task of the Jewish people. Buber no longer considers Judaism a manifestation of the innate qualities of the Jews, but rather an ideal given *to* them, one they have ever failed to realize—the ideal of true community. The "holiness" mentioned in the title is "true community with God and true community with human beings, both in one"; the "way" is the understanding of Judaism as unified, not split into the spiritless humanitarian ethics of reform, the dead rigidity of religious conservatism, and the realpolitik of purely political Zionism.[153] In the name of this Judaism, Buber nearly seems to found a new sectarianism, proclaiming, "Individuals who consider themselves members of either the Jewish confession or the Jewish nation, who worship the idols of this world and observe its commandments, usurp the name of Jew, whether they wear the ceremonial fringes under their coats or the Zionist button on them."[154]

This vision of Judaism comes together with a narrative of Jewish history, which also differs from Buber's earlier forays into this field. The first six "Speeches on Judaism" had featured an eclectic mix of biblical interpretation and grand narrative, as Buber wove his tale of a "subterranean" Judaism at odds with the illegitimate "official" Judaism that usurped it.[155] True to his Zionist outlook, he had portrayed the period of dwelling in the Land of Israel as the period of integral wholeness; in the Exile, true Judaism could manifest itself only in the occasional heretical movements or in the secrecy of the Kabbalah.[156] The loss of the Jewish state thus was the seminal moment in Jewish history. In *The Holy Way*, by contrast, he declares "the true turning point of Jewish history" to be the moment of the establishment of the Israelite monarchy.[157] Echoing Landauer's account of secularization in *Revolution*, but transposing it from the Reformation to ancient Israel, Buber alleges that when the Jews asked Samuel to help them "be like all the nations" (1 Samuel 8:20), the integral wholeness of life, the union of the mundane and the spiritual, was sundered, conceding the political realm to earthly kings and leaving the spiritual to God in heaven. Previously, "the idea of God as the sole owner of all land" had prevailed. This "corresponds to the idea, in the political sphere . . . of God as the sole sovereign of the community," with God as really present in his rule over daily political and economic life.[158] Now, his sovereignty is confined to "inner," "spiritual" matters, with no involvement in the independent political and economic spheres. Previously, the leaders of the people had been exceptional individuals called to specific tasks (the judges); once dynastic rule emerges, though, the rulers no longer have to prove themselves by deeds. To be sure, the prophets "do not fight the state as state," even though it dislodges the true community; they endeavor instead "to permeate it with spirit." Nevertheless, they "do not even shrink from sacrificing the independence of their state, if the sacrifice rescues a remnant of the people from utter destruction and preserves it as a nucleus for a future new community." Messianism, which looks forward to this future community, is thus the "creative expression of [prophetic] despair."[159]

This is the core of the argument that Buber will make in *Kingship of God* in 1932 and continue in his subsequent biblical works. In 1918, Buber writes: "I am not concerned here with the question of whether the written account of this event and its presuppositions are historical fact, or whether they bear the imprint of a later period and point of view; their inner truth is unmistakable."[160] By 1932, however, he has moved on to a richly textured scholarly account that does argue for historicity, rooted in a decade of biblical studies and reflecting his collaboration with Rosenzweig. Although Buber does not yet use the word, 1918 may be conceived as a "theopolitical" turn, to which he will devote himself throughout the course of the 1920s. Placing this emphasis on *The Holy Way* helps us to see these years as something other than a mere prelude to *I and Thou*, and to imagine a different arc for Buber's Weimar career.

The Unspeakable Jewish Tragedy: The Revolution

Buber did not remain in Munich in December 1918 but returned to his home in Heppenheim, while Landauer continued his efforts on behalf of Kurt Eisner and the Bavarian Revolution. Buber next visited Munich in February 1919; in his detailed reflections on that visit he found himself again disagreeing with his friend, although with less bitterness than in their quarrel over the war.[161] Buber now senses that Landauer, by taking part in an ostensibly ordinary political revolution, is the one not living up to his own ideals, such that Buber has become more Landauerian than Landauer himself. However, although Buber thinks Landauer is wrong, he does not accuse him of moral failure; to the contrary, Landauer's involvement in the revolution provokes worry rather than anger. Buber would later say that "no man has ever erred out of purer motives."[162]

In 1907, Landauer had quoted the poet Gottfried Keller: "Freedom's last victory will be bloodless."[163] It is thus hard to imagine him turning down the plea of Eisner, who proclaimed an independent Bavarian republic, ending seven centuries of rule by the Wittelsbach monarchy without firing a shot. Landauer understood that Bavaria, a conservative state, lacked necessary conditions for lasting social revolution. At the beginning of the revolution he wrote that "the very difficult and almost discouraging situation demands that I do not push from behind but pull from the front."[164] Later, less than a month before his death, he said: "If I'll have a few weeks, I hope I can achieve something; however, it is very likely that it will only be a few days, and then all this will have been but a dream."[165] Perhaps he was enticed, in part, by the prospect of participating in freedom's last victory. Buber, by contrast, felt that Jewish revolutionaries, driven to realize true community, must fail repeatedly if they neglect to realize that "the upheaval too takes place within the life of a nationality, that even the revolution is deeply linked to a tradition."[166] The Jewish revolutionary will cease to fail only when "he realizes his truth on his own soil and with his own nationality." Furthermore, during this period, Buber assessed both the German and the Russian revolutions in accordance with Landauer's teaching:

> [The revolution today is] no consummation but a beginning. On the surfaces of political life, rubble is cleared away; immeasurable stores remain in the depths of social life. Legal realignments have given rise to emergency actions; these will not transform the internal fabric of human life in common. Such a transformation cannot ever be enacted or decreed by institutions, but only through an inner germinating, gradually spreading rejuvenation of the cell tissue.

Nonetheless, Buber wrote, "Standing on their ground, not wanting that any good come to us as a by-product, not as beneficiaries, but rather as fellow-fighters and fellow-bearers, we salute the revolution."[167]

Buber's view of the German Revolution, though Landauerian in principle, may have also stemmed from his greater connection to the Jewish community. In general, German Jews reacted to the revolutionary upheavals in the same way as the more progressive elements among their bourgeois Christian countrymen: weathering the political storm, hoping that the Republic would win out over efforts at radicalization, anticipating a return to normality. They feared the rising wave of antisemitism bolstered by the perception that the revolution had too many Jewish leaders; they considered men like Eisner and Landauer "tactless" for ignoring the effects of their actions on other Jews.[168] Finally, also relevant is the fact that Buber in 1919 was still an Austrian citizen; he gained his German citizenship only in 1921. In the nationalistically charged atmosphere of the time, many foreigners avoided expressing opinions that deviated from the mainstream. Karl Barth, for example, reported that as a Swiss national he felt constrained in his arguments with Emanuel Hirsch, his nationalist colleague on the theological faculty at Göttingen.[169] Thus, while Buber had felt free to praise the German war effort, taking part in the revolution as an Austrian would have been another story. This would not have been a concern to internationalist communist revolutionaries (Rosa Luxemburg was Polish; Anton Pannekoek was Dutch), but neither Buber nor Landauer would think along such lines in the wake of the war and the collapse of the Second International.[170]

Compared to the rest of Germany, Bavaria under Eisner had been relatively stable.[171] Buber's second visit to revolutionary Munich coincided with its last week of stability; Eisner was assassinated the day he left—February 21, 1919. Upon his return home, Buber wrote to his son-in-law of the "profoundly stirring week" he had spent with the revolutionaries:

> The deepest human problems of the revolution were discussed with the utmost candor: in the very heart of events I posed questions and offered replies; and there were nocturnal hours of apocalyptic gravity, during which silence spoke eloquently in the midst of discussion, and the future became more distinct than the present. And yet for all but a few it was nothing but mere bustle, and face-to-face with them I sometimes felt like a Cassandra. As for Eisner, to be with him was to peer into the tormented passions of a divided Jewish soul; nemesis shone from his glittering surface; he was a marked man. Landauer, by dint of the greatest spiritual effort, kept up his faith in him, and protected him—a shield-bearer terribly moving in his selflessness. The whole thing, an unspeakable Jewish tragedy.[172]

Buber understood, however, that Landauer could not share his view of the revolution as tragic: "To Landauer himself, who witnessed the assassination of Eisner and who refused to take the opportunities to escape that were offered him, it was more: the road into the future that could come only through self-sacrifice."[173] The assassination of Eisner threw Bavaria into a chaotic power struggle between the Landtag (the state parliament), the workers' and soldiers' councils, and their Council Congress; it was during this time that Landauer made what Buber believed to be the most serious of his mistakes.

Eisner was killed on his way to resign from the office of minister president after a devastating electoral defeat for his party, the USPD. Landauer had believed the elections premature and unnecessary. He favored leaving power with the workers' and soldiers' councils, delaying the re-formation of parliament for as long as possible so that eventually all would come to see the wisdom of a permanent system of council democracy. He considered Eisner "by far the best of everyone in power."[174] But he also refused to take sides in many disputes because he believed "all positions are equally wrong."[175] He despaired of the revolutionaries' continuing faith in parliamentarism; he understood that the military and the conservative elites wished to saddle a new, left-wing civilian government with responsibility for the harsh demands of the Entente. Landauer also offered this prediction: "If, as it will probably be the case, the conditions for the working class will become so bad that it resists, then Caesarism will come, some Napoleon III, only worse than the original. . . . A shrewd, brutal military officer with an organizing talent who joins the SPD has great chances to become Germany's dictator within two years."[176] Such views naturally put Landauer and his Munich comrade, Erich Mühsam, in conflict with the new SPD-led Bavarian government as well as with the KPD.

On April 4, 1919, in response both to Augsburg workers on general strike and to reports of the Landtag's imminent reassembly, the leadership of the Bavarian Council Congress instructed Landauer and Mühsam to draft a declaration for the Bavarian Council Republic. They did so, and the *Räterepublik* was proclaimed on April 7.[177] To the surprise of both men, the KPD refused to recognize or take part in it. The SPD majority in the Landtag responded by retreating to the northern Bavarian town of Bamberg, launching a military attack on Munich a week later. This attack was repelled by a hastily formed Red Army, following which the KPD took control of Munich affairs and proclaimed the Second Council Republic. Once the communists were in charge, Landauer's services were declined; he ultimately spent less than a week in his "official" position as *Volksbeauftragter*, people's delegate, for culture and education.[178] Many years later, Mühsam wrote of the ironies of those chaotic weeks:

> On the crucial night from April 4 to 5, Landauer and I decided, against our usual convictions, that it did not really matter whether or not the proclamation of the council republic happened with the mandate of the factory workers. Furthermore, despite certain concerns, we had decided to participate in a provisional "government," thinking that this was a historical necessity. The party communists, on the other hand, who generally imposed authoritarianism on the masses, criticized our actions, because they insisted that a council republic could only be built from the bottom up. Nonetheless, on April 13, the pressure of the events forced them to do exactly what we had done a week earlier.[179]

A second attack on Munich began on May 1, this time with Freikorps units and central government troops sent from Berlin. This attack, followed by the bloody White Terror, ended the Munich revolution and claimed the life of Gustav Landauer, who was captured, taken to prison, and beaten to death.[180] He was forty-nine years old. No one was charged with his murder.

Landauer's friends could not, for some time, obtain accurate information about his whereabouts. They were sure the revolution would be short-lived but thought that Landauer might survive; Buber, Mauthner, and Margarete Susman corresponded about setting up a legal defense fund for Landauer in the event that he was tried for treason.[181] On May 7, Buber wrote Mauthner that he was sure Landauer was dead but still placed hope in a wire he had received from

Landauer's daughter Lotte on May 4 that read: "Father not in danger." Eventually, Buber wrote an extended eulogy for Landauer in the journal *Masken*, of which Landauer had been slated to become editor before the breakout of revolution. The conclusion of this eulogy has been quoted elsewhere, but it is worth reproducing:

> Gustav Landauer had lived as a prophet of the coming human community and fell as its blood-witness. He went upon the path, of which Maximus Tyrius— whose words Landauer used as the motto of his book, *Die Revolution*—said:
>
> > Here is the way of the Passion, which you call a disaster, and which you judge according to those who have passed upon it; I, however, deem it salvation, since I judge it according to the result of what is still to come.
>
> In a church at Brescia I saw a mural whose entire surface was covered with crucified individuals. The field of crosses stretched until the horizon, hanging from each, men of varied physiques and faces. Then it struck me that this was the true image of Jesus Christ. On one of the crosses I see Gustav Landauer hanging.[182]

The passage can easily be taken as the highest praise; Buber calls his friend a prophet, a martyr, and a face of Christ. And that may be the way Buber intended the text. But this passage has another, more ambiguous connotation. The image of myriad crucifixions stretching to the horizon is most commonly associated not with Jesus, who was crucified with only two others, but with Spartacus, whose defeated rebels lined the Appian Way.[183] The figure of Spartacus had already been adopted by two martyrs of 1919, Rosa Luxemburg and Karl Liebknecht, whom Landauer had eulogized despite political differences with them. Spartacus was in the air; conservative and even social-democratic forces frequently referred to the entire radical left as Bolshevist and Spartacist. Perhaps Buber, eulogizing his friend and mentor, whom he saw as an honest revolutionary who took a wrong turn, could not help but evoke all these crucifixions together: Landauer, like Luxemburg and Liebknecht, was killed by the counterrevolution; Jesus, like Spartacus and his army, was crucified by Rome. The true revolution suffers the same fate as the false—until that day when all the failures of the past will be gathered up and redeemed.

Conclusion: In Memoriam

In 1923, the Munich Anarchosyndikalistische Vereinigung (Anarcho-Syndicalist Association) erected an obelisk at Landauer's grave. Ten years later, shortly after the Nazi ascension, the obelisk was destroyed. Buber aimed to raise a literary monument to Landauer, which would be more enduring.[184] Throughout the 1920s, Buber vigilantly consecrated the memory of his friend. As executor of Landauer's literary estate, Buber often had instructions provided for his editing of Landauer's unfinished projects, but he also made his own creative decisions. First came Landauer's lectures on Shakespeare, *Shakespeare: Dargestellt in Vorträgen* (1920). That same year, Buber gave a short address to the world conference of the Zionist socialist movement, *Ha'poel Ha'tzair*, eulogizing Landauer as "the hidden leader."[185] In 1921, he followed up with *Der werdende Mensch: Aufsätze über Leben und Schrifttum*, and in 1924 he published *Beginnen: Aufsätze über Sozialismus*. In 1929, Buber brought out a two-volume edition of Landauer's correspondence, *Gustav Landauer: Sein Lebensgang in Briefen*. This edition contains only Landauer's own letters, not responses, but Buber provides context and extensive commentary on the letters. On the tenth anniversary of Landauer's murder, Buber published "Erinnerung an einen Tod" (Recollection of a Death). Then his urge to commemorate his friend seems to have finally subsided, and he did not pick up his pen to discuss Landauer for another ten years.[186]

"Recollection of a Death" beautifully demonstrates Buber's fidelity to Landauer's definition of anarchism and revolution: not as class struggle between the proletariat and the bourgeoisie, or between the masses and the state, but between individuals and themselves, between groups and themselves, in a transhistorical struggle to realize true community. Buber calls this polarity "the true front." The true front does not lie between one soldier and another. Rather, it runs through the heart of each soldier, who struggles with doubt as to whether "what stands opposite him is not at all inimical."[187] Nor does the true front lie between the revolutionary and his internal enemy, the government or the capitalist class. "The revolutionary stands, according to the situation, in the tension between goal and way, and within its responsibility, neither of which the soldier knows. . . . [T]he revolutionary lives on the knife's edge . . . here again the true front runs through the center."[188] If the revolutionary chooses means destructive of his ends, he renders those ends meaningless. This brings Buber back ten years, to his visit with Landauer in Munich in February 1919:

> I was with him, and several other revolutionary leaders in a hall of the Diet building in Munich. The discussion was conducted for the most part between me and a Spartacus leader, who later became well known in the second communist revolutionary government in Munich that replaced the first, socialist government of Landauer and his comrades. The man walked with clanking spurs through the room; he had been a German officer in the war. I declined to do what many apparently had expected of me—to talk of the moral problem; but I set forth what I thought about the relation between end and means. I documented my view from historical and contemporary experience. The Spartacus leader did not go into that matter. He, too, sought to document his apology for the terror by examples. "Dzertshinsky," he said, "the head of the Cheka, could sign a hundred death sentences a day, but with an entirely clean soul." "That is, in fact, just the worst of all," I answered. "This 'clean' soul you do not allow any splashes of blood to fall on! It is not a question of 'souls' but of responsibility." My opponent regarded me with unperturbed superiority. Landauer, who sat next to me, laid his hand on mine. His whole arm trembled.[189]

Even in 1919, in a city in the grip of a revolution, at a revolutionary council as the guest of a revolutionary leader, Buber was expected to handle "the moral problem," which his interlocutors imagined to be separate from the political questions at hand. But he and Landauer knew otherwise: "The true front runs through the licentious soldiery, the true front runs through the revolution, the true front runs through the heart of the soldier, the true front runs through the heart of the revolutionary." The ones who fight on the true front are the ones accused of weakening their own side, but "those are the men who keep alive the truth of the battle."

Buber lamented the continuing lack of understanding of Landauer, even after ten years of continuous publication on his behalf: "Landauer fought in the revolution against the revolution for the sake of the revolution. The revolution will not thank him for it. But those will thank him for it who have fought as he fought, and perhaps some day those will thank him for whose sake he fought." Not by way of the past Passion, which appears disastrous, would Landauer be judged, but by the path of future salvation, the path of victories on the true front. In the next chapter, I turn to Buber's own contribution to this path, the idea of theopolitics. Throughout the 1920s, Buber struggles to define the relation between religion and politics in a way that can provide support for Landauer's hope: "*without domination: _____.*"

Notes

1. FMD 93–126.

2. Ibid., 108–109.

3. Gilya Gerda Schmidt, *Martin Buber's Formative Years: From German Culture to Jewish Renewal, 1897–1909* (Tuscaloosa: University of Alabama Press, 1995), 118; Howard Sachar, *A History of Israel: From the Rise of Zionism to Our Time* (New York: Knopf, 1986), 180.

4. MBEY 193; cf. MBLY 400–401.

5. Martin Buber, *Briefwechsel aus sieben Jahrzenten, Band III: 1938–1965* (Heidelberg: Lambert Schneider, 1975), 597–599, 608 (hereafter *Briefwechsel III*).

6. Buber may be read as avowing anarchism in his neglected 1904 essay on Landauer. Mendes-Flohr, however, argues that there Buber "celebrated Landauer's anarchism as a metaphysical solipsism. . . . The emphasis here is on a personal, aesthetic anarchism." FMD 110.

7. Peter Marshall, *Demanding the Impossible: A History of Anarchism* (Oakland, CA: PM Press, 2010), 574.

8. George Woodcock, *Anarchism: A History of Libertarian Ideas and Movements* (Toronto: University of Toronto Press, 2009), 421–422.

9. The claim that Buber criticizes the "too-sweeping anarchist position" of Kropotkin fails to see that Buber has simply adopted Landauer's critique of Kropotkin, which is itself an anarchist critique; Bernard Susser, *Existence and Utopia: The Social and Political Thought of Martin Buber* (London: Associated University Presses, 1981), 186n56. Susser nevertheless employs the useful term "anarcho-theocratic" to describe the politics of Buber's biblical works. Ibid., 178n54.

10. PC 173; GLPU 14; Wolf-Dieter Gudopp, *Martin Bubers dialogischer Anarchismus* (Bern: Herbert Lang, 1975); Stephen Eric Bronner, ed., *Twentieth Century Political Theory: A Reader*

(New York: Routledge, 1997), 115–116, 120–126; Shalom Ratzabi, *Anarchism in "Zion": Between Martin Buber and Aharon David Gordon* (Tel Aviv: Am Oved, 2011) [Hebrew].

11. MBLY xiv.

12. Gustav Landauer, *Revolution and Other Writings: A Political Reader*, ed. and trans. Gabriel Kuhn (Oakland, CA: PM Press, 2010), 175.

13. PU 48.

14. Ibid., 16.

15. Meier-Cronemeyer makes this point himself in his letter to Buber; Buber, *Briefwechsel III*, 598.

16. Alexander S. Kohanski, "Martin Buber's Restructuring of Society into a State of Anocracy," *Jewish Social Studies* 34.1 (January 1972): 42–57; Laurence J. Silberstein, *Martin Buber's Social and Religious Thought: Alienation and the Quest for Meaning* (New York: New York University Press, 1990). Kohanski's usage derives its justification from Buber's claim that Kropotkin's "'anarchy,' like Proudhon's, is in reality 'anocracy' (ἀκρατία); not absence of government but absence of domination." PU 43.

17. Buber, *Briefwechsel III*, 598.

18. Standout recent works on anarchism include Andrew Cornell, *Unruly Equality: U.S. Anarchism in the Twentieth Century* (Berkeley: University of California Press, 2016); David Graeber, *Fragments of an Anarchist Anthropology* (Chicago: Prickly Paradigm Press, 2004); Maia Ramnath, *Decolonizing Anarchism: An Antiauthoritarian History of India's Liberation Struggle* (Oakland, CA: AK Press, 2011); James C. Scott, *Two Cheers for Anarchism: Six Easy Pieces on Autonomy, Dignity, and Meaningful Work and Play* (Princeton, NJ: Princeton University Press, 2014); Kenyon Zimmer, *Immigrants against the State: Yiddish and Italian Anarchism in America* (Urbana: University of Illinois Press, 2015).

19. The exact date of their meeting is difficult to establish, but it seems that it must have immediately preceded or followed Landauer's prison term. With reference to 1899, Buber says, "Ich habe Landauer damals kennengelernt." Buber, "Vorwort" to Landauer, *Sein Lebensgang in Briefen, Band I* (Frankfurt: Rütten & Loening, 1929), vii. Landauer served his sentence from August 1899 to February 1900; see Charles Maurer, *Call to Revolution: The Mystical Anarchism of Gustav Landauer* (Detroit: Wayne State University Press, 1971), 47–49; GLPU 50; PC 128.

20. Landauer, "Der Dichter als Ankläger," *Der Sozialist*, February 5, 1898; Landauer, *Der Fall Ziethen: Ein Appell an die öffentliche Meinung* (Berlin: Hugo Metscher, 1898); Landauer, "In Sachen Ziethen," *Sozialistische Monatshefte* 3, 1899.

21. Maurer, *Call to Revolution*, 44.

22. Selections from von Egidy's journal *Versöhnung*, printed in *Der Sozialist* 9.2 (January 1899), cited in PC 139.

23. FMD 110.

24. Karl Marx himself responded to the formation of the SAPD by arguing that the Liebknecht-Bebel faction, to which he and Engels were close, had conceded too much to the Lassalle faction to achieve the union; Marx, "Critique of the Gotha Program," in *The Marx-Engels Reader*, 2nd ed., ed. Robert C. Tucker (New York: W. W. Norton & Co., 1978), 525–541.

25. PC 29.

26. Many studies address the creative appropriation of Nietzsche by the widest variety of followers: Steven E. Aschheim, *The Nietzsche Legacy in Germany, 1890–1990* (Berkeley: University of California Press, 1992); Jacob Golomb, *Nietzsche and Zion* (Ithaca, NY: Cornell University Press, 2004); John Moore, ed., with Spencer Sunshine, *I Am Not a Man, I Am Dynamite! Friedrich Nietzsche and the Anarchist Tradition* (Brooklyn, NY: Autonomedia, 2004). Only in the 1890s did the "Nietzsche craze" really begin in Germany; the young Landauer was part of the avant-garde of his era. Aschheim, *Nietzsche Legacy*, 17.

27. Wille preceded Landauer to a synthesis of Nietzsche with socialism; Aschheim, *Nietzsche Legacy*, 170.

28. PC 39; Pierre Broué, *The German Revolution: 1917–1923*, trans. John Archer (Chicago: Haymarket Books, 2006), 15–16.

29. Broué, *German Revolution*, 17; PC 53–54; Gabriel Kuhn and Siegbert Wolf, introduction to Gustav Landauer, *Revolution and Other Writings: A Political Reader*, ed. and trans. Gabriel Kuhn (Oakland, CA: PM Press, 2010), 20.

30. Landauer, "Twenty-Five Years Later: On the Jubilee of Wilhelm II," in *Revolution and Other Writings*, 62–67. Landauer flirted with Marxism in the fall of 1891 but may have "failed to emphasize certain central tenets of Marxian thinking" in his Nietzschean stress on voluntarism and activism. PC 43.

31. Kuhn and Wolf, introduction to *Revolution and Other Writings*, 21.

32. "Unser Zweck," *Der Sozialist*, November 15, 1891; Lunn, 56. The SPD returned the venom, calling the Jungen "decadent youth, exploiters of rot, and rummagers in ruins"; Aschheim, *Nietzsche Legacy*, 19.

33. Friedländer argued that the SPD was a microcosm of an authoritarian state that foretold what would occur after a Marxist victory. I have not seen any indication that Landauer or Friedländer, both Jews, were aware of Dühring's virulent antisemitism. John Henry Mackay, the Scottish-born "individualist anarchist" and popularizer of Stirner's work, also lived in Friedrichshagen at that time; PC 66–71.

34. Landauer, "Anarchism-Socialism," in *Revolution and Other Writings*, 70. In general, it was common for anarchists at this time to insist on "anarchism" and "socialism" as synonyms, against both nonsocialist anarchists like Stirner and nonanarchist socialists like the SPD.

35. PC 64.

36. Scholars disagree about the latter elements of Landauer's thought. See PC 142–148; GLPU 115n111; Kuhn and Wolf, introduction to *Revolution and Other Writings*, 19; Breines, "A Völkisch Left?"; Bernard Susser, "Ideological Multivalence: Martin Buber and the German Volkish Tradition," *Political Theory* 5.1 (February 1977): 75–96.

37. PC 96–100. Later success of Weise's Berlin cooperative is uncertain.

38. PC 77.

39. Bakunin was "the first, as it were, to infer Leninism from Marxism." Leszek Kolakowski, *Main Currents of Marxism*, trans. P. S. Falla (New York: W. W. Norton & Co., 2005), 210. Bakunin's critique of Marx was echoed by Landauer's opposition to SPD leader August Bebel; PC 84–85.

40. Kuhn and Wolf, introduction to *Revolution and Other Writings*, 24. Whenever anarchists were excluded, they responded by organizing their own conference. There Landauer gave the 1896 report on Germany he had planned to give to the Socialist International. Landauer, "Social Democracy in Germany," in *Anarchism in Germany and Other Essays*, trans. Stephen Bender and Gabriel Kuhn (San Francisco: Barbary Coast Publishing Collective, 2005), 36–42.

41. PC 87, 94.

42. Landauer, "A Few Words on Anarchism," in *Revolution and Other Writings*, 80.

43. Landauer, "Anarchism in Germany," in *Anarchism in Germany and Other Essays*, 14–20.

44. Landauer, "Anarchic Thoughts on Anarchism," in *Revolution and Other Writings*, 85. The German reads "Die Anarchisten sind mir nicht anarchisch genug." To translate this as "*The* anarchists are not anarchic enough for me" would imply a distancing from anarchism as a whole, negating the article's distinction between the anarchism of political violence and Landauer's own anarchism. Correspondence with the translator, Gabriel Kuhn, indicated that he had precisely this concern in mind when he chose "these" to render *Die*.

45. Ibid., 87.

46. PC 122; cf. Kuhn and Wolf, introduction to *Revolution and Other Writings*, 26.

47. Kuhn and Wolf, introduction to *Revolution and Other Writings*, 27; FMD 54.

48. FMD 55–57; Paul Flohr and Bernard Susser, "*Alte und Neue Gemeinschaft*: An Unpublished Buber Manuscript," *Association for Jewish Studies Review* 1 (1976): 41–56.

49. MBEY 37. The characterization of salon culture is Friedman's.

50. MBEY 8.

51. MBEY 31. Buber learned that a well-known Polish author was working on this project and abandoned the translation.

52. Cited in Schmidt, *Martin Buber's Formative Years*, 24–25.

53. FMD 15–16; Martina Urban, *Aesthetics of Renewal: Martin Buber's Early Representation of Hasidism as Kulturkritik* (Chicago: University of Chicago Press, 2008).

54. Schmidt, *Martin Buber's Formative Years*, 56–57.

55. Ibid., 19.

56. Gilya G. Schmidt, ed. and trans., *The First Buber: Youthful Zionist Writings of Martin Buber* (Syracuse, NY: Syracuse University Press, 1999).

57. "Thus, Buber's early Zionism, which envisioned the redemption of the Jew to lie in a 'renaissance' of the Jewish spirit and 'primordial' sensibilities, is perhaps best understood as a species of *Kulturpolitik*." FMD 16; cf. MBEY 54–55.

58. Landauer, *Skepsis und Mystik: Ausgewählte Schriften, Band 7*, ed. Siegbert Wolf (Hessen: Verlag Edition AV, 2010), 131–147.

59. Flohr and Susser, "*Alte und neue Gemeinschaft*," 44.

60. Landauer, "Through Separation to Community," in *Revolution and Other Writings*, 95.

61. Ibid., 92.

62. Ibid., 97–99. I differ here from Mendes-Flohr, who reads Landauer as referring to a popular exaggeration of Wilhelm Dilthey's epistemology, which distinguishes *Erfahrung* (ordinary cognitive experience of sense data that passes through the a priori categories of understanding) from *Erlebnis* (intuitive, inner experience that makes direct contact with things in themselves). Although Landauer uses *Erlebnis* language, I take him to be making a point simultaneously expressible in mystical and materialist vocabularies (skepticism and mysticism, like his book title). From a materialist standpoint, this emphasizes the possibility of gaining knowledge from the study of the self, recognized as continuous with all other phenomena. This would not be "noumenal" knowledge, however, because in Landauer's understanding there is nothing "behind" or "above" the totality of phenomena. Individuation may be mere appearance, but recognizing this does not reveal a noumenal world—only the truth of the phenomenal world ("dem wahren Wesen der Welt"). The difference is subtle enough that many in Landauer's circles, including Buber himself, likely missed it.

63. Ibid., 101–102.

64. Ibid., 104.

65. The first letter from Buber to Landauer in Buber's correspondence is from February 10, 1903. Martin Buber, *Briefwechsel aus sieben Jahrzenten Band I:1897–1918* (Heidelberg: Lambert Schneider Verlag, 1972), 186. The first letter from Landauer to Buber in Landauer's correspondence is from April 9, 1907. Landauer, *Sein Lebensgang in Briefen I*, 165.

66. Flohr and Susser, "*Alte und Neue Gemeinschaft*," 53; Landauer, "Durch Absonderung zur Gemeinschaft," 133. Cf. Schmidt, *Martin Buber's Formative Years*, 11–16.

67. Flohr and Susser, "*Alte und Neue Gemeinschaft*," 47, 53.

68. Landauer is arguing against abstract, philosophical contemplation: "We do not want to *perceive* the community which I advocate . . . we want to *be* and *live* it." But he also stresses that "any understanding of individuality based upon our individual memory is superficial,

momentary, and fleeting too." Landauer, "Separation to Community," 105. Contrast with Buber, who focuses on "this *Erlebnis*" that interrupts our loneliness, so that "like a nuptial festival we were freed from all restraints and found the ineffable meaning of life"; he dwells on "the hours of consecration—in the crystallization of an instant, in a short festive communion—[in which] we met in a feeling of co-essentiality, of blissful, blessed fusion with all things in time and space." Flohr and Susser, *"Alte und Neue Gemeinschaft,"* 46–47, 53.

69. Landauer, "Separation to Community," 107.

70. Ibid., 104–105.

71. Buber, "Judaism and the Jews," in *On Judaism*, ed. Nahum N. Glatzer (New York: Schocken Books, 1995), 15; Buber, "Renewal of Judaism," in in *On Judaism*, ed. Nahum N. Glatzer (New York: Schocken Books, 1995), 44, 49.

72. According to Rocker, "Gustav Landauer was without doubt the greatest mind among all of Germany's libertarian socialists; it was in a certain sense his curse that, of all places, he had to live and work in Germany. The majority of the era's German anarchists understood him even less than others did; most of them had no idea what a precious gift he was." Rocker, *The London Years* (Oakland, CA: AK Press, 2005), cited in Kuhn and Wolf, introduction to *Revolution and Other Writings*, 26. Landauer published an article on Kropotkin, a Russian prince who forsook his lands and title when he became an anarchist, "Fürst Peter Kropotkin," in 1900, and translated three of his books.

73. Included in *Macht und Mächte* were *Arnold Himmelheber* and *Lebendig Tot*, Nietzschean narrative experiments that Landauer had written in prison in 1894.

74. Buber, "Gustav Landauer," *Die Zeit* 39.506 (June 11, 1904), 127–128. (This is the weekly *Die Zeit* edited by Isidore Singer, Hermann Bahr, and Heinrich Kanner, not the daily newspaper *Die Zeit*). Cf. *Martin Buber Werkausgabe Band 2.1, Mythos und Mystik: Frühe religionswissenschaftliche Schriften*, ed. David Groiser (Gütersloh: Gütersloher Verlaghaus, 2013), 102–107.

75. Notably, the two essays on anarchism Buber mentions are from *Zukunft*, not *Der Sozialist*. It is unclear whether Buber was a reader of *Der Sozialist* at that time, although he definitely subscribed to the revived version of the journal after 1909; FMD 177n189.

76. The references to "the two articles" are, unfortunately, vague; they allow for the possibility that Buber only knows of two articles by Landauer on anarchism, as well as for the possibility that he is simply referring to the two that appeared in *Zukunft*.

77. "Anarchie ist in Wahrheit eine Grundstimmung jedes Menschen." This phrase, with its continuation "who wishes to form from within himself a new being," is cited as evidence for reading the essay as an adoption by Buber of anarchism as a metaphysical, aesthetic stance; FMD 110. Although Buber clearly aestheticizes Landauer, he would have to willfully ignore or misread the rest of Landauer's essay to achieve a complete depoliticization, and indeed, he links Landauer's novels to his "brave, reckless, and significant activity in public life." In the very essay Buber praises, Landauer stresses, "One would misunderstand me deeply if one believed that I preach quietism or resignation, or that I demand the renunciation of action or social engagement." Landauer, "Anarchic Thoughts on Anarchism," 88–89.

78. In his discussion of *Skepsis und Mystik*, Buber again cites "Separation to Community" regarding the blood community as linked to innermost being.

79. Buber, "Gustav Landauer," 128.

80. The emergence from seclusion is a trope found frequently in the scholarship. Landauer's is said to have occurred in 1907–1908, with the publication of *Die Revolution* and the founding of the Sozialist Bund; Buber's in 1909 with the first of the "Speeches on Judaism" to the Bar Kochba Society of Prague. However, the years of Buber's editorship of *Die Gesellschaft*, 1906–1912, overlap with both the "seclusion" and the "renewed activity."

81. FMD 25.

82. Selected volumes of Buber's *Die Gesellschaft* are being republished by Marburg's Metropolis Verlag, including those by Simmel, Sombart, Ular, and Bernstein.

83. FMD 83–85.

84. For a complete list of the volumes in the series, see ibid., 88–89.

85. Sombart had not yet developed his "Jewish thesis" identifying capitalism with the Jewish spirit. Reiner Grundmann and Nico Stehr, "Why Is Werner Sombart Not Part of the Core of Classical Sociology?" *Journal of Classical Sociology* 1.2 (2001): 257–287; cf. Paul Mendes-Flohr, "Werner Sombart's *The Jews and Modern Capitalism*: An Analysis of Its Ideological Premises," *Leo Baeck Institute Year Book XXI* (London: Secker & Warburg, 1976), 87–107.

86. Von Gerlach (1866–1935) was a former civil servant and journalist. A well-known liberal, he edited the Berlin weekly *Die Welt am Montag*. Oppenheimer (1864–1943) and Landauer were members of the German Garden City Society, a group dedicated to socially conscious urban planning (cf. Kuhn and Wolf, introduction to *Revolution and Other Writings*, 29; GLPU 115n111; PC 148–149). Oppenheimer later became known as an economic adviser to the World Zionist Organization and transferred to the Palestinian context his plans for "internal colonization" of Germany by means of *Siedlungsgenossenschaft* (cooperative settlement), becoming the principal architect of the moshav of Merhavia. In *Der Staat*, Oppenheimer argued that the social contract was a myth and that the state could arise only through the domination of one class by another. He opposed private ownership of land and capital, and corresponded with Kropotkin, but considered himself a "liberal socialist" rather than an anarchist.

87. Buber to Landauer, July 26, 1906, *Briefwechsel I*, 245.

88. Landauer, *Revolution*, in *Revolution and Other Writings*, 110–185.

89. Ibid., 112.

90. Ibid., 135.

91. Ibid., 179n32.

92. Ibid., 130.

93. Ibid., 135.

94. Ibid., 123.

95. Ibid., 142.

96. Ibid., 144. Emphasis Landauer's: "I cannot emphasize this enough."

97. Ibid., 142–145.

98. James B. Atkinson, introduction to Etienne de La Boétie, *Discourse on Voluntary Servitude* (Indianapolis: Hackett, 2012), xxxiii–xxxv.

99. Landauer, *Revolution*, 157. Buber echoes this point, without attribution, in his accounts of the emerging Israelite monarchy, *Kingship of God* and *The Anointed* (see chapters 3 and 4 of this volume). The "outside attack" in the ancient Israelite context comes from the Philistines; the "internal corruption" comes from Samuel's introduction of the dynastic principle, encouraging a tendency to prefer the safety of life under a human monarch to freedom under God's rule.

100. Cited by Landauer, *Revolution*, 158–159.

101. Ibid.

102. "Anyone who had heard those speeches by Buber has not forgotten them and cannot forget them to his dying day." Hugo Bergmann, cited in Aharon Kedar, "Brith Shalom," *Jerusalem Quarterly* 18 (Winter 1981): 58.

103. Buber had written about "Jüdische Renaissance" in 1901, but from 1909 he seems to explicitly prefer "renewal"; Buber, "Renewal of Judaism," 53.

104. "I have not translated the tales of Rabbi Nachman, but retold them. I have done so for my purpose is not philological." In the 1916 edition the sentence is: "I have done so in full freedom, yet out of his spirit as it is present to me." Translation from Urban, *Aesthetics of Renewal*, 16.

105. Landauer, "Die Legende des Baal Schem," in *Philosophie und Judentum: Ausgewählte Schriften, Band 5*, ed. Siegbert Wolf (Hessen: AV, 2012), 345–347.

106. Landauer, *For Socialism*, trans. David J. Parent (St. Louis, MO: Telos Press, 1978), 130; this interpretation of the Sabbatical and Jubilee was widely influential; it was taken up not only by Buber but also by the young leader of the Ha'poel Ha'tzair movement, Chaim Arlosoroff; Shlomo Avineri, *Arlosoroff* (London: Peter Halban, 1989), 30–31. By some circuitous route, it was even echoed by Vladimir Jabotinsky, who interpreted it as antisocialist; Michael Stanislawski, *Zionism and the Fin-de-Siècle: Cosmopolitanism and Nationalism from Nordau to Jabotinsky* (Berkeley: University of California Press, 2001), 215.

107. Landauer Archives (Hebrew University of Jerusalem), MS Var. 432, File 23, cited by Michael Löwy, *Redemption and Utopia: Jewish Libertarian Thought in Central Europe: A Study in Elective Affinity*, trans. Hope Heaney (Stanford, CA: Stanford University Press, 1992), 136.

108. Ibid. Löwy rightly notes that the mutual influence of Landauer and Buber on each other drew from the same German neo-romantic sources, and he distinguishes this romanticism from conservative and reactionary interpretations. However, he overstates the political differences between the two. Cf. Löwy, "Romantic Prophets of Utopia: Gustav Landauer and Martin Buber," in *Gustav Landauer: Anarchist and Jew*, ed. Paul Mendes-Flohr and Anya Mali, with Hanna Delf von Wolzogen (Berlin: De Gruyter, 2014), 64–81.

109. Landauer, *Revolution*, 175.

110. Landauer, "Dreißig sozialistische Thesen," *Die Zukunft* 15 (Jan. 12, 1907). When Buber edited Landauer's writings, he added "Volk und Land" to the beginning of the title, working from Landauer's handwritten manuscript. The "twelve articles," a reference to the Peasants' War, were published in numerous anarchist journals, and revised substantially in January 1912. Landauer, "The 12 Articles of the Socialist Federation," in *For Socialism*, 144–145; cf. Landauer, "The Twelve Articles of the Socialist Bund, Second Version," in *Revolution and Other Writings*, 215–216.

111. Kuhn and Wolf, introduction to *Revolution and Other Writings*, 31; also see Erich Mühsam, *Liberating Society from the State and Other Writings: A Political Reader*, ed. and trans. Gabriel Kuhn (Oakland, CA: PM Press, 2011), 6.

112. Kuhn marks a talk given in that month, "Vom freien Arbeitertag," *Der Sozialist*, October 1, 1911, as the transition to "desperate defense against the war." Kuhn, note on Landauer, "A Free Workers' Council," in *Revolution and other Writings*, 218.

113. Landauer, "Martin Buber," *Neue Blätter* (Hellerau and Berlin: n.p., 1913), 90ff.; in Landauer, *Philosophie und Judentum: Ausgewählte Schriften, Band 5*, ed. Siegbert Wolf (Hessen: AV, 2012), 351–362.

114. Buber publicly joined the Bund in advocating community control of local schools but never contributed to *Der Sozialist*; FMD 177.

115. Richard Faber and Christine Holste, eds., *Der Potsdamer Forte-Kreis: Eine utopische Intellektuellenassoziation zur europäischen Friedenssicherung* (Würzburg: Konigshausen & Neumann, 2001); Landauer, *Sein Lebensgang in Briefen*, 2:1–16 and 2:77–92; FMD 92.

116. "We no longer need our old motto, *Not by might, but by spirit*, since power and spirit are now going to become one. *Incipit vita nova*." Buber to Hans Kohn, September 30, 1914, in LMB 160.

117. FMD 93–126.

118. Broué, *German Revolution*, 43–53.

119. Gary Dorrien, "Barthian Dialectics : 'Yes' and 'No' on the Barthian Revolt and Its Legacy," in *The Weimar Moment: Liberalism, Political Theology, and Law*, ed. Leonard V. Kaplan and Rudy Koshar (Lanham, MD: Lexington Books, 2012), 219.

120. "The Watchword" was adapted from Buber's Hanukkah address to the Berlin Zionist Union on December 19, 1914. Judah Magnes, in response to the same statement, resolved never to read Buber again; MBEY 400.

121. Buber's private epistolary debate with the Dutch poet Frederik van Eeden yielded two published pieces: "Bewegung: Aus einem Brief an einen Holländer" (in January–February 1915) and "Richtung soll kommen!" which was published in *Masken*, the journal of a Düsseldorf theater company, of which Landauer nearly assumed the editorship in 1918 before the November Revolution erupted.

122. "*No* government is fighting for the freedom of peoples; that is not in the nature of states. . . . German militarism differs from Russian or French militarism only in being better organized." Buber to Frederik van Eeden, October 16, 1914, LMB 162.

123. Scholem to Buber, June 25, 1916, LMB 193.

124. Schwarzschild, who denies that Buber deviated from his pro-war line until the war was over, ignores a new, politically radical tone; for example, in Buber's solicitations for his planned "book of essays directed against the threatening intrusion of the European malady (mercantilism, imperialism, etc.—in a word, covetousness) into an incipient Jewish Palestine"; Buber to Ernst Eliyahu Rappeport, January 28, 1918, LMB 227. Beyond that, there is the fact that Landauer once again agreed to appear in *Der Jude*, as early as March 1917, and was communicating with Buber about this as early as August 1916; LMB 199–201; FMD 101. Benjamin never wrote for *Der Jude* but did write for Buber's next journal, the interdenominational *Die Kreatur*. Magnes forgave Buber to the extent that he made great efforts to hire him at the Hebrew University.

125. Landauer to Buber, May 12, 1916, LMB 188–192.

126. FMD 101, 173n98.

127. How contorted these statements are has been noted by Steven Schwarzschild, "Buber and his Biographer," *Judaism* 34.3 (Fall 1985): 439.

128. MBEY 192–193.

129. MBEY 178. Schwarzschild uses this fact to support his claim that Buber never changed his mind on the war, but this seems strange; why wouldn't Buber then have set the cutoff at 1918? Add the fact that Buber's volte-face occurred before the notorious *Judenzählung* of October 1916, an official army census that aimed to determine how many Jews served at the front. The *Judenzählung* disillusioned many Jews who had thought of using their service as a way to bond more closely with Germany. Buber only commented dryly: "We are used to being counted." *Der Jude* 1.8 (November 1916): 564.

130. FMD 172n82, 172n84.

131. Arthur Cohen, introduction to *The Jew: Essays from Buber's Journal Der Jude, 1916–1928* ed. Arthur Cohen and trans. Joachim Neugroschel (Tuscaloosa: University of Alabama Press, 1980), 7.

132. Buber did not include the letter of May 12, 1916, in which Landauer accuses Buber of making him feel "personally disavowed," in his edition of Landauer's correspondence. He also asked Hans Kohn to soften the section on the war period in his authorized biography of Buber in 1929 and omit the controversies with Landauer and van Eeden; FMD 102.

133. The debate was conducted in four articles: Cohen, "Zionismus und Religion: Ein Wort an meine Kommilitonen jüdischen Glaubens," *K.-C. Blätter* 11 (May–June, 1916): 643–646; Buber, "Begriffe und Wirklichkeit: Brief an Herrn Geh. Regierungsrat Prof. Dr. Hermann Cohen," *Der Jude* 1.5 (July 1916): 281ff.; Cohen, "Antwort auf das Offene Schreiben des Herrn Dr. Martin Buber," *K.-C. Blätter* 12 (July–August, 1916): 683–88; Buber, "Zion, der Staat und die Menschheit: Bemerkungen zu Hermann Cohens Antwort," *Der Jude* 1.7 (October 1916): 425ff.

134. The debate is currently available in English only in excerpts: Buber and Cohen, "A Debate on Zionism and Messianism (Summer 1916)," in *The Jew in the Modern World: A Documentary History*, 3rd ed., ed. Paul Mendes-Flohr and Jehuda Reinharz (New York: Oxford University Press, 2011), 651–655; Cohen, "A Reply to Dr. Martin Buber's Open Letter to Hermann

Cohen," in *Reason and Hope: Selections from the Jewish Writings of Hermann Cohen*, ed. and trans. Eva Jospe (Cincinnati, OH: Hebrew Union College Press, 1993), 164–170; Buber, "Zion, the State, and Humanity: Remarks on Hermann Cohen's Answer," in *The Jew*, 85–96.

135. Daniel Weiss and Paul Nahme have both made this point to me in conversations about their work on Cohen.

136. Buber, "A Debate on Zionism and Messianism," 654. Landauer sent Buber an approving letter after reading "Zion, the State, and Humanity," and another when Buber collected his articles on Cohen and Zionism together in 1917 and published them as *Völker, Staaten, und Zion*. Landauer to Buber, October 12, 1916, LMB 199; FMD 110, 177n187. An October 17, 1916, follow-up on the matter of the last Cohen piece is the first letter postdating May 1916 from Landauer to himself included in Buber's edition of Landauer's correspondence; *Sein Lebensgang in Briefen II*, 163.

137. Buber eventually expressed his fear that this idea might "lure us into the glittering notion that God is an idea which can become reality only through man, and, furthermore, induces the hopelessly wrong conception that God is not, but that He becomes—either within man, or within mankind." "Preface to the 1923 Edition," *On Judaism*, 8.

138. Buber, "A Debate on Zionism and Messianism," 654.

139. Written before Landauer's death but published after it, the text carries the dedication: "Dem Freunde Gustav Landauer aufs Grab."

140. Buber, "The Holy Way," in *On Judaism*, 108.

141. FMD 175n159.

142. *Sein Lebensgang in Briefen II*, 296.

143. Landauer to Buber, November 15, 1918, *Sein Lebensgang in Briefen II*, 298. I have combined translations from LMB 232 and from Gabriel Kuhn, ed. and trans., *All Power to the Councils! A Documentary History of the German Revolution, 1918–1919* (Oakland, CA: PM Press, 2012), 172. The comments that Buber makes throughout *Sein Lebensgang in Briefen* are rarely treated as independent "works" of Buber's, but they provide insights into Buber's view of Landauer's life.

144. Landauer to Buber, November 22, 1918, *Sein Lebensgang in Briefen II*, 299. Buber annotates this comment to provide evidence for Landauer's claim by directing the reader to certain of Eisner's speeches. Translation from *All Power to the Councils*, 172–173.

145. Landauer soon wrote Buber another letter commenting on Buber's idea to write an article on the revolution for *Der Jude*. Landauer praised its "very fine theme, the revolution and the Jews," and exhorted Buber to expand on "the leading part the Jews have played in the upheaval," referring to the work of Eisner, Mühsam, and Ernst Toller; Landauer to Buber, December 2, 1918, LMB 234. However, the eventual article, "Die Revolution und Wir," took a different tack.

146. Landauer, *Revolution*, 158–159.

147. Buber, *The Holy Way*, 146–147.

148. Landauer, *Revolution*, 175.

149. Buber, *The Holy Way*, 147–148.

150. Between the volte-face of 1916 and *The Holy Way* in 1918 came the British conquest of Palestine and the Balfour Declaration, which promised a "Jewish national home" in Palestine. The appearance of the term "imperialism" in Buber's vocabulary and his condemnation of realpolitik in Zionism must be understood against this background.

151. FMD 107–109. I thank Michael Morgan for emphasizing this point.

152. Buber, *The Holy Way*, 108–109. Here Jospe's translation may be misleading: she renders "europäischen Dualismus" as "Occidental dualism," exaggerating the continuity with the fourth Speech on Judaism, "The Spirit of the Orient and Judaism."

153. Ibid., 111. The English translation omits two epigraphs from Isaiah to *Der Heilige Weg*, both of which speak of a way (German *Weg*, Hebrew *derekh*): Isaiah 62:10 and 35:8. The latter, the source for "der heilige Weg" (Heb. *derekh ha-kodesh*), prophesies the safe return of the exiles.

154. Ibid., 112. I have altered the translation to reflect Buber's use of *Individuen* and *Konfession*.

155. This constant theme is summarized in the fifth speech, "Jewish Religiosity," in Buber, *On Judaism*, 83.

156. An extreme portrayal of the Second Commonwealth as a creative era is found in the fourth speech, where Buber writes of the "fateful disaster" of "the downfall of their state" as an event that "split Judaism's history in two." Buber, "The Spirit of the Orient and Judaism," in *On Judaism*, 71–73.

157. Buber, *The Holy Way*, 117; "Dieser Augenblick ist die eigentliche Wende der jüdischen Geschichte." Buber, *Der Heilige Weg: Ein Wort an die Juden und an die Völker* (Frankfurt: Rutten & Loening, 1919), 30.

158. Buber, *The Holy Way*, 116.

159. Ibid., 118–119.

160. Ibid., 116–117.

161. Buber to Ludwig Strauss, February 22, 1919, in *Briefwechsel II*, 29, in *Letters of Martin Buber*, 242.

162. MBEY 247.

163. Landauer, *Revolution*, 174.

164. Landauer to Margarete Susman, November 14, 1918, in *All Power to the Councils*, 171.

165. Landauer to Fritz Mauthner, April 7, 1919, in *Revolution and Other Writings*, 323.

166. Martin Buber, "Die Revolution und Wir," *Der Jude* 3, nos. 8–9 (November–December 1918): 345–347. Translations from this text are my own.

167. Ibid.

168. Donald L. Niewyk, "The German Jews in Revolution and Revolt, 1918–19," in *Studies in Contemporary Jewry, Vol. IV: The Jews and the European Crisis, 1914–1921*, ed. Jonathan Frankel (New York: Oxford University Press, 1988), 41–66. The perception that Jews were the driving force of the tumult was common to left and right, Jews and non-Jews, although statistically it has been shown to be incorrect—a bias resulting from the greater tendency to notice prominent Jews.

169. Christophe Chalamet, "Karl Barth and the Weimar Republic," in *The Weimar Moment*, 245.

170. Landauer had an ambivalent attitude towards the Spartakusbund:

> A difficult case are the Bolsheviks (Spartacus). They are pure centralists like Robespierre and his men. Their aspiration has no content, it only knows power. They advocate a military regime that would be uglier than anything the world has seen. Dictatorship of the armed proletariat? I'd rather have Napoleon! Unfortunately, the best of the country have ended up in their ranks.

Landauer to Margarete Susman, December 13, 1918, in *All Power to the Councils*, 182. Landauer nonetheless advised Eisner to "win back the Spartacists." Landauer to Eisner, January 10, 1919, in *All Power to the Councils*, 183. He also eulogized Luxemburg and Liebknecht in Munich on February 6, 1919, in the wake of their assassinations; MBEY 248.

171. Hans Mommsen, *The Rise and Fall of Weimar Democracy*, trans. Elborg Forster and Larry Eugene Jones (Chapel Hill: University of North Carolina Press, 1989), 47.

172. Translation from Paul Mendes-Flohr, "'The Stronger and the Better Jews: Jewish Theological Responses to Political Messianism in the Weimar Republic," in *Jews and Messianism in the Modern Era: Metaphor and Meaning*, ed. Jonathan Frankel (New York: Oxford University Press, 1991), 159–185.

173. Buber to Ludwig Strauss, February 22, 1919, LMB 242.

174. Landauer to Hugo Landauer, January 17, 1919, in *All Power to the Councils*, 188.

175. Landauer to Georg Springer, January 25, 1919, in *All Power to the Councils*, 189.

176. Landauer to Hugo Landauer, January 29, 1919, in *All Power to the Councils*, 190.

177. The German word *Rat*, "council," is often used to translate the Russian "Soviet." However, Kuhn is right to avoid "English terms that evoke the Soviet Union's political order—such as 'soviets' and 'people's commissars'—as the situation and the debates in Germany were quite different." Kuhn, introduction to *All Power to the Councils*, xv.

178. "In translations, this has sometimes been shortened to 'minister.' However, the distinction between the position of a *Minister* and a *Volksbeauftragter* was important to the council republicans." Kuhn and Wolf, introduction to *Revolution and Other Writings*, 47n5.

179. Mühsam, *From Eisner to Leviné*, in *All Power to the Councils*, 205–263. "I especially think that I have the duty to clear the memory of the great revolutionary Gustav Landauer, my teacher and best friend, who was slaughtered on May 2, 1919, by White Guards," in *All Power to the Councils*, 210–211. *Von Eisner bis Leviné* is the only firsthand account of the Bavarian Revolution by an anarchist; it provides a salutary corrective to accounts of the Bavarian Revolution that group all the leading figures together, such as his claim that Eisner had his opponents arrested to prevent them from disrupting his plans for the Landtag elections. See *All Power to the Councils*, 217. Also see Ulrich Linse, *Gustav Landauer und die Revolutionszeit 1918–1919* (Berlin: Karin Kramer Verlag, 1974).

180. Mommsen, *Rise and Fall of Weimar Democracy*.

181. Mauthner, conveying his consent to Buber with respect to this project, refers to a previous letter from Buber proposing the committee, but that letter is not included in the *Briefwechsel*. Mauthner to Buber, Easter Sunday 1919, and Susman to Buber, May 4, 1919, in LMB 243.

182. Buber, "Landauer und die Revolution," 291, cited in Mendes-Flohr, "The Stronger and the Better Jews," 184n105.

183. The mural Buber saw in the Italian church likely represented the medieval Christian legend of the ten thousand martyrs, a popular theme for Renaissance art. Since Buber does not name the church or the work, I thank Heba Mostafa for suggesting this possibility to me.

184. Rudolf Rocker cited in Kuhn and Wolf, introduction to *Revolution and Other Writings*, 54n101.

185. Buber, "Der heimliche Führer," *Die Arbeit* 2.6 (1920): 36–37. A Hebrew translation of "Landauer und die Revolution" appeared in the Zionist paper *Ha'adama* in 1920.

186. Buber, "Erinnerung an einen Tod," *Neue Wege* 23.4, April 1929, 161–165. Cf. "Recollection of a Death," in PW 115–120. In 1939, Buber published a short piece entitled *Landauer b'sha'a zo* (Landauer in This Hour); cf. *Ha'poel Ha'tzair*, vol. 10, no. 29, June 27, 1939, 8–9. Also that year, Hebrew translations of "Landauer and the Revolution" and "The Hidden Leader" were collected with the new article into a Hebrew collection *Al Gustav Landauer* (On Gustav Landauer), published by the Histadrut (Federation of Hebrew Workers in the Land of Israel).

187. Buber, "Recollection of a Death," 117. Buber's early wartime argument that soldiers participate together in a shared *Erlebnis* of action and commitment to die for a cause has become a shared struggle not to battle but to perceive the non-inimical nature of the enemy.

188. Ibid., 118. The soldier-revolutionary comparison strikingly resembles a 1921 discussion of Carl Schmitt, *Dictatorship*, trans. Michael Hoelzl and Graham Ward (Malden, MA: Polity Press, 2014), 151. Schmitt, however, equates soldier and revolutionary, where Buber distinguishes them.

189. Buber, "Recollection of a Death," 119. The German officer walking "with clanking spurs through the room" is most likely Eugen Leviné (1883–1919), who served in the German army in World War I, joined the KPD, and may have ordered the shooting of hostages by the Red Guards toward the end of April 1919.

2 The Serpent

Theopolitics from Weimar to Nazi Germany

We have come to recognize that the political is the total, and as a result we know that any decision about whether something is *unpolitical* is always a *political* decision.

— Carl Schmitt

Here is the serpent in the fullness of its power!

— Martin Buber

1919 and After: The Shape of the Theopolitical Problem

Buber's version of the "theologico-political predicament" was strongly influenced by his understanding of the legacy of Gustav Landauer's anarchism, on the political side of the hyphen, and by his work with Franz Rosenzweig, on the theological side. Buber began this struggle after the failure of the Bavarian Revolution, during the turbulent life of the Weimar Republic. From the outset, many Germans did not welcome the rise of parliamentary democracy. Liberalization and universal suffrage had been discussed throughout the war years, but conservative and military elites resisted; the most prominent move of the Supreme Military Command toward democratization came only when the war was nearly lost, in an attempt to shift blame for the defeat from the military to a new civilian government.[1] This strategy of blaming the home front for the military loss continued into the peace years. But the theme of "legitimacy" signaled the questionable nature of the Weimar Republic in intellectual discourse across political divisions, as Hans Mommsen has written: "Even its strongest supporters were ambivalent toward the new political order."[2] Meanwhile, the radical left attempted to prevent and preempt the birth of the Republic in order to foster either dictatorship of the proletariat or decentralized democracy in council form. Throughout the 1920s, the specter of revolution was frequently used to justify states of emergency and repressive measures.

Ambivalence about the Republic crossed denominational as well as political divides. As Klaus Tanner points out: "The majority of Protestants considered the new constitution of 1919 a document of 'western liberal' thinking. . . . [T]here was a broad consensus in the [19]20s regarding the rejection of the new political order."[3] This consensus held for intellectuals as much as for the general public; it comprised religious socialists like Karl Barth and Paul Tillich as well as nationalists and authoritarians like Friedrich Gogarten and Wilhelm Stapel, for whom "models of legitimization based on religion and metaphysics had a de facto delegitimizing effect for the parliamentary democracy of Weimar."[4] On the Catholic side stood Carl Schmitt, the most prominent anti-liberal intellectual of the time (although, to be sure, his orthodoxy was suspect, he was eventually excommunicated for remarrying, and he was only one pole of a Catholic spectrum that contained significant variety).[5] Although most of the "political theology" discourse came from Protestant sources, it was Schmitt who initiated the trend with his *Politische Theologie* (1922). The Catholic Center Party, a well-established group compared to the hastily formed and regionally divergent Protestant parties, focused primarily on its old agenda of securing the autonomy of the ecclesiastical hierarchy to determine its internal cultural program. As for the Jews, they were caught on the horns of an ideological dilemma: stereotyped as left-wing radicals but also as primary forces behind the new Republic. The visibility of Jews in the Republic, the flowering of Jewish culture during this period, and the desire of Jews for equal civil and political rights fed the ire of the anti-Republican majority.[6] The figure of "the Jew" came to stand in for modernity itself: "'The Jew' became the standard negative symbol in the cultural criticism of the political right against modernity. The *Judenfrage* displayed Jews as the deputies of modernity in a culture war against modernity."[7]

How does Buber fit into this picture? He was a religious critic of liberal political thought, but also a Jew, and no conservative. Although as a Zionist he saw the Jewish future in Palestine, he himself remained in Germany.[8] He did not publish in Hebrew for years and did not visit Palestine until 1927.[9] Politically, he was perhaps closest to the religious socialists, represented by the Swiss Protestant Leonhard Ragaz. He contributed to the *Blätter fur Religiösen Sozialismus* and reviewed Ragaz's work *Weltreich, Religion und Gottesherrschaft* for the *Frankfurter Zeitung*.[10] Buber also cited Ragaz in an epigraph to his own brief "theses" on religious socialism: "Any socialism whose limits are narrower than God and man is too narrow for us."[11] Here he had comrades, Jewish and Christian, who saw the sovereignty of God as a guarantor of human freedom and sociality. The religious socialist position distinguished itself from two main opponents: a secular valorization of the autonomy of the political sphere from any religious or ethical strictures, and a conservative political theology that conceived of God's monarchy as a model for an autocratic system of earthly governance. This latter position, paradoxically, also proclaimed the autonomy of the political from religion, as it required the gravitas of the divine to serve earthly politics. From the perspective of religious socialism, the new political theology was not merely a matter of the reassertion of the previous "alliance of throne and altar," since it sought to divinize the political itself.

The foremost representatives of both these tendencies, Max Weber and Carl Schmitt, were, like Buber, present in Munich during the revolution of 1919—Weber to deliver his famous lecture *Politik als Beruf* (*Politics as a Vocation*) to an audience of left-wing students, and Schmitt to work in the censorship section of the regional martial-law administration.[12] A focus on their arguments for the autonomy of the political reveals that the relation of ends and means, a primary focus of Buber and other religious socialists, was not "merely" an "ethical" question but the consummate political question of the time. "Socialism must know," Buber wrote in 1928, "that the decision as to how similar or dissimilar the end which is attained will be to the end which was previously cherished is dependent upon how similar or dissimilar to the set goal are the means whereby it is pursued."[13] This claim raises the larger issue of whether politics and the political should be defined as a sphere of life with its own rules, alongside aesthetics, religion, ethics, and so on.

The idea that politics is a craft demanding special knowledge is as old as Plato's inquiry into the *arête,* or excellence, of the statesman. But the idea of the autonomy of politics, the claim that politics issues its own laws to itself, may be much younger. Machiavelli is said to have emancipated politics from its subordination to ethics or religion, enabling it to be studied in its own right. Political theorists might, then, be defined as those who follow in Machiavelli's footsteps, presupposing the autonomy of politics at the foundation of their work. There is a logical slippage here, however. Acknowledging that politics is a craft, like shipbuilding or medicine, that demands a particular talent or excellence is not yet to declare it autonomous, because it fails to articulate the telos, or purpose, of politics. Both Plato and Aristotle, in different ways, do subordinate politics to a telos, namely the Good. With Machiavelli, however, the move that allows his laserlike focus on political technique is precisely the refusal to articulate any task for politics beyond the desire of the prince to "maintain his state," that is, to continue being a prince. The *virtù* of the prince, then—a complex term for Machiavelli, but an integral one, which partially draws on the classical philosophical meaning of *arête*—becomes identified with whatever techniques do in fact maintain the state. In line with what Weber called the rationalization of every sphere of human life, this isolation of the technique of politics can then be maintained as the sine qua non for the existence of political science as a scholarly discipline. This claim serves as the foundation for many shades of political "realism," including Weber's own distinction between a politics founded in an ethics of responsibility, which pays political science its due, and one rooted in an ethics of conviction, which naïvely allows for comprehensive conceptions of the good to determine political action. The latter is vulnerable to the charge that it is antipolitics, since by refusing to stipulate that the purpose of politics is to maintain the state, it refuses to allow politics the autonomous existence presumed necessary for political science to exist. The plea for objectivity that inaugurates political science, namely the demand that we describe the world as it is, and not as we think it ought to be, smuggles ontology and ethics through the back door, as it first tells us how the world really is, and then demands that we recognize this state of affairs in our actions, in order to be responsible.

As the preeminent social scientist of his day, Weber sets the terms of the discussion for much of Weimar thought. Maturity in politics for Weber is defined by the ability to recognize and endure the irreconcilable clashes of value between ethics and religion, on the one hand, and politics on the other. Meanwhile, the rationalization of every sphere of life attendant to modernity encourages the growth of bureaucracy, which in turn endangers "the political" itself, defined in a Nietzschean manner as *Herrschaft* (authority or domination) of one person or group of people over another. These basic claims serve as the nodal point around which numerous "symmetrical counter-concepts" form concerning the question of the autonomy of politics.[14] Theopolitics, I argue, develops as one such counterconcept, as does Schmitt's political theology. The two concern themselves with the same Weberian problems—from secularization and technicity to representation and charisma—and think through them with a similar vocabulary but reach diametrically opposite conclusions. Both question the continuing intellectual validity of the liberal border between religion and politics but to radically opposed ends: if political theology deploys the power of the divine to serve the authoritarian state, then theopolitics denies any possibility of permanently legitimizing institutional human power. If political theology borders on the fascistic, then theopolitics is its anarchistic antipode. But it is Weber who sets the scene for both.

A Bourgeois Politician: Secularism, Polytheism, and Anarchism in Max Weber

Wolfgang Mommsen argues for a connection between Weber's political doctrines and his conception of scholarship. Both date to Weber's early studies of the increasing population of Polish migrant agricultural workers in the East Elbia region, as demonstrated by his 1895 inaugural address at the University of Freiburg.[15] Weber argued against protectionist policies that would artificially freeze German agriculture at its current point of development. He also opposed allowing the high rate of Polish immigration to continue, despite the fact that the Junker landlords benefited economically from employing lower-paid Poles. Weber's primary concern was the "German character" of the national economy, and to that end he supported state subsidization of German small farmers in

East Elbia, even if that ran afoul of the Junkers and the march of capitalism. "Ostensibly pure scientific value systems of whatever variety always appeared to stand in the way of such a consciously national economic policy," according to Mommsen. "Therefore Weber strove to refute the very existence of scientifically-valid normative categories. At the outset, his program for a value-free science rested largely on an effort to establish the ideal of the national state as the sole indisputable standard."[16] Mommsen's "therefore" may be too strong. Nonetheless, he demonstrates a connection between Weber's understandings of power and of scholarship. Weber himself once put it this way:

> Politics is a tough business, and those who take responsibility for seizing the spokes of the wheel of political development in the fatherland must have strong nerves and should not be too sentimental to practice secular politics. Those who wish to involve themselves in secular politics *must above all be without illusions* and . . . *recognize the fundamental reality* of an ineluctable eternal war on earth of men against men.[17]

This eternal war, according to Weber, is what social science, including the science of politics, must acknowledge first if it is to maintain its status as a science. This science, in turn, is the necessary basis of what Weber repeatedly calls "secular" politics. As Leo Strauss would later comment: "Conflict was for Weber an unambiguous thing, but peace was not: peace is phony, but war is real."[18] This view of conflict as fundamental extends to the realm of values. Some scholars, drawing on Weber's own image of incommensurable values as warring gods demanding allegiance, have called this his "polytheism."[19] For Weber, political decisions always refer to values and are ultimately nonrational. This is another reason why they cannot be based on an objective social science (which can recognize the fact of eternal conflict but cannot tell us what to do about it), and why the increasing bureaucratization of politics, the attempt to make it function according to set regular laws, endangers the ability of politics to preserve a space for individual decision at the highest level.[20]

Weber defined himself on many occasions as a "bourgeois" politician. This meant that he lacked sympathy for the claims of the dying aristocratic landowner class, which was struggling during the Wilhelmine twilight to retain its oligarchic privileges. However, he also cast a skeptical eye on the quest of the organized working class to seize power. He argued that Marxism could have validity either as a diagnostic scholarly apparatus submitting falsifiable claims to social science in an attempt to increase understanding of modern capitalist societies or as a purely ethical call to overthrow an unjust social order, but never both. Because the majority of the organized working class in Germany operated through the German Social Democratic Party, which was officially committed to an "orthodox" formulation of Marxist doctrine, this meant that few socialist activists framed their work in a manner acceptable to Weber. When he encountered ones who did, however, he treated them with great respect and even befriended them. Such figures, including the sociologist Robert Michels and the playwright Ernst Toller, leaned more toward anarchist syndicalism or Tolstoyan thought than Marxism.

Despite his friendly relationships with such figures, however, Weber considered the anarchist quest for a society free from domination as the very paradigm of utopianism in politics. In fact, he may have based his famous description of the "ethics of conviction" on Michels.[21] Weber believed that an anarchist society was both impossible, because contrary to human nature, and undesirable, because in eliminating *Herrschaft*, a primary source of human excellence, it would create a bleak world of passionless Nietzschean "last men." But he admitted that this was a value judgment and that he could not dismiss anarchism on the basis of reason. Rather, he shifted the grounds of disagreement to the ethics of practice. Weber described an anarchist committed to revolution no matter what the short-term consequences of revolutionary actions might be, in contrast to a sober politician concerned primarily with taking responsibility for such short-term consequences. This contrast reaches its sharpest point when it touches the question of violence. Here Weber reaches the borders of politics, explaining that if his student audience ignored the distinction between ends and means, they would exit the realm of the political:

> In the last analysis the modern state can only be defined sociologically in terms of a specific *means* which is peculiar to the state, as it is to all other political associations, namely physical violence. "Every state is founded on force," as Trotsky once said.... If there existed only social formations in which violence was unknown as a means, *then* the concept of the "state" would have disappeared; *then* that condition would have arisen which one would define, in this particular sense of the word, as "anarchy."[22]

For Weber, the state is the only locus of the political. The political is defined by the deployment of the means of violence by associated groups of people; the state then claims a monopoly over this means, concentrating the "legitimate" use of such violence in one particular association. Here Weber's "polytheism" manifests in the form of a clash between secularism and the ethics of conviction: "Anyone who makes a pact with the means of violence, for whatever purpose—and every politician does this . . . is becoming involved . . . with the diabolical powers that lurk in all violence."[23] To attempt to create a society consisting only of formations "in which violence was unknown as a means" would be to attempt "anarchy." This, of course, is what many in Weber's original audience of student radicals, inspired by Landauer and his comrades, had been attempting—for Weber, they were seeking a kingdom "not of this world."[24]

This specific goal links Buber and Schmitt to central themes of Weberian thought. Both were concerned not just with the immediate question of the Bavarian Revolution but also with the challenge posed by anarchism and non-violence to the existence and coherence of the "political sphere." Their approaches form mirror images: Schmitt tried to solve the problem by assimilating the kingdom of God to Weber's political; Buber by proclaiming that, at least for the people Israel, "there *is* no political outside the theopolitical."[25] For both Buber and Schmitt, the anarchist vision would become a seminal influence—a resource for the former, a bête noire for the latter—which each would articulate within the field of Weberian political concerns. Schmitt's *Politische Theologie* had its origins in a festschrift for Weber, whereas Buber's theopolitics, first fully articulated in *Königtum Gottes*, admits its debts not just to *Economy and Society*, with its famous sociology of domination, but also to Weber's magisterial representation of Israelite life in *Ancient Judaism*. The relationship between anarchism and the kingdom, or kingship, of God, stands behind each thinker's grappling with the nature of representation, the role of charisma in authority, the state of emergency, the nature of secularization, the ethics of political decision making, and the political significance of rationalization and technicity in modernity. But whereas Weber always insisted that one had to choose either secular politics and polytheism or the otherworldly anarchist kingdom of God, Schmitt and Buber rejected this choice, in opposite ways. For Schmitt, a "secularized" theology was at work behind and for the legitimation of secular politics and domination; whereas for Buber, the kingship of God was always actually this-worldly, embracing and encompassing political life, as long as that life remained anarchistic.

The *Charis* above Every Law: Anarchy, Legitimacy, and Theology in Buber and Schmitt

Although Schmitt does not explicitly deal with Buber, and Buber rarely deals with Schmitt, they fit into each other's worldviews as perfect foils.[26] In his study of Buber's polemic against Schmitt in "The Question to the Single One" (1936), the intellectual historian Christoph Schmidt argues that Buber's use of the term "theopolitical" serves as a Jewish *Erledigung*, or "closure," of political theology, parallel to Erik Peterson's attempt to do the same from the vantage point of Catholicism.[27] Schmidt finds that Buber uses "theopolitics" only to define the proper relationship between the religious and the political; "political theology" would then describe what theopolitics becomes if it betrays its proper task. The disagreement is about legitimacy, not legality.[28] From Buber's point of view, Schmitt epitomizes the excesses of modern power politics; from Schmitt's point of view, Buber at first appears to epitomize an antipolitical tendency to remove personal strife from society and to transform politics and government into "administration," by eliminating domination.[29] Leo Strauss once noted that for Schmitt, "the ultimate quarrel occurs not between bellicosity and pacifism (or nationalism and internationalism) but between the *"authoritarian* and *anarchistic* theories."[30] If so, and if Schmitt takes up the authoritarian position, Buber might be the contemporary of Schmitt's who best assumes the parallel anarchist position.

Schmitt, who may have attended Weber's public lectures in Munich, also came to center violence in his concept of the political. This is stated most famously in the "friend-enemy" criterion of *Concept of the Political* (1932), but it can be seen already in *Political Romanticism* (1919), which, while ostensibly concerned with the correct understanding of an eighteenth-century literary phenomenon, can easily be seen as an oblique response to contemporary political circumstances. Schmitt argues that political romanticism is found on both the left and the right. It occurs wherever one seeks to evade a final political decision, since romanticism aesthetically prefers to avoid confining reality within the limits of the single outcome that attends any decision: "In commonplace reality, the romantics could not play the role of the ego who creates the world. They preferred the state of eternal becoming and possibilities that are never consummated to the confines of concrete reality. This is because only one of the numerous possibilities is ever realized."[31] For the political romantic, Schmitt claims, decision itself is violence and therefore must be avoided. This is the origin of the preference for "eternal discussion," the critique of which will soon become a theme of Schmitt's attacks on liberal parliamentarianism.

The most extreme embodiment of antiparliamentarian, antiromantic will to decision is the dictator, and Schmitt made dictatorship the topic of his next major work, *Die Diktatur* (*Dictatorship*, 1921). The book was timely in light of the failed Kapp Putsch of March 1920, in which right-wing nationalist and monarchist forces within the military attempted to reverse the results of 1918–1919 and sent the Berlin government into exile; the attempt was met with a general strike and an armed revolt, the Ruhr Uprising, which sought to establish a dictatorship of the proletariat. Thus multiple parties had enacted or promised dictatorships in their contest for power.[32] Here, as in his book on romanticism, Schmitt laments the general confusion surrounding the concept in question and offers as an antidote a history of the concept of dictatorship that would distinguish it from absolutism, despotism, and tyranny. For Schmitt, the fundamental characteristic of any dictatorship is that dictatorship is "an exception that remains in functional dependence upon that which it negates," namely the normal situation. The norm is negated by the dictatorship, but the dictatorship also draws its authority from the norm and seeks to guard and protect it. In essence, then, what separates dictatorship from "arbitrary despotism" is that it pursues the goal of restoring the norm, seeking to make itself redundant; whatever extraordinary measures it takes are "determined from the perspective of the intended success."[33] Schmitt then distinguishes two types of dictatorship: "The commissary dictator is the unconditional commissar of action of a *pouvoir constitué* [constituted power], and sovereign dictatorship is the unconditional commission of action [*Aktionskommission*] of a *pouvoir constituant* [constituent power]."[34] In other words, the former acts under authorization and in the name of a previously constituted order to protect what exists; the latter appeals directly to "the people," that "constituent power" responsible for the authorization of any order whatsoever, in the name of an order still to come. While *Dictatorship* maintains a diagnostic tone, one can detect a clear normative preference in Schmitt for the commissary dictatorship; the sovereign dictatorship appears as a dangerous metastasizing of modern secularization, wherein the previous "constituent power," God, is replaced by an unchecked nation.

Arguably, Schmitt at one point understood Roman Catholicism to commend a middle way between romantic indecision and sovereign dictatorship. In *Roman Catholicism and Political Form* (1923), he argued that the church was not romantic, as commonly alleged, but rather was poised to become the last remaining home of true political "form" on Earth. Marxist socialism, anarchist syndicalism, and American capitalism all line up on the side of the increasing depoliticization of the world that comes with the rationalization of industry: "There must no longer be political problems, only organizational-technical and economic-sociological tasks."[35] If these ideologies spread further, only the Roman church would preserve Weberian *Herrschaft* against the onslaught of modern bureaucracy. True representation empowers one person to act in the name of another—to act freely, without needing to check with the represented to reconfirm authority, in the manner of the workers' and peasants' councils of the revolution. The pope, as Vicar of Christ, is infallible and sovereign; his decisions carry weight because of his representative function and therefore do not depend on the personal charisma of the holder of the office.

Schmitt's interest in the ability of true representation to maintain the personality of decision, even beyond the charismatic stage of authority, is found again in the famous claim in *Political Theology*: "Sovereign is he who decides the state of exception."[36] Schmitt was keenly aware of the potential of religious faith to undermine such personal human sovereignty, however, and in his later years he wrote of the need to "de-anarchize Christianity" in order to render it useful for legitimation:

> The most important sentence of Hobbes remains: Jesus is the Christ. The power of such a sentence also works even if it is pushed to the margins of a conceptual system of an intellectual structure, even if it is apparently pushed outside the conceptual circle. This deportation is analogous to the domestication of Christ undertaken by Dostoevsky's Grand Inquisitor. Hobbes expresses and grounds scientifically what Dostoevsky's Grand Inquisitor does: to render harmless Christ's impact on the social-political realm; to de-anarchize Christianity while still leaving it with a certain legitimizing effect and in any case not to renounce it. A clever tactician renounces nothing unless it is totally useless. Christianity was not yet spent. We can thus ask ourselves: to whom is the Grand Inquisitor closer, the Roman church or Thomas Hobbes's sovereign?

Reformation and Counter-Reformation revealed themselves as related in direction. Name me your enemy, and I will tell you who you are. Hobbes and the Roman church: the enemy is our own question as form.[37]

The claim here is that despite its ostensible reference to the Catholic Church in Dostoevsky's text, the Grand Inquisitor more closely resembles the modern state itself, as represented by Hobbes's Leviathan. Schmitt does Machiavelli one better here: lip service to the minimalist formula "Jesus is the Christ" is sufficient to claim absolute divine authority for human sovereignty and to short-cut apocalyptic attempts to delegitimize the state by means of theology. Furthermore, as Tracy Strong has pointed out, "The leviathan (as mortal God, hence as Christ/Messiah) *holds back* the kingdom of God on this earth or at least makes no move to bring it about. This is why this is political theology and not theological politics."[38] In one of his overtly antisemitic moods, Schmitt claims that it was Spinoza, the first "liberal Jew," who undid the great serpent and "mortal god" Leviathan by denying it the right to the formula "Jesus is the Christ" in the name of religious freedom.[39]

Such a concern with legitimation reveals a preoccupation with the potential failure of representation to be accepted by the represented. Unlike the aristocratic reactionaries with whom he associated during the Weimar era, Schmitt presented himself as highly preoccupied with political legitimacy per se and not merely with the legitimacy of the new liberal-democratic Republic. For political theorists concerned with legitimacy, anarchism often plays a role analogous to that of skepticism for philosophers concerned with the ultimate grounding of truth claims: it is like a boogeyman, lying in wait, suggesting by its very existence the possibility of the necessary failure of all projects of legitimation. Schmitt's student turned critic Waldemar Gurian sees Schmitt as always seeking a "highest instance of decision" that would bring an end to his "despair at an anarchy identified behind all its facades."[40] Indeed, Schmitt respects the anarchists' clearcut opposition to his thinking, unlike liberals who dismiss anarchism as unserious. He mentions anarchism in nearly all his works of the Weimar period and describes the conflict between the optimistic anthropology he ascribes to anarchism and the pessimistic anthropology of the Counter-Revolution as "the clearest antithesis in the entire history of political ideas."[41]

There is a strange duality to Schmitt's view of anarchism. On the one hand, he sees anarchism as atheistic and dependent upon a radically optimistic view of human nature. He links it intimately to the progressive secularization of modernity and to the corresponding increase of technicity. In this sense, anarchism aligns with liberalism and Marxism, the other secularizing and depoliticizing forces descended from the American and French Revolutions. On the other hand, Schmitt's rhetorical presentation of anarchism emphasizes its radicalism; the bloodlessness of the technical society is balanced out by the "Scythian fury"

of Bakunin, "the greatest anarchist of the nineteenth century," who "had to become in theory the theologian of the anti-theological and in practice the dictator of an antidictatorship."[42] In this sense, anarchists would be the very incarnation of the political, which Schmitt defines as "the most intense and extreme
antagonism, [which] becomes that much more political the closer it approaches
the most extreme point, that of the friend-enemy grouping."[43] Anarchists thus
embody a fascinating paradox for Schmitt: by declaring war against the political,
they instantiate the political.[44] Whereas Weber had characterized anarchism as
utopian, Schmitt does not see the anarchist ideal as utopian and admits that he
does not know whether it can be realized. Rather, he simply abhors it. In it he
recognizes a powerful enemy.[45]

But what about an anarchist who forswears violence as a means? Would
Schmitt see such a figure as irredeemably romantic? If Tolstoy, or Landauer, is
our model anarchist rather than Bakunin, is our anarchism depoliticized? Or
does the decentering of violence, precisely as the criterion of the political, constitute an even more radical attack on the political, such that by Schmitt's criteria the nonviolent anarchist is an even greater instantiation of the paradox? The
paradox may be irresolvable, by Schmitt's criteria. Let us, then, turn to Buber for
an alternative set of criteria. Against political theology's demand for hierarchical,
"representative" authority, Buber's theopolitics asserts precisely the mere "del-
egation" that Schmitt scorns. Against political theology's deployment of God's
messiah as a legitimating metaphor, even in a secularized world, theopolitics asserts the direct, literal rulership of God—and sees human rule, even a human
"anointed" by God, as the beginning of secularization. Against political theology's attempt to freeze charisma into an enduring office, theopolitics ensures that
authority comes and goes, requiring proof through deeds, like the fleeting charisma itself: "The *charis* accordingly stands superior to every enchantment as well
as every law."[46] All this works to decenter violence as the criterion of the political:
the state of emergency, in which according to Schmitt the location of sovereignty
is revealed and dictatorship is enacted, is a time for theopolitical faith to act, but
also to wait expectantly on God. It is only the failure to do so, and the succumbing to fear, that institutes violence at the heart of social life and thereby creates
the purely political sphere: "Give us a king like all the nations have, to go out
before us and fight our battles."

Hallowing the Serpent: Political Success as Religion's Trial by Fire

The claim of a necessary linkage of politics and violence, whether in Weberian or Schmittian form, implies that Landauer's murderers were engaged
in political action while their victim was an unpolitical anarchist romantic.
Buber's rhetoric develops two types of response to this implication (although
without ever framing the problem explicitly). The first accepts Weber's general

framework, in which the political equates to violence, and therefore devalorizes the political. In this case anarchism becomes proudly nonpolitical or antipolitical, standing with the "social" as opposed to politics. The second response maintains the value of the political by asserting its irreducibility to Weber's terms. At one point or another, Buber, like Landauer himself in his writings on anarchist "propaganda by the deed," embraces both strategies, although the antipolitical response does predominate.[47] No matter which rhetorical strategy he chooses in a given essay, however, the underlying intent is the same: to champion Landauer's assertion of the consonance of ends and means, against any demand for their separation.

Buber's most thorough explication of the theopolitical stance comes in *Kingship of God*, a difficult work that presents itself as biblical scholarship. It is the full explication, backed by evidence accumulated over the course of Buber's bible study during the 1920s, of the thesis of *The Holy Way*. And it can be read, in many ways, as an oblique response to Schmitt's ideas about dictatorship, emergency, and secularization. Before addressing it, however, several sources from the 1920s in which Buber deals more directly with the issues mentioned earlier, and particularly with the relationship between religion and politics in light of the question of ends and means, can illuminate how Buber considers these themes in general and make for a better entrée into the specific context of the history of ancient Israel.

In the early 1920s, between the death of Landauer and the beginning of the work on the Bible translation, Buber's publications—apart from *I and Thou*—consisted largely of reissues of his older collections of mystical and Hasidic tales and lectures on Judaism in new editions, as well as volumes of Landauer's work edited by Buber in accordance with his role as literary executor. Buber often explored his wide-ranging interests in lectures, many of which remain unpublished. *Kingship of God* has its roots in a lecture course given in Frankfurt in 1924–1925, and was updated for a small invited circle at Ponte Tresa in 1928.[48] The apparently hodgepodge nature of Buber's publication during these years makes it easy to understand why *I and Thou* dominates the scholarship on his productivity at the time. It is only in 1928 that the themes of theopolitics gain momentum in Buber's published work. Nonetheless, it is worth recalling Buber's statement, in the essay in which he referred to the political theologian Wilhelm Stapel as "the most perceptive of [the] antagonists [of our translation]," that Stapel had correctly perceived "what danger to his conception of a 'Christian statesman'—i.e., a sham Christian offering religious sanction to all the violences of the state—would be entailed among the German people by the dissemination of the actual Scriptures, which demand the shaping of society on the basis of belief."[49] Even the seemingly nonpolitical, purely "religious" activity of the Bible translation receives a theopolitical inflection here; the mere dissemination of the "actual" Scriptures undermines the effort to theologically legitimate state violence.

Of course, Buber contests the possibility of a purely religious sphere of life, just as he contests the existence of a political sphere. In 1923, the same year that *I and Thou* was published, Buber wrote that religion was "only the highest sublimation of the force that manifests itself in all life spheres in their cruder autonomization, in their tearing loose from the whole life and in the attempt, instead of subsuming conditionally autonomous multiplicity under the one world law, to allow a unity-blind being-a-law-unto-itself to dominate." If religion is not to be understood as *the* reality, then "it would be right promptly and completely to replace its rituals by art, its commands by ethics, its revelations by science." Buber praises his comrade Leonhard Ragaz for posing "the question of questions, that concerning the *kingdom*," since the proof of whether one really takes religion seriously is provided by whether one takes it politically seriously.[50] Yet Buber recognizes that there are different ways of combining religion and politics and that the predominant ones are uncongenial to his political and social aims. For the particular way of combining religion and politics that he favors to prevail, Buber needs to flesh out his description of what is at stake, and he seeks to do just this over the course of the 1920s. By 1933, just after the Nazi rise to power, he arrives at the following position:

> It is not valid to pursue a special "messianic" politics. But there is a certain manner of participation in public life by which in the midst of the interaction with world and politics the glance can be kept directed to the kingdom of God. There is no religious sanction for the setting of political aims. There is no political party that can assert that only it is willed by God. But it is also not so that one could say that before God it makes no difference whether this or that is done.[51]

Is this nuance, or simply confusion? A full answer would require a thorough engagement with the categories of theopolitics as laid out in *Kingship of God* and its subsequent biblical works, as that is where Buber considers and theorizes the widest range of examples. However, there are a few texts of the late 1920s and early 1930s that provide essential insights into the development of Buber's view. These focus for the most part on the theme of success and failure: if political seriousness is a litmus test for taking religion seriously in the whole of life and not restricting it to a powerless, meaningless sphere, then the question of political success or failure is the one on which the real commitment of real communities is likely to turn. To be politically real, it would seem, religion has to be materially effective. Yet this is exactly what it so often seems to be unable to do while remaining true to itself.

In "Biblisches Führertum" (Biblical Leadership, 1928), Buber sketches five types of leader found in biblical texts. He excludes "figures who appear as continuators, all those who are not called, elected, appointed anew, as the Bible says, directly by God, but who enter upon a task already begun without such personal call."[52] However, he has not yet developed the sophisticated distinctions he will later introduce between the types that he here groups together under the singular banner of "leadership": Father, Leader, Judge, King, and Prophet. All exemplify biblical leadership in being chosen against the laws of nature and history: against nature because they are typically weak and humble instead of strong and impressive, to demonstrate that God achieves not by might or power but "by my Spirit"; against history, because world history records importance according to the scale of conquest and success, whereas when the Bible "announces a successful deed, it is duty-bound to announce in complete detail the failure involved in the success." Moses is frustrated and thwarted by the people and does not enter the Promised Land. David fails ethically and politically over and over again. The narratives of the prophets amount to a veritable "glorification of failure." This experience of repeated failure begets messianism, an expectant hope that nonfailure will somehow emerge from failure, which must mean the overcoming of "history" understood as a record of successes: "The way, the real way, from the Creation to the Kingdom is trod not on the surface of success, but in the deep of failure. The real work, from the biblical point of view, is the late-recorded, the unrecorded, the anonymous work. The real work is done in the shadow. . . . Official leadership fails more and more, leadership devolves more and more upon the secret."[53] Yet although Buber is highly attracted to this position, and never fully abandons it, he also articulates an alternative view of the prophetic standing in tension with this one, namely that the prophetic depends on a confidence in the *possibility* of fulfillment in the present or near-future. Too much delay into the future risks despair, and with despair comes the transformation of the prophetic into the apocalyptic (for Buber, these are opposites). But this idea of the messianic transmutation of failure into success persists, perhaps because of the powerful service it performs as consolation for present political failures, such as that of Landauer in the Bavarian Revolution and Buber's own efforts at the Twelfth Zionist Congress.[54]

In 1928, Buber also published "Three Theses on Religious Socialism." Only three pages long, this is a dense and rich text that represents much of Buber's mature theopolitical position. First, it continues Buber's argument that while neither religion nor politics may be permitted existence as a separate sphere, religion suffers more under contemporary circumstances from the attempt to carve out such a sphere: "Religion without socialism is disembodied spirit, therefore not genuine spirit; socialism without religion is body emptied of spirit, hence also not genuine body. But—socialism without religion does not hear the divine address, it does not aim at a response, still it happens that it responds; religion without socialism hears the call but does not respond."[55] Second, it notes that both *Religio* and *Socialitas* have real and fictitious forms, and that the false forms may not only fail to achieve their stated goals but actually work against the real responsibilities of the human being to God and to human fellowship. At present, nearly every religious and socialist institution, whether a denomination, a party, or an intellectual tendency, counts as fictitious. This partially explains why religion and socialism are so often found in opposition, rather than in alliance. But there is hope: "Today appearance is currently opposed to appearance. But within the hidden sphere of the future the meeting has begun to take place." This confidence presumably derives from the activity of the religious socialists themselves. The final thesis reiterates Buber's Landauerian conviction regarding ends and means. Just as one must "live one's beliefs" in religion, so one must "live one's accomplishments" in socialism, which is to say, one must prefigure in one's forms of organization the kind of society sought by that organization. Violence and hierarchy must now and always fail to achieve an egalitarian, nonhierarchical society, no matter how expedient they seem.

In addition to his considerations of religion and politics in the Bible and in theory, Buber sought to work out his theopolitical quandaries through the study of an admired hero. "Gandhi, Politik, und Wir" (1930) was published in the transdenominational journal *Die Kreatur*, the editorship of which Buber shared with a Catholic and a Protestant; this context reveals something about who the "we" of the title might be. Buber singles out Gandhi, who at the time of his writing was leading thousands of Indians in civil disobedience along the course of the Salt March, as the contemporary exemplar of the theopolitical problematic. The Salt March itself was not merely a tactic, deploying tax refusal as a weapon against British colonial authority, but a religious experiment by Gandhi to discover just "*how much* is Caesar's." But how does one read the results of such an experiment? What does it mean for religion if the tactic is successful? If it fails? Gandhi, "as no other man of our age, shows us the difficulty of the situation, the depth of its problematic, the manifoldness of the battle fronts, the potency of the contradiction, which is encompassed by paradox and must be endured in every hour."[56]

The essay opens with a consideration, once again, of the question of success, in relation to Gandhi's efforts. Gandhi knows that the British fear him because of the masses he appears to command; that is to say, he seems to wield power of a type that the British recognize. However, Gandhi himself fears this power, unable to gauge to what extent his followers internalize his religious message as opposed to following him blindly. Buber quotes Gandhi to the effect that he would be more comfortable in a minority of one, standing firmly on his own truthful ground, and asks: "That is unquestionably the statement of a truthful man. . . . But can this also be regarded as the statement of a political man, that is, a man who undertakes to influence the formation of institutions and their operation? In other words: is the statement of Gandhi's that we have quoted a declaration against lies in politics or is it a declaration against politics?"[57] It seems at first that it may be the latter. "I seem to take part in politics," Gandhi writes, "but this is only because politics today strangles us like the coils of a serpent out of which one cannot slip whatever one tries. I desire, therefore, to wrestle with the serpent. . . . I have experimented with myself and my friends in order to introduce religion into politics." In this simile, Gandhi is the representative of religion, and he wrestles with the serpent of politics. Yet Gandhi's goal is not simply the victory of religion, a mass conversion. He seeks *Swaraj*, the independence of India. Can these two be linked? "Does religion allow itself," Buber asks, "to be introduced into politics in such a way that a political success can be obtained?" Gandhi seems to see the two goals as linked; in 1920 he had written that if the Indian people conducted themselves with virtue and discipline then Swaraj could be obtained in a year. Buber, in contrast, in line with his position that God's love is not measured by success, worries: "One may be certain of the truthfulness and non-violence of the love of God, but not of the attainment of Swaraj in one year. 'In one year' is a political word; the religious watchword must read: Some time, perhaps today, perhaps in a century. In religious reality there is no stipulation of time, and victory comes, at times, just when one no longer expects it."[58]

Gandhi thus risks failing to introduce religion into politics, instead merely allying his religion with the politics of others. "He cannot wrestle uninterruptedly with the serpent; he must at times get along with it because he is directed to work in the kingdom of the serpent that he set out to destroy. . . . The serpent is, indeed, not only powerful outside, but also within, in the souls of those who long for political success."[59] How can one guard against this risk? Buber's answer relates, as we have seen, to the question of success in time. "Religion means goal [*Ziel*] and way [*Weg*]; politics implies end [*Zweck*] and means [*Mittel*]."[60] The latter is achievable in time and measurable according to success, the former provides direction but does not seek historical consummation. But what does this mean for Buber's contention that God intended not to give Israel a religion but to found a kingdom? Wasn't the taking seriously of God's political rule the measure of Israel's religious seriousness? Can it now be that the realization of this kingdom becomes a "religious" goal, not to see fulfillment in historical time? Did the ancient Israelite achievement of direct theocracy in fact constitute not religion but "politics of religion, that is, the opposite of what Gandhi proclaimed: the introduction of politics into religion"?

Buber's argument snakes back and forth like the serpent Gandhi wrestles. To read "Gandhi, Politics, and Us" is to watch Buber's struggle take place on the page. He strives for the elimination of the autonomous spheres of religion and politics, but, as he already admitted in 1923, they do have a certain provisional autonomy. "Only in the great *polis* of God," he writes, "will religion and politics be blended into a life of world community, in an eternity wherein neither religion nor politics will any longer exist."[61] What, then, is theopolitics, and who is the theopolitician? "The most natural of all questions, the question concerning success, is religion's ordeal by fire. If religion withdraws from the sphere where this question is asked, it evades its task, despite all hosts and sacraments of incarnation; and if it sinks into that sphere, it has lost its soul." No simple resolution can resolve this tension once and for all in a way that would apply to every situation. The only thing that can be done is to repeatedly check, on an ad hoc basis, that one is conforming to the manner and tempo of the religious even when immersed in the political. Even Gandhi is not always successful at this, tipping occasionally to one side, occasionally to the other—Buber faults him for not seeing that the quasi-anarchist proposal of his political rival, Chittaranjan Das, for India to form a system of nested autonomous village communities that would network into larger delegated decision-making bodies, "was a political vision that supplemented his own religious one."[62] Buber also doubts that Gandhi can be successful in his polemics against "modern civilization." Technology, like politics itself, cannot simply be eschewed—instead, it must be hallowed.

Ultimately, Buber has recourse again to the prophets, his best models, who stood for justice and opposed the kings with "the firebrands of religio-political words." They did this not because they had a blueprint for God's kingdom but because the situation demanded a response: "One should, I believe, neither seek politics nor avoid it, one should be neither political nor non-political on principle. . . . There is no legitimately messianic, no legitimately messianically-intended, politics. But that does not imply that the political sphere may be excluded from the hallowing of all things. The political 'serpent' is not essentially evil, it is itself only misled; it, too, ultimately wants to be redeemed." Although Buber has yet to adopt the term "theopolitical" (he comes close with the "religio-political words" of the prophets), this is the core of the position that he will elaborate in all his biblical writings—and a radical refutation of Schmitt's attempt, following Thomas Hobbes, to base the authority of the Leviathan on a messianic formula. On the one hand, we seem to have come a long way from an endorsement of anarchism; Buber explicitly denies that theology can ever serve the purpose of legitimating a polity, or a politics. On the other hand, if it is true that "in public life (as elsewhere) it is possible and necessary to employ religious instead of political means; to win others through helping them to open out," a politics of consonance of ends and means must be adopted. For Buber, that politics remains the one he inherited from Landauer, which seeks to create community by maximizing freedom and equality simultaneously, focusing on process as much as on goal. It is not understandable except as an anarchism.

Notes

1. Hans Mommsen, *The Rise and Fall of Weimar Democracy*, trans. Elborg Forster and Larry Eugene Jones (Chapel Hill: University of North Carolina Press, 1989), 11.

2. Ibid., 71.

3. Klaus Tanner, "Protestant Revolt against Modernity," in *The Weimar Moment: Liberalism, Political Theology, and Law*, ed. Leonard Kaplan and Rudy Koshar (Lanham, MD: Lexington Books, 2012), 5–6.

4. Ibid., 12.

5. Michael Hollerich, "Catholic Anti-Liberalism in Weimar: Political Theology and its Critics," in *The Weimar Moment*, 17–46.

6. Michael Brenner, *The Renaissance of Jewish Culture in Weimar Germany* (New Haven, CT: Yale University Press, 1996); Donald L. Niewyk, *Jews in Weimar Germany* (New Brunswick, NJ: Transaction Publishers, 2001).

7. Ulrich Rosenhagen, "'Together a Step towards the Messianic Goal': Jewish-Protestant Encounter in the Weimar Republic," in *The Weimar Moment*, 51.

8. This had been typical of German Zionists for the period before World War I, compared to their counterparts among the *Ostjuden*, or Eastern European Jews; Jehuda Reinharz, *Fatherland or Promised Land: The Dilemma of the German Jew, 1893–1914* (Ann Arbor: University of Michigan Press, 1975), 144–170. It was more unusual in the 1920s.

9. The official bibliography lists only one Hebrew publication in 1923 and three short pieces in 1926, with none in the other years of the early 1920s; Margot Cohn and Rafael Buber, *Martin Buber: A Bibliography of his Writings, 1897–1978* (Jerusalem: Magnes, 1980), 28–32. Cf. MBMY 5.

10. Buber, "Religiöses Wirken," *Blätter fur Religiösen Sozialismus* 3.9 (September 1922): 34–36; Buber, "Religion und Gottesherrschaft," *Frankfurter Zeitung* (April 28, 1923); cf. Buber, "Religion and God's Rule," in *A Believing Humanism: My Testament, 1902–1965*, trans. Maurice Friedman (New York: Simon & Schuster, 1967), 109–112.

11. Buber, "Drei Sätze eines religiösen Sozialismus." *Neue Wege* 22.7–8 (July–August 1928): 327–329. Cf. Buber, "Three Theses of a Religious Socialism," in PW 112–114.

12. Max Weber, "The Profession and Vocation of Politics," in *Political Writings*, ed. Peter Lassmann and Ronald Speirs (New York: Cambridge University Press, 1994), 309–369.

13. Buber, "Three Theses," 114.

14. For "symmetrical counter-concepts," see Reinhart Koselleck, *Futures Past: On the Semantics of Historical Time* (Cambridge, MA: MIT Press, 1985), 197.

15. Max Weber, "The Nation State and Economic Policy (Inaugural lecture)," in *Political Writings*, 1–28.

16. Wolfgang J. Mommsen, *Max Weber and German Politics, 1890–1920*, trans. Michael S. Steinberg (Chicago: University of Chicago Press, 1984), 40.

17. Cited in Mommsen, *Max Weber and German Politics*, 41 (my emphasis).

18. Leo Strauss, *Natural Right and History* (Chicago: University of Chicago Press, 1950), 65.

19. David Owen and Tracy B. Strong, "Introduction: Max Weber's Calling to Knowledge and Action," in *The Vocation Lectures*, trans. Rodney Livingstone (Indianapolis: Hackett, 2004), xlvii–xlviii.

20. "If you choose this particular standpoint, you will be serving this particular god and will *give offense to every other god*. . . . As long as life is left to itself and is understood in its own terms, it knows only that the conflict between these gods is never-ending. . . . Which of the warring gods shall we serve?" Weber, "Science as a Vocation," in *The Vocation Lectures*, 26–27. This is literally a recipe for pan-demon-ium, as noted by Strauss, *Natural Right and History*, 45.

21. Wolfgang J. Mommsen, "Roberto Michels and Max Weber: Moral Conviction versus the Politics of Responsibility," in Wolfgang J. Mommsen, *The Political and Social Theory of Max Weber: Collected Essays* (Chicago: University of Chicago Press, 1989), 88. When Toller was tried for treason for having held the position of president of the Bavarian Council Republic, Weber defended his friend by pleading that he was *Weltfremd*, a stranger to the world.

22. Weber, "The Profession and Vocation of Politics," 310.

23. Ibid., 364–365.

24. The lecture was delivered to the Freistudentische Bund of the University of Munich. Weber resisted giving the lecture at first, urging that the convener, rector Immanuel Birn-

baum, replace him with Friedrich Naumann, founder of the German Democratic Party, whom he called a "representative German politician," yielding only when Birnbaum threatened to invite Kurt Eisner instead. Owen and Strong, "Introduction," xxxv.

25. KG 136.

26. Although "The Question to the Single One," originally a November 1933 lecture, is Buber's only explicit critique of Schmitt, decades later he attacks "teachers of the law . . . who . . . defined the concept of the political so that everything disposed itself within it according to the criterion 'friend-enemy,' in which the concept of enemy includes 'the possibility of physical killing.' The practice of states has conveniently followed their advice." Buber, "The Validity and Limitation of the Political Principle," PW 216.

27. Schmidt, "Die theopolitische Stunde. Martin Bubers Begriff der Theopolitik, seine prophetischen Ursprünge, seine Aktualität und Bedeutung für die Definition Zionistischer Politik," in *Die theopolitische Stunde: Zwölf Perspektiven auf das eschatologische Problem der Moderne* (Munich: Wilhelm Fink, 2009), 205–225.

28. Buber lacks the commitment to formal legalism that anti-liberals like Schmitt saw as typically Jewish—neither halakha, nor constitutional law, nor neo-Kantian moral law. In his talk at the 1936 antisemitic conference he convened titled "Judaism in Legal Studies," however, Schmitt claimed: "*The remarkable polarity of Jewish chaos and Jewish legality, of anarchistic nihilism and positivistic normativism, of crudely sensualistic materialism and the most abstract moralism,* now stands so clearly . . . that we can count on it as a decisive scientific basis." Cited in Raphael Gross, *Carl Schmitt and the Jews: The "Jewish Question," the Holocaust, and German Legal Theory,* trans. Joel Golb (Madison: University of Wisconsin Press, 2007), 74 (italics in original).

29. Whether Schmitt read Buber is not known. Ludwig Feuchtwanger sent Schmitt a lengthy review of KG he had written anonymously; Schmitt's reply implies that he read Feuchtwanger's essay carefully ("Über Martin Buber kann ich nicht mitsprechen, doch habe ich Ihre Kritik aufmerksam und mit Nutzen gelesen"). *Carl Schmitt/Ludwig Feuchtwanger: Briefwechsel 1918–1935,* ed. Rolf Riess (Berlin: Duncker & Humblot, 2007), 377–379, 381–382. I thank Thomas Meyer for directing me to this source. It was Buber who, as part of his series *Die Gesellschaft,* first published Franz Oppenheimer's *Der Staat,* which Schmitt singles out for condemnation in 1932 as "the best example" of "the polarity of state and society," which has as its aim "the destruction of the state"; Carl Schmitt, *Concept of the Political,* expanded ed., trans. George Schwab (Chicago: University of Chicago Press, 2007), 76. Schmitt also read Landauer's German translation of Kropotkin's history of the French Revolution, to which he refers several times in the footnotes to *Die Diktatur.*

30. Leo Strauss, "Notes on Carl Schmitt, *The Concept of the Political,*" in *Concept of the Political,* 113. Strauss is quoting Schmitt himself in the latter part of this sentence: "I have pointed out several times that the antagonism between the so-called authoritarian and anarchist theories can be traced to these formulas"; Schmitt, *Concept of the Political,* 60.

31. Carl Schmitt, *Political Romanticism,* trans. Guy Oakes (New Brunswick, NJ: Transaction Publishers, 2011), xv.

32. Schmitt averred that "the intention of this book has not been ignited by the current discussions on dictatorship, violence and terror," and pointed to his previous considerations of decision and law in *Gesetz und Urteil* (1912) and *Das Wert des Staates* (1914); *Dictatorship,* xlv.

33. Schmitt, *Dictatorship,* xliii.

34. Schmitt, *Die Diktatur* 146; Schmitt, *Dictatorship* 127. N.B.: Schmitt uses *kommissar* and *kommission* throughout these discussions. English translations of Buber often speak of "commission" as well, but he uses *Auftrag,* and the commissioned one is *Beauftragter.* This is politically significant, as previously noted.

35. Schmitt, *Roman Catholicism and Political Form,* trans. G. L. Ulmen (Westport, CT: Greenwood Press, 1996), 65. Schmitt holds that "American financiers, industrial technicians,

Marxist socialists, and anarchic-syndicalist revolutionaries unite" on this point, with the result that "The modern state seems to have actually become what Max Weber envisioned: a huge industrial plant."

36. Schmitt, *Political Theology: Four Chapters on the Concept of Sovereignty*, trans. George Schwab (Chicago: University of Chicago Press, 2005), 1.

37. Schmitt, *Glossarium: Aufzeichnungen der Jahre 1947–1951*, ed. Eberhard Freiherr von Medern (Berlin: Duncker & Humblot, 1991), 243. Cited in the combined translations of Gross, *Carl Schmitt and the Jews*, 85–86, and Tracy B. Strong, "Carl Schmitt and Thomas Hobbes: Myth and Politics," in Carl Schmitt, *The Leviathan in the State Theory of Thomas Hobbes: Meaning and Failure of a Political Symbol*, trans. George D. Schwab and Erna Hilfstein (Chicago: University of Chicago Press, 2008), xxiv. Weber had also mentioned the Grand Inquisitor as a cogent analysis of the problems attending an ethics of conviction; see Weber, "Profession and Vocation of Politics," 14.

38. Strong, "Carl Schmitt and Thomas Hobbes," xxv.

39. Schmitt, *Leviathan*, 57.

40. Paul Müller [pseud. of Waldemar Gurian], "Entscheidung und Ordnung: Zu den Schriften von Carl Schmitt," *Schweizerische Rundschau: Monatsschrift für Geistesleben und Kultur* 34 (1939): 566–576. Cited in Gross, *Carl Schmitt and the Jews*, 92–93.

41. Schmitt, *Political Theology*, 55.

42. Ibid., 50, 66.

43. Schmitt, *Concept of the Political*, 29.

44. Sorel is relevant here. See Carl Schmitt, *The Crisis of Parliamentary Democracy*, trans. Ellen Kennedy (Cambridge, MA: MIT Press, 1988), 65–76.

45. Strauss, "Notes on *Concept of the Political*," 113.

46. KG 140.

47. Such rhetoric has also been adopted in some recent discourse; Siegbert Wolf entitles two volumes of his edition of Landauer's writings *Antipolitik*.

48. KG 14. For the Ponte Tresa lectures, see Buber, "Arbeitsgemeinschaft zu ausgewählten Abschnitten aus dem Buche Samuel," in SM 46–91.

49. Buber, "The How and Why of Our Bible Translation," in ST 217.

50. Buber, "Religion and God's Rule," 111.

51. Buber, "Politics Born of Faith," in *A Believing Humanism*, 178.

52. Buber, "Biblical Leadership," in *Israel and the World: Essays in a Time of Crisis*, trans. G. Hort (Syracuse, NY: Syracuse University Press, 1997), 122.

53. Ibid., 133.

54. See chapter 7 for more on Buber's effort to convince the 1921 Twelfth Zionist Congress to adopt an anti-imperialist resolution committing Zionism to cooperation with the Palestinian Arabs.

55. Buber, "Three Theses," 112.

56. Buber, "Gandhi, Politics, and Us," in PW 131 (emphasis Buber's).

57. Ibid., 127.

58. Ibid., 130.

59. Ibid., 129.

60. Buber, "Gandhi, Politik, und Wir," *Die Kreatur* 3 (1930): 333.

61. Buber, "Gandhi, Politics, and Us," 131.

62. Ibid., 134.

3   God against Messiah

The Kingship of God *and the Ancient Israelite Anarcho-Theocracy*

I will cause your judges to return as before, / your counselors as at the beginning.
—Isaiah 1:26

The sociological "utopia" of a voluntary community is nothing else but the immanent side of the direct theocracy.
—Martin Buber

Introduction and Methodological Remarks

Martin Buber, a man noted for much both before and beyond *Religionswissenschaft*, the scientific study of religion, deployed biblical scholarship on the ancient
Israelite monarchy and the period immediately preceding its establishment to
articulate a polemical theopolitical position. This position has been described as
"anarcho-theocratic." Other scholars have noted that Buber's *Königtum Gottes*
(hereafter *Kingship of God*) of 1932, which appears to be his most "scientific"
work, is fraught with political and theological implications.[1] The work presents
itself as a historical-critical study of the Bible and duly employs the professional
vocabulary of that field. The book's first readers, to whose criticisms Buber replies
in the second and third editions, were primarily biblical scholars. Although the
book does not engage explicitly with political philosophers or legal theorists, it
does do so implicitly. While developing his theopolitical thesis as an alternative
reading of certain key biblical passages, Buber arrives at a full-fledged conception
of an anarcho-theocratic essence of Judaism. He presents the theopolitical, anarcho-theocratic, faithful tendency in Jewish history as involved in a kind of transhistorical spiritual conflict with an opposite tendency, the political-theological,
authoritarian, idolatrous. By "transhistorical," I mean that he sees the spiritual
conflict as continuous throughout the whole span that the Bible claims to report,
lasting into the period of rabbinic Judaism and persisting up to the present—
when it informs Buber's own arguments against those who would contest his
interpretations of ancient evidence.

Here, I address the theopolitical dimension of the text rather than the extent to which its arguments "hold up" today as claims about the Bible. My focus is on *Kingship of God* as a work produced in late Weimar Germany, in the context of the theological and political debates of the time. Examining Buber's readings of biblical evidence requires understanding the relation of those readings to the scholarship of his time, as well as his own interpretive strategies.

The Title, Origin, and Structure of *Kingship of God*

Sacred Kingship and Political Theology

The title *Kingship of God* situates Buber simultaneously in two conversations. The first is about sacred kingship in comparative perspective. Starting with James George Frazer's *The Golden Bough* (1890), a huge literature emerged on the theme of religious legitimation and the justification of kingship as an institution. Many anthropologists and historians of religion hold, in the words of one recent author, that "in terms . . . of its antiquity, its ubiquity, its wholly extraordinary staying power, the institution of kingship can lay strong claim to having been the most common form of government known, world-wide, to man."[2] Once we recognize that "it is not the interpenetration in public life of what we in the West have become accustomed to classify as the 'political' and the 'religious' that needs explaining, but, rather, the novel Western distinction between the two," interest in sacred kingship may be seen as expressing a desire to explain as much as possible about human political life by focusing on a single phenomenon.[3] The idea of sacred kingship also offers a range of case studies, principal among which for Western scholars is the ancient Israelite monarchy. That Buber's *Königtum Gottes* was meant to reflect this current of thought can be inferred from some of the other titles contained in his copious footnotes, such as *Die sumerischen und akkadischen Königsinschriften* (*The Sumerian and Akkadian Royal Inscriptions*) and *Die Vergöttlichung der babylonisch-assyrischen Könige* (*The Divinization of Assyrian-Babylonian Kings*).[4] He kept abreast of the scholarship in this field after the first edition of the book. However, the title *Kingship of God* announces that Buber will be discussing divine kingship *itself*—the kingship *of God*, not a human monarchy considered divine by its subjects; that is, not how kings are thought of as gods, but how one particular god is thought of as a king.

Beyond this discourse, *Kingship of God* may also be related to Carl Schmitt and *Political Theology*. As we have seen, Buber and Schmitt share many assumptions but proceed in radically different directions. This proximity is uncomfortable, given the likelihood that Schmitt's critique of liberalism was intended to undermine the intellectual bases of the nascent Weimar Republic.[5] Schmitt joined the Nazi party and curried favor with Nazi elites before running afoul of official dogma around 1936, never repenting for his actions once the war ended. Buber clearly states that he thought Schmitt exemplified the problems he saw in contemporaneous political thought. *Kingship of God* addresses Schmitt's favored themes, from the state of emergency to the secularizing of political concepts, although without naming him as interlocutor. In most cases, we find the Schmittian theme inverted: the commissarial dictator protecting the human constitutional order becomes the charismatic judge acting on God's behalf; the secularization of political concepts occurs with the very institution of human monarchy claiming God's authority rather than with the later transfer of that authority from the sovereign to the people.

Buber dedicated *Kingship of God* to two friends who had passed away in the 1920s and whom he credited with "helping me to read the Scriptures": one was Franz Rosenzweig, with whom Buber began translating the Hebrew Bible into German; the other was Florens Christian Rang, a conservative Lutheran theologian. Rang, like Buber, began World War I as a strident nationalist but later turned strongly against nationalism, perhaps influenced by his friend Walter Benjamin in a similar trajectory to Landauer's influence on Buber (all four were affiliated with the Forte circle, and Benjamin had special respect for Rang). Rang may have exemplified a noble and upright Christian path in Buber's eyes, by contrast to that of Schmitt. At any rate, if kingship is the most common form of the state, then to discuss kingship is to discuss the political. And to speak of God is precisely to engage in theology. To study the kingship of God, then, is to enter the sphere of political theology—or the theopolitical.

Origins of the Work: From Biblical Faith to Messianism in Israel

In the preface to the first edition of *Kingship of God*, Buber describes his original plan for the work and its place in a projected broader scheme, which he later abandoned.[6] First, he had planned together with Franz Rosenzweig "to combine the results of many years of Bible studies in a theological commentary which would have to treat Old Testament problems in the exact order of succession in which the text presents them; since these were entirely . . . problems of faith, it was to be called *The Biblical Faith*."[7] Buber persisted in this plan for a year after Rosenzweig's death but eventually realized that he would have to prioritize "those subjects which seemed of special consequence to me and on which I would soonest have something to say which would advance knowledge." From this we learn both that what we are about to read is urgent for Buber, and that here as elsewhere Buber moves easily between "theological commentary" and work that would "advance knowledge." Indeed, it is questionable whether he allows for any boundary between the two categories at all.[8]

Buber names this newly foregrounded topic "the question of the origin of 'messianism' in Israel" and relates it to "another, concerning which I had begun, more than twenty years ago, a slowly growing, subsequently postponed, essay-project and which now . . . begged to be taken up again anew, the christological question [*die christologische*]."⁹ This provides context for the intended title of the trilogy of which *Kingship of God* was to have been the first installment: *Das Kommende: Untersuchungen zur Entstehungsgeschichte des messianischen Glaubens* (*The Coming One: Investigations into the Origin-History of the Messianic Faith*). This title appears on the inside front page of the first edition, but by the time of the third edition in 1956 it had been abandoned. Explanatory footnotes thus needed to be added to reprints of the 1932 preface, to clarify what Buber meant when he indirectly referenced *Das Kommende* with asides about "the three-fold division of the subject."¹⁰ Buber sees a disquisition on the idea of God's kingship as a necessary first stage in an argument about the historical origins of the Jewish idea of the Messiah, and thus also of the Christian idea of Christ (the Greek χριστὸς, or Christos, is a direct translation of the Hebrew משיח, or *mashiach*, both literally meaning "anointed"). In the original three-volume plan, the mission of *Kingship of God* was to discuss "the religious idea of a folk-kingship of God as an actual-historical one for the early period of Israel," whereas *Der Gesalbte* was to show how "the sacral character of the Israelitish king as one 'anointed' of JHWH is related to this." It would then be left to the third, unnamed volume "to portray how both conceptions—already in the period of the kings—change from history into eschatology." In other words, Buber intended to demonstrate that a single process leads from the exclusive kingship of God, without human intermediary, to the rise of a human king, God's "anointed" one, and from there to the idea of the awaited Messiah who brings cosmic, eschatological closure.

A Difficult Structure

While the goals of *Kingship of God* and its position in the projected trilogy may be clear enough, the argumentation of the book, as it emerges from the structure, is far less apparent. Here is how Buber lays out the eight chapters of *Kingship of God* in the 1932 preface:

> The present volume starts out from a particular literary-critical question, that of Judges 8:22ff (first chapter). In order to clarify this question as far as befits the limitations of this volume (the pertinent texts in Samuel cannot be examined until volume two), the genre, structure, and origin of the Book of Judges must be investigated anew (second chapter). The historical-political concreteness of a fundamental idea of the Biblical faith, disclosed in this manner, is now religio-historically elucidated and confirmed by the consideration of related ancient-oriental ideas in general (third chapter) and west-Semitic ones in particular (fourth chapter). It is then, to be sure, ranged alongside of them (fifth chapter), but only in order to be rightly contrasted with them and to cause the divine kingship of Israel to be recognized in its uniqueness (sixth chapter), a uniqueness to which the beginning of the book had expressly referred—a consciously "theological," but in every point hermeneutically verified recognition. In order that the origin of this uniqueness, which is not to be sought upon a

level of the "development of ideas," but only in the three-dimensionality of a living fact of folk history, be understood and attested, a literary-critical investigation is again necessary, this time of several Pentateuch passages (seventh chapter). This clears the way for the venture of an historical outline of the pre-state Canaan-period of Israel in its relation to a primitive-theocratic tendency and to its transformations (eighth chapter) up until the crisis of the tendency which is to be treated in the second volume.[11]

This order of exposition is puzzling. Buber seems to veer wildly both chronologically (beginning with Judges and then moving back in time to the desert wanderings, then forward again to the Sinai covenant and the conquest) and disciplinarily (beginning with literary and source criticism, then moving to comparative history of religions, then to exegesis). The principles that determine when certain subjects should be raised, when digressions are necessary, et cetera, are unclear. As a result, the book is even more difficult than one might expect given its subject matter and subtle, complex argument. Buber may have seen these eight chapters as a satisfying narrative arc, beginning with an illustration of his thesis (the Gideon passage), then anticipating a series of challenges to the thesis, and arriving at the dramatic claims of the conclusion. However, if we are to gauge by the book's reception, Buber was mistaken in this judgment. It is among the least studied of his works, and its difficult structure surely contributes to that fact. The few studies that do exist confine themselves mainly to the first and second chapters, thereby missing the larger picture that emerges in a full reading.

Here we ignore Buber's order of exposition and begin by articulating his theopolitical thesis; we go on to apply this thesis to each of his subjects in turn. In some cases, the scholars whom Buber disputes actually tailor their objections directly to the theopolitical thesis; in most cases, however, they simply represent the current scholarly consensus on questions of the dating or provenance of biblical texts, contesting individual claims without regard to broad theopolitical implications. Nonetheless, Buber's defenses always keep the theopolitical thesis in view, and the fact that he defends a point is often more important than the substance of his defense. On other occasions, however, the nature of Buber's argument in defense of his claim will in itself be important. Throughout his discussion, Buber strategically identifies theopolitical factions described within the biblical text with factions among the editors of the biblical text, and he further depicts these factions as manifest in contemporary scholarly camps arguing about the biblical text, using academic language to create a kind of transhistorical conflict between political theology and theopolitics in which he himself is a partisan.

The Theopolitical Thesis

In *Kingship of God* the theopolitical thesis operates on two levels: that of content, the level of events described in the biblical text, and that of scholarship, the level at which the thesis itself is affirmed or denied by arguments about how to read the text.

The Theopolitical Thesis: Ancient Israel and Anarcho-Theocracy

The theopolitical thesis holds that throughout the prestate history of the tribes of Israel, and continuing well into the monarchical period, the true King of Israel was held to be YHVH, the God who had led the Exodus, and that no human institution could usurp his sovereignty.[12] This belief is only rarely dominant, never hegemonic, in the Israelite population; most often it contends with various types of idolatry and differing political conceptions. However, Buber maintains that for a significant minority, such a consciousness did exist in ancient Israel, despite scholarly claims to the contrary. The best statement of this thesis occurs early in chapter 8, "On the Theocracy":

> The covenant at Sinai signifies, according to its positive content, that the wandering tribes accept JHWH "for ever and ever" as their King. According to its negative content it signifies that no man is to be called king of the sons of Israel. "You shall be for Me a kingly domain," "there was then in Jeshurun a King"; this is *exclusive* proclamation also with respect to a secular lordship: JHWH does not want, like the other kingly gods, to be sovereign and guarantor of a human monarch. He wants Himself to be the Leader and the Prince. The man to whom he addresses His will in order that he carry it out is not only to have his power in this connection alone; he can also exert no power beyond his limited task. Above all, since he rules not as a person acting in his own right, but as "emissary" [*Entbotener*], he cannot transmit power. The real counterpart of direct theocracy is the *hereditary* kingship. . . . There is in pre-kingly Israel no externality of ruler-ship; *for there is no political sphere except the theo-political* [*denn es gibt keine politische Sphäre außer der theopolitischen*], and all sons of Israel are directly related (*kohanim* in the original sense) to JHWH, Who chooses and rejects, gives an order and withdraws it.[13]

For Buber, the Sinai covenant is theopolitical and not "merely" religious. This means, first and foremost, that the belief in the sole kingship of YHVH is no mere liturgical formula: many people take it literally and seriously; it determines their political organization.

Buber distinguishes between "prestate" and postmonarchical conceptions of divine kingship. Before the institution of a human monarchy, the divine *melekh* (king) demands of his subjects unconditional devotion, of which the ritual symbol is sacrifice. With the founding of the monarchy, however, the divine demand is compromised by the demands of the *human* monarch, from tithes to military service; the result is a kind of secularization, a separation of the religious from the political. Buber thus has a low opinion of King Solomon, despite his status as folk hero in most Jewish literature. He sees "syncretistic faithlessness" in the man who, "as hospitable as a Roman emperor, allotted holy high-places to the *melakhim* of the neighboring peoples."[14] Buber reads Solomon's pious proclamation that one's heart should be satisfied with YHVH as a crafty retreat from the unconditional insistence on heart and soul and might.[15] God "is not content to be 'God' in the religious sense," to claim only inner devotion, but demands outer devotion as well, not just in ritual but also in the full conduct of life, not just from the individual but from the people:

> The striving to have the entirety of its life constructed out of its relation to the divine can be actualized by a *people* in no other way than that, while it opens its political being and doing to the influence of this relationship, it thus does not fundamentally mark the limits of this influence in advance, but only in the course of realization experiences or rather endures these limits again and again. . . . He will apportion to the one, for ever and ever chosen by Him, his tasks, but naked power without a situationally related task he does not wish to bestow. He makes known His will first of all as constitution—not constitution of cult and custom only, also of economy and society—He will proclaim it again and again to the changing generations, certainly but simply as reply to a question, institutionally through priestly mouth, above all, however, in the freedom of His surging spirit, through every one whom His spirit seizes. *The separation of religion and politics which stretches through history is here overcome [aufgehoben] in real paradox.*[16]

Buber's polemic here is directed against both kings and scholars—especially scholars who take the side of kings or who make it easier to do so. The warning against marking the limits of divine influence "in advance," along with the claim that God's will determines cult and custom as well as "economy and society" (*Wirtschaft und Gesellschaft*, the title of Max Weber's magnum opus in sociology), suggest that Buber may be thinking of Weber's lecture "Politics as a Vocation" and may be suggesting that Weberian political realism cannot be reconciled with the faith of Israel. The position is illiberal in that it excludes the possibility of separate "spheres" for religion and for politics. The very idea of "religion" as a "sphere" unto itself is presented here as an impoverishment of divine rule.

The tendency toward direct theocracy expresses itself in two ways: first in the community's choice of a charismatic leader, a nonroyal figure whom it recognizes as temporarily inhabited by the *charis* of divine spirit.[17] This is the case of Moses, Joshua, and the various *shoftim* (judges) in the book of Judges, who arise to deliver the people from emergencies. The second aspect of theocracy occurs between the death of one charismatic leader and the rise of another. This interregnum is most appropriately called anarcho-theocracy. Israel has neither (human) ruler nor corresponding institutions. The separate tribes tend to their own business, confident that YHVH still rules as King even when he declines to issue new orders.

To explain the movement between these two stages, Buber turns to Max Weber's analysis of charisma and its "routinization." He also borrows from Weber the concept of hierocracy, rule by priests (or some other religious caste claiming to speak for the divine), as a name for what is most commonly called "theocracy"—in contrast to direct theocracy, which is the topic of *Kingship of God*.[18] The historical form of direct theocracy, according to Buber, is a charismatic leadership in which the recipient of the temporary *charis* is commissioned to some particular task (never to unlimited leadership). But what is *charis*, exactly? According to Buber, "there is here no charisma at rest, only a hovering one, no possession of spirit, only a 'spiriting,' a coming and going of the *ruach*; no assurance of power, only the streams of an authority which presents itself and moves away.... Authority is bound to the temporary proof of the charisma."[19] Charisma is thus a fleeting quality, even for the recognized charismatic, and it requires proof through deeds.

Yet its very transience renders charisma supreme: "The *charis* accordingly stands superior to every enchantment as well as every law." Problems occur, however, with any effort "to exercise theopolitics even when it is a matter of letting the *charis* hold sway beyond the actual charisma," or in Weberian terms, to base an enduring institutional structure upon manifestations of *charis*.[20] Most fundamental is the question of succession. A dying charismatic leader leaves the community with these options:

1. Waiting for a successor to have an epiphany and to demonstrate his or her qualifications (allowing for an interregnum, potentially endangering the cohesion and continuity of the community)
2. Securing continuity by one of the following methods:
    i. The charismatic leader designates a successor
    ii. If not the leader, then the followers identify a qualified candidate
    iii. The community recognizes the possibility of transmitting charisma through blood ties or ritual anointing and coronation (*Salbung und Krönung*, a process that can lead to hierocracy)

Buber seems to prefer the first option, waiting: "Certainly the faithful wait for the grace as that alone which they want to follow."[21] He also claims, however, that the Bible itself favors the first option; according to Buber, the history of prestate Israel knows only one instance of the transfer of charisma to a successor, namely the succession to Moses by Joshua.[22] That succession is unique, since Joshua dies without establishing succession and without leaving clues regarding the structure of permanent institutions.

The arrival at full anarcho-theocracy, however, and the embrace of the interregnum on the part of its supporters, sharpens what Buber calls the "paradox of theocracy." This paradox consists in the fact that "the highest commitment according to its nature knows no compulsion," that it applies in all its "existential depth" on both individual and general levels. For the individual, it is possible at any time to "either strive toward a complete community out of free will [*Gemein-schaft aus Freiwilligkeit*], a divine kingdom, or . . . to an indolent or brutalized subordination."[23] On a political level, the same principle confirms "the rightful possessor of the commission, the 'charismatic' man," in his authority, yet also sanctions the misappropriated and abused authority of pretenders and the empty anarchy (*leere Herrschaftslosigkeit*) of those who indulge in "enmity not merely to order [*Ordnung*] but to organization [*Gestaltung*]."[24] Theocracy is thus "a strong bastion for the obedient, but also at the same time can be a shelter to the self-seeking behind which he exalts his lack of commitment as divine freedom." This double-tiered double bind produces a social existence fraught with conflict:

> The result of this is that the truth of the principle must be fought for . . . religio-politically. The venture of a radical theocracy must therefore lead to the bursting-forth of the opposition latent in every people. Those, however, who in this fight represent the case for divine rulership against that of "history," experience therein the first shudder of eschatology. The full, paradoxical character of the human attitude of faith is only begun in the situation of the "individual" with all its depths; it is developed only in the real relationship of this individual to a world which does not want to be God's, and to a God who does not want to compel the world to become His. The Sinai covenant is the first step visible to us on the path through the dark ravine between actualization and contradiction. In Israel it led from the divinely proud confidence of the early king-passages . . . to that first form of resignation with which our Book of Judges ends.[25]

However theologically inflected this rhetoric may be, Buber intends to remain within the realm of historical description. The "first shudder of eschatology" occurs for the partisans of the kingship of God when they imagine a society in which all are reconciled to divine rule and no longer seek to usurp or undermine it; in other words, a sustainable anarcho-theocracy. Moreover, Buber believes he is describing a general phenomenon of which the story of Israel as presented in the Bible is only one instance. Recognition of the paradox of theocracy leads to the breakout of conflict within every people, and within every people the two sides are the same: they "contend in the same name, and always without a clear issue of the quarrel."[26] What Buber here counterposes to divine rulership and calls "history" he refers to elsewhere as realpolitik, and what he calls realpolitik is identifiable, still elsewhere, as political theology.[27] Thus the contemporary proponents of realpolitik and political theology are analogous to those Israelites who misunderstand and abuse the anarcho-theocracy.

The hero of Buber's story, in contrast, is Gideon, to whom Buber devotes the first chapter of *Kingship of God*. In the moment that Gideon refuses the principle of hereditary monarchy, he endorses the theopolitical thesis: "A will of a religious and political kind in one, historically localizable in this its stage, a will towards constitution combined with faith, found here the straight-forward expression of its demand, as afterward in the Samuelic crisis it found the discordant expression of its defensive fight and its resignation."[28] Buber emphasizes that he means only a *will* toward constitution; as the rest of the book of Judges demonstrates, Gideon's proud declaration of direct theocracy does not hold sway for long. What matters, nonetheless, is simply the existence of that will, the "real, struggling, religious-political will to fulfillment, wresting ever and again from the changing resistance of the times a fragment of realization, however altered; a will not just late-prophetic, but inseparable from the historical Israel." In other words, in accordance with the principle that antiquity confers legitimacy, Buber seeks continuity between the theocratic aspect of the late prophetic spirit and the earliest existence of the people.

But perhaps we should not overemphasize the concern for origins and beginnings. As Buber concludes his discussion of the Gideon passage, he proclaims the following:

> The kingship of God is a paradox, but an historical one: it consists in the historical conflict of the subjected person against the resisting one, a conflict which, without its naïve, but on that very account most important, original form, cannot be grasped. It is the most visible appearance of that kingdom-dialectic [*Reichsdialektik*] which educated the Israelitish people to know history as the dialectic [*Zwiegespräch*] of an asking divinity and an answer-refusing, but nevertheless an answer-attempting humanity, the dialogue [*Zwiegespräch*] whose demand is an *eschaton*.[29]

Buber claims to have isolated the essential dynamic of God's relationship with the Jewish people, in purity and clarity, in its "original form," in the Gideon passage. It demonstrates a dialectic that is constant, from the point of view of the Israelite view of history, in its most visible form. Buber proposes the seemingly paradoxical idea of an "original constant" at the end of the chapter:

> That this dialectic [*Dialektik*] has its quite earthly form, that it embodies itself not on theological heights, but in the midst of the whirl of political actualities, and that, robbed of these, the constant historical consciousness of a people, Israel, as bearer of the kingdom-message could not be understood—all this allows, yes commands, us to recognize the will toward constitution (that is, to actualization) as an original constant [*ursprünglichen Bestand*] in the dynamic of this folk life, which functions in the *historiography* because it has functioned in *history*.[30]

Many of Buber's philosophical and political preoccupations enter into this argument: the emphasis on the concrete, indeed the "earthly," as opposed to the imposing heights; the theme of realization or actualization (*Verwirklichung*); the idea of "folk life." The key, however, is the idea of a historical dynamic conceived as a kingdom-dialectic (*Reichsdialektik*). One side of this dialectic consists of a will to realization, or a will to constitution, which seeks to take seriously the exclusive kingship of God over historical reality. The other side is a resistance, a desire to replace God with some sort of human ruler. When Buber centers the Gideon passage, as the "most visible form" of the will to realization, his engagement with his opponents reveals that he views himself as engaged in a second-order form of the same struggle. Buber seeks to affirm the will to realization in the Gideon passage, acknowledging that the Israelites once proclaimed the exclusive kingship of God, while Wellhausen and his school deny its presence there, placing it in a much later, reflective context—that of a reaction to a human king.

The Theopolitical Thesis on the Level of Scholarship

It is important to recognize Buber's emphasis not only on the nature of anarcho-theocracy in the biblical sources but also on the role of historical-critical method in confirming it:

> The messianic faith of Israel is, as is to be shown, according to its central content the being-oriented-toward the fulfillment of the relation between God and the world in a consummated kingly rule of God. That Israel perceives this believing expectation and its living expression as belonging to, and entrusted most peculiarly to, it among all the nations is based upon the believing memory that it once proclaimed JHWH as its direct and exclusive folk-king. Whether the memory—necessarily mythicizing—of such an occurrence originated from its historical actuality or signifies only a late illusion, a theological art-product, is *decisively important* for our method of proceeding; for only if the memory is historical can the expectation, even in its oldest utterances, be traced back to it.[31]

Here Buber highlights the most "scientific" part of his thesis (in the sense of subject to disconfirmation). It is critical for him that the textual evidence he finds in the Bible of a theopolitical relationship between Israel and its God be derivable from a historical condition that actually existed, not from a "theological art-product" created in later times and projected back onto Israelite antiquity. While Buber himself may believe, as a matter of faith, that the God of the Bible really did have this relationship to ancient Israel, this is not what he argues here. Rather, he tries to show that the texts that report this relationship are rooted in a tradition, based on a memory of a time when the people of Israel thought that this was their relationship to their God and would have described it in that way if asked to do so. This framing makes it possible for other biblical scholars, Jewish or non-Jewish, to engage Buber's hypothesis on its merits and to challenge both the evidence he advances and his interpretation of that evidence.

Buber is keenly aware that the theopolitical thesis runs counter to the biblical scholarship of his time. Therefore, he takes seriously his obligation to confront the arguments of his opponents and to anticipate objections:

> One must attempt to establish anew, upon the basis of critical research, the thesis of an early direct-theocratic tendency in Israel, a thesis penalized because of its untenable precritical formulation—a thesis by means of which, allegedly, "a real insight into the folk history of Israel" becomes "impossible."[32] It will have to stand a double test: whether its taking with historical seriousness the Biblical pre-kingly texts of direct-theocratic tendency—in their being dated contrary to the prevailing opinion and in their interpretations which likewise diverge from that opinion in many ways—is philologically justified; and whether this taking-seriously, where . . . it progresses to historical reconstruction, attains an historical picture which can be scientifically justified.[33]

Philological rigor and historical scrupulousness are the primary scholarly tests to which Buber puts the theopolitical thesis. This passage also reveals Buber's sense of another, less "scientific" and more "cultural" obstacle to his endeavor: by daring to allege that "critical research" could rehabilitate a "precritical formulation," Buber attacks not the methodological necessity of proceeding critically, but the assumption on the part of some biblical scholars that the aim of any critical procedure is to demolish some cherished precritical belief. Rather than pursue the rejectionism of much traditionalist adherence to "precritical formulations," Buber throws in his lot with philological justification.

Of course, this self-identification by Buber as a *Religionswissenschaftler* is always ambivalent. Buber immediately reminds the reader just how far he stands from the general scholarly community on several important points, from the source-critical distinction between the J and E documents to the methodology of dating biblical texts.[34] Buber knows that because *Kingship of God* and its intended sequel *Der Gesalbte* deal respectively with the books of Judges and Samuel, they will be perceived "essentially as a contribution to the problem of the 'Elohist' or 'Elohists'" to whom the source-critical consensus of the time attributed those books. Buber himself is "not able to believe in a separable, coherent original document to be regarded as 'Elohistic,'" and he has great reservations about the "logograms" J and E, but he nevertheless regards it as securely demonstrated that there are at least two great types of tradition and compilation represented in their differentiation.[35]

It is in connection with his discussion of J and E as literary or redactional trends rather than discrete "sources" that the concept theopolitical first appears in *Kingship of God*. Buber holds that the texts commonly designated as J material originate among early circles of courtly compilers, "resolutely attentive to religious tradition, but in the treatment of contemporary or recent history prone to a profane-political tendency."[36] The E materials, however, originate among the circle of the *nevi'im*, the prophets. In contrast to the J circle, they are "independent of the court, supported by the people, less gifted in narration, but inspired in message, experiencing and portraying history as a theo-political occurrence, contending for the interpenetration of religion and politics against every principle of partition which would place them in opposition." Thus the dichotomy between the profane-political and the theopolitical is introduced in connection with the J-E distinction, that is, with editors, even before it is ascribed to specific Israelite figures and factions described in the text.

Against the trend toward late dating of biblical materials, even to the Persian or postexilic periods, Buber asserts that the material upon which he draws reflects ancient tendencies in the life of Israel. He carefully qualifies his formulations: "No dating has yet been decided, since we are dealing here not with a source, but with a manner of manipulating traditional material, and indeed with a manner which is *already established in the oldest formation of tradition*. The question about dating was therefore to be established by itself with every text."[37] When Buber questions dating proposed by other scholars, he first confronts the most recent dates suggested for particular texts, and he counterposes those to a reading that either discerns a "manner of manipulating traditional material" that allows the text to be dated earlier, or suggests that the "traditional material" that forms the core of the text may antedate the text's final literary form. Frequently, he associates his opponents on a particular philological or historical question with one of the inner-textual or editorial factions he has identified, thus reenacting with them the conflict between the theopolitical thesis and its antithesis.

Buber expounds the theopolitical thesis starting with a discussion of Judges, emphasizing the "Gideon passage" in 8:22 and offering a textual analysis of the redaction of Judges as a whole. Then he entertains possible objections to his thesis. These fall into two categories: (1) the theopolitical thesis must be false because the era to which Buber assigns it was not intellectually "advanced" enough, so that the idea of YHVH as king, for example, could not have developed prior to the historical human monarchy; (2) the theopolitical thesis must be false for lack of a textual basis. Buber addresses the first objection in two ways: first, by using the tools of comparative religion (cultural studies, Semitics, philology) to discuss the concept of YHVH as exclusive folk king in the context of the political theologies of Israel's neighbors in the ancient Near East, and second, by enlisting historical-critical biblical studies in his argument for the continuity of the theopolitical idea from Sinai to the Judges. Finally, he addresses such topics as sacrifice, holy war, and prophecy, in his effort to ground the theopolitical thesis in texts.

Kingships of the Gods: The Theopolitical Thesis and Comparative Religion

Of Kings, Gods, and Covenants: Ancient Israel in Context

Buber seeks to defend the possible historicity of the theopolitical thesis against charges of inconsistency with the "religio-historical level of that epoch."[38] Both Buber and his opponents take for granted the notion of "the character of a folk-epoch." The history of ancient peoples is often conceived according to the idea of "stages of development," which proceed teleologically toward what are viewed as most characteristic features of modernity. This alleged progress moves from the sensuous, embodied religion of paganism to the abstraction of pure monotheism; and if the story is continued through the advent of Christianity, it balances abstraction and concreteness in the concept of the God-man. When taken up by biblical scholars, such schemes can produce fine-grained distinctions between earlier and later periods. Much contortion is then required to demonstrate "progressive" movement between different textual strata, though "regression" or backsliding may also sometimes be allowed.[39] Buber accepts many of these categories but rejects particular conclusions, especially those related to the development of the Israelite conception of YHVH.[40]

Buber's basic comparative principle is that "every great religion arises before a background which more or less resembles it typologically, with which it, however, nevertheless contrasts decisively. . . . [T]he incomparable in it can be scientifically grasped only from the point of view of the comparable."[41] From this perspective, he considers how ancient Near Eastern peoples viewed their gods as kings. Buber's academic contemporaries admitted that these cultures deified their kings but considered the concept of gods as kings a more abstract, and therefore later, development.

Buber creates an additional schematic layer by arranging Egyptian, Babylonian, and South Arabian material according to how closely it approximates the Israelite idea of immediate and exclusive divine rulership. There is also a general theory of cross-cultural exchange operating here. Buber avoids the difficult concept of influence, which is often loaded with normative biases in favor of originality (consider religious leaders who recoil from suggestions that their holy texts took ideas from previous sources). He argues instead that "everything flows together and yet marks itself off from everything else again, since form always originates because there follows upon surrender a resistance, a new independence."[42] Buber thus turns away from asking who took what idea from whom and when, asking instead: what did each culture do with these ideas once they had them?

For this investigation, images of and analogies between cosmic and earthly kingdoms are irrelevant. What matters is neither the god's domination of nature nor even his rule over a pantheon as "king of the gods"; Buber is interested in the political relationship between the god and the people, however manifested in the title and responsibilities of the human king. This focus is especially important in Semitic studies, since for Buber the Semitic root *m-l-k* (מ-ל-ך) did not originally mean "to rule as king," but "leader," in the literal sense of "guide who goes in front," and in the oracular sense of guiding with counsel.

Buber delves just deep enough into Egyptology to retrieve the case of the hierocracy of the Theban priests of Amun, which he portrays as continuous with earlier Pharaonic practice.[43] He downplays the period of Isis and Osiris worship, as well as the earlier interlude of monotheism under the iconoclastic Pharaoh Akhenaten, to focus on what he characterizes as an Egyptian mainstream, consisting of several elements: Amun-Re, the sun god, unifies Egypt and rules over both the upper and lower countries; he departs for heaven and is succeeded by a human dynasty as that of father to son. For Buber, the replacement of Pharaohs by priests does not change things in this regard, which reflects his view of the authoritarian nature of hierocracy. Amun remains in regular communication with his sons, who are themselves divinized and immunized against death, and he helps them make just decisions. Verbal appeal can be made to Amun if his sons abuse their power. Although this is a hierocratic structure, and Buber presents it as the furthest from the Israelite case, it nonetheless admits the idea of a god as true political ruler (albeit "behind the scenes" as a guide) and therefore can serve Buber's point about the "religio-historical level of that epoch" (the Theban hierocracy being roughly contemporary with the rise of the Israelite monarchy).

Buber refers to the Babylonian-Assyrian example as a "preliminary form" of Israelite theocracy. Here we have more concrete representations of gods as political rulers; they are referred to as "genuine kings" and depicted as the signers of peace treaties. The human king, chosen by the god, is legitimized as sovereign through the god's pronunciation of his name; he is the adopted son of the god and not generated by the god directly. As such he is mortal, but a vessel of the divine splendor. Buber sees the human regent as invested with a stronger sense of responsibility to his divine master in Babylon than in Egypt; he is called on to establish the god's law in the land, and if he fails, the god is expected to set things right.[44]

Finally, in South Arabia, there is no question of a context for considering ancient Israel, since the evidence available to Buber about the Minaean and Sabaean cultures dated back only to the beginning of the first millennium BCE. Despite this, Buber takes up this case because it closely follows his view of the Israelite distinction. He sees here an example of "a theocratic *constitution of society*." The legal formula for the state comprises god, king, and people; a recurrent feast commemorates and renews this relationship as a covenant, through the transfer of land and rule from the property of the god to the king as regent. Divine ownership of the soil is accepted as a real principle; "private property is feudal tenure."[45] The king, living symbol of the covenant, is simultaneously its "servant"; in this respect the analogy to Israel is closest.[46]

Buber also sees South Arabia as analogous to Israel in a more politically and historically resonant sense. He evokes the moment of the priest-king's mediatory announcement during the renewal ritual, in which he takes the title of *malik*. Following Nikolaus Rhodokanakis, Buber refers to this moment as a "world-ing" (*Verweltlichung*), in that the rulership is transferred to the human king; he argues that this initiates the human control of the land itself.[47] In Israel, in the same way, with the rise of the monarchy, "the theocratic principle begins to lose its comprehensive power and to be limited to the merely-religious in order finally merely to provide the intangible shielding of autocracy, as in Egypt and Babylon." Here again is the *Reichsdialektik*: the Sabaean ritual proclaims their god as real king and simultaneously weakens this rulership through the institution of a human kingship. "If anywhere," Buber asserts, "there is world-history in such an event, in which the problematics of the relation between religion and politics assumes its climactic manifestation."[48]

Having presented the three cases, Buber claims that they have served his dual purpose. On the one hand, they show that the idea of a kingship of God was not merely a vague formula but denoted a real political relationship between heaven and earth: "In Egypt he is first only the primeval king who, withdrawn into heaven, holds his protecting and guiding hand over his human followers. In Babylon he looks down upon his regent as though examining the guardian of his law and, if it must be, ready to judge him. In South Arabia, he is constitutionally related to his people, founder and partner of the covenant on whose fulfillment the preservation of the commonwealth hangs." On the other hand, Buber argues that other Near Eastern cultures did not conceive this relationship in the same way as did Israel, as "immediate, unmetaphorical, unlimitedly real," and thus that, despite the influence of other cultures on the Israelites as they moved into Canaan, "the kingship of God is not to be derived from this influence."[49] At this point Buber has laid the groundwork for his real interest: the Semitic case.

The West Semitic Tribal God: On Baal and M-L-K

Buber comes to address the linguistic-historical significance of the Semitic root *m-l-k*, which overlays a field of terms related to kingship in the Phoenician, Aramaean, Ammonite, Moabite, Israelite, and Arabian languages. His main interest is in its specific function, as distinguished from that of *el* or *baal*. This is the point in *Kingship of God* at which Buber most combines his own research and experience in biblical Hebrew with the history-of-religions paradigm, acknowledging the powers attributed by ancient peoples to earth and sky, fertility and magic, and the various ways people conceive of themselves in relation to all the mysterious forces at work in the world.

Buber first distinguishes the term *el* from *baal* and *malk*. *El* denotes naked potency, pure divine efficacy, experienced as part of one's regular contact with nature and the world, whereas *baal* and *malk* indicate "in which respect a potency is potent and in which way." *Baal* is what Buber describes as "*encountered* divinity," a manifold power met with in a particular place and providing for the fruitfulness of that place by mating with consorts. *Malk*, in contrast, is the singular god of the tribe, the god of wandering, "the *accompanying* god" who helps the tribe realize its own unity, increase its own power, and succeed in all efforts. *Baal* is stationary "master" or "owner" of a place, but *malk* is "leader" of the mobile tribe. Buber thus separates the *malk* from any sociological or anthropological schema in which all religion serves the same purpose. The *baal* carries out the holy copulation that fertilizes the fields, but the tribe looks to the *malk* for the increase of its own numbers in the form of children.[50] "The consecration of a city is not earth-magic," Buber writes, "but social-magic; not the power of earth and also not that of the sky, only that of the people's destiny, is represented." Buber also denies the contention of "the French school of the sociology of religion" (i.e., Durkheim) that the *malk* is "the personified spirit of the community"; he argues, rather, that "he represents the power which transcends it, happens to it, which *changes* it, even historicizes it." To be sure, it can happen that over the course of history the *malk* and the *baal* can combine. The *baal* can be hailed as the *malk* and can come to be seen as identical with the *malk*. It may be that the wandering desert people, once settled, allow themselves "to be initiated by the indigenous population into Canaanitic Baal-customs, into sexual myths and sexual rites as into the standardized basis of blessed agriculture." But Buber insists that it was not the *baal*, but the *malk*, who was the tribal god, accompanying the nomadic people in their wandering.[51] Buber's treatment of YHVH, as the *malk* of Israel, serves as a transition from comparative history of religions to the field of biblical studies.[52]

The Kingship of God: The Theopolitical Thesis in the Bible

YHVH as M-L-K of Israel

For Buber, YHVH is paradigmatically manifest as *malk*, as leader-god of the wanderers. He is not a sky god, although he is often said to dwell in heaven, and he is not a mountain god, despite his manifestation at Sinai. When he attaches to a place, prior to the establishment of the Temple, Buber reads the biblical text as always making clear that he is not the *baal* of that place; the Bethel of Jacob and the Sinai of Moses are prominent examples. In each case a theophany occurs and the place is marked, but the recipient moves on, knowing that "God is not bound to the spot at which he appears; He lingers at it . . . only as at a place of manifestation."[53] Rather, God leads his chosen ones, individually and as a people, from one place to another, traveling before them.[54] After Sinai, the Ark of the Covenant exemplifies YHVH's nature as *malk*, a "*movable place*" (Buber's italics) that goes with and before the tribe in the wilderness; Buber emphasizes that the ark, like the later Temple, is not a permanent dwelling place for YHVH but more like a guesthouse upon which YHVH may descend at will. In a description fraught with significance for Buber's own readings of prophets and politics, Buber claims that "the tent is the corporeal sign against that Baalization [*Baalisierung*] of the God Who does not allow Himself to be attached to any natural spot, not even to Zion, the original spot of his habitation."[55] With respect both to Bethel and to

Sinai, Buber's insistence on YHVH's *malk* nature can be read as doubly directed, as conflating his scholarly opponents with their ancient Israelite antecedents. Buber simultaneously challenges both those among the ancient Israelites who viewed YHVH as a *baal* and those contemporary scholars who treat the Bible as though it concealed hidden traces of YHVH's true or original *baal* nature, whether in Canaanite cult places or Moabite shrines.[56]

Perhaps the ultimate proof of YHVH's *malk* nature, in Buber's eyes, emerges from the passages in which YHVH reveals his name. Both the Jewish exegetical traditions and the modern documentary hypothesis attach great importance to the names of God in the text, and in particular to the Tetragrammaton. And much scholarship addresses the question posed to God by Moses in Exodus 3:13: "When I come to the Israelites and say to them, 'The God of your fathers has sent me to you,' and they ask me, 'What is His name?' what shall I say to them?" Medieval exegetes worried about this verse—these are the descendants of Abraham, Isaac, and Jacob, so why wouldn't they know the name of their own God? Biblical criticism scrutinizes this apparent cleavage between the God of Abraham and the God of Moses.[57] Buber, however, recalling the powerful ancient Egyptian belief in name magic, cannot imagine that Moses is asking what he should do when he comes to the people at the behest of the God of their fathers, and they ask him the banal question "Well, what is he called?" Rather, they will ask for the meaning of the name YHVH, the hidden truth behind the name that when learned will grant assurance and power. "*To this*," Buber emphasizes, and not to a simple inquiry about a name, "JHWH replies with his *'ehye asher ehye,'* which discloses in the first person what the name in the third person hides—hides, to be sure, since it was out of the original 'God-cry' *yah* or *yahu* as the primeval name of invocation . . . that the Tetragrammaton grew." The secret of YHVH's name is his *malk* nature; it means "I will be there with you."[58]

But what distinguishes YHVH as *malk* from any other West Semitic *malk* god, besides the fact that He is the god of Israel? Although Buber does not ask this question, he answers it, by opposing a second contrast to *malk*, one simultaneously starker and more complex than the contrast with *baal*: *molekh*. Buber defines the special *melekh*-hood of YHVH as a claim on all of life: "The *melekh*-ship is undetachable from the characteristic demand by YHVH, among all *melakhim*, of unconditionedness, immediacy, and unreserved completeness." In taking seriously such a demand, one discovers how difficult it is to obey. Buber calls this error "according to that transformation of vowels which makes out of 'king' a 'pseudo-king'—'Molechization.'"[59]

The Faith of Israel: Theocracy and Idolatry

Buber elaborates on the distinction between true and false belief in the Bible, especially concerning the concept of idolatry. True belief for the Israelite, according to Buber, revolves around the "unconditionedness" of God and the awareness of and receptivity to that unconditionedness. The familiar distinction between "mere" henotheism, the belief that one's god is the most powerful of all gods, and true monotheism, the belief that one's god is the only real one, is at work here in the background. Buber takes it further: "The doctrine of uniqueness has its vital ground not only in this, that one formulated thoughts about how many gods there are and perhaps also thought to establish this, but in the exclusiveness which rules over the faith-relation as it rules over the true love between man and man; more precisely: in the total validity and the total effect of the exclusiveness."[60] The commitment to this exclusiveness in all areas of life is the mark of the Israelite faith.

However, this faith does not simply come upon the people at a stroke. It must be fought for, and "the inner fight for JHWH, for exclusiveness, and for dealing seriously is to be regarded as the genuine form of movement in the history of faith of Israel."[61] It stands in contrast to other, idolatrous possibilities, which seek to make truth and error appear compatible by juxtaposing true and false service. Buber names two such tendencies: "Baalization" and "Molechization." The former assimilates foreign powers to YHVH in an effort to gain control over those powers; the latter attempts to control and domesticate YHVH himself, making him one's own. The golden calf incident in Exodus 32 is the prime instance of Baalization. Even from the standpoint of the calf worshippers, the calf does not represent some god other than the one who led them out of Egypt; rather, that very god is the one said to be located in and possessing the molten calf. The prime example of Molechization, however, is found in the thread of references in the historical and prophetic books to the practice of passing children through fire as a dedication *le-molekh*, which Buber construes not as "to Molekh" as though Molekh were the proper name of a rival god, but as a polemical device signifying the distortion of true service *l-melekh*, to the King: "The service of *molekh* demonizes an actual and characteristic essential demand of JHWH. The demand, posed by the nature of JHWH Himself as the unconditional king of existence, for unconditioned surrender, for that 'with all your heart, with all your soul, with all your might,' finds its ritual response in the usage of the *s'mikha* which we scarcely meet with outside Israel." The *s'mikha*, the expiatory sacrifice of an animal that transfers identity from the self to the animal, is the true form of service to which child sacrifice stands in opposition.[62]

To make this argument, however, Buber must trudge once again through some philological thickets. He has many potential allies in the belief that passages like Jeremiah 32:35 make no sense without the assumption that the child sacrifices were offered to YHVH rather than to another god.[63] Who could ever believe, even mistakenly, that the jealous YHVH would command sacrifices to "Molekh"? However, many scholars take the view that biblical passages mentioning child sacrifice should be read to mean that in the ancient past, the "correct" or normative form of the YHVH religion itself may have mandated human sacrifice.

This Buber cannot accept, although he thinks he understands what misleads these scholars. Because while YHVH, "according to His nature, has nothing at all to do" with orgiastic Baalism, he "is brought into association [with *molekh*-ism] by virtue of the very fact that He is a *melekh*-God, and the child-sacrifice, apparently that of the first-born, is the fitting offering to the King as to the augmenter of the tribe."[64] Buber sees this perhaps as the supreme challenge for YHVH believers, and as an intentional paradox in the biblical text.

According to Buber, the final text as redacted first admits the possibility of human sacrifice as a logical response to the divine demand for exclusivity, but then radically rejects it, thus allowing it to serve as an example of a spiritual and logical error that remains a persistent temptation—most dangerous precisely to those who most desire to take the divine demand seriously:

> So long as God contends against the idols there prevails for the people a clear demarcation: one's own and that which is alien stand in opposition to one another. It is a matter of withstanding the allurements of the alien and to keep one's vows to one's own. But where God rises against the idolization of Himself the demarcation is clouded and complicated. No longer do two camps stretch out opposite to one another: here JHWH, there Astarte!, but on every little spot of ground the truth is mixed with the lie. The struggle of exclusiveness is directed toward unmixing, and this is a hard, an awesome work.[65]

Even the recognition of the problem and the determination to resist temptation do not guarantee success against such a persistent and pervasive possibility.

Buber sees this understanding of Molechism as enabling him to resolve one of the most perplexing verses for biblical commentators, Ezekiel 20:25–26: "Moreover, I gave them laws that were not good and rules by which they could not live. When they set aside every first issue of the womb, I defiled them by their very gifts—that I might render them desolate, that they might know that I am the Lord."[66] The startling statement that God gave the Israelites an ungood law is followed by the even more shocking proclamation of punishment for those who obeyed this law! Buber points out that this threat of punishment also contains "the only sentence of Scripture in which the deity Himself utters the predicate *malakh*, to have kingship, to act as king, about Himself."[67] Against scholars who would chop up this section of Ezekiel, assigning different verses to different authors, Buber argues that God's use of *emlokh* ("I will reign") at 20:33 unifies the passage around its central point: the polemic against the pseudo-kingship, the confusion of *melekh* and *molekh* on the part of those who made the idolatrous mistake. The crux of Ezekiel 20:25 is explained by Buber as meaning, "I allowed an ambiguity to exist in the law, namely that since I only mention the redemption of the first-born in some places that I command the sacrifice and not others, it became possible to interpret this redemption as only allowed, and not commanded. This tested the hearts of the people; those who failed decided not to choose redemption and instead to pass their children through the fire. These are the ones I will punish."[68] In addition to resolving the crux in a way that conforms to Buber's theological assumptions, this interpretation avoids implying that the biblical author and editor intended for God to declare here that he meant to punish the people for something he himself had just commanded them to do.

From Abraham to Moses: Sacrifice, Covenant, and Theopolitical Emergence

Buber seeks to establish the continuity of this interpretation of sacrifice from Abraham through the prophets. The significance of the *Akedah*, the binding of Isaac, is that God commands Abraham to sacrifice "that creature which the loving man, who presents it as himself, simply was not able to offer with lessened reality of intention. Indeed the essential action is even more final than if one had to offer only one's own body.... [N]othing but the intention was demanded, but the intention could only then become actual if the deed itself was demanded in utmost seriousness."[69] This deed symbolizes the wholeness of devotion that YHVH demands from his tribe as their rightful *melekh*; the expiatory sacrifices are intended in the same spirit. The prophets eventually decry the decay of the intention behind such sacrifices, demanding the restoration of actual willingness to sacrifice oneself for one's true King.[70] Thus Buber finds an essential continuity in the biblical description of the relationship between YHVH and Israel, one that transcends all shifts of authorship and editorial complexities; this continuity is contained in the demand of totality that JHWH as *melekh* makes on his people as subjects: "The patriarchal narrative of Genesis is not 'religious,' but religio-political . . . *as soon as JHWH and Israel encounter one another in history, the kingship of God as such emerges.*"[71]

The relationship symbolized in the *Akedah* is formalized in the *brit*, or covenant, at Sinai. For Buber, the sacrificial ritual Moses performs at Exodus 24:5–8 constitutes a unique ceremony, to which "none of the parallels adduced by the comparative science of religion offers a real correspondence. . . . The deciding factor is here that both partners, the altar as representative of the deity, and the people, are treated in the same way as the two parties of a *sacral-legal act of reciprocity*."[72] This ceremony is unique, not just because only Israel performs it (and Buber rejects suggested parallels from other cultures), but also in its singular occurrence in the Bible (Buber rejects the possibility of any analogous ritual). Neither the *brit* with the patriarchs, which was not signified by a similar ritual and did not establish a community that embraced a reciprocal duty to God, nor the post-Sinaitic covenant renewal ceremonies, which only recall and recommit the people to the existing covenant, can be compared to the Mosaic instance.

Etymologically, Buber argues, *brit* connotes confinement or restriction; applied to a pact between two parties, it links them and restricts at least one of them. In its "maximal" meaning, realized at Sinai, both partners are confined "into a relationship of unconditional super-ordination and sub-ordination, each of which has its own, its characteristic binding form in the reciprocal connection." Buber warns against identifying *brit* with the contemporary concept of contract: "*Berith* is not limited to an agreement which establishes a 'community of interest' between two partners until then strange to one another." It can also redefine existing relationships, consecrate them anew, and reestablish them when the covenant is broken. Above all, the *brit* is not "purely religious" in character; rather, it is religio-political, religio-national:

> There is by this time a people Israel, enabled to be partner of a sacral-legal reciprocal act. A people can, however, be partner of such an act only if it already has the power to act and to operate as a unity, in other words: if it is national-politically constituted. The liberation, the fearful flight of liberated wandering, the destruction of the pursuers, promise and leadership, welded together the shepherd tribes into a people. . . . It is able only then to become partner of an act of covenant which can be consummated between a God and a *people*—no purely religious, but only a religio-political, a theo-political act. . . . JHWH is not just the exclusive "Protector-God of the group"; He is its exclusive, political Head.

Buber appeals to Weber, who also saw the covenant as "political-legal throughout, nothing merely theoretical," on the question of the theopolitical character of the covenant, and adds that while Urukagina of Lagash (the early Akkadian lawgiver) and Kariba-ilu Watar (the seventh-century Arabian) each concluded similar compacts with their gods, both, unlike Moses, sought to transform their positions as mediatory priest-princes and to claim the title of king. Only Moses saw that title as already claimed.[73]

Here Buber must again defend a position embraced by few other scholars—that a united Israelite people already existed before it settled Canaan. He takes issue with those who read the Sinai account as a historicizing version of a cultic drama or as an interpretation of some mysterious festival rite from the E author's own time. Buber assumes that the Israelite faith is itself "historical" and does not "historicize" contemporary events with imaginary projection into the past: "*This spirit would not be, if there were no experience and memory to which it bears witness.*" Buber admits that such projections may occur with respect to specific ritual practices, but not with respect to the central narrative of the religion. Such a projection would violate the spirit of a "historical religion."[74] He accuses these scholars of speculation, of imposing arbitrary restrictions while ignoring specific elements that contradict their efforts, and of unnecessarily doubting ancient reports preserved in the oral tradition.[75]

Buber's argument for the theopolitical nature of the covenant is bolstered by the fact that the text places its enunciation into the mouth of YHVH himself:

"You shall be to me a kingdom of priests, a holy nation" (Exodus 19:6). Buber turns this statement against the classical interpretation of "theocracy" in ancient Israel: the only way to understand a "kingdom of priests" in this context is to imagine priestly service to a king as the model for service to God by all the people of Israel. Buber also sees the Song of the Sea (Exodus 15), which ends with the exultant cry "YHVH will reign [*yimlokh*] forever and ever," as a precursor to the covenant establishing: "The shout runs ahead . . . like a herald." He sees the indwelling of YHVH in the Israelite camp as endowed by the covenant with "a theopolitical character."[76] The people themselves, through their shouts of joy outside the tent of meeting, showed that they knew their King dwelled among them and that Moses was meeting with him inside.[77]

From Moses to Joshua: Holy War and Theopolitical Reduction

Moses never enters the Promised Land; he transfers the responsibility of leadership—and conquest—to Joshua. Buber, now undermining "pre-critical formulations," writes that although the book of Joshua itself may say (23:1) that Joshua died having completed his conquest, "historical investigation" determines otherwise, indicating an extended period of Israelite "infiltration" of the land of Canaan attended by short bursts of violent conquest. Buber therefore turns to the discussion of the holy war, "a war which was experienced, not first by its chroniclers, but already by its fighters, as one commanded by and under the command of JHWH." Buber denies that YHVH is a war god, any more than a sky god or an earth god. While war gods help their fighting peoples, they do not wage their own wars, as does YHVH, wars that are listed in a "Book of the Wars of JHWH" (Numbers 21:14). Like any king deciding whether to wage war, YHVH considers the moment at hand: "He *is* not a 'man of war' (Exodus 15:3); He *becomes* one when it is necessary. 'JHWH'—the Present One—'is His name.'" So the heroes of the holy war, from Samson to Deborah, understand with "naïve-theocratic enthusiasm" that they are serving in their King's army, "coming to the help of JHWH among the heroes" (Judges 5:23). Naïve-theocratic enthusiasm, however, cannot survive the institution of the dynastic principle and ends with the kingship of David.[78]

The text clearly demarcates the two periods, according to Buber, at 2 Samuel 7:10: "I will appoint a place for my people Israel, and will plant them, that they may dwell in their own place." Ordinarily understood as foreshadowing the establishment of Solomon's Temple, Buber reads the verse as a farewell to the past: "One cannot say more clearly that here an era comes to an end, the era of that historical action which we call the wandering and settlement of Israel—and therewith also the era of the JHWH-war." Not just any campaign or raid of an Israelite tribe, however, counts as a YHVH war. Nor does just any war waged in the name of YHVH become a YHVH war; it is not the Israelite war per se. Rather, it refers to the "one action, taking place on many fronts and covering many generations, which begins with the downfall of the Egyptian pursuing army and ends with the entrance of the ark into the recently conquered Jerusalem. . . . [T]he JHWH-war is the war of the *melekh* Who fulfills His promise."[79] It refers to the concerted action of all the separate tribes, in common purpose, in pursuit of a goal ordered by YHVH and under the command of YHVH.

Thus it becomes easier to understand Buber's view that "for the expression of the theocratic idea, the book of Joshua is indeed only a trough between Moses and Judges-Samuel."[80] He has a similar view of Joshua himself, "whom we glimpse in shadowy fashion, but like the real shadow of a real person"; he holds that Joshua lacked Moses' inherent understanding of the theopolitical task to which YHVH had committed them. Allowing himself to imagine the psychological state of this "real shadow of a real person," Buber engages in some creative exegesis:

> He is a military man, and he is pious. A theopolitical founder has trained him and has committed him to his work, a theopolitical work, to be continued. He has continued it; he has never felt the theopolitical ardor of his master. The political expression of the theocracy, its only political expression, has been for him the JHWH-war, and this is now at an end. The community led by the charismatic person was necessary for the sake of victory; now it is no longer necessary. He needs to name no successor; the office is disposed of. . . . Outside of the JHWH-war he understands the theocracy in a purely religious fashion, and he gives it a purely religious description [at the assembly at Shechem].[81]

Buber's theopolitical principles are at work in this disdainful understanding of the human need to view divinity as bound primarily to war and victory. Thus Buber refers to Joshua's "purely religious" covenant at Shechem as a "reduction" of theocracy. Joshua emphasizes cultic centralization around a primary sanctuary and attends far less to the political centralization around the invisible king. Joshua considers the YHVH war the tribal confederation's central project, and when that project is completed, he does not think the confederation has any more to do. Nor does he transfer the *charis* to a successor. For Buber, this explains the lack of a succession crisis following Joshua's death. Joshua dissolves the confederation, apportions lots to the tribes, and assumes that they can manage their own business without a central leadership.

Joshua's death "strips theocratic reality of its severe garments of power: now it is surrendered unarmed to the freedom of man," and battle lines are drawn around theocracy itself. Only in the absence of charismatic leadership appears "the kind of man for whom really 'nothing remains but the countenance of his King'; the King which stands on alert for a kingly covenant which now dispenses with an earthly executive."[82] Buber refers to this moment as the "second stage" in the history of direct theocracy, when a community emerges "whose nature is only to be surmised by us." Now the problematic of anarcho-theocracy first arises.[83]

In response to difficulties besetting tribal unity, theocratic leadership, and the incomplete YHVH war, "there arises in the passion of the spirit an association of 'speakers' which as association attempted to fulfill that which Moses intended." They preach in favor of the Mosaic project and in opposition to the Joshuanic reduction, calling for the renewal of a politically functioning confederation under the rule of its *melekh*, capable of waging a new, defensive YHVH war. These speakers actively engage in the battles of the people and eventually produce those "judges" whom they perceive as temporary holders of the *charis*: "They appear to me as the divine-militant society distributed over the land which gives birth to and supports the judges." Some, such as Deborah, serve as judge and prophet. Over time, the title of *navi* acquires a certain respect and currency, and forces opposed to theocracy later attempt to appropriate it. But "the tradition of the pre-Davidic period . . . knows no other reception of the charisma than the prophetic; even the judge, such as Gideon and Jephtha, also the great berserker, such as Samson, must first of all become a *nabi*" by declaring the Spirit to have come upon him.[84]

The Song of Deborah (Judges 5:2–31), considered "the oldest coherent historical source of Israel, absolutely contemporary," exemplifies these traits: the view of YHVH as a *melekh*-leader who goes before the people, whose throne moves with the people, and who commands the heavens and the people Israel.[85] Merely human kings are instructed by this singer to listen to the tale of the true, divine king's victory. Buber designates this personality type as "primitive-prophetic," although he knows some scholars consider the term *navi* a late artifact. Therefore, he defines the prophetic office contrary not just to the views of other scholars, but even to the views of those biblical writers who think of the *navi* as an accredited court prophet who would use his divine connection to see the future and to reveal hidden things. For Buber, however, *navi* designates a "'pronouncer,' who announces that which is communicated to him from above in intelligible manner to those below—and that which is addressed to him from below in acceptable manner to that which is above."[86] This argument serves one of Buber's larger purposes: to establish a continuity from the covenant through the prophetic and postexilic periods without involving the monarchy, thus establishing the antimonarchic essence of Judaism. By claiming that the societies of *nevi'im* first emerged after Joshua's death, preaching in the name of Mosaic theopolitics against the Joshuanic reduction, giving rise to the judges, and continuing to support the ideal of a unified and politically focused Israel under the rule of a divine *melekh* throughout the monarchical period, Buber traces his line of continuity throughout the historical span covered in the Bible.

Der Gideonspruch: Gideon's Refusal of Kingship as Primal Moment of Theopolitics

For Buber, the period described in the book of Judges, in which the people vacillate between charismatic leadership and anarcho-theocracy, is the time when political and theological conflicts within Israel become most intense. The ultimate expression of anarcho-theocratic idealism for Buber is the passage in which

Gideon refuses kingship for himself and rejects the principle of hereditary monarchy. Buber's account of this passage has attracted the lion's share of the scholarly attention devoted to *Kingship of God*. Here we place it in a more comprehensive
context.[87]

Buber's argument seems straightforward enough: Judges 8:22–23 means
just what it appears to say. Buber accuses other scholars of retreating from this
truth and introducing unnecessary hypotheses to support faulty assumptions.
When Gideon refuses the offer of hereditary rulership, saying: "I will not rule
over you, my son shall not rule over you, YHVH shall rule over you," he asserts
the exclusive kingship of YHVH. Scholars who deny the validity of this reading discount the plain sense of the text and distort the history of ancient Israel.
Unlike Gideon, they cannot "dare to deal seriously with the rulership of God."[88]
Instead, because the statement "does not occur eschatologically but historically,
not as prophecy but as political declaration," scholars commonly view it as "a
risk to be regarded as almost contrary to history." After all, Buber argues, theocracy is usually seen as "a form of rulership in which the power of men over
men is fundamentally at its strongest, [and] is, according to its constitution,
unlimited, because it is derived from divine authority, or is itself believed to be
divine."[89]

Buber addresses the two chief arguments of those who read Judges 8:23
against its plain sense. First is the claim that a straightforward reading is incon-
sistent with Judges 9:2, in which Gideon's son Abimelech, whose name means
"my father [is] king," challenges the town leaders to help him attain the power his
father supposedly rejected; he asks them: "Which serves you better, that seventy
men rule over you, all sons of Jerubbaal, or that a single man rule over you?"
Since Jerubbaal is another name for Gideon, this passage would indicate that at
some point, despite what Gideon says at 8:23, he must have eventually accepted
the rulership and passed it on to his sons; how else could Abimelech have acquired his name?

Buber sees no contradiction between his reading of 8:23 and the formulation in 9:2. Noting that the root *mashal* (משל), "to rule," is used in 9:2 rather
than *malakh* (מלך), "to be king," he argues that Abimelech's statement refers to
the de facto power of the sons of Gideon in Israelite life and offers to institute a
de jure alternative. *Mashal* "signifies not the formal possession, but rather the
factual practice of a power which can also be affirmed of a 'kingship' as predicate
(Psalm 103:19). Thus Joseph 'rules' ['*waltet*'] in Egypt (Genesis 45:8, 26); thus also
Abraham's chief steward 'governs' ['*gewaltet*'] his house (24:2)."[90] Employing the
Leitwort technique he had laid out with Rosenzweig in *Die Schrift und ihre Ver-
deutschung*, Buber argues that the redactor of Judges wanted 8:22 and 9:2 to be
read together, and that he indicated this by the repetition of *mashal*: "No matter
whether 8:22ff and 9:2 spring from the same tradition or from two different ones,
in the version which lies before us they form an intelligible and stylistic unity.

There is no contradiction in content, and the stylistic connectedness is expressly brought to the fore."[91]

In Buber's reading, Abimelech repudiates his father's renunciation of monarchical authority, because it led to a situation in which too many men could accrue power. As for Abimelech, Buber argues that he obviously named himself. As one of Gideon's lowborn sons, his mother a Shechemite concubine, he asserts proudly that his father was actually a king.[92] Worse still, Abimelech's is the first Israelite name to contain the term *melekh*, although the Canaanites previously used it to connect "two different orders of divine denotation, the father-order and the king-order, thus the biological (the god as primeval father of the tribe) and the political conception (the god as overlord of the tribe). In the adoption, the name's constituent parts referring to the divinity were here as well as on other occasions applied to JHWH"—an especially offensive act of usurpation.[93] In fact, Buber argues, Abimelech appears as a villain, as "the demonically intended adversary of the thought of the exclusive kingship of God." Everything in his story pairs with something in the Gideon story; his narrative is the doppelgänger of the Gideon passage. Gideon correctly understands the role of the charismatic leader under anarcho-theocracy: "a completely personal and wholly once-for-all commission [*Auftrag*] which can neither be continued, handed over nor dynastically exploited. Every attempt to do this, as well as every step into an authority-less self-rule [*auftraglose Selbstherrlichkeit*], would be betrayal of the giver of the authority [*Auftrags*], the one ruling Lord."[94] Abimelech takes just such a step, inciting a bloody civil war in the process. The contrast between Gideon and Abimelech extends to the style of the passages. Buber, like Wellhausen, finds little supernatural embellishment in the Abimelech story:

> The redactor sees in him, the enemy of the theocratic bias, the man who wishes—expressed in our language—to politicize history, rather, to make it into an arena of *merely* political interests. The style of the legend *must* give way here to that of the profane chronicle: God allows the adversary to set the tone—until the moment of annihilation. With the report of divine punishment the legendary style could resume again.[95]

As Carl Schmitt might say, "Tell me who your enemy is, and I will tell you who you are." This characterization of Abimelech—that he wants to make history into an arena of merely political interests—could also apply, from Buber's perspective, to scholars who deny the historicity of the Gideon passage because they deny the possibility of primitive theocracy. The importance of Abimelech is merely the shadow of the importance of Gideon.

Buber sees Gideon as "the genuine hero of the primitive-theocratic legend . . . the only one among the pre-Samuelic judges whose call is actually narrated;" he thus opposes any negative interpretation of Gideon's character, whether as ambitious or as idolatrous.[96] Gideon's other name, Jerubbaal (Judges 6:32 and

7:1; 1 Samuel 12:11), read as "Baal will contend," is still taken by some to suggest that the Gideon of the most ancient legends was a Baal worshipper; the incident in 8:24–27 (the construction of the "ephod") is adduced in further support of this reading.[97] In this interpretation, Gideon's more pious acts (tearing down his father's altar to Baal at 6:27, and refusing the kingship) are apologetic interpolations by a late editor. However, this alleged editor left inconsistencies, leaving a contradictory Gideon in the final redaction.

In Buber's harmonizing account, by contrast, Gideon remains heroic throughout. The name Jerubbaal does not imply that Gideon aligned with Baal, and the ephod was not an idol. In a deft hermeneutical maneuver, Buber interprets Jerubbaal as analogous to the name Israel itself, referring to the view in Hosea 12:4 that "El" is the object, not the subject, of the verb *sara*, "to fight." Similarly, he vindicates the folk etymology for Jerubbaal given in 6:32 (*yarev bo ha-ba'al*, or "Let Baal contend with him"), which others read as late and apologetic: "Beside the former who fought the El, the redactor places the latter who fought the Baal; thus, beside the wrestler for the blessing of the genuine numen he places the annihilator of the anti-God and false God—both 'fighters of God.'" Not only does he reject the picture of Gideon as an idolater; he deems him worthy of comparison to Jacob/Israel himself.[98] In the light of Buber's claim that Abimelech is the first usurper of anarcho-theocracy, hubristically naming himself *melekh*, we can read the analogy of Gideon to Jacob as an identification with the spirit of Israel itself. Kingly qualities are first attributed to Gideon by foreigners, themselves kings—Zebah and Zalmunna, the kings of Midian. The people take their inspiration from these foreigners and seek to imitate them; the redactor answers the people with the Gideon passage, which preserves the theocracy and thereby the identity of Israel. As for the ephod, Buber "cannot understand by this an idol in spite of all that has been adduced." But he speculates that a Deuteronomist editor may have disapproved of Gideon's founding an independent oracle location. If the people later dedicated the spot to a syncretistic Baal, Gideon is hardly to blame, since his career began with the destruction of a Baal cult: "In Gideon's speech the mute saga has its banderole; in the saga Gideon's speech has the biographical foundation and authorization without which, notwithstanding its concreteness, it would be only a splendid aphorism."[99]

The second critical argument against Buber's reading lies in the fact that the passage in which it occurs is dated late. Wellhausen and others assert that the theopolitical sentiment expressed by Gideon in 8:2 is too abstract to have been conceived during the primitive, nomadic stage of Israel's development. More likely that a far later writer, perhaps in the time of Hosea's prophetic condemnation of the monarchy, conceived the theopolitical idea and projected it back onto an imagined predecessor. Against this objection, Buber does *not* argue for the "actual historical" existence of a man named Gideon who actually said the words ascribed to him. Indeed, he questions the scientific basis of any such procedure. In the absence of other evidence, it would be impossible to distinguish the "natural" historical content from the "religious" layer of legend. Fundamentally, "it is not as if saga had joined itself to history and accordingly had to be detached from it, but the holy saga is for this reporter the immediate and single way of articulating his 'knowledge' about the events," which is itself a "legendary knowledge," representing a believing narrator's view of history. Buber views the question in this way: "A time has been given, a saying has been given—can the saying, according to its nature, have been spoken in the time, according to its nature? That is all I mean to affirm for the Gideon passage and for the epoch of history between Joshua's death and Saul's ascension to the throne . . . proof of the historical *possibility* of the Gideon passage would be at the same time the proof of its historical *truth*."[100] If his early dating of the Gideon passage is admitted as possible, then his whole argument may follow.

Richterbuch und Richterbücher: The Book(s) of Judges between Monarchy and Anarchy

In the second chapter of *Kingship of God*, "Books of Judges and Book of Judges," Buber reenacts the tension between Gideon and the men of Israel, which prefigures the tension between his reading and Wellhausen's. This time, he sees it as a conflict between two earlier groups of "historians," namely the redactors of the two "books of Judges," which Buber sees in the canonical book Shoftim as we have it: "The work is composed of two books between which stand the two dissimilar Samson legends. Each of the two books is edited from a biased viewpoint, the first from an anti-monarchical, the second from a monarchical."[101] The final redactor of the book, faced with these two separate texts, aligns them from a particular political-historical standpoint: "Something has been attempted—about which the first part reports; but it has failed—as the last part shows. This 'something' is that which I call *the primitive theocracy*."[102] Tradition then adopted the redactor's view, perhaps influencing its eventual, habitual veneration of the House of David.

The prevalent critical view of Judges in Buber's time, according to his own account, divided the book into even more parts than Buber does himself. It was held that there was no "people Israel" in the time Judges describes, only separate tribes and their chieftains. Much later, the alleged Deuteronomist wove disparate legends about the exploits of these chieftains into a chronological narrative of successive "judges" of the united people Israel. Buber does not entirely disagree with this picture. He admits the presence of a "schema," even a "literarily stiff" one, imposed on the events described. However, he asserts once again that the schema "is in no way contrary to history." Insisting on the need to account for the horizon of faith of the compilers and redactors, Buber asks:

> But does the lively opposing power of historical destiny allow itself to be mas-
> tered by a pragmatism?[103] Only if in that pragmatism a deeper reality dwells,
> even if deficiently . . . cannot it be assumed that just as at one time the believ-
> ing experience of an event constituted the people, so the specific conversion
> to the believing experience of history again and again revived anew the power
> of unity in the people? That it did not prove itself strong enough gives to the
> Book of Judges its melancholy character, to the whole, not just to the closing
> section.[104]

On the one hand, this reads more like philosophy of history, or nationalism, than
like source criticism. On the other hand, Buber claims that this view clarifies
difficult passages. He contests seemingly minor points to show that his hypothesis precludes the need for many unconvincing explanations his critics offer.[105]
Buber's impression that the book of Judges has an overall "melancholy character"
meshes tightly with his general analytical stance.

Buber's preference for the antimonarchical book extends beyond theopolitics to questions of composition, dating, and priority. He refers once to the antimonarchical book, which extends roughly from Judges 1 to 12, up to the story of
Jephthah, as "the original Book of Judges"; the monarchical book, which includes
chapters 17–21, he calls an "appended chronicle." Buber's arguments in favor of
the traditional material of the Gideon story, and the oral memory that lies behind
written accounts, do not recur in connection with the monarchical book, which
"has no pre-literary existence." Rather, it came into existence in a reactionary
fashion:

> It is plain that the monarchical book followed after the antimonarchical book
> just as a disputation follows the disputed thesis. Oral form and written form,
> compactness and confusion, but also information and correction, religious-
> political theory and its "purely political" counterpart, in any case thesis and
> counter-thesis, thus the two books stand beside one another, books which a
> remarkable spirit of balancing has linked together, the same spirit in which,
> then, the canon originated.[106]

Buber asserts that the monarchical book originated at a time when the stories of
the judges were first collected and redacted—not into the antimonarchical portion of our book of Judges, nor into a version contemporary with the redactor of
the final book of Judges, but rather into some very rough early cycle with a clear
antimonarchical intent. The monarchical book was then composed all at once
and circulated in answer, although our redaction bears the marks of later editing. The cycle that would result in the antimonarchical book, involving the first
stories of the Judges, dated from the so-called Samuelic crisis, a turbulent epoch
in which the tradition of anarcho-theocracy was questioned.[107] Then, during the
period of the monarchy, the partisans of the anarchy finally felt it necessary to
inscribe and circulate their cycle as propaganda, evoking a response from court

circles in the form of the monarchical book, which sought "rejection of a 'romantic' error."[108]

The thesis of the monarchical book of Judges is expressed in the slogan: "At that time there was no king in Israel, and every man did what seemed right in his own eyes." This slogan attaches to two stories that portray Israel as unstable during the period of the judges, consumed by its inner immorality and disorder and its vulnerability to attack from without. The first story, in two chapters, tells of Micah, a man who sets up an illicit ephod and altar site, recruiting his son and a passing Levite to serve as priests for him. When some men from the tribe of Dan, on a military expedition, pass Micah's house, they steal the ephod and other altar objects and hire away the Levite priest. Micah fails to resist and the Danites set up their altar once they conquer their new land, where they live "until the land went into exile" (Judges 18:30). The second story, contained in the final three chapters of Judges, is much grander and more terrible. The brutal rape and murder of a woman in Gibeah leads to a league of Israelite tribes seeking to punish the offenders. When the tribe of Benjamin protects those accused, a civil war breaks out and Benjamin is all but destroyed. Finally, after some debate, the remaining men of Benjamin are allowed to marry and reproduce. Their wives are abducted from Jabesh-Gilead, after the slaughter of the men there, and from Shiloh, and carried off to live with the defeated remnant of Benjamin. For Buber, the pro-monarchical intent of the author of this tale is transparent: "A people without a king plunders; a people without a king is plundered—that is the opinion."[109]

Great claims had been made for the anarcho-theocracy: it maintained order, it defeated kings of other nations, it served God according to His will, and allotted power only to those with recognized qualifications, and to them only temporarily. To this outlook, in Buber's summary, the monarchical book responds: "'That which you pass off as theocracy has become anarchy [*Das, was ihr für Theokratie ausgebt, ist Anarchie gewesen*],' and: 'Only since this people, as is fitting for human beings, took unto itself a human being for a king, has it known order and civilization.'"[110] Buber's description of its style reflects his disdain for this thesis: "One sees the shrugging of shoulders, hears the superior, regretful tone: 'At that time they simply didn't have a king in Israel!'" Unimpressed by the monarchical book's tales of terror, he explains its inclusion in the final book of Judges by the historical standpoint of the redactor.[111]

Ultimately, Buber argues, neither the authors of the monarchical book nor the final redactor of the book of Judges understood the nature of the judgeship. A noninstitutional institution, relying wholly on divine call and charismatic authority, it was well suited to the anarcho-theocracy. The futility of kingship is proclaimed most strongly in the story that Buber regards as the counterpart to the Gideon passage: the Jotham fable (Judges 9:7–21). If the Gideon speech is the mind of the anarcho-theocratic antimonarchical book, the Jotham fable is its heart. A son of Gideon who escapes Abimelech's slaughter of the rest of his brothers, Jotham emerges from hiding at the moment of Abimelech's coronation and preaches to the citizens of Shechem. He tells of the trees going to anoint (*limshoach*, the same root as *moshiach*) a king over themselves. One by one, each tree to which they offer the honor refuses. The olive tree would rather produce its rich oil, the fig tree its sweet and delicious fruit, the vine its cheering wine. None wants to give up these useful pursuits "to go and sway above the trees." Finally, the thornbush or bramble accepts but warns of dire consequences if the other trees later change their minds. Buber's description of this passage is effusive:

> The Jotham fable, the strongest anti-monarchical poem of world literature, is the counterpart of the Gideon passage. Independently of the latter it could be understood anarchistically [*anarchistisch*]. Fitted into the strict context it functions as a keenly realistic illustration of that fundamental manifesto. The kingship, so teaches the poem . . . is not a productive calling. It is vain, but also bewildering and seditious, that men rule over men. Every one is to pursue his own proper business, and the manifold fruitfulnesses will constitute a community over which, in order that it endure, no one needs to rule—no one except God alone (so the Gideon speech interprets the doctrine which, without it, appears to embody a primitive belief in freedom). The "commonwealth without government" is thought of by the author or the redactor of the antimonarchical Book of Judges as a commonwealth for which an invisible government [*unsichtbare Obrigkeit*] is sufficient.[112]

For Buber, the Jotham fable makes an even stronger claim than the Gideon passage considered in isolation. From the simple assertion that anarcho-theocracy is the way of Israel, we move to the considered rejection of an alternative. Monarchy has been considered, then found wanting. Buber takes his description of this rejection to rhapsodic heights as he details his own longing for true *Gemeinschaft*, a perfect combination of individual freedom and collective solidarity, the anarchist ideal at its purest, where "no one needs to rule." Yet Buber adds a twist to the old anarchist slogan "No gods, no masters." "*One* God, no masters." Instead of no government whatsoever, which would represent a "primitive belief in freedom," he sees the antimonarchical author as calling for an *invisible* government.[113]

In the conclusion to his discussion of the redaction of Judges, Buber offers a detailed description of the redactor's worldview and editorial strategy:

> The readers received in the totality of the book, in various gradations between dimness and clarity, an aspect of history . . . which perhaps corresponded to the assertion of contemporary historiography that a people in a given epoch was not 'ripe' to actualize a structure intended for it . . . by its spiritual leaders. This aspect was supported or corroborated by the fact of the pause, for a time, between *shophet* and *shophet*, thus of a *normal* 'interregnum'; a fact which was inseparable from the institution of the judgeship, as an institution again and again in an extraordinary period of emergency [*Notzeit*] resulting, only in

such a time, in vocation of the liberator and unification of the tribes. Continuity of the union was not guaranteed; without judges, thus without unified and superior earthly government, the people was not able to maintain order and civilization. The primitive theocracy therefore was plunged again and again into anarchy [*Anarchie*], as is demonstrated for us in the five closing chapters in two examples.[114]

Buber asserts that the intermittent character of the judgeship, crucial to anarcho-theocracy itself, could no longer be comprehended after a period of monarchy.[115] If the monarchical book polemicized against anarcho-theocracy, the redactor scarcely even understood it. The period between the calling of each judge was a terrifying pitfall for Israel; the redactor and the later readers of Judges yearned for the safety and security that they saw in the monarchy. Thus the tradition came to identify the anarchy of interregnum, which was theocracy, with the anarchy of emergency, which was chaos.[116]

The editorial conflict between the antimonarchical writers, on the one hand, and the pro-monarchical writers and the redactor of Judges, on the other hand, itself only continues the conflict that runs through the period from Joshua to Saul, between those who see in the absence of a human leader an opportunity to approach the ideal order and those who perceive it only as a danger. Eventually, the latter group points to enough physical and historical evidence to overcome the assertions of the prophets and judges, which will seem distant and abstract to a people living in harsh conditions: "Disorder, completely unconquered by the prophetic community, is almost the only universal constant. Only trouble and tribulation again and again pull together a few tribes for a while and up from flightiness to theocratic obedience."[117] Eventually, a military crisis allows the latter group to gain control—the threat of the Philistines, no mere local tribe but a well-organized people, ruled by a powerful human king. It is at this moment that the people rebels against their anarcho-theocracy, as Buber puts it in the final words of *Kingship of God*:

> Then for the first time does the people rebel against the situation which the primitive-prophetic leaders tried, ever anew and ever alike in vain, to inflame with the theocratic will toward constitution. The idea of monarchic unification is born and rises against the representatives of the divine kingship. And the crisis between the two grows to one of the theocratic impulse itself, to the crisis out of which there emerges the human king of Israel, the follower of JHWH (12:14), as His "anointed," *meshiach* JHWH, χριστὸς κυριου.[118]

Although Samuel receives most of the attention that Western political theory pays to the Bible, Buber insists that Judges, too, deserves to be considered a biblical *Politeia*.[119] Hidden in its pages, in the separate sources as well as in the tradition of the redaction, is a profound historical struggle with the paradox of the two senses of anarchy, as chaos and as utopia; the paradox, that is to say, of the kingship of God. The triumph of the monarchical faction is the triumph of the one they ask for: the anointed one, the messiah, the usurper, against the anarcho-theocratic ideal of unmediated rule by God. In this sense, it is the victory of political theology over theopolitics—of Messiah over God.

Conclusion

Over the course of part 1 of this book, we have traced an arc following more than three decades of Martin Buber's life and work. At the turn of the twentieth century, he was a young neo-romantic poet and Zionist activist. His initial meeting and friendship with Gustav Landauer overlapped with a decade when he rose to prominence as a Jewish thinker whose writings on mysticism and Hasidism appealed to a generation of acculturated Central European Jews. The peak of this early activity came just before World War I, when Buber clashed with Landauer and drastically reevaluated his philosophy and political priorities. In 1918's *The Holy Way*, he had already moved, under Landauer's influence, from a fairly standard cultural Zionism, one that imagined the restoration of Jewish creativity and vitality that would come with the restoration of the Jewish people's contact with the Land of Israel, to a rather more iconoclastic position: that it was not primarily cultural creativity that was at stake, but faithfulness and obedience to God, manifested through a principled rejection of any politics of statehood and sovereignty. Over the course of the 1920s, Buber memorialized his martyred friend while simultaneously pursuing the other projects for which he is better known. It was also during this period that he tested and developed the thesis of *The Holy Way*, both measuring it against challenges from intellectuals like Weber and Schmitt and working to increase and improve his knowledge of the Bible itself. By the late 1920s and early 1930s, Buber is ready to offer a sustained and detailed book-length version of this thesis: *Kingship of God*.

Buber argues that some ancient Israelites imagined a unique theopolity, echoes of which can be found in the layered strata of the Hebrew Bible. From the Bible we also learn of the paradoxes in this theopolitical structure and of the tensions that emerged during the periods of waiting that followed the death of each successive charismatic leader. Eventually, the internal and external pressures on the people, especially from military threats, led to the success of the monarchical faction, the historical-political defeat of the anarcho-theocracy, and the institution of the human monarchy, justified by the claim that the king was the anointed of God. Despite this victory, the conflict between the two factions continued in the opposition of the various editors and redactors of what became our book of Judges, between prophets and kings up until the Babylonian Exile, between scholarly camps over the biblical evidence, and finally in the contest between theopolitics on the one hand, and realpolitik and political theology on the other, for the direction of contemporary life.

For the ancient Israelites, theopolitics may have meant alternating between a family-centered, tribal home life and a collective existence as "Israel," a nation ruled by an invisible king. But Buber never entertains the notion that modern Jews should attempt to reconstitute themselves into tribes. Instead, it seems that he believed that the anarchist vision of Landauer, of a decentralized network of internally democratic local councils, could come to form the modern version of a Jewish theocratic politics. The mission of his Zionism then became an effort to counteract the political-theological tendency, which risked repeating the ancient monarchical mistake (even if it too attempted to update its vision, substituting a liberal parliamentary system for the House of David). Buber addressed the issue head-on in his Zionist polemics, but he also considered it important to keep telling his biblical story. In part 2, we will see how Buber told the stories of Moses, of Samuel and Saul, and of the prophets of Israel, further elaborating his vision of a Judaism simultaneously anarchic and theocratic.

Notes

1. KG 139. "Die soziologische »Utopie« einer Gemeinschaft aus Freiwilligkeit nichts andres als die Immanenzseite der unmittelbaren Theokratie." Buber, *Königtum Gottes* (Berlin: Schocken, 1932.), 144. Citations are usually to SM unless otherwise noted.

2. Francis Oakley, *Kingship: The Politics of Enchantment* (Oxford, UK: Blackwell Publishing, 2006), 4. For a counterclaim that most humans have lived without states, see James C. Scott, *The Art of Not Being Governed: An Anarchist History of Upland Southeast Asia* (New Haven, CT: Yale University Press, 2009), ix.

3. Oakley, *Kingship*, 5.

4. Cited in KG 165n15, 170n11, 170n21, 171n31.

5. John P. McCormick has argued that Schmitt provides "a blueprint for the permanent supersession of [the liberal-legal parliamentary components of the Weimar constitution] by [the democratic-plebiscitary presidential components.] . . . [This] may not be 'Nazi' in 1932, but certainly is fascist." McCormick, "Identifying or Exploiting the Paradoxes of Constitutional Democracy? An Introduction to Carl Schmitt's *Legality and Legitimacy*," in *Legality and Legitimacy*, by Carl Schmitt, trans. and ed. Jeffrey Seitzer (Durham, NC: Duke University Press, 2004), xlii.

6. We should bear in mind Buber's desire to obtain an official position at the Hebrew University, and his need to produce a scholarly work worthy of habilitation. This need sharpened after the first edition, with the Nazi rise to power.

7. KG 13.

8. Buber, *Königtum Gottes*, IX. The word *Erkenntnis* can be rendered as "insight," "understanding," or "comprehension," all perhaps having less "hard" scientific connotations than "knowledge" does in English. However, Scheimann writes that Buber approved his translation; Scheimann, "Translator's Foreword," 10.

9. KG 14.

10. Ibid. In one of these notes, presumably added for the 1956 third edition, Buber writes that the second volume, *Der Gesalbte*, "was half finished in 1938 and had already been set up in type when the Schocken Press, Berlin, which published the work, was officially dissolved. For many years external and internal causes hindered continuation of the work; not until recently could it be resumed. Sections from the still uncompleted second volume have been printed in

advance in German and Hebrew publications. I plan to publish it as a separate book." However, in the 1964 edition of Buber's *Werke*, Buber updates this note to say that he never finished the book; ZWB 489. Confusingly for English readers, Scheimann's 1967 translation of KG, despite having been largely finished in the mid-1960s while Buber was still alive, reproduces the 1956 version of the note rather than the updated 1964 version from the *Werke*. As for the projected third volume, which was never titled, Buber's 1956 footnote states: "I have abandoned the writing of the third volume; nevertheless its fundamental ideas have been set forth in my book *Der Glaube der Propheten* (1950), 180–334 (cf. also my book *Zwei Glaubensweisen*, 1950, pp. 103–16)." Thus our discussions of PF in chapter 6 and of *Two Types of Faith* in chapter 8 both keep *Das Kommende* in mind as the original framework for the ideas in these books.

11. KG 18–19.

12. I prefer the use of "YHVH" to "the LORD." See Note on Translation and Transliteration.

13. KG 136; Buber, SM 174.

14. KG 118.

15. Classically represented by Deuteronomy 6:5, and later the opening line of the first paragraph of the Shema prayer in rabbinic liturgy. Most scholars, however, believe Deuteronomy was written later than other books of the Torah, certainly long after the monarchy had arisen. To represent Solomon as retreating from this motto, Buber first must suggest that the written motto is only a latter-day transcription of ancient oral wisdom, a suggestion characteristic of his biblical scholarship.

16. KG 119. Emphasis Buber's. The term *aufheben*, often translated as "overcome" or "sublate," is freighted with Hegelian philosophical ballast.

17. The continual use of the Greek term *charis*, rather than a Hebrew term, probably reflects the influence of Weber's widely known theory of charisma. *Charis* has connotations of gratuitousness, of free gift, comparable to the Hebrew *chesed*.

18. Buber acknowledges that Weber's account of hierocracy in *Economy and Society* does not "touch upon our problem," but he appropriates the term anyway, because it aids him in drawing the contrast to theocracy; KG 215n15.

19. KG 140.

20. Ibid., 141.

21. Ibid., 149. The continuation of the text in English, together with the fact that Buber supposedly reviewed Scheimann's translation, poses a problem for us here. The English continues: "And the most faithful of all profess to do it in order to have to follow no one." The German text, however, reads: "Freilich, die Gläubigen harren der Gnade, als der allein sie folgen wollen, und die Allerungläubigsten geben vor es zu tun, um niemand folgen zu müssen"; SM 186. Scheimann has "most faithful" where Buber has *Allerungläubigsten*, the most unfaithful ones! This drastically changes his meaning; what seemed like an intensification is really a contrast. The context helps clarify: the unfaithful say that they are waiting, like the faithful, for a new charismatic leader, but in fact they want only to gain from the perceived absence of authority to assert their own power. (It may also matter whether we read *geben vor* as "profess" or "pretend": Should we understand that the unfaithful are also dishonest, feigning allegiance to the idea of freedom? Or are they forthrightly declaring their intention to do what they will?) I thank Eric Santner for noting this, and Ari Linden for his thoughts. My earlier discussion of this passage neglected this item; Samuel Hayim Brody, "Is Theopolitics an Antipolitics? Martin Buber, Anarchism, and the Idea of the Political," in *Dialogue as a Trans-Disciplinary Concept*, ed. Paul Mendes-Flohr (Berlin: Walter de Gruyter, 2015), 79.

22. In a remarkable literary-critical footnote on this passage, Buber suggests an emendation of Numbers 27:18–21, the calling of Joshua, to eliminate references to Eleazar the priest, characterizing them as "hierocratizing revision." KG 215n21.

23. Ibid., 138.

24. Ibid., 148–149. Scheimann has "anarchy" here, although Buber seems to distinguish between *Herrschaftslosigkeit*, here clearly negative, and *anarchische*, used elsewhere to describe the characteristic psychological inclination to freedom of desert tribes.

25. Ibid., 139.

26. Ibid., 148. The form and nature of this conflict, however, can vary. For example, Buber contrasts the "spiritual" polemic of the antimonarchical judges and prophets against their fellow Israelites with the "attitude of opposition, determined by religious commandment and urging on to the most gruesome massacres," assumed by the Kharijite sect of early Islam to the whole body of their coreligionists. Buber otherwise considers the Kharijites to parallel the anarcho-theocratic attitude found in Judges, except that "the Kharijites want to prevent any one from ruling upon whom the Spirit does not rest; by Gideon's mouth, however, the person on whom the Spirit rests says that he does not want to rule." Ibid., 159–160.

27. "History" is a term with many valences in Buber; here, in quotation marks to show that it is being spoken by the opponents of anarcho-theocracy, referencing the notion that force and necessity govern the temporal realm. Cf. Buber, "What Is to Be Done?" in PW 109–111; and Buber, "The Question to the Single One," in *Between Man and Man*, trans. Ronald Gregor-Smith (New York: Routledge, 2007), 46–97.

28. KG 64.

29. Scheimann renders *Zwiegespräch* in this paragraph as both "dialectic" (for which Buber already used *dialektik* earlier in the sentence) and "dialogue." There might be some value in distinguishing paradox, dialectic, and dialogue here, if only to show the degree to which Buber treats them as interchangeable. The italicized *eschaton* is Scheimann's, not Buber's.

30. KG 65. I have restored these italics, omitted in Scheimann's English translation, from the 1932 edition of *Königtum Gottes*, 12, which reads "der in der Geschicht*schreibung* wirkt, weil er in der *Geschichte* gewirkt hat."

31. KG 15. My italics.

32. The reference is to Wilhelm Caspari's 1928 essay "Der Herr ist König," *Christentum und Wissenschaft* 4 (1928): 23–31.

33. KG 15.

34. Readers unfamiliar with the terminology of biblical scholarship will benefit from consulting John J. Collins, *Introduction to the Hebrew Bible* (Minneapolis: Fortress Press, 2004). Source criticism assumes that the final text of the Bible is compiled or redacted from parallel, originally independent source documents. The most famous attempt to identify these documents, for the Pentateuch in particular, is Wellhausen's documentary hypothesis, which assigns texts to J (for Jahwist source), E (Elohist), P (Priestly), and D (Deuteronomist).

35. KG 16.

36. Ibid., 17.

37. Ibid.

38. Ibid., 85.

39. The intellectual origins of this progressive schema include Hegel's history of religion and liberal Protestant theology more broadly. Weber, a closer resource for Buber, often polemicized against facile and reductionist attempts to divide history into preconceived systems of "stages," although he himself may not always overcome this tendency.

40. For example, against the allegation that the exile introduces either "new values of the spirit and of morality" or "a loss in reality-content" to the Israelite conception of God—the latter a view he had once held—Buber argues that "The God of Whom it is known that His kingship rules over all (Psalm 103:19) is neither more spiritual nor is He less real than He of whom it is only known that He 'was King in Jeshurun' (Deuteronomy 33:5)." The theisms of the

Exodus and the Exile relate to each other "as the folded-up leaf is related to the unfolded leaf." KG 108.

41. Ibid., 48.

42. Ibid., 90.

43. Buber corresponded with the Egyptologist Kurt Sethe, author of *Amun und die acht Urgötter von Hermopolis* (1929) and *Urgeschichte und älteste Religion der Ägypter* (1930), about textual points in the works of other Egyptologists (including Alexandre Moret's claim that there was a "leaderless primeval period" in Egypt, a claim Sethe disputed) and sided with his correspondent against earlier scholarship; KG 170. He also maintained interest in the topic, adding sources to the notes of the third edition of KG, including Ivan Engnell, *Studies in Divine Kingship in the Ancient Near East* (1943), and Henri Frankfort, *Kingship and the Gods* (1948).

44. KG 88–90. Here too, Buber plays the specialists off against each other in the notes. For example, he marshals Francois Thureau-Dangin against a claim, made by Johannes Hempel in his 1930 work *Altes Testament und Geschichte*, that the uniqueness of the Israelite king is that he is called and adopted, whereas both Babylonian and Egyptian kings are generated. The preponderance of the evidence shows that the Babylonian king was considered adopted, so Buber rejects this particular attempt at an Israelite distinction. Buber maintained interest in the topic, adding sources such as René Labat, *La caractère religieux de la royauté assyro-babylonienne* (1939) and C. J. Gadd, *Ideas of Divine Rule in the Ancient East* (1948) to the third edition.

45. Buber takes this example to be a refutation of those who consider the biblical verse "Mine is the land, for you are guests and sojourners with Me" (Lev. 25:23) to be a "theological utopia" that cannot truly represent a historical, political attitude towards land ownership.

46. KG 90–92. Buber considers the evidence for the South Arabian case "scanty" and delves less deeply into the scholarship here. His primary source is Nikolaus Rhodokanakis, "Altsabäische Texte" (1930) and "Die Bodenwirtschaft im alten Südarabien" (1916).

47. The term *Verweltlichung* is often translated as "secularization." Etymologically and semantically, however, the connotations of *Verweltlichung* differ from what is commonly thought of as secularization; today's German usage prefers *Säkularisierung* for that purpose. It would be anachronistic for Buber to posit that the South Arabian *malik* ceremony involved the kind of rationalization process we associate with "secularization"; rather, he means that a certain orientation toward transcendent authority is redirected toward something worldly. Modern secularization is here reconceived as continuous with its ancient form.

48. KG 91–92.

49. Ibid., 92–93.

50. This point was important enough that when Otto Eissfeldt published *Molk als Opferbegriff im Punischen und Hebräischen und das Ende des Gottes Moloch* in 1935, arguing "that the biblical *lam-molekh* has nothing to do with a *malk*-divinity, that it should be understood after the manner of the Phoenician *molk*—which signifies promise, vow, sacrifice—'as a technical term for this kind of sacrifice,' namely, for the offering of children," Buber added an eight-page footnote to the second edition making a point-by-point refutation. He followed up again in the third edition, noting subsequent scholars who had supported his position.

51. In the preface to the 1956 edition, Buber addresses the contention of the Uppsala school that the texts describing opposition between YHVH and Baal would merely refer to a familiar mythic conflict between two gods, not to two radically different ways of worshipping or to two types of gods being worshipped. Buber argues that the role of Baal in the Ras Shamra pantheon fails to account sufficiently for the biblical examples, much less to diminish the functional contrast between the *baal* and the *malk*, the leader who decides on the path for the tribe.

52. KG: "in which respect a potency is potent," 94; "not earth-magic but social-magic," 96; "the power which . . . historicizes it," 97; "sexual myths," 51.

53. Ibid., 100.

54. Buber cites numerous scriptural proof texts; perhaps the one that best encapsulates the argument is Exodus 19:4: "You have seen what I did to the Egyptians, how I bore you on eagles' wings and brought you to Me." The combination of "bore you" and "to Me" is the essential thing, and Buber sees it as supported by the placement of "He who led us/caused us to go [*molikh*] through the wilderness" as second in rank among YHVH's titles of glory, behind only "He who led us out from the land of Egypt" (Jeremiah 2:6; Amos 2:10; Psalms 136:16).

55. Ibid., 102. In the first edition, Buber also cites Micah 2:13 to demonstrate continuity into prophetic images of redemption of the relationship between kingship and literal leading: "Und so bleibt es auch in dem Bilde der künftigen Befreiung; wie der Leitwidder das Gatter des Pferchs aufstößt, so »steigt der Durchbrecher vor ihnen, / sie brechen durchs Tor, ziehn heraus, / ihr König zieht ihnen voran, / JHWH ihnen zu Häupten« (Micha 2,13)." This passage is missing from later editions and the translation.

56. In a two-page footnote, Buber disputes the view of Gerhard von Rad that the ark is of Canaanite origin and that it was conflated with the Tabernacle through a later maneuver of the priestly editor. If von Rad were right, Buber would lose the ability to link the mobile ark to the earliest form of the YHVH religion, as one more example of YHVH's essential *malk* nature. The arguments are technical, but in one Buber substantiates my claim about the targets of his polemic: he accuses von Rad of misunderstanding the significance of the terms "*bet* JHWH" and "*aron* JHWH" as genitive forms for the containment or possession of JHWH in perpetuity, "as the Philistines apparently misunderstood it, in the same way as several modern historians of religion have done so." Ibid., 187. The direct equation of a faction from within the text to a faction among modern interpreters of the text is evident.

57. This passage is an entry point for supporters of the "Kenite hypothesis," which maintains that YHVH was foreign to the Israelites before Moses, who converted them to the worship of a Kenite god appropriated from his father-in-law, Jethro, priest of Midian. In the preface to the second edition of KG, Buber devotes ten pages to refuting Walter Baumgartner, a supporter of the Kenite hypothesis, on methodological and textual grounds. Ibid., 27.

58. Ibid., 105. Buber reads this revelation in line with Freud's *Fortschritt in der Geistigkeit*, an advance in rationality and spirituality (despite Buber's low opinion of Freud's 1943 *Moses and Monotheism*). Although the secret of the name was requested under the influence of a magic-based culture that inculcated a desire for numinous power, its granting reveals the insufficiency of the magical understanding that informed that request. The name means "you do not need to conjure Me, but you cannot conjure Me either," thus constituting "the 'de-magicizing' of faith"; Ibid., 106. Such "de-magicizing" directly relates to the *malk* relationship and the kind of trust the people are asked to place in a *malk* god.

59. "Unreserved completeness," ibid., 117; "Molechization," ibid., 111.

60. KG 109. This passage marks Buber's only explicit use of I-Thou language in the book: "The uniqueness in 'monotheism' is accordingly not that of an 'exemplar,' but it is that of the Thou in the I-Thou relation so far as this is not denied in the totality of the lived life." Buber also writes here that the believing Israelite is unable "to conceive seriously concerning his divine Thou that it have only *more* power and not *the* power," and "Whoever to his King and God speaks this ardently singular Thou, cannot in the meantime remain in domains for which He is not pertinent; he must subject them all to the One." This theopoliticized "Thou" language designates a demanding, hierarchical, militant relationship, in a way it does not in the dialogical philosophy (although Buber cites *Ich und Du* here).

61. Ibid., 110. Buber uses *Kampf*; Scheimann renders it "fight" (110), "battle" (110), and "struggle" (112).

62. KG 115. The *s'mikha*, a laying on of hands that signifies an identity transfer, has several important parallels, including Moses' transfer of leadership to Joshua and the high priest's transfer of sins to the scapegoat on Yom Kippur.

63. "And they built the shrines of Baal which are in the Valley of Ben-Hinnom, where they offered up their sons and daughters *le-molekh*—when I had never commanded, or even thought that they should do such an abomination and so bring guilt on Judah." The valley of Ben-Hinnom eventually gives rise to a Jewish concept of hell.

64. KG 113.

65. Ibid., 112. This passage is full of Buber's favored theopolitical concepts, such as demarcation and the true front. One striking example is appropriate here: "We have passed from the difficult period of the World War into a period which outwardly seems more tolerable, but on closer examination proves still more difficult, a period of inner confusion. It is characteristic of this period that truth and lies, right and wrong, are mingled in its various spiritual and political movements in an almost unprecedented fashion." Buber, "Nationalism," in LTP 48.

66. Scholars commonly understand the verse to reference Exodus 13:2: "Consecrate to me every first-born; man and beast, the first issue of every womb among the Israelites is Mine."

67. KG 114.

68. My paraphrase of Buber's argument on 113 and 195n32.

69. Ibid., 116.

70. Here Buber plays into a Protestant conception of "mere" ritual embedded in contemporary *Religionswissenschaft*; he even refers to "the great Protestantism of the prophets," meaning a kind of general "religio-historical category" that could potentially apply to any tradition. Ibid., 116, 199n32.

71. Ibid., 118. My emphasis.

72. Ibid., 121.

73. Ibid., 124–125, 126, 128.

74. Ibid., 126. *Religionswissenschaft* of the time contrasted "historical" religions with "nature" religions. The latter interpret historical events according to a cosmic conception that reads them all as part of an eternal, natural movement.

75. Gerhard von Rad's challenge stems from textual evidence rather than a general theory of religion; Buber responds to him in the 1936 preface; ibid., 37.

76. Ibid., 133. Buber rejects efforts to date the Song of the Sea to make it contemporary with the Psalms, just as he rejects efforts to regard a verse in the Blessing of Moses, Deuteronomy 33:5, "There was a king in Jeshurun," as an alternative to the Sinai covenant. These arguments preserve the singularity of the Sinai covenant as a theopolitical occurrence.

77. Buber devotes a four-page footnote to refuting scholars who assign the Balaam passage (Numbers 23:21) to a postmonarchical period. He also notes that the rabbis of the Tannaitic period combined these three verses (the Song of the Sea, the Blessing of Moses, and the praise of Balaam) to form the *malkhuyot*, recited in the Rosh Hashanah liturgy.

78. KG 142–145.

79. Ibid., 144–145.

80. Ibid., 131. One might expect a different conclusion, considering the use of the book of Joshua by Zionist thinkers. Chapter 7 returns to this point. On David Ben-Gurion's use of the book of Joshua, see Rachel Havrelock, *River Jordan: The Mythology of a Dividing Line* (Chicago: University of Chicago Press, 2011), 85–105.

81. KG 146–147.

82. Ibid., 149.

83. Ibid., 158.

84. Ibid., 154–156.

85. The citation is from Karl Budde. Buber is no doubt glad to discuss a source considered early by consensus.

86. Ibid., 151.

87. Avishai Margalit, "Prophets with Honor," *New York Review of Books*, November 4, 1993; Sufrin, "History, Myth, and Divine Dialogue in Martin Buber's Biblical Commentaries," *Jewish Quarterly Review* 103.1 (Winter 2013): 74–100; Kotaro Hiraoka, "The Bible and Political Philosophy in Modern Jewish Thought: Martin Buber's Theocracy and Its Reception in an Israeli Context," *Journal of the Interdisciplinary Study of Monotheistic Religions (Isshinkyou Gakusai Kenkyu)*, 6th issue (CISMOR: Doshisha University, 2010), 53–66.

88. The debate is still live: "Gideon's refusal to rule as king is interpreted by scholars in different ways. Some see it as an early text connected to the ideology that God alone may be king; others claim that it is a later interpolation critical of the monarchy; still others suggest that . . . Gideon is simply offering a polite refusal, although the text then depicts him as a king." Adele Berlin, Marc Zvi Brettler, and Michael Fishbane, eds., *The Jewish Study Bible* (New York: Oxford University Press, 2004), 529; cf. Dennis T. Olson, "Buber, Kingship, and the Book of Judges: A Study of Judges 6–9 and 17–21," in *David and Zion: Biblical Studies in Honor of J. J. M Roberts*, eds. Bernard F. Batto and Kathryn L. Roberts (Winona Lake, IN: Eisenbrauns, 2004), 199–218; Michael D. Coogan, *The New Oxford Annotated Bible* (New York: Oxford University Press, 2001), 368–369.

89. KG 59.

90. Ibid., 61. Buber uses the German *walten* to render *mashal*, although Scheimann departs from this consistency in his English translation.

91. Ibid., 62. The *Leitwort* technique assumes that the Bible uses repetitions of roots in different forms to emphasize particular concepts; this only emerges in oral readings.

92. Ibid., 74.

93. Ibid., 73.

94. Ibid. Scheimann alternates between "commission" and "authority" to render *Auftrag*, which for Buber refers to a divine commission to a circumscribed task. To attempt to continue the commission beyond the task betrays it; to institute permanent authority forfeits true authority. In a compound, *Auftrag* has uses both nontechnical (as in *Lehrbeauftragter*, the "adjunct lecturer" position Buber held at Frankfurt) and technical (as in *Volksbeauftragter*, the "people's delegate" position Landauer held in the Bavarian Council Republic).

95. Ibid.

96. Ibid., 70–71.

97. E.g., Collins, *Introduction to the Hebrew Bible*, 208.

98. Ibid., 71.

99. Ibid. "Cannot understand," 166n9; destruction of a Baal cult, 73, 168n32; "splendid aphorism," 73.

100. Ibid., 63–64. My italics.

101. Ibid., 68.

102. Ibid., 83.

103. "Lively opposing power" is Scheimann's rendering of *widerspruchslebendige Gewalt*. I might suggest something like "the vitally contradictory force."

104. Ibid., 67–68.

105. The charge has recently been leveled at Buber himself. Olson writes that Buber's hypothesis of an antimonarchical book, made up of Judges 1–16, can be sustained only at the cost of admitting "that several parts and details of the book did not deal with kingship at all and

had to be ignored in determining the book's structure"; Olson, "Buber, Kingship and the Book of Judges," 203.

106. Ibid., 78–80. This narrative order has a philosophical-normative dimension as well, namely the priority Buber always gives to speech over writing.

107. Buber supposes that the narrative of Samuel's resistance to the people's demand for a king corresponds to a real historical tension, between groups, if not between a real judge named Samuel and the entire people; ibid., 82. He later speaks of "the religio-political group for which the 'Elohistic' narrative knows only the person-like designation 'Samuel'"; ibid., 159.

108. Ibid., 82.

109. Ibid., 80.

110. Ibid., 78.

111. Ibid., 82.

112. Ibid., 75. The phrase "commonwealth without government" refers to Wellhausen's 1900 address *Ein Gemeinwesen ohne Obrigkeit*.

113. The term recalls Immanuel Kant's "invisible church," itself taken from Lessing's "On the Education of the Human Race," and stems from Joachim de Fiore. I speculate that the reference is not coincidental, though perhaps unintentional.

114. Ibid., 83–84.

115. Cf. Landauer's exegesis of Étienne de La Boétie in *Revolution*, to the effect that after one generation surrenders its freedom, subsequent generations no longer remember it.

116. Putting words into the redactor's mouth, Buber uses *Anarchie* here in a negative sense, similarly to how he contrives an accusation for the monarchical authors to hurl at the theocratic authors. Buber uses *Anarchie* negatively in his own voice to describe the Jotham fable, when he contrasts the *anarchistisch* reading of the fable with the *unsichtbare Obrigkeit* it actually advocates. However, this instance is outweighed by Buber's positive uses of the term, especially when he speaks of the "anarchic psychic foundation" (*anarchischer Seelengrund*) on which the ancient Israelites erect their theocracy; ibid., 138, 161.

117. Ibid., 161.

118. Ibid., 162. *Christos kuriou* means "anointed of the lord." The shift to Greek at the conclusion, at the moment the partisans of the monarchy betray the theocracy, is no accident. It recalls the position of *Kingship of God* as the first in the *Das Kommende* trilogy, focusing on messianism and "the christological question."

119. Ibid., 84. *Politeia* is the Greek title for the work of Plato usually translated as *Republic*.

PART II

THE ANOINTED AND THE PROPHET: THEOPOLITICS IN ISRAEL FROM EXODUS TO EXILE

The Lord has chosen to abide in a thick cloud; I have now built for You a stately House, a place where You may dwell forever.

—1 Kings 8:12–13

From Moses to Samuel is only a step in the history of faith, whereas from Samuel to Solomon, the son of his protégé, is a long way.

—Martin Buber

BUBER NEVER FULFILLED his aim to follow *Kingship of God* with a trilogy on *Das Kommende*, "The Coming One" of Israelite messianism. He abandoned work on the second part of the trilogy, *Der Gesalbte* (*The Anointed*), after the Nazis shut down the Schocken Press, and he did not take it up again upon his 1938 emigration to Palestine.[1] However, Buber did end up producing a biblical trilogy of sorts. *The Prophetic Faith* and *Moses* are identical in genre to *Kingship of God* among Buber's biblical studies; although they do not share its biographical genesis, they do show a relatively relaxed scholarly attitude and a greater freedom of expression. In part 2 of this book, I argue that they also reiterate, develop, and clarify the central concern of *Kingship of God*: theopolitics. Theopolitics is not just an incidental concern in what are otherwise works of edifying religious commentary; rather, it is the unifying theme that combines with the historical-critical genre to render these works into one integral whole, in contrast to the anthological form in which Buber's commentary is so often presented by English-language publishers.

One way to emphasize the theopolitical nature of *Moses* and *The Prophetic Faith* would be to enumerate the individual topics they share with *Kingship of God*. For example, all three examine the matter of the Divine Name and its revelation of YHVH as a God who descends to the earth at his pleasure, manifesting where and when he wills, while also promising to be with Israel in its trouble. The

Song of Deborah is repeatedly mined for its "primordial" information about the Israelite faith in the direct kingship of YHVH, and the contrast between YHVH and the Baalim is drawn repeatedly. Buber retreads all this ground, I suspect, so that each book may stand alone as containing the rudiments of his overall view. To avoid such repetition myself, I focus on what each work uniquely adds to the theopolitical picture and on ways they clarify matters touched on but left undeveloped in *Kingship of God*.

Although *The Anointed* came first chronologically, having been written in German in the mid-1930s, while *Moses* and *The Prophetic Faith* were first published in Hebrew in the mid-1940s, I treat them in their biblical order, in accordance with the project for *The Biblical Faith* that Buber planned with Rosenzweig even before thinking of *Das Kommende*: *Moses* first, the paradigm and founder of the biblical faith and its archetypal expression; *The Anointed* second, to follow up on the tension-filled conclusion of *Kingship of God* and to show how Buber deals with the transition from divine to human kingship; and *The Prophetic Faith* last, as the monarchy calls forth opposition from the prophets and the theme of subsequent Israelite history takes shape. I thus draw the sequence of my discussion from the works themselves, in which the triad Moses-Samuel-Jeremiah serves to illuminate the continuity of the theopolitical vision that Buber considers the essence of the project that goes under the name "Israel."

4 Between Pharaohs and Nomads

Moses

The Lord makes a distinction between Egypt and Israel.
—Exodus 11:7

The tradition of the pyramid faces that of the campfire.
—Martin Buber

Introduction

Buber's treatment of Moses reveals the extent to which he sees the people Israel as both a distinct historical phenomenon and a transhistorical theopolitical project.[2] Moses is presented as visionary, founder, and revolutionary paradigm: many of the obstacles he faces are perennial. Moses foresees a certain kind of life for his people but also expects a struggle to achieve it. In this sense, Buber's Moses is a militant, defending his theopolitical vision from the Egyptian oppressor and from idolaters within his own camp. These struggles illuminate what Buber sees as essential to Moses' vision. Just as in *Kingship of God*, Buber polemicizes against those scholars who would foreclose the theopolitical possibilities that he desires to keep open.

Organizing his text around the idea of Moses as both an effective revolutionary and a witness to a personal divine encounter, Buber sets himself against several competing tendencies in Moses scholarship. First, he opposes any view of Moses as primarily concerned with cultic purity, whether as priest or legislator; he concurs with critical scholarship in regarding the priestly code as almost entirely post-Mosaic. Second, there is the notorious viewpoint represented by Sigmund Freud (whose *Moses and Monotheism* is dismissed by Buber in a single footnote), wherein Moses is the product of Egyptian culture who molds the Israelites into a neo-Egyptian, Aten-worshipping splinter group.[3] Finally, those who might agree with Buber's depiction of Moses as revolutionary raise the question of revolutionary ethics; here Buber rejects any notion of a "red terror of God" against Egypt or of Joshua as violent enforcer of Moses' edicts.[4] However, he cannot completely absolve Moses of complicity in means destructive of his ends; this contributes to what Buber calls "the tragedy of Moses."

On Methodology and Radicalism

In one approach to historical-critical biblical scholarship, the words "conservative" and "radical" denote the degree to which methods and conclusions diverge from the Hebrew Bible's self-representation.[5] In this view, *Moses* is the most "conservative," perhaps even reactionary, of Buber's biblical writings, even though he promises us an "unprejudiced critical investigation, dependent neither on the religious tradition nor on the theories of scholarly turns of thought."[6] He intends to separate older from newer passages, to isolate original reports from later accretions, and to hypothesize about the "historical nucleus" of those reports, which to his mind stem from even more ancient oral traditions. But unlike in *Kingship of God* or *The Prophetic Faith*, where he deals with the "historical books" of the Bible, *Moses* is concerned primarily with the Pentateuch—the five books of Moses. Buber's interest in salvaging historical information through inspired interpretation of legends and sagas thus takes on a more contentious, rearguard cast.[7] While *Moses* contains several footnotes in which Buber battles regnant scholarly opinion, he largely confines his polemics to one methodological chapter, "Saga and History."

Even readers lacking expertise in biblical scholarship can discern that there is no necessary connection between historical-critical "radicalism" and political radicalism.[8] Buber proves this by placing his "conservative" faith in the possibility of gleaning historical information about Moses from the Pentateuch in the service of his "radical" theopolitics. What he says about Moses can usually be read as a microcosm of what he says elsewhere about Judaism. Even when engaged in typical historical-critical moves, as when he accepts the proof that six hundred thousand Israelites could not possibly have left Egypt, he neutralizes the importance of this fact by claiming that "the inner history of Mankind can be grasped most easily in the actions and experiences of small groups."[9] Lest others perceive incongruity between his method and his theopolitical conclusions, Buber justifies his method in a political way:

> The historical song and the historical saga exist as spontaneous forms, not dependent upon instructions, of a popular preservation by word of mouth of "historical" events; such events, that is, as are vital in the life of the tribe. . . . [T]he saga is the predominant method of preserving the memory of what happens, *as long as tribal life is stronger than state organization*. As soon as the latter becomes more powerful . . . the unofficial popular forms are overshadowed through the development of an annalistic keeping of records by order of the governing authority.[10]

Thus Buber simultaneously affirms that sagas predate annals, an assumption that enables venturesome dating of legendary narrative texts, and that this sequence is itself bound up with transition from the anarchic, nomadic, tribal way of life (and the acceptance of the kingship of God) to the sedentary, agricultural, nation-state way (and the sovereignty of the human monarchy). The social transitions that the Bible narrates thus affect the editorial composition of the Bible itself, a fact long emphasized by critical scholarship.

In what follows I trace the implications of Buber's intertwined methodological "conservatism" and theopolitical radicalism through the examination of two of the main struggles he presents for Moses and his project. The first is the contrast with Egypt; the second, the contrast with what Buber calls "the contradiction," namely misunderstanding and idolatry on the part of the people. Together, these form a common Buberian trope: the "narrow ridge" between two abysses, which must be walked by the one who hears the divine call and seeks to answer it.

Against Egypt

The contemporary German philosopher Peter Sloterdijk sums up a discussion of Régis Debray on the Exodus as follows:

> The myth of exodus is tied to that of total mobilization, in which an entire people transforms itself into a foreign, movable thing that abducts itself. At that moment all things are re-evaluated in terms of their transportability—at the risk of having to leave behind everything that is too heavy for human carriers. The first re-evaluation of all values therefore concerned weight. Its main victims were the heavy gods of the Egyptians, whose immovable stone bodies prevented them from travelling. The people of Israel were able to change into a theophoric entity from that point on . . . because it had succeeded in recoding God from the medium of stone to that of the scroll.[11]

Sloterdijk here captures one of the primary concerns of Buber's *Moses*: the total contrast between Israel and Egypt, in which Israel carries out a revaluation of Egypt's values, especially the relationship between mobility and divinity.[12]

Buber thus stands in a long tradition of Moses commentary, critically assessed by Egyptologist Jan Assmann, in which "'Egypt' stands not only for 'idolatry' but also for a rejected past. The Exodus is a story of emigration and conversion, of transformation and renovation, of stagnation and progress, and of past and future. Egypt represents the old, while Israel represents the new."[13] Assmann's controversial argument, especially his claim that the Exodus story creates for the first time in history a so-called Mosaic distinction between true and false religion, and as such could be held responsible for substantial intolerance and violence, has formed a framework for subsequent discussion of the relationship between Moses and Israel and Egypt, in history and memory.[14] Buber himself rejects one of Assmann's central categories, "monotheism," as irrelevant to his project in *Moses*: "It is a fundamental error to register the faith with which I deal as simple 'Monotheism.'"[15] As Paul Yorck von Wartenberg wrote to Buber's teacher Wilhelm Dilthey, such categories as monotheism, polytheism, pantheism, and so on "constitute only the outline of an intellectual attitude; and only a formal projection even for this." Whether one thinks there is one god or many does not determine how one seeks to fulfill one's obligations in relationship to that god. Divisions within "so-called monotheism" can be far more important than the boundary separating all monotheism from all polytheism.[16]

To substantiate this point, Buber argues that "The universal sun-god of the imperialist [*imperialistischen,* אימפריאליסטי] 'Monotheism' of Amenhotep IV is incomparably more close to the national sun-god of the ancient Egyptian Pantheon than to the God of early Israel, which some have endeavored to derive from him."[17] Buber's use of the term "imperialist" in the description of Akhenaten's religion points to the first element of the Israel-Egypt contrast, the political. Assmann, summarizing the work of the pioneering Egyptologist James Henry Breasted, notes that "the concept of a universal god as the religious counterpart of political imperialism originated in Heliopolis . . . while the Egyptian armies were conquering the world, the Heliopolitan priests were drawing the concomitant theological conclusions."[18] Eventually, Akhenaten radicalized the Heliopolitan concept of a universal god, "giving it the character of an intolerant monotheism." The intolerance of this monotheism is manifest for Assmann in what he calls its "untranslatability": the name of the monotheist god cannot be exchanged for the names of the most-high gods of neighbor nations. But cosmotheism, which he seems to prefer, is itself rooted in a cosmopolitan-cum-imperialist political project. Assmann's ancient gods may be translatable as part of a general cultural background shared by different peoples, but their human political masters, kings and emperors, are not. They demand exclusive allegiance from their subjects.[19] For Israel, by contrast, it is political allegiance that is exclusively and directly owed to the invisible king. All the political leaders of the nations round about are insignificant; it is they who are interchangeable—translatable.[20] It is telling that Assmann argues that "Breasted's correlation of monotheism and imperialism echoes the political theology of Eusebius of Caesarea, who pointed out to Constantine the correspondence between terrestrial and celestial monarchy, that is, the Roman Empire and Christian monotheism."[21] In addition to ignoring the many centuries in which the Roman Empire conquered without being Christian, while Christians did little conquering, this leap from Akhenaten to Eusebius disregards the life of Moses himself, and the contrast that might be drawn along political lines between Egypt and Moses' vision for Israel. This is precisely Buber's focus, and he too marshals Breasted to his cause.

In a chapter called "Israel in Egypt," Buber correlates the agricultural and architectural innovations that made Egypt "the starting point of what we call civilization." The comprehensive system of dams and dykes that enabled the Egyptians to harness the power of the Nile, a massive effort to regulate nature for human ends, familiarized human beings "with the character of a perfectly organized duty of collective work, which ascribed no greater value to the foot of the living human being than to the water-wheel which that foot turned." This pervasive impersonality, however, also required absolute hierarchy: "As the pyramid culminates in its apex, so the Egyptian state culminates of almost mathematical necessity in the Crown, the 'red flame,' which is addressed in the pyramid texts as living Godhead. . . . [E]verybody received from the King the function which made him a man."[22]

This combination of hierarchy and anonymity is compared with examples both ancient and modern. In contrast to ancient China, "no less conservative" than Egypt according to Buber, no civil society was allowed to flourish alongside the all-encompassing Egyptian state. Buber cites Breasted's "fine book," *The Dawn of Conscience*, to support the claim that the first ideas of social justice developed in Egypt, but he notes that this could be only a hierarchical, centralized justice, leaving no room for individual freedom: "The perfect economic and political centralization which characterized Ancient Egypt has led certain students to speak of it in terms of State socialism [*Staatssozialismus*/סוציאליזם של מדינה]."[23] From the many possible contrasts to the striking anachronism "state socialism" here (e.g., free-market capitalism, fascism), we should not be surprised that Buber presents the "Israelite" critique of Egyptian institutions in terms of libertarian-socialism (i.e., anarchism). This plays out on the micro level of specific Israelite versus Egyptian social practices, as well on the broad civilizational level, where the sedentary agricultural and architectural society opposes the organization of the nomadic tribe.

The concept of a civilizational contrast between sedentary and nomadic societies was familiar to Buber from his studies in comparative religion, especially in the fields of archaeology and anthropology. The discourse around this contrast is always freighted with implied normative assumptions, even if these are not always framed in an explicitly political way. Buber claims that mutual distaste, even revulsion, exists between the two types of societies. From the perspective of the great civilizations, the nomad is dangerous, threatening, wild, and unpredictable. Buber quotes a Sumerian hymn that refers to the Amorite of the western hills, "who knows no submission . . . who has no house in his lifetime," and an Egyptian document that describes "the miserable stranger. . . . He does not dwell in the same spot, his feet are always wandering. From the days of Horus (i.e., since time immemorial) he battles, he does not conquer, and is not conquered." As Buber puts it, "Here can be heard the deep animosity of the settled State form of life towards the unstable elements of the wilderness, yet also the knowledge of their indomitability."[24] In the language of the great civilization, such people are commonly given a name that means "detached, dissociated, not-belonging." These designations, according to Buber, are not ethnic or clan related.[25] Both Semites and non-Semites, for example, were included among the Habiru people of the regions stretching from southern Mesopotamia through Anatolia to Syria,

Palestine, and Egypt. Rather, these are polemical terms expressing the discom-
fort of the settled civilizations toward those who wander outside.

The nomads are also seen as threatening. The refusal of structured hierarchy, characteristic of state-based civilizations, grounds the nomadic view; Buber
quotes the historian Eduard Meyer, who describes their disdain for "the peasant
tied to his clods, and the cowardly townsfolk, who seek to protect themselves behind walls and who serve a lord as slaves."[26] The conflict between these societies
is mischaracterized if described as occurring between a more and a less advanced
"stage of development" (rhetoric that serves the "civilized"). Rather, at issue is a
perennial conflict between two principles, and therefore between two options:

> The stable oasis society, however, with its State trends and closed culture,
> fights against a fluctuating cultural element which, its small units linked by
> a strong collective solidarity, organizes itself in closer tribal association solely
> for war or cult activities, and recognizes personal authority solely in so far as
> the bearer of the latter evinces it by his direct effect.... Here the dynastic prin-
> ciple faces the charismatic one; a thoroughly centralist principle faces one of
> primitive federalism. State law faces tribal law; and beyond this a civilization
> established in rigid forms faces a fluid element which rarely condenses into a
> comprehensive structural form of life and work. The tradition of the pyramid
> faces that of the campfire. It is precisely when the nomads or semi-nomads
> receive the alien State form in their power, and take possession of leadership,
> that they fall most rapidly under its sway.[27]

Buber sees Israel and Egypt as exemplifying these types.

Egypt, then, represents rigidity, and Israel fluidity. Egypt committed itself
absolutely to "the tendency to persist," which was "operative in Egypt with a
degree of exclusiveness which has been achieved by no other civilization. In its
double expression—the wisdom of knowing what should persist, and the art of
ensuring that it should persist—it produced a gruesomely consistent world in
which there was every kind of ghost; but in which each ghost carried out the
function assigned to it."[28] Egypt is thus the settled civilization par excellence, as
its entire culture is dedicated to the principle of immobility; its greatest achievements, the pyramids, testify to this. To make the case that Israel represents the
other type, Buber draws on the well-known scholarly identification of Abraham
"the Hebrew" in Genesis with the migrant Habiru.

Buber does not identify the Israelites with the Habiru, because they comprised many non-Semitic elements and only part of the Semites. But his focus
on the Habiru provides an interesting counterexample to Assmann's focus on
the Hyksos. Assmann imagines that the traumatic invasion and rule of Lower
Egypt by the Hyksos, an ancient Semitic tribe, left a scar in the cultural memory
of the Egyptians. The memory of this event later combined with the repressed
trauma of the heretical rule of the monotheist Pharaoh, Akhenaten, to form
Egyptian legends about the expulsion of foreign tribes who worshipped strange

gods and brought misery and disease to Egypt. These legends lacked historical accuracy, since the historical Hyksos apparently conformed to Egyptian customs, their kings styling themselves sons of the sun god; in contrast, Akhenaten was a domestic phenomenon, an eruption of intolerant monotheism from within Egyptian culture itself. However, Assmann hypothesizes that in later years when Egyptians had forgotten these particulars and had learned of the customs of their neighbors the Israelites, history and legend became mixed, resulting in the kind of anti-Israelite, counter-Exodus narratives reported by Strabo, Manetho, and others. Whatever the merits of Assmann's "mnemohistorical" hypothesis, he combines, as two possible historical precedents for the activity of Moses (in both the Egyptian imagination and the reality of history), the actions of two political rulers, representatives of the principle of settled civilization.

Buber reaches back to the Habiru migrants. For him it is not ultimately important whether there is a real etymological connection between *Habiru* and *Ivri* (Hebrew), or what these terms mean in themselves (options include "unsettled," "rovers," "comrades," "those who come from beyond"); what matters is that the archaeological reports of Habiru activity match the "human type" exemplified by Abraham and his descendants.[29] In negotiating with the Philistine king, Abraham says that the Elohim, the divine forces, made him stray from his father's house; Buber links this to what he believes to be the oldest language from the prayer for the first fruits, *arami obed avi* ("A wandering Aramean was my father"; Deuteronomy 26:5). Thus Buber maintains the connection between Abraham and Moses, now along the lines of the cultural-political struggle between nomadism and settlement. Abraham can serve as the proper precedent for Moses, the man who "came back to his forefathers by way of his flight" to Midian, where he resumed the seminomadic shepherd life his people lost under enslavement: "A man of the enslaved nation, but the only one not enslaved together with them, had returned to the free and keen air of his forebears."[30] The theme of the conflict between the settled and the nomadic thus finds expression in Moses' own biography.

While Buber seems to prefer nomadic to settled civilizations, he does not valorize nomadic life per se. His attitude towards it can be quite detached:

> They seemingly . . . wander to and fro in the wilderness with their flocks of sheep and goats, they hunt wherever they can do so; they conduct a fleeting form of cultivation with primitive tools wherever they find suitable sites; they pitch their tents near towns with which they exchange their produce; but they also endeavor to establish themselves more securely. . . . If a warrior band cannot advance on its own, it temporarily becomes a mercenary body for some party waging war. If it is broken up, the individual members gladly accept service in public works as overseers, scribes, etc.; they are given preference on account of their qualifications and achievements, and rise to leading positions. What this type of life requires is a "particular combination of the pastoral with

the military virtues"; but it also calls for a peculiar mixture of adaptability and the urge to independence. The civilizations into which they penetrate are their opportunity; they are also their danger.[31]

Missing from this account are the usual signs of normative privilege within a Buberian schema. There is no claim that life within nomadic bands especially encourages I-Thou relationships, that families and clans combine into larger confederations to form a *Gemeinschaft der Gemeinschaften*, that such life lends itself to the greater development of human capacities. We should take this as a sign that Moses still has something to contribute.

Nomads believe in their lifestyle; Buber calls it, following the anthropologist Marcel Mauss, "a kind of faith." They find settlement both alluring and threatening. They may seek control of the settlement, even assuming positions of power in settled societies if possible. But this provides for the tribe at the expense of that which defined it. This is what Buber thinks happened to the Hyksos. Moses and his mission offer one possible resolution of this ambivalence: settlement without rule, without masters, except for the invisible One who makes the settlement possible through his emancipatory action on behalf of the people.[32]

The broad civilizational contrast denoted by the Israel-Egypt dyad has its counterpart in innumerable individual institutions and practices that model the contrast in microcosm. The way Moses appoints Joshua as his successor is one example. According to Buber, "It is entirely in harmony with the nomadic and semi-nomadic style of life that Moses should by choice educate his spiritual son and successor" rather than his biological son.[33] Although Buber is ambivalent about Joshua—both the book and the man—this is no recommendation for the dynastic alternative of the settled states. A second example is land tenure practice. In Egypt, "the King . . . exercises a strict, unremittent supervision over all landed property, so that all landed property merges in that of the King. 'The land,' as the Bible expresses it in full accordance with the historical reality, 'became Pharaoh's'; and every worker-family was left with just as much of the yield of the soil as was required for bare subsistence."[34] In contrast to this, one could easily imagine a system of private property that empowers smallholders to invest and undertake enterprises through the promise of profit. Buber hints at this possibility in his discussion of the ideal vision of Israel in the proclamation of Balaam: "Moses had wished for such an Israel, he had desired life, marriage and property to be secure, and envy to be eradicated among the people."[35]

This quasi-Lockean formulation is undermined, however, by Buber's eventual description of the Mosaic alternative to Egyptian land-tenure practices. As a nomad by tradition and commitment, Moses would have had trouble imagining the transformations involved in switching to agricultural life. At Kadesh, however, on the verge of crossing into the Promised Land, the people began sustained farming. At this point, Moses "would have had to start out from his basic idea, that of the real and direct rule of God; which would necessarily have led to the postulate that God owns all land." The Sabbatical is one expression of this conviction; Moses "conceived the idea of overcoming the continually-expanding social harm forever by ensuring the restoration, in each ensuing Sabbatical year, 'of the normal situation of the national community of Israel after all the deviations and wrong developments of the preceding six years.'"[36] God's ultimate ownership of the land facilitates the redistribution of that land after seven years of private accumulation, thus preventing any permanent class structure from developing. This harks back to the discussion in *Kingship of God*, where Buber argued against the claim that Leviticus 25:23 ("Mine is the land, for you are only guests and sojourners with Me") had to be a late text and a "theological utopia" rather than reflecting an actual ancient view that could have become manifest in political practice. The ultimate consequence of this view is that "private property is feudal tenure"—there is ultimately no right to hold property that cannot be undone after a number of years by redistribution, since the true owner of the land has stated that this is how he wishes to dispose of it.[37] Indeed, Buber sees the Sabbatical year, whose purpose it was "to lead to a renewal of the organization of the society, in order to start afresh," as having the status of "a renewal of the Covenant" itself.

For Moses, social law and religious vision are inseparable:

> Above all this there hovers the consecration to YHVH, to whom the earth belongs and who, by means of that earth, nourishes His dwellers and sojourners. They ought not to thrust one another aside, they ought not to impoverish one another permanently or enslave one another; they must again and ever again become equal to one another in their freedom of person and free relation to the soil; they must rest together and enjoy the usufruct together; the times dedicated to God make them free and equal again and again, as they were at the beginning. The land is given to them in common in order that in it and from it they may become a true national Community, a "Holy People" . . . in order that they might become a *berakah*, a blessing power.[38]

The gift of the land is a reminder to the Israelites not simply of the author of their prosperity, to whom they owe gratitude, but also of the purposes for which the giver of the land intends it to be used. If they honor these purposes, their activity will serve as a "blessing power" to all the other peoples of the earth, who will have the opportunity to observe justice in action. If they fail, they will desecrate the name of God and dishonor the mission for which they were brought into existence as a people.

Just as the civilizational contrast between Israel and Egypt is illustrated through concrete social practices, so is it illustrated by contrasting ideas and concepts. The concept of miracle stands out here as exemplary. In his chapter "The Wonder on the Sea," Buber discusses the miracle of the splitting of the waters and the drowning of Pharaoh's army. The discussion is almost self-parody in its naturalism; Buber wants simultaneously to dismiss the simplistic notion of supernatural intervention while preserving the possibility that Exodus 15:21 reflects a real historical memory: "Sing to YHVH for He has raised Himself high, horse and charioteer He flung into the sea."[39] But this is not the core of the discussion. Far more important than what happened is how the people perceived it. This perception "had a decisive influence . . . on the development of the element 'Israel' in the religious history of humanity." An event in history is perceived as an act of God; it inspires an abiding astonishment, which cannot be neutralized by any knowledge or explanation of the event's causal chain. "Any causal explanation only deepens the wonder." In fact, Buber argues, the miracle can be "fully included in the objective, scientific nexus of nature and history"; however, at the same time, the meaning of the event destroys that very nexus for the one who experiences it, "and explodes the fixity of the fields of experience named 'Nature' and 'History.' Miracle is simply what happens; in so far as it meets people who are capable of receiving it, or prepared to receive it, as miracle." The attribution of the miracle to God is not an "explanation" in the fashion of scientific cause and effect, because unlike scientific explanation it does not do away with wonder. Rather, the entire cause-and-effect system is revealed in its ordinary operation to be the sphere of this same power, and the one who recognizes this must recognize that power at work on every occasion, in every time and every place. "That is the religion of Moses, the man who experienced the futility of magic, who learned to recognize the demonic as one of the forms by which the divine functions, and who saw how all the gods of Egypt vanished at the blows of the One, and that is religion generally, as far as it is reality." Buber deduces a final theopolitical conclusion from this account of miracle: "Whoever recognizes the one effective power on every given occasion must desire that the whole life of the community should be made subject to that power." Here, the *melekh* is revealed as leader of the people and the world at the same time, and the Song of the Sea closes with the proclamation that YHVH *yimlokh*, "will reign," for all time.[40]

Moreover, the miracle is an event in time, not an object in space. It is preserved in memory and later in text, but not in physical form as a mummy. By its very nature, then, it opposes Egyptian staticism. Thus, the Enlightenment thinkers, whom Assmann praises for attempting to substitute "natural religion" for the Mosaic distinction, were wrong when they suggested that miracles were merely a condescending, magical "accommodation" offered by Moses to a people too primitive to understand his true message.[41] Buber adheres to the distinction between nature religions and history religions; Judaism for him is without doubt a history religion. YHVH is *melekh* of both nature and history, but the two are not of equal importance. It is the liberatory and emancipatory action of YHVH, taught as miracle by Moses and received as such by the people Israel, that creates this people for the first time and brings it together as the people of YHVH. Thus the Israel-Egypt opposition, conceived as a contrast between dynamism and freedom on the one hand versus staticism and hierarchy on the other, reproduces itself here at the level of theology.

Finally, it is worth recalling that for Buber, Moses' entire mission, as embodied in his most enduring theopolitical contribution, namely the conclusion of the covenant between God and Israel, can be represented as a critique of Egypt. This critique is summarized in the so-called eagle speech of Exodus 19:4–6: "You have seen what I did unto the Egyptians, and how I bore you on eagles' wings, and brought you to Me. / Now therefore, if you will indeed hearken unto my voice, and keep my covenant, then you shall be mine own *segula* [treasure] from among all the peoples; for all the Earth is Mine. / And you shall be a kingdom of priests and a holy nation."[42] Buber devotes an eight-page chapter to these three verses, which express as no other text "the theo-political idea of Moses, namely, his conception of the relation between YHVH and Israel, which could not be other than political in its realistic character, yet which starts from the God and not from the nation in the political indication of goal and way." The eagle hovers over the nest to teach his young how to fly; the bird picks up one that needs special attention and carries it in his pinions until it can dare the flight itself. "Here we have election, deliverance and education all in one."[43] The word *segula*, rendered in many translations as "treasure," Buber interprets as "a possession which is withdrawn from the general family property because one individual has a special relation to it and a special claim upon it."[44] Such is the people Israel among the family of nations, *if* they fulfill the Covenant ("It is impossible to express more clearly and unequivocally that the liberation from Egypt does not secure the people of Israel any monopoly over their God"). What is established here is "a prestate divine state": the *mamlekhet kohanim*, the kingdom of priests, who constitute the new sphere of the rule of the Lord, are those who attend him—his retinue, but extended to encompass the entire kingdom, each individual in an identically close relationship to their King. The *goy kadosh*, the holy nation, suggests that it is not the behavior of the individual members of the nation that is most important, but "the behavior of the national body as such. Only when the nation with all its substance and all its functions, with legal forms and institutions, with the whole organization of its internal and external relationships, dedicates itself to YHVH as its Lord, as its *melekh*, does it become His holy people; only then is it a holy people."[45]

The historical reality that Buber takes to lie behind these texts is a "challenge offered by the Hebrew tribes, departing from Egypt into freedom, to Pharaonism." The people, freed from slavery, acclaim a leader who refuses leadership. Their freedom is God's freedom; God is their king. Buber then recapitulates the theopolitical thesis of *Kingship of God*, this time placing a greater emphasis on justice and law:

Historically considered, this means the rule of the spirit through the persons charismatically induced and authorized as the situation warrants; its rule on the basis of the just laws issued in the name of the spirit. The entire conception of this royal Covenant, which aims at being all-embracing, is only possible when and because the God who enters into the Covenant is just and wishes to introduce a just order into the human world. . . . The just law of the just *Melek* is there in order to banish the danger of "Bedouin" anarchy, which threatens all freedom with God. The unrestrained instinct of independence of the Semitic nomads, who do not wish to permit anybody to rise above them and to impose his will upon them, finds its satisfaction in the thought that all the Children of Israel are required to stand in the same direct relation to YHVH; but it achieves restraint through the fact that YHVH himself is the promulgator and guardian of the law. Both together, the kingship of God as the power of His law over human beings and as the joy of the free in His rule, achieve expression in the ideal image of Israel which is found in an old lyric utterance attributed to the heathen prophet Balaam: "One beholds no trouble in Jacob and *melek* jubilation is in him." YHVH the "Present One," is really present among his people, who therefore proclaim him as their *Melek*.[46]

This whirl of prepositions offers many insights into Buber's theopolitics. Rule of the spirit, through the charisma, on the basis of the just laws, which are over human beings, who will not allow any other mere humans to be above them or lay things upon them; freedom is with God, the joy of the free in his rule. The relation of overness and aboveness is clearly reserved for YHVH and prohibited to humans, but this does not mean that the relation to YHVH is defined only by overness and aboveness. It is also a with-relation, and an in-relation, specifically when the subject of freedom is mentioned. The freedom of YHVH makes possible and guarantees the freedom of Israel, and thus the rule of YHVH has just freedom as its telos.

Against the Contradiction

Just as important as the struggle with Egypt is the one between Moses and those within Israel who resist his vision and program. Occasionally, these tendencies manifest as simply a continuation of the struggle with Egypt, a failure to convey his vision. At other times, however, unique challenges arise as a result of Moses' success. These challenges outwardly conform to the new order by accepting the rule of YHVH, and because of this they may be even more dangerous than the desire to return to the fleshpots of Egypt. Buber often sees such misunderstandings as a failure to grasp the meaning of freedom with God, the difficult dialectic of the yoke of heaven.

The general unfaithfulness of the people Israel is manifest in both their stubborn resistance and their spectacular bursts of rebellion. The "murmuring" in the desert stands for the "stiff-necked" nature of the people, while the golden calf and the revolt of Korach are indications of deep errors.[47] Moses wages "the primal fight from which everything subsequent, including the great protests of the prophets against a cult emptied of intention, can find only its starting-point. . . . The people wish for a tangible security, they wish to 'have' the God, they wish to have Him at their disposal through a sacral system; and it is this security which Moses cannot and must not grant them."[48]

The biblical narrative singles out the desert generation as particularly wicked, a great irony given its status as the generation of the Exodus, which witnessed the miracles and was privileged to receive the Torah. Yet these miracles seem to make little impression on them; scarcely days after YHVH performs wonders for them, they begin to "murmur" against Moses and to indulge in nostalgia for Egypt. This unrest has a special theopolitical status that distinguishes it from the sins of later generations, which place the people in opposition to the later prophets. According to Buber, the prophet arises first and foremost to chastise the monarch, the wielder of power, and only secondarily to chastise the people for going astray. The prophets are powerless and officeless spokesmen of the spirit, standing against institutional power. Moses, however, wields power himself, "though his power is a doubtful one. He is the leader who demands no dominion for himself." Buber traces this attitude to Moses' Midianite background, which stresses the nomadic rather than the settled approach to leadership. But Moses adds his own great mission, "the passionate wish to make a serious political issue of the faith in the earthly dominion of the god." As in *Kingship of God*, this wish gives rise to the noninstitutional institution of charismatic leadership, in which the leader led by God resists the temptation of dynastic power. But the charismatic idea is easily misunderstood, and Buber makes it more explicit in *Moses* than in *Kingship of God* that the cause of this misunderstanding is the people's longing for visible signs of victory and success, which Moses opposes in a "never-interrupted, never-despairing struggle":

> Only as long as the leader is successful is he regarded as equipped with the authority of Heaven. As soon as something goes wrong, or unsatisfactory circumstances ensue, people are swift to detect a rift between him and the God, to whom appeal is made against his unworthy because unlucky representative; if indeed they do not prefer to draw the conclusion from the mishap that it is impossible to depend on the favor of YHVH. . . .
>
> Always and everywhere in the history of religion the fact that God is identified with success is the greatest obstacle to a steadfast religious life.[49]

In their impatience, the "murmurers" assume at the slightest negative turn that Moses, and by extension they themselves, have lost divine favor. The "stiff-neckedness" of Israel, for Buber, is nothing other than the "permanent passion for success." The tragedy is that this passion emerges from the very same "unbridled craving for independence" that refuses to submit to any man.

This murmuring, then, is deeply rooted. It may be that the other forms of rebellion derive from it. All three can and do recur, but the underlying passion for victory and the rejection of suffering are constant, while the others come in waves. Perhaps this is why Moses' response to the murmuring is different from his response to the sin of the calf or to the rebellion of Korach. In a speech filled with "words that cannot be surpassed, words of the most intimate knowledge and the most intimate daring," Moses addresses God: "Indeed, a people stiff of neck are they—forgive then our transgression!" For Buber, there are two ways to understand this plea. The first emphasizes the people's weakness and inability to change: "Where and when a person or a people are just what they are, nothing, so to say, is left except for God to forgive them."[50] The second, however, points to the hidden dialectic of theopolitics, and to its tragedy. Hidden deep within their very stiff-neckedness, there is "a kind of secret virtue, which only rarely comes to light. This is the holy audacity which enables the people to do their deeds of faith as a people. Here Moses and Israel become one, and he genuinely represents his people before YHVH." What we have here is a restatement of the theopolitical paradox: the same stubbornness and inability to endure suffering that leads to the rejection of God's kingship also allows the people to achieve great things.[51] It is this audacity that allows Moses to speak to God in the way that he does, as no one else since Abraham.

Turning to the episode of the golden calf, Buber must address a different kind of rebellion against Moses. In this case, the Bible relates that Moses react-ed by "reduc[ing] all resistance," as Buber euphemistically puts it. He begins by emphasizing the connection between the golden calf story in Exodus and the section of the book of Kings (1 Kings 12:28) in which Jeroboam, the new king of the northern tribes, erects golden statues of bulls at the entrances to Bethel and Dan. There he proclaims the same words as Aaron: "These are thy Elohim, O Israel, who brought thee out of the Land of Egypt!" Surprisingly, however, Buber maintains the antiquity of the Exodus tradition rather than regard the period of Jeroboam as the source of the Exodus passage.[52] He accepts that the passage in Kings is tendentious and intended to portray the northern kingdom in a negative light; he nonetheless doubts that Jeroboam really intended to worship other gods or even to represent YHVH in the form of a bull. If he constructed bulls, Buber said, they would serve the same purpose as the oxen that carried the basin in Solomon's Temple: they are god bearers, not gods. They are meant to create the impression of an empty seat, to be filled by the god when he chooses to visit. The problem arises when this purpose is misunderstood, and the sculptures are taken for gods or even representations of God. Similarly, the worship of the calf could not have been intended for a god other than YHVH; an explanation must thus be provided for the violent reaction to the people's intention to represent YHVH corporeally, especially before the delivery of the Decalogue.

Buber argues for the historicity of the calf episode by tying it to the origin of the Ark of the Covenant. The ark crystallizes two major issues related to the calf: the question of guidance (leadership) and the location of the throne of the invisible king. Buber postulates that the ark was the product of Moses' own imagination, synthesizing elements from the surrounding areas (the litter, the sacred vessels, the god-bearing animals) into something new, to meet the challenge of the calf episode.

Buber formulates the problem of guidance ("leadership," as with *melekh* in chapter 3) as follows: Moses has promised the Israelites that the God who freed them also wishes to lead them, to protect them, and to be with them constantly. But the people lack anything like a "constant and uniformly functioning oracle"; instead, they wait for Moses to receive some sign, frequently one that they cannot see.[53] How can one follow a leader one cannot see? Moses thinks he can: "We may call it intuition or whatever we like. He calls it obedience, and if we wish to understand him we must take cognizance of his view and build upon it."[54] Yet the people find it difficult to share Moses' faith: "They can all see how often he is uncertain, when he withdraws himself into his tent and broods for hours and days on end, until he finally comes forth and says that what has to be done shall be done in this and this way. What kind of guidance is this, after all?" The people wonder why Moses cannot produce the god for them to view; in Egypt all gods could be represented in images. When Moses disappears on the mountain, they assume that perhaps he and the god fought, or that he displeased the god, and that it would fall to them to do what he failed to do. When representatives appointed by Moses attempt to intervene in the construction of the calf-god, they meet with violence. Aaron's attempts to serve as a go-between fail, and a bloody riot ensues.[55]

According to Buber, the aftermath of the riot results in the first major change in the relationship of Moses to the people, as Moses moves his tent outside the camp. He can no longer meet with God in a place polluted by idolatry and bloodshed; he designates it "the tent of meeting" and places it outside, with Joshua guarding it. Moses sees an altered relationship of God to the people; God no longer dwells in the camp with them. However, in Buber's reading God himself rectifies Moses' new impression. First God promises Moses that his "face" will still go before them (Exodus 33:14), and then he tells him, in an echo of his name at the burning bush: "I will be gracious to whom I will be gracious, and show mercy to whom I will show mercy" (Exodus 33:19).[56] At this point Moses requests that God travel in the midst of the people (Exodus 34:9), which gives rise to the ark.

Neither the response to the request nor the establishment of the ark by Moses is recorded in the biblical text (Buber considers the detailed instructions for the Tabernacle to be separate, later, and "literary" in origin), but for Buber its purpose is clear: "It was necessary to give the people legitimately, that is, in a fashion corresponding to the character of YHVH, that which they had wished to fashion illegitimately; that is, after a fashion running counter to the character of YHVH."[57] This fashion is a throne upon which the king does not always sit; he comes and goes as he pleases, and he sits there only when he wishes to become manifest in his function as ruler. The wings of the cherubim extend and touch one another to form the seat. Against other scholars who connect the imagery of the cherubim to Babylonia, assuming it symbolizes God's cosmic nature, Buber argues that the ark is purely the empty throne for the *melekh* of Israel. Only much later, "in the period of the State, when the theopolitical realism succumbed to the influence of the dynastic principle and the kingship of YHVH was transfigured and dissipated into a cosmic one lacking all direct binding force, did the nature symbolism prevail; since the aim then was to abstract living history from the domain of God."[58] The effect was not to provide a permanent dwelling for God, but to represent God's movement, paradoxically conferring visibility not on the corporeal presence of God but on his coming and going. Thus, it became possible for the people to feel that God stayed with them even in battle while also helping them fulfill his command that they become holy. This was the solution of Moses to the crisis of the calf, and it lasted until the ark and the tent were later separated—first when Israel lost the ark to the Philistines and later when the ark was brought to the Temple. That later period honored the ark, but so disregarded the tent that no record tells what became of it; this discrepancy indicates a return of the errors that first led Moses to build the ark.

Finally, the revolt of Korach represents a third possible misunderstanding of the theopolitical covenant, alongside the permanent expectation of success (the murmurers) and the desire to represent and "have" God at all times (the calf). The people do not have to become holy because the presence of YHVH in their midst and their being chosen by him mean that they already are holy. Therefore, whatever they will is blessed by God; in other words, their will can be taken for God's will.

Buber entitles this chapter "The Contradiction" because it represents the most subtle and difficult of Israel's misunderstandings. It is easy enough to read the revolt of Korach as a democratic one, seeking to take the teaching of the eagle speech and render it even more real by removing Moses as the one who seems to stand above the people. Yet according to Buber, this "converts the words of Moses into their opposite, changing as it does request and hope into insolent self-assertion."[59] The very establishment of the ark created the conditions of possibility for this new misunderstanding. Moses thought that placing the shrine with the Law tablets at the feet of the ark might remind the people that their freedom came with duties, but he was unable to overcome the people's assumption that God's presence with them represented prior sanction of their will. Thus, the contradicion embodied by Korach's revolt is none other than the contradiction of freedom itself, the primary theopolitical problem.

The urge to freedom stems from two sources: a negative source, seeking to eliminate anything that is "over" the individual to unleash the individual's will without obstruction, and a positive source, seeking to eliminate illegitimate authority to pursue some project. In the first case, the desire for freedom has a dictatorial side; inasmuch as the mere existence of others, whose desires may not match one's own, constrains one's will, one seeks to overcome others and impose one's will. In this instance, freedom for one thus excludes freedom for others. In the second case, one's desire for freedom comes together with a commitment to freedom; one therefore attempts to discern how everyone in the community might possess equal freedom. However, one can immediately see that equal freedom for everyone places a restriction on the freedom of each individual ("my freedom to swing my fist ends where your nose begins"). This is a paradox, unless one admits that the dictatorial nature of the first type of freedom means that it is not really freedom at all, only a desire to remove obstacles from the path of the will. This is the type of freedom that the dictator possesses, and from Buber's perspective this type of freedom usurps the prerogative of God:

> The people who set rebellions of this kind under way are not merely endeavoring to find a sanction for the satisfaction of repressed lusts, but are in all seriousness desirous of gaining power over the divine might; or more precisely, of actualizing and giving legitimacy to the god-might which a person has in himself, the "free" one, as against the one which is "bound" by the chief or shaman, with all the taboos used to fetter it. This tendency can admittedly be realized only by placing [others] in a state of non-freedom and exposure, such as is in many cases far worse than any previous abuse ever was; but this is only, as one might say, a secondary effect, which is regarded as being unworthy of any consideration.[60]

Indeed, God himself already set an example in this regard, restricting his own freedom by cutting the covenant with Israel and making promises to them. Self-restriction too is *imitatio dei*, if the people understand how to do it in order to empower others.

In this context we find a highly sympathetic discussion of law.[61] According to Buber, the history of antinomian movements, which are "developed" versions of the kind of tribal schism represented by Korach, shows that these movements always seek to set divine freedom (*Gottesfreiheit*, חירות-אלהים) against divine law (*Gottesgesetz*, חוקת-אלהים). Antinomians argue that "the law as such displaces the spirit and the freedom," and thus come to the false conclusion that "that [the law] ought to be replaced by them." Isolated divine freedom alone, however, "abolishes itself" in paradoxical fashion:

Naturally God rules through men who have been gripped and filled by His spirit, and who on occasion carry out His will not merely by means of in-stantaneous decisions but also through lasting justice and law [*überdauerndes Recht und Gesetz*/לחוק ומשפט מתמיד]. If their authority as the chosen ones is dis-puted and extended to all, then the actual dominion is taken away from God; for without law [*Gesetz*/חוק], that is, without any clear-cut and transmissible line of demarcation between that which is pleasing to God and that which is displeasing to Him, there can be no historical continuity of divine rule upon earth.[62]

How can Buber, after painstakingly taking so much care to elucidate and demon-strate the errors of Egyptian staticism, now aver the necessity of "lasting justice and law"?

The answer harks back to one of Buber's oldest ideas: renewal. Structures do become shackles, and institutions continue to claim their original justification and authority long after the spirit has left them. Thus, the argument of a true ver-sion of Korach's rebellion would be that "the law must again and again immerse itself in the consuming and purifying fire of the spirit, in order to renew itself and anew refine the genuine substance out of the dross of what has become false." Renewal in the context of the law is another instance of Buber's narrow ridge: one neither upholds the law as eternally fixed nor abandons it for some notion of absolute freedom; instead, one constantly renews the law, one inspirits it. And this is, according to Buber, a "Mosaic principle . . . a 'Mosaic' attitude," believing in the future of a "holy people" and preparing for it within history.

Here eschatology enters into the discussion in an interesting way. As long as the eschatological expectation is maintained, which imagines "the coming of the direct and complete rule of God over all creatures, or more correctly of His presence in all creatures that no longer requires law and representation," it is impossible to perceive the necessity of the Mosaic solution, namely renewal. The slackening of the eschatological belief, however, results in the restriction of God's rule to the purely "religious" sphere, following which "everything that is left over is rendered unto Caesar and the rift which runs through the whole being of the human world receives its sanction." Thus eschatology appears as the inverse of the narrow ridge of law. It is certainly true that if the eschaton were realized, there would be no need for law because God would be immediately present to the hearts and minds of all creatures. Living too far inside this expectation, however, leads to the kind of enthusiasm that wants to dispense with the law now, while forsaking the expectation abandons the world to the rule of force—a betrayal of the law in the name of the law. Understanding this narrow ridge is what differen-tiates the partisans of the anarcho-theocracy, whose eschatological expectation takes the form of wishing that they no longer had to wage a battle against their countrymen for the kingship of God, from the messianists—who paradoxically form the other side of the coin from realist politicians.

For Buber, the Baalism of Korach is more significant than the Baalism of the golden calf, which holds a much greater place in the folk memory. Buber completely rejects the view that the uprising was merely against the restriction of cultic priestly functions to Moses or to a certain class of Levites, not only because he doubts that Moses was ever a priest but also because he thinks that Korach shows that "the eternal word is opposed by eternal contradiction." Tragedy, another element not often associated with Buber's worldview, enters the picture here. Moses places a wager on the people of Israel: that their urge to freedom from any human master will lead them to recognize their true master in the Lord of the world. And "until the present day," for Buber, "*Israel has really existed in the precise degree in which Moses has proved right.*"[63] Moses' wager, however, depends on the very same personality traits in Israel that give rise to the rebellion of Korach, who is able to use Moses' own words against him. Moses can never secure his goal completely as long as he refuses to impose his will by force, yet imposing his will would negate his project. And while he stands back in humility, others step in to fill the void.

The Uncategorizable Man

This idea of the tragedy of Moses reaches to the heart of Buber's conception of theopolitics, and even further, to his conception of revelation and thus of Judaism itself. Moses' tragedy does not reflect the failure of any particular institution or office, because theopolitics does not allow him to be defined by any one role: he is not priest, prophet, judge, ruler, or even legislator. If Moses' failure and tragedy were traceable to his institutional role, some kind of reform of either institution or role would suffice to eliminate the problems. A remediable problem, however, is not a tragedy.[64] It is Moses' uncategorizability that allows him to stand in for Israel itself, and thus his tragedy represents Israel's tragedy.[65]

That Moses is not a priest is the easiest of these claims to grasp. The text never sees a special priestly role for Moses, even when it outlines the duties of the priestly class; in any case, Buber is in good historical-critical company when he holds that the earliest textual strata report nothing about such a class. Far more likely is the possibility that a centralized cult developed during the period of the settlement of the land. Moses does perform occasional sacrifices, usually without assistance; he does this "not as a professional priest but as the leader of the people, as we afterwards also find, for example, in the case of Samuel."[66] The same is true for Moses' transmitting God's will in a unique way, independent of any priestly tradition of divination. The Urim and Thummim are dated by most scholars to a post-Mosaic period. "The priest is the greatest human specialization that we know," Buber writes. "In his mission and his work Moses is unspecialized; he is conditioned not by an office but by a situation, a historical situation."[67]

That Moses is not purely a prophet is a much stranger claim. Deuteronomy concludes with the statement that "there has not since arisen in Israel a prophet like unto Moses, whom the Lord knew face to face" (Deuteronomy 34:10). Buber's own emphasis on Moses' role as a historical actor who receives and conveys God's word also seems to cement Moses' prophetic status. What separates Moses from all the subsequent prophets, however, is his political function. Moses is "leader of the people . . . legislator." He is not comprehensible "within any exclusively 'religious' categories," since every such category marks out a specific area of duty from the rest of life, rendering it a specialization. Moses, however, is unspecialized, uncategorizable; his whole work is a single unity:

> What constitutes his idea and his task: the realization of the unity of religious and social life in the community of Israel, the substantiation of a ruling by God that shall not be culturally restricted but shall comprehend the entire existence of the nation, the theopolitical principle; all this has penetrated to the deeps of his personality, it has raised his person above the compartmental system of typology, it has mingled the elements of his soul into a most rare unity.
>
> The historical Moses, as far as we are capable of perceiving him, does not differentiate between the spheres of religion and politics; and in him they are not separated.[68]

The fact that Buber crosses the line here into a romantic exegesis, mingling "the historical Moses" with talk of the "elements of his soul," tends to add to our understanding of Buber's Moses. The normative cast of Buber's description of Moses' unification of religion and politics suggests that he finds a model here for contemporary practice. And yet it is precisely by accepting this model that we are left to deal with the tragedy of the *Reichsdialektik*, on the one hand, and of Moses himself, on the other.

It may even be possible that two tragedies arise from the union of religion and politics in Moses. The first emerges from his singularity, the fact that no one is able to follow him who is "like" him. Moses contemplates Joshua as successor and realizes that "Joshua lacks that which is the constituent element in the attitude and actions of Moses; he does not receive revelations."[69] This gives rise to an unprecedented thought: the necessity of the division of powers. The functions that Moses had united, the oracular utterances and performance of communal offerings, as well as the political and military leadership, must be divided. What begins with Joshua eventually gives rise to the dual roles of priest and judge in Israel, and the very existence of the separate, specialized functions has the effect of splitting the religious from the political in the minds of the people, making it easier for them to eventually demand the monarchy. Moses, like most revolutionaries throughout history, eventually chooses means that are contrary to his ends:

> Moses does something, for the sake of maintaining the work, as a consequence of which a central part of the foundation of his work is broken down. The final

scene in the tragedy of Moses, like those which had preceded it, derives from the resistance of the human material. Moses wished for an entire, undivided human life, as the right answer to the Divine revelation. But splitting up is the historical way of mankind, and the unsplit persons cannot do anything more than raise man to a higher level on which he may thereafter follow his course, as long as he is bound by the law of his history.[70]

In almost any other context, Buber would treat such a choice as an avoidable error, but in this one he ties it to an elemental tragedy.

There is a parallel here to one of the strangest episodes in the biblical text, Exodus 4:24–26. Immediately after meeting God at the burning bush, Moses sets off on his journey, whereupon God comes upon him and tries to kill him. The murder attempt is halted by Zipporah, Moses' wife, who performs an impromptu circumcision on her baby. The passage is puzzling because the attack comes without warning or explanation, and seems to run completely counter to the mission God has just given to Moses. Some scholars propose that the story originally told of a demon, rather than YHVH, attempting to kill Moses, and that it was revised by later editors who were theologically opposed to the notion of any divine powers apart from YHVH. Buber, however, sees the opposite: YHVH was the original actor in the story, and later editors felt that even to render the story comprehensible from the standpoint of later theology, it was impermissible to alter it. Only this assumption "reveals the whole significance of the tale for the history of faith," which goes far beyond the role of the rite of circumcision in the ancient West Semitic clan structure.[71]

Buber connects the attack on Moses to the attack on Jacob; both represent a "dread night" (*grausige Nacht*, ליל הזוועה) or "event of the night" (*Ereignis der Nacht*, מאורע של הלילה), in which takes place "the sudden collapse of the newly won certainty, the 'deadly factual' moment when the demon working with apparently unbounded authority appears in the world where God alone had been in control but a moment before."[72] Yet because there is no dualism in Israelite religion, no realm given over to Satan, any power that attacks a man must be recognized as YHVH, "no matter how nocturnally dread and cruel it may be; and it is proper to withstand Him, since after all He does not require anything else of me than myself." Yet Buber goes further, connecting the literal circumcision that stops the attack to the metaphorical one applied to Moses' speech: "For I am uncircumcised of lips" (Exodus 6:12, 30). "This is a kind of uncircumcision which cannot be eliminated by any circumcision, an absence of liberation which is clearly not organic but penetrates to the core of the soul, an absence of liberation and *an impossibility of liberation*; not a mere defect in the instruments of speech but a fundamental inhibition of expression."[73] Moses has been chosen to deliver God's word to Israel, but he lacks mastery over his own speech. He is thus separated from his fellow humans by a basic and insurmountable barrier: "Teacher, prophet, law-giver; yet in the sphere of the word he remains insurmountably lonely; alone in the last resort with the word of heaven which forces itself through inflexible soul into inflexible throat." And when Moses' relationship to Aaron, his brother who speaks for him, is characterized in Exodus 4:16 as analogous to the relationship between God and Moses ("you shall be as god to him"), the point is hammered home: "The tragedy of Moses becomes the tragedy inherent in Revelation. It is laid upon the stammering to bring the voice of Heaven to Earth."

Despite these emphases, neither Buber nor Buber's Moses possesses a vision of Israel that is ultimately tragic. An appreciation of tragedy is necessary, perhaps, for hope and optimism to be warranted, to avoid the traps of sunny naïveté. Hope cannot survive if it flies in the face of all evidence. Turning, then, to Moses' legacies, Buber notes first that Moses writes: "What Moses says may be clumsy, but not what he writes; that is suitable for his time and for the later times in which the stone will testify."[74] And when the stone passes out of memory, when the ark and tent are lost, the Word endures. Second, Moses promises. He relays to the people a promise from God:

> At times he would send the people a prophet like to Moses, in whose mouth he would place His words like Moses, and to whom they would have to hearken. This, going far beyond the problem associated with the succession, is an admission of a higher continuity resulting from the ever-repeated renewal out of the spirit. We are entitled to regard this as containing, at its core, a genuine hope on the part of Moses.[75]

The leadership, of course, does not return; the later prophets do not have the same political function that Moses had, which is why there was never another prophet like him. But what does return is sufficient for renewal, if the people hearken to the prophetic voice. The prophets carry on the work of Moses, striving to bring Israel into being.

Notes

1. As late as 1950, Buber still referred to an "as yet unpublished book" titled *Hamoshiach*; *Torat Ha-Nevi'im* (Tel Aviv: Mossad Bialik, 1950), 6. The choice of *Hamoshiach* to render *Der Gesalbte* in Hebrew creates an interesting translation problem. It is a literal rendering, but the connotations of "the anointed" and "the messiah" differ in both German and English, which cannot be captured in Hebrew where they are the same word.

2. Originally published in Hebrew as *Moshe* (Tel Aviv: Schocken Press, 1945); shortly followed by the first English edition in 1946, and then the German *Moses* (Zürich: Gregor Müller, 1948). Because the language of the original composition is unclear, I provide Hebrew and German alternatives when necessary. German citations are to WZB 11–230.

3. "That a scholar of so much importance in his own field as Sigmund Freud could permit himself to issue so unscientific a work, based on groundless hypotheses, as his 'Moses and Monotheism' (1939), is regrettable"; MRC vii. Although this is the only reference to Freud in *Moses*, Buber repeatedly cites Ernest Sellin, the source of Freud's claim that Moses was an Egyptian.

4. For these ideas: Lincoln Steffens, *Moses in Red: The Revolt of Israel as a Typical Revolution* (Philadelphia: Dorrance and Co., 1926); Thomas Mann, *The Tables of the Law* (1944; Philadelphia: Paul Dry Books, 2010).

5. John Rogerson, *Old Testament Criticism in the Nineteenth Century: England and Germany* (Eugene, OR: Wipf and Stock, 1984), 21, 29.

6. MRC vii.

7. In some ways this position identifies Buber with eighteenth-century German neologist scholarship, which held that one could salvage history from the "myths" of the Pentateuch; Rogerson, *Old Testament Criticism*, 56. However, the movement of "tradition-criticism" to the forefront of biblical studies during the period of Buber's work on the topic may have retroactively rendered his method less "conservative" (Buber cites many of the most prominent tradition critics). Buber occasionally agrees with Wellhausen, such as by assenting to the Pentateuchal order of events (Exodus, wandering, settlement, monarchy). Douglas A. Knight, *Rediscovering the Traditions of Israel*, 3rd ed. (Atlanta: Society of Biblical Literature, 2006), 54; 67–69, 172.

8. *N.B.*: Buber is careful to avoid the type of conservative apologetics wherein scholars attempt to demonstrate the historicity of biblical personalities (e.g., Darius the Mede in the book of Daniel); John J. Collins, *Introduction to the Hebrew Bible* (Minneapolis: Fortress, 2004), 554.

9. MRC 74.

10. Ibid., 15 (my italics). The Hebrew word rendered as "saga" is *aggada* (cf. *Moshe*, 1–7), which in its rabbinic sense has neither an English nor a German equivalent. However, Buber uses it in a mundane sense, to mean *Legende*, or *Sage*, as given in the German (WZB 16–23).

11. Peter Sloterdijk, *Derrida, An Egyptian: On the Problem of the Jewish Pyramid*, trans. Wieland Hoban (Malden, MA: Polity Press, 2009), 47; cf. Régis Debray, *God: An Itinerary*, trans. Jeffrey Mehlman (New York: Verso, 2004).

12. Relevant is Gershom Scholem's "whimsical" definition of Zionism "as a movement against the excessive inclination of the Jews to travel." The whimsy masks a clear divide between Scholem's vision of Zionism and Buber's, which, from Buber's perspective, may readmit a significant quotient of Egypt into the affairs of Israel; Scholem, "What Is Judaism?" in *On the Possibility of Jewish Mysticism in Our Time and Other Essays*, ed. Avraham Shapira, trans. Jonathan Chipman (Philadelphia: Jewish Publication Society, 1997), 116.

13. Jan Assmann, *Moses the Egyptian: The Memory of Egypt in Western Monotheism* (Cambridge, MA: Harvard University Press, 1997), 7.

14. In reply to critics, Assmann claimed that he never wanted to "revoke" the Mosaic distinction, only "sublimate" it; Jan Assmann, *The Price of Monotheism*, trans. Robert Savage (Stanford, CA: Stanford University Press, 2010), 120.

15. MRC ix.

16. Assmann acknowledges that the Mosaic distinction is not merely about quantifying the number of gods as "one" rather than "many," but about the notion of true and false in religion. But he neglects to examine the diverse attitudes one might take towards such truth and falsity.

17. MRC x; WZB 14; *Moshe* viii.

18. Assmann, *Moses the Egyptian*, 152–3.

19. "To every worldly empire belongs a certain relativism with respect to the motley of possible views, ruthless disregard of local peculiarities as well as opportunistic tolerance for things of no central importance." Carl Schmitt, *Roman Catholicism and Political Form*, trans. G. L. Ulmen (Westport, CT: Greenwood Press, 1996), 5–6.

20. Buber's claim for this gains some historical justification from the rootedness of the form of the literary version of the Sinai covenant in Hittite vassal treaties; Collins, *Introduction to the Hebrew Bible*, 122.

21. Assmann, *Moses the Egyptian*, 152–153.

22. Ibid., 20–21.

23. Ibid., 22; WZB 26; *Moshe*, 10.

24. MRC 25.

25. In argumentation strikingly close to Buber's, James Scott holds that this process initiates ethnogenesis. Over time, the outsider group is seen as separate because of "ethnic" characteristics distinct from the state dwellers; initially, however, "ethnic" difference simply is the difference between owing obeisance to a government or not. James C. Scott, *The Art of Not Being Governed: An Anarchist History of Upland Southeast Asia* (New Haven, CT: Yale University Press, 2009), 125.

26. MRC 26.

27. Ibid., 28.

28. Ibid., 22.

29. MRC 30. Abraham does differentiate himself from the average Habiru type, by refusing to be identified as a mercenary (Genesis 14:23) and by identifying the God that leads him and his men in their wanderings "with that particular one among the gods of the settled people who is recognized by them as the 'Most High God'" (Genesis 14:22).

30. Ibid., 38.

31. Ibid., 24–25. No source is provided for the citation here, but elsewhere Buber repeats it and credits Arnold J. Toynbee; PF 42.

32. Ibid., 28–30.

33. Ibid., 197.

34. Ibid., 21.

35. Ibid., 171.

36. Ibid., 175, 179. The citation here is to Alt, *Die Ursprünge des israelitischen Rechts* (Leipzig: S. Hirzel, 1934), 65. In associating the Sabbatical year not just with letting land lie fallow but also with economic redistribution, Buber assumes as correct the view of some scholars that the Sabbatical was originally as forceful as the Jubilee, which was introduced only later, after the Israelites persisted in viewing the Sabbatical as impracticable and thus failing to observe it.

37. Such a view would naturally bring Buber into conflict with libertarians and so-called anarcho-capitalists, who criticize redistribution of the kind instituted by the sabbatical as inherently coercive and counter-productive. Recent protest campaigns have called for broad debt relief, referred to as a "Jubilee." David Graeber, *The Democracy Project: A History, a Crisis, a Movement* (New York: Spiegel & Grau, 2013).

38. MRC 179, 181.

39. The highlight of this overly serious "scientific" effort occurs when Buber discusses the chase: "We do not know where the pursuers caught up with the fugitives; whether in the neighborhood of the present Suez or . . . further north . . . or even, as some suppose, only at the Gulf of Akaba (though in that case it is hard to understand why the pursuing chariots should not have caught up with them sooner)." MRC 75.

40. Ibid., 75–79. Contrast Schmitt's account of miracle in *Political Theology* as a suspension of natural order, analogous to the power of emergency of the state and ruler. Many see Schmitt's conception of miracle as a weak point in his political theology. Cf. Erik Peterson, "Monotheism as a Political Problem: A Contribution to the History of Political Theology in the Roman Empire," in *Theological Tractates*, ed. and trans. Michael Hollerich (Stanford, CA: Stanford University Press, 2011), 68–105; Bonnie Honig, *Emergency Politics: Paradox, Law, Democracy* (Princeton, NJ: Princeton University Press, 2009).

41. Buber's critique applies by extension to Maimonides, and any other medieval rationalist exegetes who appeal to the principle of accommodation.

42. Buber cites Volz and von Rad as sharing his view that the passage is old and "genuinely traditional," rather than a late interpolation; MRC 101. "Der Adlerspruch" (The Eagle Speech) is the single chapter specifically noted as found in German manuscript in the *Nachlass*.

43. Ibid., 102.

44. Ibid., 105.

45. Ibid., 106–107.

46. Ibid., 108.

47. Compare the distinction between Molechization and Baalization in KG.

48. Ibid., 128.

49. Ibid., 87–88.

50. MRC 89.

51. Cf. *Genesis Rabbah* 9:7.

52. Considerations include the strangeness of the plural "Elohim" in the late period, and the retention of the theme of Aaron's share of guilt in idolatry, which by the time of the divided kingdom would have been highly inconvenient for the authorities of the Jerusalem Temple, who presumably backed the writing of this anti-northern passage.

53. MRC 151.

54. Ibid., 77.

55. Buber's claim that a riot took place in the camp derives from a number of textual considerations but also mitigates the brutality of Moses' response to the idolatry. If the rioters already used violence against their fellow Israelites, Moses seems less bloody in reply. Riot suppression as revolutionary means presents a problem from the standpoint of Buber's general theopolitics; however, it ultimately does not constitute Moses' fundamental mistake for Buber. Cf. Buber's 1913 treatment of this subject, in which he not only adheres to the traditional picture of Moses exacting violent punishment on the idolatrous Israelites but also valorizes it in the name of "unconditionality"; Buber, "Jewish Religiosity," in *On Judaism*, ed. Nahum N. Glatzer (New York: Schocken, 1995), 88.

56. Buber interprets the promise that God's "face" will go before the people in light of the immediately preceding statement that no one can see God's face and live; it is a renewed promise of protection, since enemies along the way will be met by the "face" and die—enemies attacking from the front, that is. The lasting infamy of Amalek is that they attacked from behind.

57. MRC 156–157. This claim is a near-exact parallel to what Buber says in *Der Gesalbte* about YHVH granting the people a human monarch.

58. Ibid., 158. I have slightly altered the English wording, which renders both *Königtum* (מלכות) and *Bereich* (רשות) (WZB 182; *Moshe* 142) as "kingdom." I also translate *verflüchtigt* as "dissipated" rather than "subtilized."

59. Ibid., 184.

60. MRC 187.

61. Buber's negative view of rabbinic halakha is well known from his correspondence concerning Franz Rosenzweig, "The Builders: Concerning the Law," in *On Jewish Learning*, ed. Nahum N. Glatzer (Madison: University of Wisconsin Press, 2002), 72–92, 109–118. What he says here about the category of "law," using the Hebrew *chok* for German *Gesetz*, challenges the usual understanding of his relationship to *halakha*.

62. MRC 187–88; WZB 215; *Moshe*, 169–170.

63. Ibid., 188–189 (my italics).

64. Hence Buber refused the common identification of the Zionist-Arab conflict as a tragedy. It is not because his worldview had no room for tragedy; it is because he understood the conflict as remediable.

65. Moses Mendelssohn also stressed the uncategorizability of Moses' polity: "But why do you seek a generic term for an individual thing, which has no genus . . . which cannot be put

under the same rubric as anything else? This constitution existed only once; call it the *Mosaic constitution*, by its proper name." Moses Mendelssohn, *Jerusalem; or, on Religious Power and Judaism*, trans. Allan Arkush (Waltham, MA: Brandeis University Press, 1983), 131.

66. MRC 183.
67. Ibid., 185.
68. MRC 186; cf. PF 71.
69. Ibid., 198.
70. Ibid., 199.
71. MRC 57.
72. Ibid., 58; WZB 69–70; *Moshe*, 46.
73. Ibid., 59 (my italics).
74. Ibid., 140.
75. Ibid., 200.

5 The Arcanum of the Monarchy
The Anointed

Sie, die trauernd »nach JHWH« stöhnten, haben nur seine Siegesmacht, nicht seine Herrschaft gemeint. Das Palladium kehrt nicht heim, die Obmacht des Feindes dauert fort, die für die Stunde gegebene Antwort reicht für die Folge der Stunden nicht zu.

—Martin Buber, "Wie Saul König wurde"

Is Saul too among the prophets?

—Israelite Proverb (1 Samuel 10:12)

Introduction

In the early 1960s, when compiling the German edition of his three-volume *Werke*, Buber rejoined articles he had published on Samuel, Saul, and the rise of the monarchy under their original heading: *Der Gesalbte (The Anointed)*.[1] This marked the first publication of any work with that name, although the separate pieces had been available for over a decade.[2] In 1951 Buber estimated that when he ceased work on *Der Gesalbte*, in 1938, the work was about half finished.[3] He does not specify what the second half would have discussed. However, we may speculate that since the first half deals with the roles of Samuel and Saul in the transition from judgeship to monarchy, the second half would likely address the rejection of Saul as king, the rise of David, and the continuation of the Davidic line in Solomon, perhaps concluding with the secession of the northern kingdom and the reign of Jeroboam I.

In content and style, *The Anointed* is the direct sequel to *Kingship of God*. It starts where that book ended, with the military crisis that precipitated the end of the anarcho-theocracy and the charismatic leadership of the judges, and with the crystallization of the idea of permanent, hereditary monarchy to solve the problems of foreign domination and domestic chaos. Like *Kingship of God*, *The Anointed* belongs simultaneously to two conversations: one in the field of biblical scholarship, concerning the dating, authorship, and interpretation of scriptural texts, and another in the field of political theory. In fact, given the subject matter of *The Anointed*, one expects it to engage even more explicitly with political theory. *Kingship of God* was part of a discourse on sacred kingship taking place in anthropology and the history of religions; that discourse admittedly had great political resonance. But the primary topic of *The Anointed*—I Samuel and the founding of the monarchy in Israel—is second to no scriptural text, except possibly Romans 13, in its significance for political theory in Christian countries. Interpretations of 1 Samuel have varied widely throughout history, and differing interpretations have yielded myriad theories of state legitimation, all claiming scriptural warrant.[4] Long-standing debates on nearly every point of 1 Samuel 8 show that even small differences in interpretation beget wide political repercussions. And the chapter is filled with gaps and difficulties: What is Samuel's office when the elders come to him requesting a king? Why is he the "address" for such a request? Why are Samuel's sons mentioned? What role had he attempted to assign them? Why does the failure of Samuel's house lead to the request for an entirely new constitution of society, rather than the replacement of his house in its current office? What does God mean when he characterizes the request for a king as a rejection of his own kingship? Why, if both Samuel and God disapprove of the elders' request, does God tell Samuel to grant it anyway? What is the nature of the *mishpat ha-melekh* ("law or rule of the king") that Samuel reads to the people? Is it intended to enumerate royal prerogatives, or to dissuade the people from their course? Why, when the people reaffirm their desire for a king against Samuel's warning ("you shall become his slaves"), does he simply send the people home? All these questions pertain to chapter 8 alone, before Saul even enters the narrative, bringing along entirely new contradictions and problems.

To these exegetical questions we must add a number of biblical-critical concerns: is the book of Samuel a coherent work, and if so, what is its position on the events it narrates?[5] If not, is it possible to pinpoint which sections date to ancient Israelite factions (pro-Saulid, pro-Davidic, "Deuteronomist")? Who are the final editors of the work, and what is their ideological stance? Are they exilic Deuteronomists animated by hatred of the monarchy, or preexilic figures with a more sympathetic attitude toward the follies of the kings? Although these questions may be of merely antiquarian interest, Buber felt compelled to answer them, in order to uncover the true theopolitical history of Israel and to gain for this history the recognition he thought it was due in contemporary thought and political life.

The Anointed thus serves two purposes. First, it was intended to be the middle part of the trilogy *Das Kommende* and to narrate the transformation of the direct theocracy into the indirect through the concept of anointing, while pointing forward to the prophetic period and the eschatologization of the messianic idea. In the process, however, Buber also attempts to answer one of the greatest challenges posed by Scripture to his understanding of the history and faith of Israel, namely the apparent divine sanction of the monarchy with its attendant political and cultic centralization. His philosophical and historical probity prevents him from making simplistic theological maneuvers that could have served to further his thesis. For example, one could argue that the entire Deuteronomic history—from the fifth Book of Moses through Joshua, Judges, Samuel, and Kings—represents a strongly antimonarchical viewpoint in its final form.[6] Some would argue that therefore "the Bible" opposes monarchy, rendering efforts to valorize monarchic or authoritarian politics on scriptural grounds misguided at best. However, such an argument invites an account of the scriptural sources informed by a cynical, *realpolitisch* secular worldview: that during the time of the Davidic-Solomonic ascent, the historical texts and psalms proclaiming the divine approval of the monarchy and the eternal glory of the Davidic house were written, and that later, during the period of the exile, these texts were placed by an editor into a context that rendered them ironic, tragic, or at the very least balanced by antimonarchical voices. In such an account, the canon emerges in accordance with the caprice of human attitudes to power: in times of success people praise kings and hold them divinely appointed, but in times of failure they decide that God never really liked kings after all.

The people of Israel, as characters in the narrative, may display such caprice. But Buber finds this untenable as a scholarly view of the origin of the core narrative of 1 Samuel. He finds another voice in the text, one that expresses an intermediate position between the anarcho-theocratic vision of the judges and the revolutionary reformism of the later prophets. *The Anointed* intends to articulate this voice, which Buber links to a circle around the prophet Nathan in the court of David, and to show that it forms the basis for the rest of our Book of Samuel. Buber aims to isolate the "original narrative," and also to focus on several themes within this reconstructed source text: secrecy and mystery as keys to monarchical power; the succession of powers in Israel and the variety of offices (*kohen*, priest; *nabi*, prophet; *shofet*, judge; *zaken*, elder; *nagid*, prince) that attempt to secure the people against internal degeneration and external domination prior to the institution of the *melukha*, the kingship; and the unbreakable connection between the anointed one, the king, and the one who anoints, the prophet.

The Voice of Our Narrator: Reconstructing How Saul Became King

The book of Samuel is the object of a large and contentious critical literature, both for its political centrality and for its many apparent inconsistencies and contradictions. Well before professional biblical criticism, Baruch Spinoza wrote that he could not imagine 1 Samuel as the work of a single narrator with a single purpose.[7] And for historical-critical scholarship at large, it made sense to attribute contradictions in the text to divergent traditions and haphazard redaction. The defense of 1 Samuel's coherence, however, argues that in its final form the text does serve a discernible editorial purpose and that its "inconsistencies" are only apparent. In *The Anointed*, Buber seeks to locate and explicate the original tradition of the rise of the monarchy, not the intention of the final editors of 1 Samuel. Therefore, we will not attempt to resolve the controversy surrounding textual phenomena that are classified as difficulties and contradictions by historical criticism but that literary criticism may view as authorial artistry. It is sufficient to note that they provide Buber an entry point into a tradition-critical project of narrative reconstruction.[8] He does not accept the major historical-critical hypotheses of the text's emergence. In particular, he rejects the source hypothesis, in which there are two or three major traditional sources: a Mizpa source and a Gilgal source, corresponding to the two legends of Saul's coronation, which are later edited together. He also dismisses the fragment hypothesis, in which independent epic units are strung together according to a later editorial vision. Instead, he sees a unified narrative emerge early on, incorporating previous oral traditions into a cohesive understanding of history. To isolate this narrative, however, requires a thorough critical assessment of nearly every verse of chapters 7–13, a project Buber describes with dry understatement as "the elimination of several additions, recognizable as such."[9]

Buber's own criteria for distinguishing between earlier and later passages are both historical and literary. In assessing authorship and consistency, he considers the sound and timbre of the text, in accordance with the theory that the core of the text was originally oral. His method of tracing the *Leitwort*—that is, root sounds repeated by the text in order to draw otherwise-invisible connections for readers who are conceived of as *hearers*—is well known.[10] By reciting the text out loud, Buber argues, one hears relationships between words that may not be etymologically related but that resonate with each other; this draws us closer to the original meaning of the text as spoken. Scholars rarely note, however, the extent to which Buber deploys the *Leitwort* method in the service of his theopolitical interpretation of Israelite history. Nor is it noted how his theopolitics drive his instincts in cases in which no *Leitwort* is present, sometimes leading him to contradict what would otherwise appear to be a clear *Leitwort*. Examples include his comments on the sound א-ג-ד (*aggid*) and the root ש-פ-ט (*shafat*) in the legend of Saul's becoming king.

To start with the less surprising example: Buber reads our narrator as playing on the "weighty central word *nagid*" in a twofold theopolitical way. On the level of form, Buber calls our narrator "a master of esoteric style" (*Geheimstil*), who repeats this sound throughout chapter 9 in reference to Saul's rise to power. Only two of these uses involve the noun *nagid*, "prince"; the others are variations on the verb *higgid*, "tell": "We hear *jaggid* in v. 6, *higgid* in v. 8, in v. 16 *nagid* itself appears, then twice again, v. 18 *haggida*, v. 19 *aggid*, and finally renewed at 10:1 and the concluding *nagid*. Whoever refuses to give up maintaining that such things are random throws the key to an inner chamber of the Hebrew Bible into the sea."[11] This word choice also signifies on the level of theopolitical content. At

9:16 YHVH tells Samuel that he will send him a man from the land of Benjamin, to "anoint him *nagid*." *Nagid*, Buber argues, is intentionally chosen in contrast to *melekh*:

> Here it is to be pointed out, that on the basis of Old Testament word-usage *Nagid* is not an autocrat, but rather can only designate one commissioned [*Beauftragten*], and that hence "to anoint" someone for this purpose plainly does not mean to bestow power upon him (as had been demanded), but rather to charge him with a commission [*Auftrag*] and likewise to grant him necessary authorization to its execution. In the order to Samuel JHWH's actual answer to the desire of the people declares itself, the critical transformation of that which was granted. The event signifies to the narrator the *replacement*, ordered by God, *of the primitive direct theocracy by the indirect*. On the right understanding of this sense depends the understanding of the *Politeia* the Book of Samuel is narrating generally.[12]

Here the *nagid* is described in terms that Buber used in *Kingship of God* for the *shophet*: he is a delegate or commissioner, a *Beauftragter*, to whom a commission, an *Auftrag*, is given. In 9:17, when Samuel first sees Saul, YHVH points him out, telling Samuel, "This is the man who will protect [*ya'atzor*] my people." Buber notes that *ya'atzor*, a word that often means "detain," "prevent," or even "arrest," is used rather than *yimlokh* ("will reign," from *melekh*) or *yimshol* ("will rule") or *yishlot* ("will govern"). In this context, the word means something like "protect," but it also connotes "hold together, enclose, care for." Such is the *Auftrag* of Saul in these early moments, when he is anointed, before the narrative switches to *Melekh*.[13] This crucial distinction, for Buber, is what makes 1 Samuel a *Politeia*, a work of political thought.

There are also cases, however, in which Buber's theopolitical concerns override his *Leitwort* method. Historical-critical analysis of a more traditional sort then intervenes to separate the *Leitworter* from one another. In 1 Samuel 8, for example, the root *shafat* recurs three times: at 8:1, when Samuel makes his sons judges (*shoftim*) over Israel; at 8:5, when the elders ask for a king "to judge us [*l'shofteinu*] like all the nations"; and at 8:6, when Samuel is displeased that the elders said "give us a king to judge us [*l'shofteinu*]." These uses in turn follow on a threefold repetition: at 7:15 ("Samuel judged [*vayishpot*] Israel all the days of his life"), 7:16 ("and he judged [*veshafat*] Israel in all these places"), and 7:17 ("and there he judged [*shafat*] Israel"). Buber admits that after the first four of these six usages, "the unbiased reader . . . cannot really do otherwise but understand the same verb in like manner in v. 5 and 6."[14] Yet Buber is not the unbiased reader, and he argues against interpreting the sixfold repetition of the *Leitwort* identically at each point. To do so, he thinks, would be to fall into at least two editorial traps: one set by the author of 7:15–17, which exaggerates Samuel's temporary victory against the Philistines and wrongly describes his subsequent peacetime authority as that of a *shofet*, and one set by the editor who, in Buber's view, interpolated 8:1–3 into its present position precisely to dull the meaning of *shafat*. The first four occurrences situate Samuel in the line of *shoftim* familiar to us from the book of Judges—saviors whose charisma and military prowess indicate their selection by YHVH for a particular moment. The final two occurrences describe a request for a *melekh*, a king, to carry out the function of the *shofet*. Buber asks why, if Samuel already fills the *shofet* office, the elders request a new office to fulfill the function of an old one? Even if Samuel and his sons are filling the position ineffectively, why does he suddenly face a demand for a constitutional overhaul? To understand the section, Buber argues, we have to separate the first four uses of *shafat* from the final two.

The known meanings of the root ש-פ-ט [*sh-f-t*] according to Buber include to procure justice for someone, to make justice visible through a decision, and to demonstrate to one behaving unjustly his injustice. It is clear that of these, the elders intend the first meaning. The people themselves express this at 8:19–20, when they say: "Nay! Let a king be over us, so that we may also be like the other tribes of the earth; let our king *shafot* us and move out before us and fight our battles." If "move out before us" and "fight our battles" are roughly synonymous expressions, then "*shafot* us" is to be read through them. The implication is that Samuel is incapable of being a *shofet* in this sense, in which he procures the rights of his people through war.[15] Chapter 7 attempted to attribute military leadership to Samuel, but Buber points out that even here Samuel's intervention takes the form of prayer and response. Yet "successful prayers founded no judgeship in the sense of the history of the great judges. They were fighters, fighters chosen and dispatched by God, those he helped . . . not peaceful supplicants and petitioners for wonders."[16] The elders, then, do not seek the replacement of their current *shoftim*. They are frustrated that no *shofet* has arisen to deliver them from the Philistines, and therefore seek to establish a continuous authority. Here we have an instance in which an apparent *Leitwort* is misleading, and Buber dissects it critically in order to arrive at the reading he considers to be in accord with the political and historical context of the core narrative.[17]

Elsewhere, Buber's theopolitical outlook leads him to delete entire verses, as in his virulent polemic against 1 Samuel 8:8, which he holds to be a "rhetorically impoverished addition by the compiler" that "intolerably weakened, indeed abolished" its preceding verse, 8:7.[18] How so? In verse 8:6, Samuel is reportedly displeased with the request of the elders for a king, and prays to YHVH. In verse 8:7, YHVH responds, telling him to hearken unto the people's voice and to give them what they ask, while noting that Samuel should not feel that he himself is being challenged—rather, God's kingship is what is being rejected. Verse 8:8 then compares this rejection, in Buber's view the cardinal moment in Israelite history since Sinai, to "everything else they have done ever since I brought them out of Egypt to this day"—thus weakening what he perceives as unique. The words "so

they are doing to *you*" then contradict the previous verse even further by implying that the request *was* really a rejection of Samuel's authority after all:

> The theopolitical unity of action which was the unmistakable object of the
> accusation in 7b has made way for an irritating binary comparison . . . the
> compiler—perhaps endeavoring for the greater glory of Samuel, by then re-
> ceived in the state of historical apotheosis—easily recognizable by his sharply
> contrasting rhetorical style from the terseness of the preceding sentences, has
> here, arguably without appreciating the scope of his intrusion, obliterated the
> basic, great theme of the "biblical *Politeia*."[19]

For Buber, 8:7 by itself is a great documentary report, but 8:8 drains it of its force,
preventing a proper understanding of Israelite history. From one verse to the
next, the entire *Politeia* is undone by a pious addition. Buber criticizes not only
the intelligence of some of the biblical editors but also their spiritual stature, as
indicated by his claim that although they are "convinced that they only 'expound'
what is written," their "well-meaning intervention" for the sake of narrative unity
is rooted in their effort "not to bear" the tradition, not to trust it.[20]

Buber accuses those editors who come after "our narrator," especially the
compilers of 1 Samuel 12–14, of a panoply of stylistic offenses: "over-hasty pace,"
"undisciplined syntax," "lax use of completely foreign verbal forms"; their diction
is "derivative," "vacuous," "childish," "imprudent," "oddly inappropriate," and
indicates "imitative erosion."[21] It is no coincidence that they are also politically
benighted, although unlike the last redactors of Judges, they do not represent a
unified party. Our original narrator produces "simple, concise, powerful speech,
worthy of its object and of its narrator, and without a trace of later language,"
and Buber believes that he shares his own concerns about the origin of kingship in Israel. He is "the first answerer" to the question of "what it was to be the
anointed."[22]

The foregoing is but an exemplary selection of biblical verses illustrating
how Buber's theopolitical commitments and his scholarly analysis dovetail in
The Anointed. A final example: from the twenty-five verses of 1 Samuel 12, Buber
keeps ten, and many of these only in a shortened form. These verses comprise
two short addresses of Samuel to the people following the installation of Saul as
king of Israel. In the first (1 Samuel 12:1–5), Samuel acquits himself of wrongdoing
before ceding authority to Saul.[23] Here, for the first time, he refers to Saul as "the
anointed of YHVH." In the second address, containing parts of verses 13, 14, 15,
24, and 25, Buber has Samuel delivering this message to the people:

> And now, there is the king whom you have wished for, there, YHVH has set a
> king over you. / Therefore fear YHVH and hear his voice, so you may live, both
> you and the king, who according to YHVH your God became king over you. /
> But if you do not hear YHVH's voice, then will the hand of YHVH be against
> you and against your king. / Only fear YHVH! For see, such great things he

has done for you! / You pursue evil, but your evil that you do will sweep you away, both you and your king.[24]

This version of 1 Samuel 12 eliminates the reference to the Exodus, the litany of the *shoftim* and their involvement in a cycle of sin and redemption, the people's fear of Nachash and the Ammonites, the repeated accusation that they rejected God's kingship, the miracle worked by Samuel to prove the impudence of their demand, their confession of sin, and Samuel's reassurance that YHVH will reward their confession. It may seem puzzling that Buber eliminates the verses of 1 Samuel 12 that reiterate the people's sin in asking for a king. Is this not his own view in *Kingship of God*? Why does he excise this as a later addition, which, when removed, leaves us with a passage lacking further evidence of Samuel's opposition to the people's request?

Although Buber is sympathetic to the redactors of the antimonarchical book of Judges, he does not conflate or harmonize diverse biblical viewpoints. The narrator of the core of 1 Samuel, according to Buber, does not stand with the anarcho-theocrats of old, or with the likely authors of the antimonarchical insertions to chapter 12, but neither does he stand with the elders of the people. He is hopeful about the prospects of the monarchy but has serious reservations. He is not a propagandist but an inquirer:

> The questions, which stand over the narrators, are about the origin, purpose, and destiny of the greater Israelite monarchy, where purpose and destiny are indispensably related to the origin and the early transformations, and these questions appear answerable to the narrators only from out of the historical faith which they believe: the reciprocally-acting opposition of a God and of a people that he leads, without coercing it, and that he still leads, if it is submissive to him, but thereafter to the opposition of this God and the ones "chosen" or "seized" by him from out of the people, who nevertheless act against him over and over again. . . . [H]ow [our narrative] renders this report, how it represents particular proceedings and how it excludes other ones, what it achieves and what it only indicates, its stories and its teachings, its realism and its symbolism are essentially determined from that which for the narrator here, in the inception, hides the arcanum of the monarchy, the problematic of the divine-human encounter, the sense of faith of a historical tragedy and possibly also already of the seed of the promise of overcoming it.[25]

From Priests to Prophets: The Philistine Emergency and the Rise of Samuel

The narrative begins in a time of crisis. The Philistines have dominated Israel for generations. Attempts at liberation have failed, and YHVH has not sent a judge to redeem the people in many years. In this context Samuel, who is to anoint the king of Israel, becomes a prominent public figure. For Buber, this context colors the position of the narrator of 1 Samuel vis-à-vis the traditions of the judges, and explains his desire to account for the emergence of a new tradition, the charismatic kingship:

> Here he was dealing with another situation: in an enemy-emergency . . . longer than any previously known, the emergency of an entire era, JHWH had not helped through the empowerment of a doer, but rather the people, sated of suffering, had undertaken, finally, to provide themselves the form of help to God, so to speak, one borrowed from the surrounding world, the perennial task, the task of sovereignty.[26]

The rhetoric of Zionism resonates here (self-empowerment versus waiting for God, sovereignty versus isolation from the world and history), and Buber's elucidation of this narrator's voice parallels his struggles to articulate his own Zionist position. Our narrator willingly accepts the task of countering the inheritance of Gideon, the victorious general who refuses dynastic leadership as an offense to divine sovereignty. He must explain why divine approval is conferred on human kingship regardless of this tradition. And he does this by viewing the concept of kingship as denoting a transition from direct to indirect theocracy rather than from theocracy to human rule. Samuel, as a *navi* who at first resists but then approves the institution of the *melukha*, is the agent of this transformation.

The earliest Samuel narratives need not be attributed to the same sources as in Buber's core narrative of Saul's anointing, but in his reconstruction they become theopolitically compatible.[27] *The Anointed* is largely devoted to clarifying Samuel's status and to defending the proposition that he is a *navi* par excellence, rather than a *kohen* or a *shofet*. Samuel's prominence is unquestioned, but his specific office remains unclear:

> The narrative accepts as self-evident that this Samuel, who in the preceding passages of the book appears first as Temple attendant (2:11; 3:1), then as *Nabi* (3:20), then as sacrificer of the public sacrifices (7:9f), then as *Shophet* (7:15–17), is the man authorized and competent for the fulfillment of the demand expressed to him; but whether we have to consider him as such because he possesses an authority and it can also be conferred, or because he is intermediary between the people and its God, and therefore called by God to carry out the realization of any wish of the people, we are not told.[28]

Buber opts for the second position: Samuel can represent the will of YHVH and mediate between the divine and the human. Although the *kohen* and the *shofet* also occupy such mediatory roles, Buber argues that Samuel must be understood as a *navi*, although he defies the lines of accepted categories by performing some functions of the other offices.

Having disposed of the notion that Samuel was a *shofet*, Buber denies that Samuel was a *kohen*. He acknowledges the textual support for scholars who maintain a priestly Samuel: "Does not the supplicant of ch. 7 also sacrifice, does not the 'Seer' of ch. 9 also bless the meal, do we not hear also in 10:8 and in the continuation of our narrative of his sacrificial office? Does not the Chronicle (I 6:13) account him among the Levites?"[29] Yet Buber finds the arguments for Samuel's priesthood as unpersuasive as those for his judgeship. The legend of Samuel's childhood, which tells of his birth and childhood at Shilo, the shrine of the ark, is dismissed as pure fiction, modeled on the Samson story and inserted here by a late redactor to make the final form of the text contain the meaning of the hero's life from the beginning. The actions of the adult Samuel differ in crucial ways from priestly service. He does not sacrifice professionally, at a single sanctuary at specified times, but only on special occasions, at large public gatherings, in a variety of locations. He makes oracular pronouncements freely, when he has something to say, whereas a priest can pronounce only by consulting the ephod, and only when asked a specific question. Ultimately, Buber concludes that for our narrator, "Samuel maintains no association with the priesthood and concedes to it no function."[30]

Buber sees the story beginning with a moralistic contrast between Eli, the priest at Shilo, and Samuel, who represents the future of Israel. Eli's sons "did not know YHVH" (2:12), whereas Samuel "came to know YHVH" (3:7). Revelation from YHVH was rare in the days of Eli (3:1), whereas YHVH reveals himself to Samuel (3:21). To be sure, YHVH announces the fall of Eli and the rise of Samuel by saying, "I will raise me up a *kohen ne'eman*," a faithful priest (2:35), but when he fulfills this action Samuel is *ne'eman le-navi*, trusted as a prophet (3:20). In other words, "the new *kohen* is no longer a *kohen* in the old sense, linked to noble house and sanctuary, but rather the house should be deprived of its heads, the sanctuary should be demolished, the inheritance should default to the *nabi*. Not a priest, who would found a new priestly house and preside over another sanctuary, but a *nabi*."[31] Thus, where Samuel takes over the priestly functions, he adapts them to the needs of his own mission.

Eli's house is replaced because it attempts to usurp political authority for the priesthood, the only centralized dynastic institution in Israel, by attacking the Philistines without charismatic authorization to do so. This is the first attempt in Israel's history at "a materialization of the theocracy as hierocracy, through utilization of the acknowledged oracle-authority and the Ark as martial power. Such an attempt is dependent on military proof."[32] Yet the effort culminates in catastrophe, as the ark is taken by the Philistines, putting an end to the priestly pretensions. Much of the material about the ark is legendary, but Buber insists on the historicity of this fundamental event: "No people comes up with such a thing; no people can make such a thing credible, if it has not been passed down."[33] The narrator interprets this event to mean that YHVH punishes the people, together with its overambitious priesthood, and elevates a new prophetic leadership instead.

If Samuel ever was a temple attendant at Shilo, even without having been born and raised there, he may have himself brought the ark to the Israelite war camp, under Eli's orders, together with his sons (4:4), only to witness the unfolding disaster. Samuel experiences this event as a revelation from YHVH: the loss of the ark stemmed not from the superior strength of the Philistines but from YHVH himself. Samuel would replace the hereditary cultic leadership with a prophetic, divine leadership without the ark and without the oracle of the ephod. He spends possibly two decades (from the ark defeat to the gathering at Mizpa in 7:5), nonviolently and noncoercively building power as a counterweight to the disgraced priestly authority. He does this primarily by gathering around him a circle of *nevi'im*, men inspired by the spirit of YHVH, who travel in groups throughout the land, singing, playing instruments, dancing in ecstasy, in witness to the rule of YHVH. Against critics who contest the association of Samuel with the bands of *nevi'im* reported in the text, Buber argues for a number of connections both textual and phenomenological.[34] Samuel and the *nevi'im* exemplify a relation to YHVH that runs from God to human being, rather than the other way around. The *davar*, the word, and the *ruach*, the spirit, of YHVH descend on the *nevi'im*, whereas priests resemble conjurors in that they attempt to move upward. But there are textual connections as well: at 10:5 Samuel announces to Saul that he will receive the Spirit together with a band of *nevi'im*, and at 19:20 Samuel is "standing as head over them," like "a secret society [*Geheimbund*]: a society for speech and a society for life."[35]

The *nevi'im* are committed to the ideology of Deborah, Gideon, and the direct rule of YHVH: "The true forerunner, the true spearhead, the true leader, the true *melekh* is JHWH. That is the *nebiish* stance, with or without the name *nabi*, and wherever it manifests itself, the *nabi*-essence manifests itself. . . . From there is the catastrophe of the Ark and its consequences to be considered anew."[36] Samuel, perhaps looking back to the period of Mosaic leadership before the sin of the calf, may even see the loss of the ark as an opportunity to reeducate the people about the truth of divine leadership. The loss of the ark is a symbol that YHVH leads according to his will alone. YHVH perceived that the people believed that they "had" him when they had the ark; let them learn that "he is no pseudo-king to whom one can dictate; he is the true *melekh*."[37] The people, however, are attached to the ark; they mourn for the lost leadership of God "as for the dead."[38] Therefore Samuel convenes a sacred gathering at Mizpa, to induce YHVH to the revival of the leadership.

The Desire of the People Transformed: From Direct to Indirect Theocracy

Here the narrative pace accelerates, but there is no great rout of the Philistines in Buber's reconstructed version of 1 Samuel. Instead, the Philistines hear of the gathering at Mizpa, and, sensing a plot against their hegemony, initiate a crackdown. However, a report of their troop movements reaches the Israelites in time and the crackdown fails. This happens concurrently with Samuel's sacrifice and prayer for deliverance from the Philistines, and he interprets the momentary reprieve from attack as evidence of the efficacy of his prayerful intervention—he believes that YHVH has "answered him." Here he is out of touch with the people, who have less patience than he: "They, mourning, who moaned 'after YHVH,' intended only his power of victory, not his sovereignty. The Palladium does not come home, the supremacy of the enemy continues, the answer given for the hour is not enough for the hours that follow . . . the invisible, merely audible does not satisfy . . . what one calls the kingship of YHVH, they reject, since it is not tangible and not effective enough."[39]

Following these events, Samuel attempts to stabilize his own charismatic authority by recommending his sons as his successors. This is an unwarranted overreach on two levels: first, since he and his *nevi'im* had yet to really solve the problem of the Philistine military threat; second, because his own power was rooted in the primitive-theocratic understanding of divine rule which "did not tolerate any extra-cultic dynasty formation."[40] His attempt to establish a dynasty undermines the basis of his own authority. There is thus a late Samuelic politics, divergent from the theopolitical vision of the *nevi'ish* movement, and Samuel becomes responsible for a second hierocratizing effort following the folly of the house of Eli: "This only adds to the outer crisis an inner one. Together, the lack of foreign policy achievement and the inner-political attempt at a dynasty provide the background for the desire of the people—or better, of the people's representatives [*Volksvertretungs*]."[41]

Samuel's overreach frustrates the elders of the people, or "sheikhs" as Buber sometimes calls them, who were already suffering Philistine dominance with no end in sight. Sociologically, they belong to the class of Israelites with the greatest contact with "civilization," and furthest along the path of de-nomadizing (Buber compares them to the Spartan *Gerousia*). Nonetheless, the offense to the old antidynastic bias and their "Bedouin" passion for freedom moves them to action. They demand that Samuel find a *melekh* who can win a war of liberation against the Philistines. If there is going to be centralization, it must at least accomplish the liberation war and achieve stability and order in the land. This request, of course, goes far beyond Samuel's own missteps: "They are searching for a captive charisma. They invert the Gideon-motif (Judges 8:22): the offer precedes the deed; they take the Jephthah-motif (Judges 11:6) once more to a wider folk plane—but the invitation is issued to one who has yet to be found. This is what is new. They would offer the crown, as is often assumed, to the first victor."[42] The form of the request indicates a secularization of divine rulership, in the sense established by *Kingship of God*. The "religious" preeminence of Samuel's house remains unquestioned; in fact, the address to Samuel presumes its continued validity. However, he is asked to separate his cultic functions from political leadership (a demotion

he unwittingly invited through his initial attempt at hierocratization), by install-
ing a separate individual to assume the responsibility of war making. Buber sees
in this the outline of "a concordat delimiting worldly and sacral power."[43]

Samuel reacts badly to the request. He had thought his intervention in the
most recent battle with the Philistines sufficiently demonstrated his efficacy. Now
the elders want a new person—they haven't even identified anyone, but expect
Samuel to find and appoint him! This person will be able to fulfill the "revolutionary task" (*revolutionäre Aufgabe*): summoning the tribes, mobilizing the troops,
and uniting Israel for liberation.[44] Samuel is surprised, however, when he turns
to YHVH in prayer:

> Samuel considers the desire of the people as an incontrovertible matter, as
> something that one can only accept or reject. He rejects it and prays against it.
> But JHWH does not see it so. He commands the *transforming* fulfillment: with
> binding testimony, with diplomatic legal-obligation to God as to the giver of
> the commission. What he says to Samuel is not an echo of the soul of the
> prophets, no projection of human feeling, or such as one might formulate; it
> is an immense, manifest contradiction: against that which is said, against that
> which is meant, against everything "unconscious" along with it. Initially that
> "Not you but me," and then: Neither their demand, nor your refusal, but rather
> this third, in which the human will is elevated into my will and is transformed
> within.[45]

Here Buber provides his account of the greatest problem in the history of the
founding of the monarchy. YHVH tells Samuel: "Hearken unto the people in
all that they tell you, for it is not you that they have rejected; it is Me they have
rejected as their king." Why should such a rejection deserve a hearkening? Buber
declines an antimonarchical reading, available from Jewish tradition, that says
YHVH decides to punish the people for their request by giving them evil kings.[46]
"That would be quite abhorrent to the spirit of the genuine narrative, which anticipates nothing of the coming human transgressions."[47] Rather, for Buber, this
is a moment in which YHVH reveals himself:

> He is however even greater and more mysterious than the image that the ex-
> egetes . . . made of him, this God who called world history to happen in order
> 'to put to the test' the liberated human creature. Where he grants him permis-
> sion, he transforms the substance of his desires during the fulfillment, so that
> it is turned into a new challenge—one that is elevated towards the last, not
> passed, test. The human being has failed, and he has enveloped his failure in
> a wish and sealed it; God grants the wish and does not grant it, he prevents
> disaster and does not prevent it, and from such a Yes and No grows the new,
> higher form of the challenge.[48]

YHVH here teaches Samuel something that combines politics, logic, psychology,
and religion into a single great existential lesson.

Finally, there is the matter of the *mishpat ha-melekh*, the "law of the king," which God orders Samuel to read to the people at 8:9. In the final version of 1 Samuel, verses 8:11–18 constitute Samuel's fulfillment of this order; he enumerates royal prerogatives and privileges (e.g., "he will take your sons and appoint them unto him for his chariots"), concluding with the dire prediction "You shall cry out on that day because of your king whom you have chosen yourselves, and YHVH shall not answer you on that day." For the traditional Jewish antimonarchical exegesis mentioned earlier, Samuel clearly warns the people that they should give up their request or suffer terrible royal outrages. For supporters of the divine right of kings throughout history, though, these words make up a perfectly reasonable list of divinely conferred royal powers. In a sense, Buber agrees with both positions. He grants to the Jewish exegetical tradition that 8:11–18 creates the impression that Samuel is warning the people against monarchy, but then he denies the originality of 8:11–18, holding it to be a Deuteronomist interpolation. And he agrees with the absolutists that the phrase *mishpat ha-melekh* in 8:9 refers to the way or customs of the king.[49] But—and this is the most important move of the argument—since Buber denies that 8:9 is followed by 8:11–18, Samuel does not fulfill the command to tell the people the "way of the king" until 10:25, where it is called the *mishpat ha-melukha*, "way of the kingship," and where we are not informed of the content of Samuel's speech.[50] Buber fills in the blank by surmising that Samuel conveys the nature of the new constitutional order: the *melekh* is to be the new commissioned one, responsible to God and prophet to do justice. The *mishpat* is "the rule which *should* apply to the appointed king, the command of law to him, his legal binding." In this sense it is a constitution from above rather than below; it is adopted by YHVH to oblige the king to him, and it contains "indeed no individual duties, needing only just to include the fundamental definition of this accountability."[51] Such an obligation contains a warning, but not one to the people about the king—it is to the people and the king together that Samuel sends warning that they should not misconstrue themselves as "like all the nations," as they originally requested. YHVH does not really intend to empower someone to "nominate themselves as vicariate of God, but not in reality owe accountability to heaven and report to it, but rather real responsibility to the top, a governorship deposable by the top, 'rejectable' by the top. So does the narrator understand the foundation of the Israelite *melukha* as the passage from the direct rulership of God to the indirect." The *navi* will retain an important role as a check on the power of the king, who will be a mere governor for YHVH. Thus the people both get what they want and are refused it; thus Samuel comes around from his initial rejection of the project to support for it. He is prepared to receive instruction concerning the man whom YHVH, and not he himself, will elect to the kingship.[52]

The Arcanum of the Monarchy: The Anointing and After

Through a series of seemingly random events, narrated in the form of a saga, YHVH brings Saul to Samuel, who has kept the elders with him following his announcement to them (rather than sending them home, as the final text has it). The actual election of Saul is a hidden event that takes place inside the divine mind; we are not given access to it. What we do get through our narrative, Buber argues, is a description of the manner in which YHVH enacts his promise to Samuel to grant the people their wish while transforming it at the same time. Buber comments on even apparently insignificant elements of the saga in his portrayal of the core narrative of Saul's rise to kingship as a manifesto for indirect theocracy. From the moment Saul's father loses his donkeys, the saga follows a unifying vision of the mysterious ways of YHVH.[53] Hiddenness, secrecy, and mystery are the dominant themes of this narrative; "the anointing story and what holds it together are only to be understood from an atmosphere of conspiracy."[54] A hero so imposing that he stands head and shoulders above all others (9:2) and a prophet famous throughout the land (9:6) meet for a secret encounter (9:25) and a secret anointing (10:1); the Spirit seizes the hero and he prophesies in public (10:10) but then hides his destiny from his family (10:16) and conceals himself when others seek him (10:22); he answers doubts about himself with silence (10:27) and recruits a secret guerrilla army (10:26) for a clandestine military operation (14:11):

> The apprehension of the secret incidents serves this apparently prolix Ritardando with incomparable efficacy. The divine providence is so strongly felt because it is secretive; the straying of the donkeys and the gossip of the girls apparently determine the tempo. The fable-colored glass of this mundane-seeming saga is suitable as no other to hide the white blossom of the holy.[55]

All this, in Buber's reading, is carefully arranged by the narrator, the "master of the esoteric style," and serves to justify the contradiction of YHVH himself, in granting the kingship to Israel even though it rejected him.

Samuel invites Saul to a clandestine sacrificial meal at which (according to Buber) the elders of the people are present. Samuel signals to all, by seating him in the place of honor (9:22) and assigning him the sacrificial portion (9:24), that Saul is the one who will fulfill the elders' request. No further explanation is required; the elders have been waiting for him. Any verbal announcement would spread rapidly and reach the Philistines, thus defeating the plan. Samuel and Saul then have a discussion (9:25), whose content is hidden, but which Buber holds to be about affairs of state and military strategy. The anointing takes place the next morning.

The account of Saul's anointing begins at 9:27, as Samuel and Saul are exiting the city. Samuel has Saul send his servant ahead so he can privately tell him a *davar elohim*, a word of God. Once again, the contents of the conversation are hidden, but when Samuel pours oil over Saul's head at 10:1, and kisses him, and asks "Is it not that YHVH has anointed you to be *nagid* over his own?" the speech appears to conclude. Buber notes two changes in the phrasing from 9:16, when YHVH told Samuel he would send him a Benjaminite whom he should anoint "to be *nagid* over my people Israel." The first is that "my people Israel" is replaced with *nachalato*, "his own" or "his inheritance"; Buber reads this as increasing the emphasis on YHVH's retained sovereignty even after the anointing. The second is that this time YHVH is said to have anointed Saul personally, concretizing the theopolitical character of the act. Buber argues that the first anointing, far more than any subsequent one, concentrates all "the pathos which inheres in the concept of the anointed king in biblical history and biblical prophecy."[56] Saul is called "anointed of YHVH" ten times, David only twice, and only the Saulid instances exemplify the essential trait of anointing, its "sacral inviolability."[57]

The anointing, however, because it is a secret ceremony, takes place only between YHVH, Samuel and Saul. It is insufficient on its own to install Saul in power; there are several further stages through which he must pass before he truly becomes the *melekh*. Nonetheless, the anointing must precede these other stages: the transformation of Saul's heart and his seizure by the Spirit, which make him "into another man," would on their own render him a *navi*; the successful prosecution of the liberation war would on its own make him a *shofet*. However, our narrative is about the rise of a *new* category in Israel, and Saul cannot be either of these preexisting types of figure:

> *Melekh* is biblically something *different* from *shophet*, and therefore a categorically different event must be preceded by a categorically different action. . . . When it comes to the case of Saul, were he too only a *shophet* . . . then neither the sacral basis nor the mark of mystery would have been his, and there would have resulted no *meschiach JHWH* and no messianism.[58]

The anointing is not sufficient, but it is necessary. Yet Buber reminds us that the narrator places as much emphasis on who does the anointing as who is anointed: it is the *navi*, in his function as proclaimer of YHVH's will, who anoints Saul *nagid*, and only because he has done this can there be a *melukha* and its attendant *mishpat*.

But Saul remains unknown to most of Israel; he must still come to power. Samuel announces that Saul will encounter three signs on his way home, and they come to pass, conveying that "here a people comes towards its unknown king."[59] The third and most important sign is the only one that is both predicted and reported. Saul encounters a proclaiming band of *nevi'im*, and "in this moment the *ruach* of JHWH invades him, transforming him, and he proclaims along with the proclaimers. . . . The gift of the Spirit is not separated from human categories. Like the old *schophtim*, so must the anointed, before he can operate as commander, be prepared and inwardly held by the low-roaring power, but this means: he must be a *nabi* the transforming hour long."[60] Buber agrees with scholars who see the religious agitation of the *nevi'im* as having a patriotic, political dimension; their singing and proclaiming announce the war of liberation. Saul's prophesying is witnessed by his fellow Gibeans, who ask each other: "What is this that is come upon the son of Kish? Is Saul too among the prophets?" They receive the enigmatic response: "And who is their father?" Buber reads this as a narrative in which the provincial, sedentary, conservative villagers, who know Kish well as a respectable local pillar of the community, express shock at the sight of Kish's son engaged in such "raging, incendiary behavior."[61] Another villager, who knows a little more about the *nevi'im*, answers that one cannot consider the actions of these men according to their family lineage; entry into the society binds the group together by severing one from one's earthly father.[62]

When Saul's uncle (previously unknown to the story) asks him what happened when he met Samuel, Saul refrains from telling him about the kingship. This is the first appearance of the concept *melukhah* in the story, and it appears as a secret kept, as something not enunciated aloud. The conspiracy cannot be revealed until the proper moment. From this point, however, the idea of the *nagid*, that justified the election of Saul for Samuel, is phased out; an academic notion is being replaced by a folk-popular concept. In the brief conversation between Saul and his uncle, the *Leitwort* sound of *nagid* reappears: *haggida, hagged, higgid, higgid*—"the final fading away of a *Leitwort* dear to [our narrator] from the central chapter of his history," before the story moves to the sphere of the people.[63]

Saul sinks into the collective of *nevi'im* and then emerges from it, ready to set the liberation plan in motion. Samuel has told Saul that after the third sign he would be empowered to "do as your hand shall find, for God is with you" (10:7).[64] Buber sees this as a reference to charismatic power and comments on the extent and limits of such power: "Now do for every situation what the situation claims and vouchsafes, since you are empowered to be charismatic. That is the practical implication of v. 6b: 'there you are transformed into another man.' Whoever receives the *ruach* needs to consult within his commission for his decisions, not any oracle. He is free within his commission."[65] However, freedom within a commission means the ability to choose the appropriate means to accomplish a particular task, as the Judges were: "The man gripped by the *ruach* is *specifically* empowered and *specifically* authorized."[66]

What needs to be achieved here is a levy. Samuel calls a gathering at Mizpa and proclaims that YHVH has chosen a king, and he reads the new *mishpat hamelukha*, publicly acclaiming Saul. At 10:24, all the people shout "long live the king," but Buber notes that the people are in fact split into three groups: two extreme wings and a passive mass in the middle. At one extreme is an elite of fighters, "whose hearts YHVH had touched" (10:26); these Saul recruits to mount a surprise attack on Ammon. At the other extreme are the *bene beli'al*, the "base fellows," who grumble and doubt Saul's ability to achieve the liberation; these

Saul ignores. As for the passive mass, they bring gifts, but they are unprepared for war with the Philistines. To overcome their fear, Saul leads his secretly formed elite guerrilla troops in combat against Nachash and the Ammonites, who have encamped against Jabesh-Gilead (11:1). This inspires faith in his military prowess and provides for a full-scale tribal recruitment against the Philistines, with Saul commanding that "anyone who does not follow behind Saul and Samuel" will have his oxen cut to pieces (11:7).[67] The call is successful, and "the people came out as one man" (11:8). The liberation succeeds, and the people, no longer divided, meet again at Gilgal "to renew the kingship" (11:14).

Samuel and Saul are united in the text of Saul's call to battle, as they are throughout the text of Buber's original narrator, who is "always concerned . . . to constantly bring together the anointing one and the anointed."[68] When Samuel calls for the people to "renew" the kingship at the end of chapter 11, he is connected with the concept *melukhah* for the third time (10:16, 10:25, 11:14). Samuel mediates the sacrament that makes the kingship possible, takes the constitution of the kingship to the people, and initiates the liberation strategy that cements the kingship. The Septuagint and the Masoretic text differ over the wording of 11:15b: the MT has Saul and the people rejoicing together, whereas the Septuagint has *Samuel* and the people rejoicing at Saul's coronation. Buber accepts the Septuagint's reading unconditionally, as demonstrating that this narrator has a vision contrary to that of later editors and redactors:

> Samuel, who initially became furious about the desire of the people, has proven himself, since JHWH has made known to him his decision for the transforming concession, as the faithful servant of his master and his whole-hearted representative in this matter. The *melukha* as such, as it has been allocated to Israel by JHWH, is thus not like that of all the nations, but rather it is characterized through the sense of commission of the anointing, the sense of office of the *nagid*-ship, the sense of binding of *mishpat*; *the kingship of the indirect theocracy as such may not, according to the thought of the narrator, have the nabi for an adversary.*[69]

Thus in the long struggle within Israel over God's kingship (a struggle that Buber says probably began at the same time as "Israel" itself), we have an exception to the rule that those who believe in the kingship of YHVH oppose the human monarchy. With the anointing of the first king, we find a narrator who believes, perhaps idealistically, that indirect theocracy is possible and that the kings can be faithful to their commissions. From now on, the *navi* is not a powerless representative of YHVH's will but is included within the power structure. The *navi*, the king, and the people, as a united commonwealth, are subject to the rule of YHVH. At 1 Samuel 12:25, one of the only verses Buber retains for our narrator without modification, Samuel threatens that if the people and the king do not hearken to the will of YHVH they will be "swept away":

In all concreteness the *nabi* here places state power under the prophetic critique: his critique, the speaker for God . . . [T]*his kingship in its particular actuality must have the nabi as verifier and admonisher.* Both belong together; each complements the other for the idea of a task. But both together result also in the insight of the narrator into the real historical function of the Israelite prophet, one unparalleled in the ancient Orient, a theopolitical function only explicable from a special historical location and special dispensation.[70]

Buber attributes this ideological position to Nathan, the first and last court prophet who was a real *navi*, not merely a tool of the king.[71] He serves David, but he takes no part in the Davidic war against the first king. He combines Saulid and anti-Saulid traditions in a single vision of the emergence of the anointed kingship. He and his circle do not pit Samuel against Saul, as did all later generations of storytellers: the partisans of David, who used Samuel's authority to delegitimize Saul's line, and the proto-Deuteronomic opposition to Solomon and the Deuteronomic and Jeremianic schools, who set Samuel against the kingship as a whole because they could not conceive that the great prophet could have acquiesced in such a folly. Our narrator argues for the *navi* Samuel as "herald and custodian of the indirect theocracy," and "by waging his cause, he wages his own."

Conclusion

For Buber, as for others, the apparent incoherence of the book of Samuel reflects its being a compilation of traditions that were passed down, revised, and compiled "in an epoch of difficult inner-political conflicts or even of civil war."[72] Unbiased representations of events are even scarcer than in ordinary times; historiography is a function of politics. Where a single ruler reigns unchallenged, the state can create annals and odes to its greatness, and such a history has a chance of being coherent. But this is not our text:

> Where on the other hand the sovereign power is contested again and again, as in the Israelite political system, be it because two dynastic claims stand against each other, be it because in the people and its spiritual leaders there are vital aspirations, which have found classical expression from the "anarchistic" Jotham fable, certainly belonging to a bold early flowering of literature, to the revolutionary royal slogans of Jeremiah (22:10–23:4), there is together with the manifold of possibilities for political action also a manifold of conceptions of history.[73]

Buber sees himself as having cut through layers of contentious tradition-formation to discover a unique voice in Israelite theopolitical history, perhaps the only voice that truly explains how the monarchy came to be.

Of course, the hopes of the Nathan circle are not to be fulfilled. The kings quickly seize total power, and reduce the prophets to a position of powerlessness. The kingdom forgets that it lives only by the sufferance of YHVH, and it neglects his commandments. As a result, the later prophetic voices become increasingly rebellious, seeking to recover the old anarcho-theocratic traditions, finding little use in the possibility of the anointing, longing for theocracy not as an immanent future but as the search for "a lost world." True, "the revolutionary stance of the Judean prophets is constrained through the Davidist character of pre-exilic messianism," and prior to Jeremiah they never quite reach the point of proclaiming opposition to the kingdom itself.[74] They nonetheless seek to assert the kingship of YHVH, against the kingships of Israel and Judah. The story of this struggle is *The Prophetic Faith*.

Notes

1. WZB 725–845. Citations in this chapter will be to the new critical edition, SM 281–379. Translations from *Der Gesalbte* are my own.

2. These chapters are "Das Volksbegehren" (The Desire/Demand of the People), in *In Memoriam Ernst Lohmeyer*, ed. Werner Schmauch (Stuttgart: Evangelisches Verlagswerk, 1951), 53–66; "Die Erzählung von Sauls Königswahl," first published as מעשה המלכת שאול (*Ma'aseh Hamelukhat Sha'ul*, *Tarbitz* 22 [1950]: 1–84); and "Samuel und die Abfolge der Gewalten," first published as שמואל והשתלשלות הרשויות בישראל (*Shmu'el ve-Hishtalshlut ha-Reshuyot Be-Yisrael*, *Zion* 4 (1939: 1–29). Both the *Werke* and Buber's bibliography give the year as 1938, but the journal gives 1939, תרצ"ט). Brief excerpts of "Samuel und die Abfolge der Gewalten" appeared as "Samuel und die Lade," in *Essays Presented to Leo Baeck on the Occasion of His Eightieth Birthday* (London: East and West Library, 1954), 20–25. Michael A. Meyer's fine "Samuel and the Ark," in Buber, *On the Bible*, ed. Nahum N. Glatzer (New York: Schocken Books, 1982), 131–136, is the only English translation of this material I have found.

3. Buber, introduction to "Das Volksbegehren," in *In Memoriam Ernst Lohmeyer*, 53. In this short paragraph Buber refers to "Das Volksbegehren" as the first chapter of *Der Gesalbte* and calls the second chapter "Wie Saul König ward."

4. This variety surged in the early modern period, when the Protestant commitment to *sola scriptura* fueled a "political Hebraism"; cf. Eric Nelson, *The Hebrew Republic: Jewish Sources and the Transformation of European Political Thought* (Cambridge, MA: Harvard University Press, 2011); Gordon Schochet, Fania Oz-Salzberger, and Meirav Jones, *Political Hebraism: Judaic Sources in Early Modern Political Thought* (New York: Shalem, 2008). Take one example, from a thinker who helped define the term "theocracy" for the modern period: "If it was rightly said about the people of Israel when they rejected Samuel's rule (I Sam 8:7) that they would not allow [God] to reign over them, why might the same thing not equally well be said today about those who allow themselves license to malign all positions of authority instituted by God?" John Calvin, *On Civil Government*, in *Luther and Calvin on Secular Authority*, ed. and trans. Harro Höpfl (Cambridge: Cambridge University Press, 1991), 55. Jean Bodin offers a nearly identical interpretation: "Contempt for one's sovereign prince is contempt toward God, of whom he is the earthly image." Bodin, *On Sovereignty*, ed. Julian H. Franklin (Cambridge: Cambridge University Press, 2004), 46. Bodin's interpretation makes Samuel into a "prince" and accuses the Israelites of demanding a "different" prince. A Huguenot writer appealed to this same passage to make an opposite point: "Kings should always remember that it is from God, but by the people and for the people that they rule. . . . [T]hey should not claim that they have received their kingdom from God alone and by the sword . . . since they were first girded with that very sword by the people." George Garnett, ed. and trans., *Vindiciae, Contra Tyrannos* (New York: Cambridge University Press, 2003), 68–69. These interpretations assume that

the request for a king was not itself problematic. But Thomas Hobbes reads the passage otherwise:

> When the Elders of Israel . . . demanded a King, Samuel displeased therewith, prayed unto the Lord; and the Lord answering said unto him, *Hearken unto the voice of the People, for they have not rejected thee, but they have rejected me, that I should not reign over them.* Out of which it is evident, that God himself was then their King; and Samuel did not command the people, but only delivered to them that which God from time to time appointed him.

Hobbes, *Leviathan,* ed. Richard Tuck (Cambridge: Cambridge University Press, 2001), 283.

5. Robert Polzin, speaking for "literary" criticism, chastises biblical scholars (including Buber) for excessive concern with what he calls "genetic" questions at the expense of the final form of the text—which is the only text we actually have (as opposed to the hypothetical pretexts constructed by critics in their investigations). Polzin nonetheless cites some of Buber's more "literary" observations; Polzin, *Samuel and the Deuteronomist: A Literary Study of the Deuteronomic History, Part 2: 1 Samuel* (Bloomington: Indiana University Press, 1993).

6. A position associated with Martin Noth, who is cited frequently throughout *The Anointed.* Buber does not avail himself of Noth's authority in this matter, even though it might initially seem congenial to his political views.

7. Spinoza, *Theological-Political Treatise,* trans. Samuel Shirley (Indianapolis: Hackett, 2001), 120.

8. *N.B.:* Not textual reconstruction, because Buber generally does not seek the original text; he seeks the original tradition that he thinks lies behind the earlier forms of the text.

9. SM 295.

10. See Buber, "*Leitwort* Style in Pentateuch Narrative," and Buber, "*Leitwort* and Discourse Type," in ST 114–128, 143–150.

11. SM 307.

12. Ibid., 308.

13. Ibid., 309.

14. Ibid., 301.

15. Buber points out that 1 Samuel 4:18 even describes Eli, in the moment of his great military *failure,* as having "judged Israel forty years"; its placement shows that it designates succession to authority, not judgeship in the technical military sense. SM 373.

16. SM 300.

17. By splitting up the passage, Buber is saying that the *Leitwort* is a false *Leitwort.* He associates the *Leitwort* style with the "genuine" narrator, and accuses later editors of failing to master it. Another example of an apparent *Leitwort* that Buber considers misleading is the play on the name *sha'ul* and its seeming relation to *shemu'el.*

18. SM 287.

19. Ibid., 288.

20. Ibid., 290.

21. SM 337–338, 342.

22. Ibid., 343.

23. With the exception of 2a, from *va-ani* through *itkhem*: "and I am old and greyheaded and my sons are with you," which Buber deletes as clashing with the more authentic earlier description of the sons as a black mark on Samuel's tenure.

24. SM 339–340. This reconstructed passage evidences what Buber considers the clear and powerful style of the authentic work of our narrator.

25. Ibid., 297–298. I usually render Buber's *Geheimnis* as "secret" or "mystery." I translate *Geheimnis* as "arcanum" here because of this term's history in discussions of royal authority and ideological mystification: "To every great politics belongs the 'arcanum.'" Carl Schmitt,

Roman Catholicism and Political Form, trans. G. L. Ulmen (Westport, CT: Greenwood Press, 1996), 34.

26. Ibid., 323. Buber's use of *Feindesnot* (enemy-emergency) suggests an oblique reference to Schmittian discourse; however, he avoids an explicit link by not using *Ausnahmezustand*.

27. I treat the three chapters of *Der Gesalbte* as telling a coherent story about Samuel, Saul, and the rise of the monarchy, and I reconstruct Buber's interpretation of the core narrative and its likely historicity from all three. There are some inconsistencies between the chapters. For example, "Das Volksbegehren" implies that the elders' complaint about Samuel's sons is a post facto rationale, irrelevant to the true motivation for requesting a king, whereas "Samuel und die Abfolge der Gewalten" holds that Samuel attempted to endow his sons with some kind of power, and that this offense against the primordial Israelite love of freedom partially motivated the elders' request. The discrepancy is likely due to the incomplete nature of *Der Gesalbte*, or else the claim in "Das Volksbegehren" may intend only the interpolation of the textual mention of Samuel's sons at 8:5, not the oral tradition that Samuel somehow violated the antihereditary bias of premonarchical Israelite political culture.

28. SM 282.

29. Ibid., 354.

30. Ibid., 359.

31. Ibid., 358.

32. Ibid., 379.

33. Ibid., 361. In other words, the taking of the ark so runs against the grain of the usual naïve patriotic belief in divine protection that a mere legend about it, unsupported by memory, would be rejected as fiction and would not be handed down.

34. Primary interlocutors here include Alfred Jepsen, Sigmund Mowinckel, and Paul Volz. Buber enlists Rudolf Kittel and Abraham Kuenen to support his thesis regarding Samuel's leadership of the *nevi'im*.

35. Ibid., 370. The specific term *Geheimbund* appears in Buber, *Werke II*, 833; earlier editions had *Bund*. That Buber chose to play up the "secret" nature of the early prophetic society seems significant.

36. Ibid., 370–371.

37. Ibid., 372.

38. SM 299.

39. Ibid., 302.

40. Ibid., 374.

41. Ibid., 375.

42. Ibid.

43. SM 285. A "concordat" is an agreement between the Vatican and a secular government. The *Reichskonkordat* signed between Nazi Germany and the Catholic Church in 1933 was afterward referred to in the singular as "the Concordat." The use of the term here is suggestive, as though there were an *Urkonkordat*, setting a precedent for all the others.

44. N.B.: Buber refers to the elders as the "representative body" of the people, the *Volksvertreterschaft*, and the task of the king as *Aufgabe*. These are distinct from the terms he uses when referring to the *nevi'im*—the commissioned ones, the delegates, *Beauftragten*. Buber knew another situation in which the "people's delegates," including Landauer, stood against the "people's representatives," namely the SPD and its allies in and outside of parliament. Then, too, initial cooperation collapsed when the people's "representatives" seized all power from the "delegates." Then, too, the delegates relinquished their program and their power, though they remained committed to "meting out critique, struggling with personal dedication, and where it is necessary, preparing for martyrdom." SM 376.

45. SM 302.

46. See sources cited in Michael Walzer and Menachem Lorberbaum, eds., *The Jewish Political Tradition*, vol. 1, *Authority* (New Haven, CT: Yale University Press, 2000), 147–155.

47. SM 288.

48. Ibid., 289.

49. Buber relates this use of *mishpat* to that found at Judges 13:12, when Samson's father Manoah asks the angel who announced that Samson would be born what the *mishpat*, the rule, of the child should be once the word comes to pass. Here it clearly means instructions— "roughly the 'rule [*Richte*],' the 'guideline [*Richtschnur*].'"

50. 1 Samuel 10:25 reads: "Then Samuel told the people the *mishpat ha-melukha*, and wrote it in a book, and laid it up before YHVH. And Samuel sent all the people away, every man to his house." There is still the problem that 8:9 is often read as containing an instruction from YHVH to Samuel to "warn" the people what the king will do. Buber denies that *ha'ed ta'id* in 8:9 should be read as "warn," but argues that "*ha'ed* with *b^e* implies that a solemn testimony is erected, facing a partner, for an explanation that was or is to be delivered in respect to him." Ibid., 290.

51. Ibid., 291.

52. This point provides another textual consideration leading Buber to eliminate the version of the *mishpat ha-melekh* found at 8:11–18: In 8:18 Samuel says that "the day will come when you will cry out because of the king *whom you have chosen yourselves*." To Buber this reads like a polemic against 10:24: "Have you seen him, whom YHVH has chosen?" The people desire *a* king, but YHVH elects *this* king.

53. I highlight only central narrative elements; Buber, however, discusses everything from the lands through which Saul searches for the missing donkeys, to the conversation with his servant about the "seer" who lives in the city, to the chatter of the girls at the well, and so on.

54. SM 327.

55. Ibid., 303. However, here again I translate from the 1965 edition, for which Buber changed *buntfarbige* (colorful) to the more narrative-centric *märchenfarbige*; Buber, *Werke II*, 753.

56. SM 352.

57. Ibid. Buber considers the anointing of David by Samuel, reported at 1 Samuel 16:13, to be a literarily dubious "idealized repetition of the Saulish" anointing, and he holds David's two public anointings by the people, reported at 2 Samuel 2:4 and 3:5, to lack prophetic sanction.

58. Ibid., 353.

59. SM 314.

60. Ibid., 313.

61. Ibid., 319.

62. Buber notes that between Samuel and Elisha we encounter no prophets with patronyms, and entertains the proposal that the word *navi* led to a "joke of a folk-etymology," *en-avi*, or "fatherless."

63. Ibid., 322.

64. Buber strikes 10:8, in which Samuel issues orders to go to Gilgal and wait seven days for him to arrive to sacrifice, from the original narrative, holding it to be an interpolation by the author of 13:7b–15a. The interruption of the charismatic empowerment with a new order to wait recalls the "theopolitical hour" of Isaiah and Ahaz in PF, in which the prophet as the voice of YHVH denies the human sovereign the right to claim mastery of the logic of war. However, for this reason Buber denies it to this narrator, who is not of a late prophetic school but an early one.

65. Ibid., 317.

66. Ibid., 317n44.

67. Here the chronology of Buber's reconstructed narrative differs from the final text of 1 Samuel. Buber places the Ammonite attack roughly concurrent with the king-selection ceremony; the levy against the Philistines then follows, as the narrator assumes that by now "all those whom the call reaches now know whom this Saul is, who calls them, and also knows this, that he is able to make good on his threat 'so shall be done with his oxen.'" Ibid., 330.

68. Ibid., 331.

69. Ibid., 335 (Buber's italics).

70. Ibid., 341 (Buber's italics).

71. This is not to say that Buber considers Nathan to be a chronicler, although he does note that of the four history narratives claimed by Leonhard Rost to descend from the Davidic-Solomonic period, two of them feature Nathan in a significant position, and indeed one where he demonstrates simultaneous fidelity to and critique of the monarchy. Ibid., 348.

72. Ibid., 343–344.

73. Ibid., 344.

74. Ibid., 364.

6 The Battle for YHVH
The Prophetic Faith

Thus has YHVH, the Holy One of Israel, spoken:
In turning away and in rest you will be saved,
In keeping still and in confidence will be your strength.
But you would not.

    —Isaiah 30:15

This is a reliable political program for the people living at the time in Canaan.

    —Martin Buber

I give thee a king in Mine anger, and take him away in My wrath.

    —Hosea 13:11

Introduction: A Theopolitical History of Israel

Of Buber's biblical studies, *The Prophetic Faith* receives the most attention.[1] Harold Bloom called it Buber's "finest single book," and Gershom Scholem said that in it Buber "seems to me to have reached the high point of his efforts to understand the Bible as a great dialogue."[2] Its section on Isaiah, "The Theopolitical Hour," has been the subject of recent treatments by Nitzan Lebovic and Christoph Schmidt.[3] Nonetheless, there are relatively few studies of the work as a whole, its place in Buber's corpus, and its contribution to his theopolitics when considered with his other biblical studies. Here I argue that it is a deeply conflicted work. It is the capstone to the theopolitical history of Israel that begins with Moses, continues with the rise of the monarchy, and concludes with the Babylonian Exile (Buber virtually ignores the Second Commonwealth), yet it is riven by the tension Buber finds in the development of the messianic idea over time.[4] According to the original plan of *Das Kommende*, this should be the point at which the origin of the doctrine of messianism in Israel emerges with greater clarity. An ideal has been presented, and the departure from that ideal—indeed, the failure ever to fully realize it—has been painstakingly charted; what follows is the adaptation to new circumstances and the transformation of the ideal in the new situation. What was only touched on in *Kingship of God* and *Moses* is here given fuller exposition, as the Israelite faith transforms into the exilic tradition that will be known as Judaism.

Methodology and Structure

From the perspective of the theopolitics laid out in *Kingship of God* and *The Anointed*, Buber's primary challenge in *The Prophetic Faith* is the extent to which the prophets accept the parameters of the monarchical period. *Kingship of God*, in its discussion of the redaction of the book of Judges, placed great emphasis on how the anarcho-theocracy was forgotten after the rise of the monarchy. *The Prophetic Faith*, in accordance with this, treats the prophets as people of their own times, embedded in particular historical contexts, no matter how much legendary material has accumulated around them. As men of the monarchical period, the prophets criticize the kings, but rarely the kingship; they criticize monarchs, but not monarchy. In this sense, the "fight against the kings . . . is not fundamental."[5] Their longing for a just and righteous order usually takes the form of a longing for a just and righteous (human) king. Yet these are the figures Buber presents as the true inheritors of the tradition of Moses and Samuel as he understands it (in this Buber follows Jeremiah himself, for whom Moses and Samuel are linked as predecessors; Jeremiah 15:1). Buber relies on the proposition established in *The Anointed* that when the people asked for a king, YHVH both did and did not give them what they wanted, creating a monarch but also an independent *navi* to check the king's power.

Buber's methodological preliminaries are even shorter here than in *Moses*. Once again denying that source criticism has the ability to identify and date discrete "documents" in the larger biblical text, he proposes instead a "tradition-critical" division into three literary tendencies, defined by the authors' political interests: court prophets (interested in the monarchy and its antecedents), free prophets (interested in antecedents to the rule of the Spirit), and priests (interested in antecedents to the cult). However, in developing their material, these editors build on oral traditions; therefore, a late literary form can contain ancient content. Buber repeats his defense (from *Moses*) of legend as a source of history, as well as his emphasis (from *Kingship of God*) on moving to the very borders of knowledge to study religious phenomena.

The Prophetic Faith contains significantly less documentation of its arguments than *Kingship of God* and *Moses*; this is partially because it is less argumentative.[6] Buber sometimes asserts that scholars miss the sense of a passage when they attribute it to a later editor rather than to the prophet himself or to one of his disciples. Seldom, however, does this assertion pertain to a pivotal part of his argument, and he rarely confronts a scholarly consensus as dogmatic as that which he faced with respect to other parts of the Bible. If there is scholarly disagreement, for example, about the historical order of the prophets, or whether they lived at all, or whether they are responsible for preaching the messages reflected in the books that bear their names, such controversy has not resulted in any conventional wisdom. Nor is it particularly controversial that these books were edited extensively before their eventual canonization. There are doubts about the nature of this editing, and whether the prophets founded "schools" of disciples, who assumed the right to modify their teachers' speeches, but these doubts rarely threaten Buber's central theopolitical assertions. Thus, *The Prophetic Faith* is much less of a polemic against the scholarship of its time than *Kingship of God* or *Moses*. Its genre remains historical criticism, but of all Buber's works in that field it is the closest in character to his free-flowing religio-philosophical essays.

Of the themes that typically concern the literature on prophecy, Buber devotes the greatest attention to the biblical standard for distinguishing true from false prophecy.[7] Starting with the praise of Balaam that "there is no divination in Jacob, nor soothsaying in Israel" (Numbers 23:23), Buber assumes that merely predicting the future correctly cannot be the criterion for determining true prophets. The hearer cannot know whether a prophecy will come to pass. Moreover, a true prophet can issue one unfulfilled prophecy after another, with his prophecies unfulfilled precisely because he is successful—people hear him and repent. Even the seemingly more sophisticated criterion suggesting that false prophecy lulls the people into an unjustified sense of security, whereas true prophecy accurately warns of approaching danger, only partially captures the situation: "It is not whether salvation or disaster is prophesied, but whether the prophecy, whatever it is, agrees with the divine demand meant by a certain historical situation, that is important."[8] True prophecy confronts the people with an alternative, consisting only of possibilities actually available. The false prophecy against which Jeremiah battles is pernicious precisely because it too takes on historical form but encourages the people "to meet the historical danger with the usual historical action."[9] Nothing about the situation makes obvious the truth of the prophecy; God will not put his thumb on the scales for his spokesman:[10] "This God makes it burdensome for the believer and light for the unbeliever; and His revelation is nothing but a different form of hiding His face." False prophets are not even necessarily malicious; "certainly many of them are honest patriots," but they are deceived by their delusions, which are projections of their own desires. True prophets, however, encounter the word of God as something transcendent that subdues them.[11] Buber discusses this latter phenomenon most powerfully in the case of Jeremiah, whose arrogation of leadership to the prophets Buber contrasts with his priestly background; this is also the most "dialogical" of all the passages in his writings on the Bible. In contrast to the perception of Buber's dialogue as a mutual and reciprocal process, here the dimension of imbalance between the parties cannot be effaced:

> The divine word, which suddenly descends into the human situation, unexpected and unwilled by man, is free and fresh like the lightning. . . . He, Who speaks, is incomprehensible, irregular, surprising, overwhelming, sovereign.

> Therefore it is the virtue of this word, and of this alone, to lead, that is to say, to show the way. . . . Only Jeremiah of all the Israelite prophets has dared to note this bold and devout life conversation of the utterly inferior with the utterly superior—in such a measure is man here become a person. All Israelite relationship of faith is dialogic; here the dialogue has reached its pure form. Man can speak, he is permitted to speak; if only he truly speaks to God, there is nothing he may not say to Him.[12]

A bit of Buber's old Nietzschean vitalism returns here, with true revelation being "free and fresh like the lightning," and he joins themes of sovereignty and dialogue.

Buber treats the prophets chronologically, beginning with the legendary figures described in Kings (Elijah and Elisha), then the first writing prophets (Amos and Hosea), concentrating on the eighth-century Isaiah, and last the preexilic prophets (Micah and Jeremiah). The book concludes with Ezekiel and Deutero-Isaiah, as well as several other texts Buber dates to the same period (e.g., Job, Psalm 73). If we look at the placement of these discussions in the structure of *The Prophetic Faith* as a whole, however, the plan of the book seems obscure. The eight chapters roughly increase in length as the book progresses. The introduction and the first few chapters ("The Song of Deborah," "Origins," and "God of the Fathers," fewer than forty-five pages combined, despite forming "half" of the book by number of chapters) trace the Israelite faith back through the generations to its origin, which Buber finds in its oldest extant form in the Song of Deborah (Judges 5).[13] He then advances in time again, from the patriarchs to Sinai ("Holy Event"), and from Sinai to the period of the settlement and the rise of the monarchy ("The Great Tensions"), before finally addressing the prophetic books themselves ("The Turning to the Future" and "The God of the Sufferers," more than half the book, despite comprising only two chapters).

The reason for this structure is not obvious. Buber's movement through these topics neither charts a simple decline nor describes a single development, perhaps because he is mingling the original goal of *Das Kommende* (accounting for the origin of messianism) with the new goal of describing the teaching of the prophets. He blends fragmentary older material with new material to produce *The Prophetic Faith* as a stand-alone work, not entirely smoothly, as evidenced by his references in the introduction to "parts" of the book that are not extant in the final table of contents.[14] Moreover, Theodore Dreyfus has shown that the concluding part of the work, the section called "The Mystery," which addresses the transformation of the messianic idea in the suffering servant songs of Deutero-Isaiah, already existed in a lecture Buber gave in Berlin on April 6, 1925, in honor of the opening of the Hebrew University in Jerusalem.[15] That lecture was called "The Messianic Mystery," and it seems significant that the final fragments of *Das Kommende*, a work resulting from years of research with Rosenzweig, are combined in 1942 with a position on the climactic moment of the narrative of Israelite messianism that had already been developed before the Buber-Rosenzweig Bible translation work began in earnest, and before Buber began to compile the notes for *Kingship of God*. The inclusion of "The Messianic Mystery" at the close of *The Prophetic Faith* complicates the alliance between the theopolitical and the prophetic that otherwise prevails throughout Buber's biblical works. Buber stretches his categories to include Deutero-Isaiah, costing him theoretical coherence.

Given the odd structure of the book, one fruitful way to discuss it, without retreading ground, and following Buber's own suggestions, is to see it as divided into three main sections according to the focus of *Das Kommende*. In this light, *The Prophetic Faith* traces the historical path of the relationship between Israel and YHVH, a nonmessianic faith at its inception, to the point of accepting its first messiah (the flesh-and-blood king, who will deliver the people from military threat), the second messiah (the hoped-for king, perhaps still imminent, who will rule according to God's will), and finally to Buber's unique interpretation of the third messiah, a suffering redeemer of the uncertain future, who is still not yet the cosmic figure responsible for healing nature and ending time.

The First Messiah: A King Like All the Nations Have, to Fight Our Battles

The introduction to *The Prophetic Faith* is noteworthy for the way it employs language that Buber often shuns. He declares on his first page that his purpose is "to describe a teaching [*Glaubenslehre*/תורה] which reached its completion in some of the writing prophets from the last decades of the Northern kingdom to the return from the Babylonian exile. . . . [T]his is the teaching about the relation between the God of Israel and Israel." It is important to keep this description in mind when faced with Buber's repeated emphasis on the dynamism and unpredictability of this relation in the light of God's freedom, and when considering his repeated insistence that he himself has no "teaching."[16] Insofar as Buber adheres to his stated purpose, the changes in the "teaching" he describes give his narrative an overall mood of decline and disappointment, albeit with some complications. The "teaching," wherever it arises, is connected with figures designated as *navi*. As we have seen, the *navi* for Buber is not one who "predicts," but one who wishes "to set the audience, to whom the words are addressed, before the choice and decision, directly or indirectly."[17] The community—and the agent of *teshuva*, or "return," demanded by the *navi* is always a community, even if an individual is sometimes addressed—determines the future through the choice it makes in response to the call of the *navi*. Buber insists on this essential form of prophecy to such an extent that any step away from it is necessarily a distortion, even if he endeavors to maintain scholarly objectivity in describing the evolution of a social role in response to changing conditions.

The first five chapters trace the relationship described in the Song of Deborah, "YHVH God of Israel," back to Joshua's assembly of the people at Shechem, back further to Sinai, and back further to Abraham, then forward to Sinai again. The basic contention is that "the true original nomad faith" of Abraham is a personal revelation that prefigures the collective revelation at Sinai.[18] Abraham is compelled by his experience of God to modify the nomadic religion of the Semites, who worshipped moon gods as "gods of the way," by proclaiming a god who is also a god of the way, but with several crucial differences: he leads at all times, not only under moonlight; he leads where *he* wills rather than helping the tribe get where it wants to go; he communicates to the one he has chosen, by distinguishing the chosen one from others. Abraham's *hijra* is defined by a straying that is perceived as a being-led.[19] The decision to follow such leadership demands committed and loving devotion. These elements remain present in the move from Genesis to Exodus; the family led by the road god becomes the people led through the desert. Finally, the political rulership that is embodied at Sinai through the constitution of Israel as a people with God as its king is prefigured in the patriarchal narratives as well: "A *coming* deity like this could not acknowledge any domain in the universe or life, on which he set foot, remaining outside his sway; whoever had possession of the place and sphere was forcibly put down from his throne, or was clearly shown to be the substitute of the coming deity, or even to be identified with this very deity."[20] This explains why there is no war between YHVH and the Elim of the patriarchal age, the way there will be in later years against the Baalim—the El Elyon of Abimelech is simply recognized by Abraham to be his very own god, who subjects all of life to his rule.

What Buber says about Sinai here strongly emphasizes the fact that "Israel only exists as 'YHVH's people' . . . 'coming to YHVH's help' and 'blessing' Him, and he who does not belong in this sense to YHVH's people does not belong to Israel."[21] Indeed, Buber proclaims, "No one can declare himself [*entscheiden*/להתיחש] for Israel without declaring himself for YHVH," a statement that resonates beyond the circumscribed world of textual criticism into the contemporary political context of that criticism.[22] The entity "Israel" is created here, its very name testifying to the sovereignty of its ruler (Buber supposes, with Martin Noth, that the original meaning of the word Israel is not "God fights" but "God rules"). The "holy event" (*Heiliges Ereignis*, מאורע קדוש) that creates this people (Buber's definition of holy event parallels his description of "miracle" in *Moses*), however, creates it only as potentiality, as "holy people" that shall be, and due to the eventual failure of the people to respect the divine sovereignty and to attain this status, "after the people had broken the covenant again and again, this category changed and was replaced by the Messianic promise and hope."[23]

The institutions Moses ordained are intended to aid the people in attaining their holy status, that is, to help Israel become Israel. The chapter "Holy Event" condenses the separate discussions in *Moses* about the Passover ("A nomadic feast . . . transformed by the holy event into a feast of history"), the Sabbath ("a day . . . freed of all authority of command except that of the one Lord . . . [it] binds together the deity and the tired, exhausted slave"), the divine demonism, the covenant ("no legal agreement, but a surrender to the divine power and grace"), and God's ownership of land ("The divine ownership of the ground and the whole people's possession of it originate in a unity meant to last forever, whereas the rights of the individual are only conditional and temporary").[24] Buber cites Albrecht Alt's work *Die Ursprünge des israelitischen Rechts* in support of his own basic idea: "In Israel's apodictic law an aggressive, as yet unbroken force operates, a force which subjects every realm of life to the absolute authority claim of YHVH's will for his people, and therefore cannot recognize any secular or neutral zone."[25] The "social" laws are not a result of deliberations by wise men with expertise in a special realm, called "the social," but rather look toward "establishing a true people, as the covenant partner of the *melekh*, according as the tribes are a people as yet only by God's act and not by their own. . . . The *melekh* YHVH does not want to rule a crowd, but a community."[26] Thus, Buber claims that the prophets are conservative in their social preaching, echoing the original intention of the covenant.

The discussion of Joshua and the covenant renewal at Shechem fleshes out Buber's earlier statement that "for the expression of the theocratic idea the book of Joshua is indeed only a trough between Moses and Judges-Samuel."[27] Buber rejects claims that Joshua 24:1–28 represents the earliest covenant report, and that the later Sinai account was intended to provide a precedent for events at Shechem. However, here Buber gives Joshua more credit than in his other works: Joshua extracts from the people a commitment to recognize what their previous oath of fealty to YHVH entails: not only do they as a people serve YHVH alone, but also each individual family must cast out its subsidiary deities and private gods—something that might not have even occurred to them as interfering with the public worship of YHVH.[28] Again, this is not about enforcing cultic propriety: "Because these subsidiary private deities weaken the collection of the people around YHVH, they hinder the establishment and manifestation of a united 'Israel' acting historically as such. . . . Hitherto the conquest of the land has only partially succeeded, because there was not . . . any actual and vital unity of the people." Elimination of the family deities is a theopolitical intervention aimed at increasing cultural unity and military effectiveness. Joshua's effort, however, achieves only partial success, because the establishment of a cult center is actually the first stage in the process of reducing direct divine sovereignty, to the point where the prophets' invocations of it are experienced as new ideas.[29] The increasing difficulties of the conquest, meanwhile, give rise to the group Buber refers to here explicitly as "a 'realist-political' movement," "in opposition to this theopolitical ardor [of the Deborah circle]," demanding a kingly dynasty of flesh and blood.[30]

After recapitulating *The Anointed* by narrating the loss of the ark and the passage from Samuel to Solomon, the chapter on "The Great Tensions" introduces the "legendary" prophets with discussions of Micaiah ben Imlah, Elijah the Tishbite, and Elisha.[31] First Buber reiterates his conviction, already argued in *Der Gesalbte*, that Samuel too is primarily a prophet and not a priest. This early prophetic leadership demonstrates why the prophets are seen as the representatives of YHVH and explains that "they were the ones who anointed all the kings in Israel (except Omri) acting on divine authority, a fact the influence of which was still recognized in postexilic times (Neh. 6:6f)—they stand and summon to justice the representatives on the royal throne for their treachery against YHVH and his commandments."[32] Samuel's failures, however, play a significant role in the rise of the first messiah, whom he anoints. He is the one who attempts to pass on his judgeship to his sons; he fails to defeat the Philistines and to counter the propaganda of the realist politicians with a compelling vision of the leadership of YHVH.

Samuel's prophethood combined with his role as anointer sets the tone for the "*theopolitical supposition* of this prophetic standpoint, a supposition which is for the most part not openly expressed . . . the commission of YHVH's representative which is not fulfilled by the kings in Israel."[33] The prophet must be understood as a believer in his own role as the guardian of the divine will of the true king. The prophet's role is to keep the monarch accountable and to remind him that he is merely a governor: "In the first period it was required of the *am* that they should be a true *am*, and in the second period it was required of the *nagid* that he should be a true *nagid*." However, from the beginning of the kingdom, the monarchy is "prepared to accept the symbolic sense of the charge and authorization from on high, implied in the act of anointing, but it resists the realism, according to which orders can be given to the king and an account of his activities can be demanded."[34]

The Second Messiah: A Righteous Ruler in Fear of God, Like the Light of a Morning without Clouds

Crucial to Buber's picture is the notion that the protest prophecy of Amos and Hosea marks the end of a long process and is not an innovation of the eighth century BCE. Buber cites the last words of David (2 Samuel 23:1–7) as evidence for a view that YHVH "has" a future righteous ruler whom he keeps to himself for the present.[35] From the very beginning, the people and the kings fail to live up to the conditions on which the kingship was premised and promised, and from the beginning of the kingdom there are people who see it as their role to call the sinful kingdom to account. For the most part, however, their words fall on deaf ears: "For four hundred years they come one after the other and take their stand before the prince and reprove him because of the violated covenant, and finally Jeremiah (22:6ff), some time before the disaster, announces destruction for the king's house which had not been just, and therefore was no more justified."[36]

The prophets' battle for the sovereignty of YHVH takes two major forms: the fight for social justice and the fight against worship of other gods. Buber emphasizes that these struggles cannot really be separated. Both result from the monarchy's secularization: "There is here an acknowledgment of the Lord of the heavens and of the Lord of the cult too, but there remains no place for God as the leader of the people, and indeed Solomon did not need this. The functions of YHVH are to be reduced so that they *do not bind* the king."[37] The kings imagine that they bargain with YHVH, leaving heaven to him so long as they can have the earth. War, in particular, is an area in which the monarchy refuses to cede authority to novices. Since none of the prophets are soldiers, YHVH is shut out of war. Meanwhile, the public sacrifice, formerly offered by prophets in time of crisis, is usurped by the kings as lip service to religion—David, Solomon, and Jeroboam I all offer it themselves, and then it is delegated to priests under the monarchy's control. After Samuel, no prophet offers it again until Elijah, who is the last to do so.[38] The king assumes a monopoly on earthly power. Of course, this power is precarious; too much foreign influence in worship, or failure in war, can provoke resentment and rebellion. But even this is "obviously only in order to enforce the worship of YHVH against the Baal cult, and not in order to censure God's deputy for failing to guide the state in accordance with God's justice. From now on no one censures the king except the prophet, the man without appointment . . . a fact which the kingship naturally regards as a potential revolution."[39] The proliferation of court prophets, then, represents the monarchy's effort to co-opt this powerful counterforce.

The Man of Holy Unrest: Elijah versus Ahab

Buber's discussion of the legendary Elijah the Tishbite argues that Elijah's struggle against *baal* worship is also a struggle against social injustice. In a parallel to Joshua's covenant renewal at Shechem, Elijah opposes the *baalim* out of a desire to unite the people around YHVH. Yet the problem with *baal* worship goes deeper than the private worlds of family gods that Joshua forced the people to abandon; the problem reaches back to Moses' quandary at Kadesh, when he wondered how a nomadic people would remain faithful once it began to settle.

In *Kingship of God*, Buber defined "Baalization" as an incorrect form of divine worship in which one represented YHVH in order to "have" him at one's command; in *Moses*, he cited the golden calf episode as the prime instance of this process. Here, he describes a later phase in the struggle between YHVH and the *baalim*, during which the outer form of *baal* worship has changed. The central feature of the new agricultural existence of Israel, the fertility of the ground, seems to be a deep mystery; somewhere within the ground the *baal* and the *baalat* (literally, the "owners" of the soil) would copulate and produce the blessing of flowering and growth. Peasants had to placate these powers to ensure a successful harvest. Human sexual pairing is seen as a sacral act that can facilitate the pairing of the *baalim*. As with the household gods in the time of Joshua, overt forsaking of YHVH is not at issue: "The *baalim* were accepted by the people as a fact, but treated as the indispensable religious requisites for the successful fertilization of the soil, for which YHVH, the wanderer and warrior, was not competent. Even now they wished to *acknowledge as a people* YHVH only; whereas the fertility deities they *knew* only, and this in a private and intimate manner."[40] Nonetheless, as with the family and household gods, the separate worship of landowning gods threatened the unity of the people. The idea that the fertility of the land lay outside the purview of YHVH, meanwhile, posed a threat to the unity and universality of the dominion of YHVH; and the idea that sexual rites were holy, because connected to agricultural fertility, called into question the distinction between YHVH and the natural world over which he ruled: "YHVH by His uncompromising nature is altogether above sex, and cannot tolerate it that sex, which like all natural life needs hallowing by Him, should seem to be declared holy by its own power. There is no place here for compromise. Whoever baalizes YHVH introduces Astarte into the sanctuary."[41]

A YHVH considered a *baal*, a power accessible to the people, would no longer be capable of leading them. Elijah's task, then, is to teach that farming, too, is in YHVH's power. But Elijah faces a new obstacle: a human king, betraying his commission, encourages the idolatry. Ahab, the seventh king of the northern kingdom of Israel, has instituted worship for Baal to please his Tyrian wife, Jezebel (1 Kings 16:30–33).[42] By indulging in this worship himself, Ahab outdoes even Solomon, who built altars to foreign gods merely as a diplomatic gesture.

Despite the fantastic stories in which he figures, Elijah "is perceptible through the veil of legend as a great historical character, though he appears without a parental name and disappears without a grave."[43] This is another case in which legend yields clues to its origins: "The stern theopolitical facts in all their fullness stand opposed to every attempt of tradition to resort to legendary transfiguration."[44] Buber pictures Elijah as a wild nomad, a "man of holy unrest," who comes from the desert to the city in a microcosmic mimicking of Israel's collective journey. He teaches the people that they cannot stand on two branches, that either YHVH or Baal must be "Lord of heaven and earth." For Elijah, this phrase is not merely a euphemism for "Lord of everything"; it refers to the specific agricultural powers attributed to Baal. As at Shechem, the people unite around YHVH, indicated by Elijah's use of the twelve stones representing the tribes in his erection of the altar, and by his use of Jacob's name Israel in his prayer.[45] This creates another fleeting moment of theopolitical unity: "Only now is there again a people Israel. There is no Israel and can be none except as YHVH's people."[46]

In a final note, Buber clarifies his view of Elijah's theopolitical status and offers another example of his characteristic way of applying an unchanging teaching to changed circumstances. Elijah has taught the people that their nomad god of old is also the lord of their agricultural endeavors. His own nomadic nature sets him apart from the people and the king, establishing his credibility and his connection to Israel's past. This is not to agree with the claim that Elijah opposes a "nomadic ideal" against the cities and the farms. The Mosaic vision accepted the transfer of nomadic virtues to the settlement, replacing chaotic wandering and settled hierarchy with a new form of life, in which an invisible king maintained order while the people appeared to live anarchistically. Elijah represents this synthesis even in the monarchical period: "Elijah serves his god as a nomad, but he has no nomadic ideal. He demonstrates the futility of the Baal, who merely usurps the sovereignty of the settlement."[47] By showing YHVH as lord of the land, "the great nomad serves his God by occupation of land for him." Shortly after Elijah's time, there arises a misguided nostalgic tendency to view a nomadic ideal as the only possible form for serving YHVH. Yehonadav, who orders his sons "not to build houses, nor to sow seeds, nor to plant vineyards, but to 'sojourn' in tents all over the land," leads this movement.[48] Scholars describe it "both as 'reactionary' and 'revolutionary,'" since it invokes the past in challenging the status quo; Buber, however, faults its failure to sufficiently contest the nature of the *baalim*. It tells its followers to eschew their seductions but without denying their role as fertilizers of the soil; in fact, its rejection of agriculture relies on viewing farmland as where the *baalim* dwell. This is an intolerable position for one who sees YHVH as hallowing all nature and human activity.[49]

Fearless: Micaiah ben Imlah before Two Kings

The Elijah story, concerned primarily with Ahab's baalism, occurs on the "religious" side of the prophetic struggle. Eventually, however, Ahab's offenses against social justice (e.g., the seizure of Naboth's vineyard) cause YHVH to decree the destruction of the house of Ahab. Because Ahab initially repents in terror, YHVH tells Elijah that he will delay this destruction until the next generation, and he leaves it to Micaiah ben Imlah, Elijah's younger contemporary, to prophesy Ahab's death. If Buber says more about Micaiah ben Imlah, who is reported only in 1 Kings 22, than about the prophet Elisha, one of the main characters in the books of Kings, this is undoubtedly because "it is not enough for [Micaiah] to proclaim the rejection of a single king, as Samuel spoke to Saul, but he ventures to declare the kingdom as such to be rejected and annulled for the time being—a word which not even Hosea will be able to surpass: 'I saw all Israel scattered to the mountains as sheep which have no shepherd, and YHVH spake: these have no longer a ruler.'"[50] This reading is somewhat tendentious, since Ahab is in fact followed as king by his son Ahaziah—nor are we told of either a significant inter-regnum or a reference to the far future in Micaiah's words. Nonetheless, Buber sees in "that irrepressible fearless man, Micaiah ben Imlah," a reassertion of the united sovereignty of YHVH over both heavenly and earthly things.[51] Speaking at once to the two kings of Israel and Judah, who are sitting together at the gate of Samaria plotting military strategy, Micaiah depicts an enthroned YHVH in heaven sending a spirit to make their court prophets false. Buber is especially im-pressed that Micaiah describes this spirit as meant to "entice" Ahab. The rejected prophets are not false merely because they are wrong, nor even because they are subservient to power and prophesy salvation, "but that what they prophesy is not dependent on question and alternative. . . . The true prophet does not announce an immutable decree. He speaks into the power of decision lying in the moment, and in such a way that his message of disaster touches this power."[52] By sending the spirit to make the court prophets prophesy falsely, YHVH seeks to remind the kings that he is still lord of history, and not only of heaven.

The Word Militant: Turning to the Future

Elijah and Elisha inspire the revolt of Jehu, but the replacement of Ahab's son fails to remind the northern monarchy of its obligations. The king still behaves as though he is endowed with the power of YHVH, aided by the cultic system, which allows YHVH himself to be worshipped as an idol.[53] At this point the two contradictions (first, between the real and fictitious power of God, and second be-tween the real and fictitious worship of God) "unite and form an abyss." Against this abyss, the writing prophets wage a "new stage in the battle for YHVH, the battling by the word as such: militant script and militant speech."[54] As this stage progresses, we discern the "Turning to the Future" that Buber finds in the proph-ets of the eighth century BCE. The movement of this turning defines the remain-der of the book.

Buber's valuation of this turning is ambivalent. On the one hand, there is a clearly negative direction to the movement. As the prophets weary of the kings and their followers, they move ever closer to the common definition of prophecy as prediction, because the ability of the hearers to influence the outcome is seen as reduced. Thus, every step along the path is one step further in the transfor-mation of prophecy into apocalyptic literature, a genre for which Buber has no praise. The contrast between prophecy and apocalypse is quite clear; they form a binary, and prophecy has every quality lacking in apocalypse. Prophecy is vital; apocalypse is degenerate. Prophecy speaks to the historical situation and places a decision before the actors in that situation; apocalypse announces a script for the future that has already been written, reducing individuals to players simply acting out their destiny. Prophecy comes from hope that the chosen people of

YHVH will fulfill their task; apocalypse emerges from despair that they will not. But the "turning to the future" does not of itself transform prophecy into apocalypse; additional steps are required, which will not take place until the Second Commonwealth. What the "turning" does first is increase the willingness to denounce the failed monarchy and the Temple; it also increasingly universalizes the prophetic message and ties together the destiny of the chosen people of YHVH with that of all the other nations. The symbol of Buber's ambivalence toward the turning to the future, the prophetic doctrine whose emergence he traces with a mixture of interest and trepidation, is the idea of the remnant: the true part of the people, the faithful ones, who will survive after the destruction.

The universalization of the prophetic message and the development of the idea of the remnant are already found in Amos and Hosea. Buber imagines that Amos was a great childhood influence on Hosea, his younger contemporary. The two are discussed both as complementary, with Hosea's focus on "lovingkindness" (*Liebe*, חסד) balancing Amos's focus on "righteousness" (*Gerechtigkeit*, צדק), and progressively, with Hosea publicly teaching what Amos directs at a single disciple: the future promise of the twofold covenant, a covenant of peace with the nations and nature that is also a new marriage covenant with YHVH.[55] This comes, however, only after a holy hailstorm of criticism, in which the "whole history of Israel, beginning with the entry upon the settlement up to the time of the prophet's words, appears [in Hosea] as a succession of acts of desecration."[56]

Like Rolling Waters: Amos

The book of Amos begins with a festival at Bethel, with representatives from many nations commemorating the reconquest by Jeroboam II of areas once held by David. This festive gathering is disrupted by a stranger, "a sheep-breeder from the extreme border of the Judean wilderness," who dares to proclaim the judgment of YHVH on all the nations present, not for their plots against Israel, or even for their worship of other gods, but for their crimes against one another. Amos's ability to see YHVH in the gods of these diverse nations is a development of the ability of the patriarchs to see each new El as a manifestation of their own god; Amos goes on to declare that YHVH is the leader (9:7) and judge (1:3–2:11, 9:8) of these nations as well.[57] This does not imply, however, that the relationship between YHVH and the other nations is exactly the same as the one between YHVH and Israel. Buber's explanation of the difference can be read not just as his interpretation of Amos but as a manifesto on Israel's chosenness:

> Out of the depth of history one people appears in God's eyes as another, whereas only Israel he "knew[.]" . . . In revelation it was laid upon them to become a true people, that is the living unity of the many and the diverse. With regard to this, Israel was given the people's statute, the "instruction" (*torah*). The *torah* represses social wickedness and wards off the stumbling blocks liable

to stand up between the members of the people through the growing social division. The *torah* combats these corruptions by means of a rhythmic social restoration, by means of a renewed leveling of the ownership of the soil and the re-establishment of common freedom. And now the revealing, lawgiving God litigates with Israel. . . . The people, whom God desired to become his first fruits, has not derived anything from the holy destiny laid upon them except the summons to a historical *provision*, for which they thought to pay with a well-equipped cult, with abundance of offerings, and with instrumental music of rich artistry (5:22ff); whereas their whole politico-communal life they had withdrawn from the divine leading.[58]

What we have here is a version of the "ethical monotheist" picture common in modern Jewish thought, wherein the election of Israel is an intermediate step in God's plan for universal salvation.[59] Israel (the "first fruits") receives from God its teaching, which it then in turn shares with the rest of humankind (the full "harvest"). The specifics of this teaching, and of Israel's passing it on to the nations, vary from one ethical-monotheist thinker to another. For Buber, this teaching is the path to true peoplehood, to "the living unity of the many and the diverse," the *Gemeinschaft der Gemeinschaften*. The failure to take it seriously by splitting communal life into pieces—subjugating "the political" to monarchy and "the religious" to priesthood—incurs the prophetic wrath.[60]

Amos demands that "justice roll down like waters, and righteousness as a mighty stream" (5:24)—a demand Buber characterizes as "not ethical nor social, but religious . . . the unity of justice and righteousness is in Israelite thought one of the basic concepts of the divine-human relationship."[61] YHVH wills that the divine righteousness operate on earth through human righteousness. A water metaphor represents the duality of righteousness. Righteousness flows, meets obstacles, but keeps sweeping forward, whereas the humans who try to dam the flow (to "turn justice into hemlock, and righteousness into wormwood"; 6:12) only ensure that what was once a potential source of life must force its way through the dam, its frustrated momentum transforming it into a destructive source of judgment and punishment.

We also recognize here the theme that Buber associated with the rebellion of Korach: the presumption that the people are already holy and that their election conferred not responsibility but honor. "Seek good and not evil, that you may live, and so shall the God of hosts be with you, as you are accustomed to say" (Amos 5:14). Buber adds: "This is the saying familiar to the careless: God is with us!"[62] This point marks the first step in the turning to the future: after twice interceding with God to spare the people (7:1–6, "probably the only account written by [Amos] himself" in Buber's estimation), Amos no longer expects this people to repent when it has enslaved the poor for a debt on shoes, kicking dust on them (2:6–7). This pessimism allows for scholars to read Amos as a "prophet of doom." Unlike Elijah, who chose seven thousand from those who had already refused to bend the knee to Baal (1 Kings 19:18), Amos does not proclaim salvation; he only hopes that *perhaps* some "remnant of Joseph" (Amos 5:15) will be saved. But the destruction itself will come. "Prepare to meet thy God, O Israel," Amos announces (4:12), and in connection with this verse Buber recalls that anyone who sees God's face cannot live.

To place Amos at the earliest point in the "turning to the future," Buber must contest any perception of Amos as a prophet of doom offering the people no alternative road to salvation. This effort purports to divine the true chronology of the disordered statements in Amos, producing a quieter version of his general polemic with scholarship.[63] In the end Buber credits Amos's prophecy of the restoration of the "fallen hut of David" as authentic, whereas many scholars assume that the reference to the house of David is a postexilic addition. Buber sees Amos as referring not to Judah here but to the whole Israelite community; the hut is a shepherd's hut, the only kind worth restoring in the eyes of the shepherd prophet.

You Shall Sit Solitary: Hosea

Hosea both develops and departs from Amos. His focus is on *chesed* rather than *tzedek*, and on the idea of a love relationship between YHVH and Israel rather than YHVH's political leadership of the nations. Unlike Amos, Hosea knows of a covenant that is also a teaching (6:7, 8:1, 8:12); Buber also credits him with the correct understanding of the revelation of the Tetragrammaton to Moses.[64] Where Amos saw YHVH as Israel's divine leader, repaid with ingratitude, Hosea adheres to the Exodus tradition and conceives of the covenant as a reciprocal event, in which Israel does right for at least one moment. Perhaps this is why Hosea is more confident than Amos with respect to future redemption. On the one hand, Hosea's confidence interrupts any smooth trajectory from optimism to pessimism or from prophecy to apocalypse. On the other hand, it continues the progression, since Amos's indecision and hope represent less of a claim to future knowledge than Hosea's confidence.[65] Hosea also experiences a call that differs from that of any other prophet: he is commanded to speak God's word not only through his mouth but also through his entire life, by marrying a "wife of harlotry." Through the experience of this marriage he comes to understand the relationship between YHVH and Israel on a personal, emotional level.

The focus on *chesed* and the imitation of God through marriage to a harlot may suggest that Hosea lacks theopolitical concerns. Here too, however, "all the time that it is still possible to come to political decisions, he calls to a turning that includes the political domain," particularly in the realm of foreign policy. "They have made kings, but not from Me" (8:4) applies both to the man sitting on the throne and to the Molekh, in the form of a bull, sitting in the sanctuary at Bethel. Hosea lives at a time of extreme political turbulence; unlike Amos "he does not prophesy in an hour of triumph about coming adversity, but he sees it descending and coming at first in inner troubles, afterwards in the vain giving of tribute to Assyria, in the revolt, in the covenant war with Syria against Judah and her neighbors, in the Assyrian invasion, in the breakup of the Galilee region, in the transportation of a large section of the people to Assyria." Hosea thus begins a polemic against state policy, especially the attempt to fend off one great power by hiring the aid of another, that will culminate in Isaiah.[66]

The condemnation of *baal* worship, which reappears in a new form, is again read by Buber with an eye toward its political import; the husbandship of YHVH to the people replaces the husbandship to the land. Even God's love itself, which Hosea describes as demanding, wrathful, but merciful, is theopolitically inflected in Buber's reading. He notes that "YHVH charges Israel again and again that they commit whoredom in forsaking Him; but He does not say that He demands or expects from them that they love Him. Love is not, in the book of Hosea, a concept of reciprocity between God and man."[67] Why should this be, given the Scriptural command to love God? Buber stresses *chesed*, that "almost untranslatable concept . . . which originally may have signified the right relationship between a lord and his men, his *Hasidim*, a relationship of goodwill and loyalty." When Hosea complains that there is "no truth, nor *chesed*, nor knowledge of God in the land," he does not mean that the people should show *chesed* to God, which would be impossible, but that they should show it to the weak and helpless among them. As with his *tzedek*, God wants Israel to receive his *chesed* and then pass it on to others. This is what God would expect were Israel to be faithful in its marriage: "I will betroth thee unto Me forever, I will betroth thee unto Me in righteousness and justice, and in lovingkindness and mercy, and I will betroth thee unto Me in faithfulness, and thou shalt know YHVH" (Hosea 2:21–22).

In the future redemption that Hosea describes, Israel calls YHVH *ishi*, "my man" (*baali*, another way of saying "my husband," would be inappropriate), after they have returned to the wilderness and settled in tents again "as in the days of the meeting" (12:10). Buber sees an admission on Hosea's part that although he too has no "nomadic ideal," a simpler natural setting is required for the new covenant. The Israelites fall prey to the mysteries of agricultural fertility as far back as Baal Peor, and they must return in exile to the wilderness to undo their misdeeds. Thus "the lawsuit between YHVH and the unfaithful royal house is here brought to a close by Hosea in Samaria before its fall, as in a later age by Jeremiah in Jerusalem before its fall."[68] Here we have, albeit in veiled form, the first prophecy of a future king. In Hosea 3:3 the prophet says to his wife, "Thou shalt sit solitary for me many days; thou shalt not play the harlot, and thou shalt not be any man's wife, nor will I be thine," and this applies to Israel as well. Buber argues that this "is best interpreted as meaning that in this lengthy between-time Israel will have as king neither YHVH nor His adversary, and will not have a true representative of God nor one of the authority-usurping princes (and so . . . there will be no cult, neither true nor false)."[69] As he did with Amos, Buber takes a verse commonly held to be a postexilic addition and reads it as predicting the return of the true king and his legitimate representative. The promise is stronger than anything in Amos; God will heal both the wounds inflicted in the course of the turning away, and the turning away itself. In the meantime, however, the "many days" prevail, until "in two days He will make us whole again, on the third day He will raise us up" (Hosea 6:2). "The days are days of God," Buber comments, "and it is not known how long such are."[70] Despite this apparent tinge of apocalypticism, Hosea remains inside the true prophetic situation as Buber perceives it, because the moment of this divine turning, "in which the wrath turns and mercy awakes, YHVH makes known as a present one (11:8): 'How shall I give thee up, O Ephraim, and deliver thee, O Israel! . . . My heart turns within me, my compassions boil up together.'"

To Keep Still: Isaiah

The universalization of the divine message, the doctrine of the remnant, and the turning to the future are completed in Isaiah, the prophet of *kedushah*, "holiness." Buber says of Isaiah, though not of Amos or Hosea, that there is a "tragic contradiction in his prophetic way," that his way can "only be a tragic way and one full of contradiction," which tells us that we are dealing here with a figure of great significance.[71] Like no other prophet since Moses, Isaiah simultaneously represents and chastises his people; unlike Moses, Isaiah has to act in the name of the true *melekh* (and unlike many of the prophets Buber treats, Isaiah directly refers to "the *king* YHVH of hosts" enthroned in heaven during the vision of his call [6:1, 6:5]) against a human *melekh*.

That theopolitics is the central concern of Buber's treatment of Isaiah has not gone unnoticed.[72] It would be difficult to miss given that the heading of the section is "The Theopolitical Hour" (*Die theopolitische Stunde*, השעה התיאופוליטית). Buber refers to Isaiah 7–9:6 as Isaiah's "political memoir," focusing on this section to the exclusion of most of the forty chapters attributed to Isaiah and his disciples.[73] Here Buber offers the primary definition of theopolitics in *The Prophetic Faith*: "A special kind of politics, theopolitics, which is concerned to establish a certain people in a certain historical situation under the divine sovereignty, so that this people is brought nearer the fulfillment of its task, to become the beginning of the kingdom of God."[74]

Holiness, Buber declares, is "the greatest" of the three concepts of divine-human relationship in the early writing prophets; like the other concepts, this one indicates that "YHVH wishes to work through the independence of man created as independent and to continue His work on earth by this means."[75] In its preexilic sense, before being limited by the priesthood to the objects and actions of the cult, "holy" means "distinct but not severed, distinct and yet in the midst of the people . . . distinct and radiating . . . detached and joined at once . . . *distinction and radiation together* [*Absonderung und Ausstrahlung zugleich*/פרישה והקרנה כאחת]."[76] When Israel is commanded in Exodus to be a "holy nation," and when the later writers of Leviticus record the demand "You shall be holy as I the Lord your God am holy," the sense is that Israel must be distinct, "not in order to withdraw itself from the world of nations, but in order to influence them by the radiance of its way of life." This is the sense in which, in Amos, Israel was to be the first fruit of God's harvest. Imitation of God's righteousness and lovingkindness would influence the other nations to choose this path themselves. In Isaiah, holiness has the special political meaning of "keeping still."[77]

The root ש-ק-ט is rare in verb form. It occurs in four places in Isaiah, and these instances constitute "the core of his theopolitical teaching." When Isaiah and his son first come to Ahaz, he tells him: "Be calm, and *keep still*, and fear not, neither let your heart be faint because of these two tails of smoking firebrands," namely Aram-Damascus and Samaria (Isaiah 7:4). "Fear not" is the usual advice of court prophets to kings, a common assurance of success for a kingdom that has God on its side, but coupled with "keep still" and the silent presence of a boy named Shear-Yashuv (which means "a remnant shall return") it takes on a new meaning. More than two decades later, in a different political situation (with Judah seeking an alliance with Egypt against Assyria), Isaiah refines his earlier pronouncement: "Thus has YHVH, the Holy One of Israel, spoken: In turning away and in rest you will be saved, in *keeping still* and in confidence will be your strength, but you would not" (30:15). Buber tersely comments: "This is a reliable political program for the people living at the time in Canaan." If the community life is rightly ordered according to prophetic admonition, keeping still and refusing of Great Power politics "lends the people a downright magnetic power."[78] When this advice goes unheeded, with the Assyrian host at the doorstep of Jerusalem, Isaiah repeats these words of YHVH: "I will *keep still*, and look on my foundation place like a clear heat above light, like a cloud of dew in the heat of harvest" (18:4).[79] This means that YHVH does not intend to involve himself in the war; Israel should keep still, as he does, rather than wage war in the hope that he will take their side. If Israel imitates YHVH in holiness, righteousness, and lovingkindness, by keeping still, by distinction and radiation, then "the work of righteousness shall be peace, and the effect of righteousness *keeping still* and confidence forever" (32:17).[80] The choice belongs to the people, and Isaiah says to the king of Judah who acts in its name: "If you will not confide, you will not abide" (7:9).

All this is, for Buber, a matter of obedience to the will of YHVH as well as of realist political thinking. In contrast to those moods in which he denies that visible historical success is instructive, here Buber explains Isaiah's aversion to "covenant politics" as a matter of sound political judgment:

> Covenant policy is not suitable for such a people from a religious point of view, because it puts the people under obligations and in a position of dependence,

contrary to that one such relationship which is true; but at the same time it is unsuitable from a political point of view also, because it involves the people in other nations' wars of expansion, in wars liable to rob the people of its independence and finally to destroy it, especially when, as with little Israel, it has to live between two great powers.[81]

There are unmistakable echoes here of the situation of "little Israel" in the 1940s: of Buber's own polemics against Zionist alignment with the British Empire, and of his hope for Jerusalem as a third option vis-à-vis the ideologies of the "two great powers" of his time.[82] Buber held, "He who has dealings with the powers renounces the power of powers, that which bestows and withholds power, and loses its help; whereas he who confides and keeps still thereby gains the very political understanding and strength to hold his ground."[83] There may even be an echo of Buber's debates with the Zionists in Isaiah's meditation on speed: "The unbeliever demands acceleration of God's actions and mocks His slowness, as Isaiah related earlier (5:19), for he, the politician, cannot wait . . . the true believer does not wish to hasten God's work, the work of salvation, even if he could. Small politics is a monologue of man; great politics is a discourse with the God Who 'keeps still.'"

The remainder of Isaiah's political memoir contains some of the most controversial verses in the history of scriptural interpretation. The sign, the maiden, the child, Immanuel—these perennial topics of Jewish and Christian exegetical disputation are here treated as part of Isaiah's theopolitical manifesto. To be sure, Buber contests some well-known interpretations in support of his version of the narrative. The *ot*, or sign, for which Ahaz is permitted to ask, and which he refuses, does not indicate a miracle; the *almah* or young woman who will give birth is none other than his own young queen. The birth of a son to a king who passed his previous son through the fire (2 Kings 16:3) is the sign that Ahaz is given against his will. Isaiah states further that this son will become king and will fulfill Ahaz's neglected theopolitical commission and be called *Immanuel*, "God-with-us." Buber interprets the other epithets of Immanuel similarly:

"counsellor of the valiant God" (that is, of the God as leading the battle), "father of the spoil" (this spoil is the world of peoples delivered from the "rod" of the Assyrian tyrant), and "prince of peace" (that is, of the "peace that has no end" . . . which in the later prophecy of Isaiah is pictured in the image of the peace of the animals, 11:6–9).[84]

These are the three stages of salvation: war, victory, and peace. These titles belong not to a divine figure but to the true anointed one who stands over and against the one who defiles the title:

"Immanuel" is the anti-king but not "a spiritual anti-king," as some explain it, for the fulfilling, the messianic kingship too is a real, political kingship, or rather a theopolitical one, that is to say, it is a kingship endowed with political power to the scope of the political realization of God's will for people and peoples—no other view is held by Isaiah or by any other prophet of the period of the monarchy. Immanuel is the king of the *remnant*, from which the people will renew itself.[85]

This messiah is a king from the house of David who fulfills the promise of David's last words, that of "the right ordering of the people—and radiating from it the right ordering of the world."[86] His reign is not eschatological but historical. He could be the very next king, or the one after that. "The original Messianic faith has no reference to 'the Messiah' in the sense of a special category: the man, whose absence is felt, the expected, the promised, he is the anointed king, who fulfills the function assigned to him at his anointing. *There is no need for more than this*."[87] His royal code is not merely to avoid the overt violation of the Deuteronomic and Samuelic "kingship ordinance," but to worship YHVH by imitating him. The prescription for this imitation appears, according to Buber, in the prayer of Hannah at 1 Samuel 2, as well as in Psalm 72, which Buber dates to Isaiah's time. The king is to raise the poor out of the dust and seat them with the nobles; to vindicate the oppressed; to crush the oppressor; to "guard the feet of his *Hasidim*, but the wicked shall be put to silence in darkness, for not by strength shall man prevail" (1 Samuel 2:9).[88] The paradox of freedom, however, which held for the entire people in the days of the anarcho-theocracy and which still holds true for it with respect to the turning in the face of catastrophe, applies as well to the individual kings. Each anointed one is free to accept or reject God's will and the word of the prophets. "The 'Messianic' prophecy too conceals an alternative. This too is no prediction, but an offer. The righteous one, whom God 'has,' must rise out of this historic loam of man." Thus, it is simultaneously possible for the prophecy of Immanuel to refer to Ahaz's son Hezekiah and for Hezekiah not to fulfill the prophecy: "The prophecy remains in substance, but the reference to a particular man is suspended."[89]

Isaiah's disappointment with Hezekiah, who succumbs to alliance politics with Egypt against Assyria, is the occasion for his second messianic song, 11:1–9. Buber denies that this song refers to the same person as the song of Immanuel. A fundamental shift has taken place: "Isaiah no longer acknowledges the ruling dynasty."[90] The royal house is destroyed, reduced to a stump, and the new king emerges from the remnant, from the "rootstock" of Jesse rather than the branches of the felled tree. Isaiah reverts to an old trope of prophetic authority, emphasizing the "spirit" that comes from YHVH to endow the future king with wisdom, understanding, counsel, might, knowledge, and fear of YHVH. Even here, in the image of the wolf dwelling with the lamb, Buber denies that there is an eschatological transformation of the cosmos: "It seems to me that this idyll of the beasts of prey 'staying' with the domestic animals is intended merely as a symbol of the peace of the peoples, perhaps even a symbol in which under the name of wild beasts certain nations were to be recognized." Buber reads the conclusion of the song ("They shall not hurt nor destroy in all my holy mountain, for the earth shall be full of knowledge of YHVH as the waters cover the sea") as circling back to the seraphic proclamation that Isaiah heard ("Holy, holy, holy is YHVH of hosts, the whole world is filled with his glory"); however, this time with the idea that all human beings, and not the prophet alone, perceive and recognize the omnipresence of God.

In the end, Isaiah turns to eschatology—though not to apocalypse—with his prophecy of the *yamim acharim*, the "lateness of the days," when all nations will flow to the mountain of YHVH, and the "teaching shall go forth from Zion, and the word of YHVH from Jerusalem," and consequently the nations beat their swords into plowshares and refuse to learn war any more (2:1–5). Buber denies that Isaiah describes an end to history here, noting that the figure of the Messiah is missing from this purportedly apocalyptic prophecy. The prophecy refers to a late stage in the redemption process, after the anointed one has fulfilled his function, namely the internal right ordering of the people of Israel. Indeed, it is only because of this that the nations now hearken. But "the great arbitration and the great instruction upon the mount are YHVH's concern and not His agent's. . . . There is here no declaration about a world state under the rule of a world king, but about the reception of a universal revelation, after which . . . the peoples will continue to live their life, but they will be united in the ways of God, Whom they have come to know."[91] This is the same vision of theopolitical holiness, achieved through keeping still, that Isaiah has proclaimed from the beginning. The only "theological" evolution that has occurred in his long life is that successive disappointments have caused him to imagine a delay in the vision's achievement.

Disappointment and delay give rise to Isaiah's doctrine of the remnant, and to his introduction of concealment, if not esotericism, into the prophetic repertoire ("Bind up the testimony, seal the instruction among my disciples," 8:16). During the vision of his call, Isaiah receives a difficult and complex task. He has to harden the hearts of the people, and prevent their returning and being healed—not by deception, but in and through the word of God itself: "He is not to deceive his hearers with lying promises, as did that wind-spirit [seen by] Micaiah ben Imlah, but he is to hand on the true sayings of God. . . . [W]e cannot avoid the question as to what prophecy is fitted to act so—in other words, what prophecy of this kind we find in the extant sayings of Isaiah."[92] The answer arrives when Ahaz refuses the sign that Isaiah offers him as proof of the prophecy of the destruction of Judah's enemies. The offer and refusal have a theopolitical meaning: by allowing Ahaz to *choose* a sign, any sign, from any realm, YHVH through Isaiah makes it known that he is willing, this time, not just to offer but also to guarantee security. Ahaz's refusal ("I will not ask, nor will I try YHVH") seems on its surface like a pious statement, but in this context it means that he is unwilling to give up his original plans—which the acceptance of a sign would force him to do. "He wishes to give to religion that which appertains to it; but it must be far removed from the sphere of politics, that is from the sphere of real decisions."[93] Thus he cloaks his power play in piety, and Buber suggests that Ahaz expects Isaiah, son of a prominent family "and who can therefore be expected to adapt himself to the benefit of the state," to close the conversation there. Instead, Isaiah responds with the prophecy of the birth of Immanuel. By rejecting the first sign, Ahaz has called forth the second. Both are promises of salvation, and Isaiah sees that these harden the heart even more than his previous prophesies of judgment. Ahaz hears that his enemies will be destroyed and takes confidence from this without assuming the attendant obligation. In Buber's view, only a message of salvation—and *not* of disaster—could have fulfilled the demand laid upon Isaiah to fatten the hearts of the people, yet to do so with the truth: "A sound so new, so strong and clear, that it silences all prophecy of disaster in the ears of the many, who only long for the securing of the people's existence, for the quieting of their soul's unrest, and for the confirmation of their illusions."[94] And this is when Isaiah "chooses his way," saying "no more to Ahaz than he must hear."[95] Any further revelations of messianic hope, without orders to reveal them to specific audiences, Isaiah resolves to conceal within the "circle of the faithful, which has begun to gather around him as the original community of the holy remnant." He does this because he sees that the heart-hardening effects of the prophecy of salvation are even greater than those of the prophecy of destruction. Because he wants the people to turn, he hides what he knows, hoping that they will do God's will on their own.

Buber does not specify what makes this choice "the beginning of the tragic conflict in the prophetic way of the man, whose prophecy was itself the starting point of the special 'Messianic' hope of the people of Israel." Perhaps it is the paradox just mentioned; or perhaps it is the anticipated unsealing of the testimony, after the destruction, when the people are hungry and desperate, in a world of total darkness (8:22), and finally turn to Isaiah, his sons and disciples, despite the fact that they might perhaps have prevented the destruction (9:1–4). The decision to reveal the truth comes when the people "will come running to you who are patiently waiting, to you recognized now as the knowing ones." But the people still don't understand exactly what they expect these knowers to know, as they entreat them to engage in necromancy and to seek the truth from the spirits of the dead.[96] And the disciples are to answer: "What? On behalf of the living the dead?" and point the way instead to the testimony (*teudah*) and the teaching (*torah*).[97] The tragedy, which Buber sees but Isaiah does not, is that neither revelation nor concealment is guaranteed to turn the free people to YHVH. Future prophets experience an ever-increasing despair accompanied by ever more sweeping visions of destruction, and seek to assuage their despondency in exile by moving ever closer to apocalypse.

The Third Messiah: A Man of Sorrows, Light to the Nations in His Deaths, Amazing the Kings

Under the chapter heading "The God of the Sufferers," *The Prophetic Faith* brings together discussions of Micah, Jeremiah, Ezekiel, Job, Psalm 73, and Deutero-Isaiah, totaling eighty pages (nearly a third of the entire book). Micah and Jeremiah fall under the heading "Against the Sanctuary"; Ezekiel, Job, and Psalm 73 under the heading "The Question"; and Deutero-Isaiah under the heading "The Mystery." These divisions are more mysterious than enlightening.[98] The concept of a God of the sufferers is surely worth examining, but these pages are not primarily aimed at explicating such a concept. Rather, they continue to examine the faith of Israel historically and to correlate its changing political situation to its fundamental theopolitical commitments. In the final sections, Buber traces the relationship of the prophets to the monarchy over the last century of its existence, and then into the transformations of the Babylonian Exile.

Reform and Destruction: Micah and Jeremiah

The prophet Micah, a younger contemporary of Isaiah, may have been one of the "disciples" entrusted with continuing the teaching and testimony of Isaiah. Whereas Isaiah was a Jerusalemite aristocrat, Micah is a villager from the coastal plain. Lacking Isaiah's personal connection to the Temple, Micah is able to proclaim the inclusion of the sanctuary in the imminent general destruction. Buber sees Micah as more radical than his teacher. When he criticizes the oppressors of the poor for "eating the flesh of his people" (Micah 3:3), he speaks as one of these poor. In Micah's rebuke to a man who asks whether he should sacrifice his son, we find the "crystallization of the divine demand": "It has been told thee, O man, what is good, and what YHVH requires of you: only to do justice, to love mercy, and to walk humbly with thy God" (6:8). Finally, the destruction that Micah proclaims is complete and does not stop at the borders of the city or the sanctuary. "Because you feel safe in all this wickedness," Buber summarizes Micah's warning, "the stronghold of your safety shall fall." Perhaps his uncompromising nature is what gains Micah a hearing with Hezekiah and finally brings the prophets into the mundane world of political reform.[99] When the king refuses to acknowledge the true prophet, preferring to rely on court prophets and priests who tell him only to persist on his chosen path, the prophet is assured that his own responsibility has been fulfilled. When the king seeks to act on the prophet's words, however, while misunderstanding their full import, new problems are created. This is how Buber understands Hezekiah's cult reform in the wake of Micah's prophecy. The cult reform was necessary but insufficient; an effort at social reform had to accompany it. This had only scarcely begun when Hezekiah died and his son Manasseh rose to power. Manasseh's reign was so pervaded by iniquity that the book of Kings argues that it is his sins that caused the Babylonian defeat of Judah a hundred years later. Buber skips over this century, avoiding the short chapters of Nahum, Habakkuk, and Zephaniah, to arrive at the end of the story: the twilight of Judah.

The context for Jeremiah is the revival of Hezekiah's reform program by Josiah, after the terrible interlude of Manasseh. Buber supposes that the book "found" in the Temple, the core of Deuteronomy, which spurred Josiah's reform, was originally redacted out of disparate materials by a circle of priests and cult prophets, disciples of Isaiah, in support of Hezekiah's reform. They hid it away during the reign of Manasseh to protect it, but imagined that Josiah might prove a more receptive audience:

> In it are fused into one a legal tradition, which had grown into an organic whole, the spirit of the first writing prophets, a priestly organizational tendency and a preaching style, schooled on great examples. It may be said of this book that it is designed to bring the torrent of prophecy into a regular channel: on the one hand the realization of the social demands had to be set within the realm of the "politically possible," and on the other hand the sacred domain, which seemed menaced by the prophetic fight against the degenerate cult, had to be at once purified and supported.[100]

One could almost read Buber as implying that this book read to Josiah resembles the old Social-Democratic Party program. It seeks to co-opt the dangerous prophetic power and reharness it to the benefit of the state and the sanctuary; that is, it seeks "the closing of a social revolutionary movement."[101] Yet just as social democrats share fundamental values with radical socialists and anarchists, these establishment reformers agree with Jeremiah on a wide range of issues. They see themselves as empowered to act on his ideas and to realize them. Like Jeremiah, their goal is "the fulfillment of God's will for the order of the people and the sanctuary *as one*, in a unity of 'holy' common life."[102] Because of this, Jeremiah confronts the difficulty of assisting the reform while at the same time maintaining his status as outside critic. Buber holds that Jeremiah 8:8, a protest against the "vain pen of the scribes," is directed against Deuteronomy 12:4–12, a strong command for cult centralization which he imagines was inserted by the priesthood into the original Deuteronomic core: "In these matters we can do little more than conjecture, but the silence of Jeremiah, which extended so many years between the reform and the death of Josiah, is best understood as meaning that he did not wish, on the one hand, to oppose the action of the king, while, on the other hand, he was no longer able to approve of it."[103] As an heir to Moses and Samuel, Jeremiah is most comfortable with a vision of God as one who "will be" where he will be, unlinked to any particular place. He accepts centralization only insofar as it includes removing foreign objects and rites, and he highlights the necessary connection of cultic activity with righteousness and social justice.[104]

Eventually, however, Egyptian interference in the politics of Judah renders Jeremiah's qualms moot. Josiah is cut down at Megiddo by the Pharaoh before he can complete his work. This is a crisis on several levels. First, the king installed by Pharaoh is willing to adopt the cult reform but not the social reform, and even this ultimately fails. The centralization of YHVH worship is its only lasting fruit, which is why Jeremiah finally breaks his long prophetic silence at the Temple gate. Second, Josiah, fully committed to the will of YHVH, is cut down before his time. The question of how and why this could have happened "penetrates the innermost depths of faith. YHVH has been proclaimed by the prophets as the God of justice. The question comes to include the justice of the leadership of the world. . . . The ready teaching about reward and punishment in the life of individual and community is shaken. This deity is no more to be formulated."[105]

Jeremiah cannot explain the loss of Josiah, but he is nonetheless incensed as the panicked people stream to the Temple to say, "We are delivered" (7:10). None of his views on social justice as a complement to cultic propriety have changed, and the idea that the people still respond to crisis by making offerings in the same "den of robbers" (7:11) moves Jeremiah to bar the gate with his body. Buber notes that the litany of the people's crimes ("Stealing, murder, adultery, and false swearing . . . and following after other gods," 7:9) resembles the Decalogue, but the sins against religion are at the end. The priority of social justice over cultic propriety is the lesson that the people need to learn:

> Out of a human community He wills to make His kingdom; community there must be in order that His kingdom shall come; therefore here . . . man's claim upon man takes precedence of God's claim. . . . It is as if he, standing at the gate of the temple, put forth his hand into the innermost room and took from the ark the tablets in order to show them in a changed order to the people. Opposite the self-reliant, spirit-forsaken civilization religion there stands here for all to see God's ancient instruction of the nomad tribes.[106]

Jeremiah, true heir to Moses and Samuel, urges that YHVH will be wherever he will be and that the people cannot "have" him. Just as Moses conceded the ark only as a pedagogical tool, and just as Samuel failed to teach the people that they could experience God's leadership without it, Jeremiah prophesies that "they shall say no more: the Ark of the Covenant of YHVH; neither shall it come to mind; neither shall they make mention of it; neither shall they miss it; neither shall it be made any more" (3:6). Jeremiah, for Buber, is the last "pure" prophet, the last to speak to a specific historical situation and convince his hearers that they must make a decision. "After this the prophetic 'if' ceases."[107] The destruction comes, and with it the despair of alternatives: Jeremiah prophesies a new covenant that will be "written on the hearts" of the people (31:32)—blessedly relieving them of the necessity to choose it.

Individualizing the Remnant: Ezekiel and Deutero-Isaiah

What is only a moment of weakness in Jeremiah becomes something closer to a doctrine in Ezekiel, whom Buber views as "the man on the borderland of prophecy, between prophecy and priesthood, between prophecy and theological construction, between prophecy and apocalypse."[108] Jeremiah "has nothing to say about the future of the temple . . . the future of the priesthood . . . the future order of the relationship between God and man."[109] The prophecy of the new covenant does not come with any details about the future Israelite society. By contrast, Jeremiah's younger contemporary Ezekiel, who prophesies from the Babylonian exile in circumstances in which "the new acting force is nothing less than the force of extreme despair," describes the future Temple in all its details.[110] Ezekiel's prophecy is "becoming problematic" for Buber, because it "peeps into a future which . . . is already at hand and so describes it . . . the pure prophet is not imaginative or, more precisely, he has no other imagination than the full grasping of the present, actual and potential."[111] Ezekiel's tendency to speculate has a complex and paradoxical relationship with his most famous feature, his doctrine of individuality.

In Buber's reading, Ezekiel is less a religious or ethical genius than one who shares in the dominant trends of his time: "In the atmosphere of the catastrophe the old idea of solidarity has broken down; men rise up against the very suggestion that they should suffer and perish for the guilt of others."[112] This partially results from the people's failure to understand the prophetic: they perceive that Manasseh rose and Josiah fell, but they do not understand how Judah's present vulnerability stems from the "anti-prophetic covenant politics of the kings." They incorrectly supposed that the cult reform was another way of giving to YHVH that which belonged to him, and this increases their shock at the disastrous aftermath. Thus the notion of the remnant undergoes another transformation: Ezekiel individualizes it. Formerly a concept of a surviving community that represented in microcosm what Israel as a whole should have been, the remnant becomes "a sum of individuals: pious ones and penitents."[113] Now no one has to answer for the deeds of his fellow, but only, fully, for himself. In a sense, Ezekiel responds to the apparent destruction of the covenant by eliminating the people as covenant partner, and replacing the collective with individuals, each of whom stands before God alone. "For this hour and in reply to the doubts of the despondent, he establishes the concept of a God in Whose justice it is possible to believe, a God Whose recompense of the individual is *objectively comprehensible*."[114] The confident, near-apocalyptic visions of Ezekiel see a community restored, but their apocalyptic cast comes from the fact that he cannot imagine a way leading from his situation to theirs. Instead, he allows each individual to feel that he himself is justified. Buber sees this vision of a God whose justice is legible by rational standards as rejected by the authors of Job and Psalm 73, as well as by later generations of religious thinkers, who refer to this type of religiosity as serving the world "for the sake of receiving a reward."[115] They reject the notion of objective comprehensibility as foreign to their experience. The increasing traces of apocalypticism, however, remain, and what was once a clear prophetic alternative becomes harder to see through veils of obfuscation and mystery.

The anonymous prophet who lived toward the end of the exile, whose words are bound up with those of Isaiah, and who is usually referred to in biblical criticism as Deutero-Isaiah, is the last figure Buber discusses in *The Prophetic Faith*.[116] He could certainly have forged ahead into later Israelite history had he wished to do so. Ezra and Nehemiah describe aspects of the postexilic situation; Buber could have discussed the beginning of the Second Commonwealth while still remaining within the purview of biblical studies. He ends the discussion here, however, because this is the end of prophecy according to his definition (we hear nothing about Malachi, the last prophet according to Talmudic tradition). In fact, Deutero-Isaiah (DI) never explicitly claims to be the recipient of divine speech, despite his frequent reporting of words of God; rather, he presents himself as a *limmud*, indicating by his use of this unique Isaianic term that he is a disciple of a prophet from centuries earlier, unfolding the hidden meaning of the words Isaiah had sealed up. Yet "his conception of prophecy is different from that of all the prophets that preceded him[;] . . . his God no longer sets before men two possibilities, in deciding between which they may have a share; He has decided, and man is only the object of his decision . . . his prophecy is in Israel the first prophecy according to the accepted sense, that is to say, he has to foretell things fixed and unchangeable."[117] DI imagines a history divided into manifest and hidden things; God makes decisions about the hidden things in a way inaccessible to human beings. So DI is unable to conceive the old idea that God actually gives his creatures the power to obey or resist him, and that choosing to obey is the only route to becoming holy.

Despite this movement away from the true sense of prophecy, however, DI is still not an apocalyptist; he still directs his prophecy of comfort to the particular time and place of his audience.[118] There is a substantive contrast between him and the previous prophets, in that they foresaw danger amid complacency and false security, while he sees comfort after years of suffering; however, the form of the prophecy as one directed to God's involvement in the particular hour still holds. "He does not fix history from the sphere on the yonder side and strange to it, He does not allow history to be unrolled as a scroll, but He Himself enters into it, and conquers it in warfare."[119] This message is expressed by his adoption and refinement of Isaiah's concept "The Holy One of Israel," who also becomes the "Redeemer of Israel" by buying it back from its bond service for debt (the original economic sense of the activity expressed by the term *geulah*). Israel has paid, and it will be brought out from Babylon by its redeemer, returned to its proper place, and will finally fulfill the goal of its election: "YHVH's hallowing by Israel, that is to say, the establishment of His holy kingdom by the people hallowed by Him."[120]

The human agent of this process, however, is problematic. The Persian king Cyrus the Great defeats Babylon and repatriates Judah and thereby earns for himself the title "anointed of God," messiah, from DI, who admires his achievements (Isaiah 45:1). Later, however, DI is disillusioned with Cyrus, who continually proclaims himself the chosen one of their god to all the peoples he repatriates. DI therefore mounts a polemic against all these gods, declaring YHVH alone to be the lord of history and becoming in the process the true "originator of a theology of world-history."[121] YHVH is capable of leading the nations, just as he leads Cyrus who does not "know Him" in the way that Israel does (45:6). This much Amos had already declared, but DI asserts that one day the nations will know him as their liberator, and all peoples will be called "YHVH's people" and will recognize that all justice and liberty in world affairs flow from YHVH and from nowhere else. As DI's teacher, Isaiah, said, Israel will serve YHVH by preparing and readying themselves for this stage of redemption.

The "suffering servant," however, to whom Buber turns, cannot simply be Israel as a collective.[122] This is a classical Jewish opinion, to be sure, but it has never been unanimous, because there are textual problems with this as a "solution" to the "problem" of the servant's identity.[123] The detailed account of the servant's death, and references to his past actions, complicates efforts to identify the servant with a particular individual. Buber's analysis, tracing minute linguistic connections between the figures of Israel, Cyrus, and the servant (e.g., both Israel and the servant are fashioned by YHVH "from the womb," whereas both Israel and Cyrus are "called by name"), concludes that the servant acts as a successor figure to both Israel and Cyrus. The servant, like Cyrus, is anointed and charged with a task, which, though the same as Israel's, he will accomplish where Israel failed. The "former things" against which DI frequently sets up the "coming things" or the "new things" are Isaiah's prophecies of the child and the "shoot of Jesse"; these he interprets as fulfilled by Cyrus, who has done the work of liberating the people, and by the servant, who "does not smite except with the rod of his mouth, and does not slay the wicked except with the breath of his lips (11:4)." But since Cyrus has attempted to take glory from YHVH by attributing his victories to other gods as well, the "hour of the king of Persia, who has liberated Israel from the yoke of Babylon, passes away and the hour of the 'servant' begins, he who attends to YHVH's 'desire' to redeem the world of the nations from the yoke of its guilt."[124] This servant may initially be Israel (41:8), but soon Israel is rejected again (42:18) and replaced by an alternative, anonymous servant.

The servant thus claims the leadership of Israel, according to a new interpretation of an old leadership style. "David's throne (9:6) man shall no more sit upon; the 'faithful graces (promised) to David (53:3) pass over to Israel ("to you");

the king of Israel, in accordance with the primal covenant, is now none other than YHVH Himself (52:7 *et al.*)."[125] The passage that many consider the strongest evidence for identifying the servant with the collective of Israel ("You are my servant, Israel in whom I glorify myself," 49:3), Buber uses in support of his own view of the servant as a part, but not the totality, of Israel:

> If the saying really was directed to Israel, there was no need to say: "Thou art Israel." If, however, what is meant by the servant is a person, but a person standing in a quite peculiarly close relationship to Israel, it is fairly evident that God speaks to him: "*Thou* art the Israel in whom I glorify myself." The paradox of the two "servants" cannot be dissolved or dispelled. It is intended to be a paradox. In it we recognize the supposition necessary in order that Isaiah's messianic prophecy should be transformed into the Messianic mystery of Deutero-Isaiah.[126]

A shift of emphasis here transforms the servant into yet another version of the doctrine of the remnant: Ezekiel's individualized remnant that reduced the penitent community into a collection of penitent individuals is now concentrated even further, to become a remnant of one person. The suffering-bearing servant of YHVH stands in for the people as a whole.

Mystery remains as to the exact identity of this remnant servant. Buber notes passages in which the servant appears to be the prophet himself, and others in which this identification is rendered impossible (e.g., the report of the servant's death at 53:9). Because nothing here suggests a miraculous individual resurrection, Buber proposes the following solution:

> The substance of the servant is more than a single human person without, however, having a corporate character. Here we infer that this person takes shape in many likenesses and life-ways, the bearers of which are identical in their innermost essence, but no supernatural event, no resurrection of the dead leads from one of these figures to the next. It seems to me that we are able to take the remarkable phrase 'in his deaths' (v. 9) quite literally: it is not a single death that comes upon the servant on his way, he goes from death to death, and to new life again.[127]

Stretching beyond the life span of any individual, people across time and space participate in the life of this servant. Each recognizes that they must endure suffering for the sake of the great work of YHVH; each transforms this suffering from a passive endurance to an action for God's sake; each participates in the liberation of the oppressed peoples, contributing to the divine order and the redemption of history. "Deutero-Isaiah" felt himself to be one of these figures, the one to whom the mystery of the concealment and future revelation of the whole future series was revealed. This vision leads Buber, despite his misgivings about the style and direction of this figure, to anoint him "in truth a prophet, a *nabi.*"[128]

Conclusion

Deutero-Isaiah concludes the messianic transformations that had been ongoing since the days of Samuel and reveals a parallel transformation in the role of the prophet. The charismatic representation of YHVH's kingship through the performance of specific and limited tasks was sundered into many when the king assumed military command as well as the responsibility for public sacrifices. Yet the process of the anointing binds prophet and king, one watching over and directing the other. By turns ignored, reviled, and assaulted, prophets struggle to claim leadership, reminding the people and kings of their first leader, a liberator whom all recalled as a *navi*, a prophet. They promise a king who is to fulfill his task, who never comes. Yet after the destruction, in exile, it becomes possible once again to conceive of a kingless kingdom. In the guise of the suffering servant, Deutero-Isaiah reclaims leadership for the prophets, this time not just for Israel but for the entire world. "The suffering *nabi* is the antecedent type of the acting Messiah."[129] This messiah is not sent to Israel from an other-worldly divine realm but emerges from within Israel itself as its remnant. The struggle that began in the anarcho-theocracy continues:

> There is a nucleus of Israel, preserved through the generations, that does not betray the election, that belongs to God and remains His. Through this nucleus the living connection between God and the people is upheld, in spite of the very great guilt: not alone by interposing on behalf of Israel, but far more by being the true Israel. God's purpose for Israel has put on skin and flesh in these powerless combatants. They are the small beginning of the kingdom of God before Israel becomes a beginning of it; they are the beginning before the beginning. The anointing of the kings was unfulfilled, and Deutero-Isaiah no longer awaits a king in whom this anointing should be fulfilled; the anointing of the *nebiim* has been fulfilled, and therefore it is from their midst that the figure of the perfected one will rise.[130]

For Buber, the first messiah is the only one who ever really came, and his coming must be understood as an occasion of much grief, no matter how gladly the people perceived it at the time. The second messiah was mere prophetic fantasy, and the third messiah recasts that fantasy into a revised form of the premessianic Israelite faith. The suffering servant assumes the role of Israel among the nations, taking upon himself the role that Moses had intended for the entire people.[131] And where Deutero-Isaiah himself may have viewed the identity of the coming servants as a mystery, Buber provides a simple formula for their identification: "As far as the great suffering of Israel's dispersion was not compulsory suffering only, but suffering in truth willingly borne, not passive but active, it is interpreted in the image of the servant. Whosoever accomplishes in Israel the active suffering of Israel, he is the servant, and he is Israel, in whom YHVH 'glorifies Himself.'"

The Second Commonwealth failed to realize the dreams of Deutero-Isaiah. The people went into a second exile, so long it seemed permanent. Prophecy ceased, and the people awaited their messiah as one who would end both the exile and the world. The "great scattering, which followed the splitting up of the state and became the essential form of the people, is endowed with the mystery of suffering as with the promise of the God of sufferers," until, in Buber's own time, a movement arose that sought to end this suffering by ending the exile. Buber's relationship to this movement cannot be fully understood without an understanding of his theopolitical history of Israel.

Notes

1. The text was published first in Hebrew as *Torat Ha-Nevi'im* (literally "Torah/Teaching of the Prophets"). As with *Moshe*, the language of composition is unclear; I therefore cite both Hebrew and German. Hebrew citations are to the second edition of *Torat Ha-Nevi'im* (Tel Aviv: Mossad Bialik, 1950). German citations are to *Der Glaube der Propheten*, in WZB 233–484.

2. Bloom, introduction to *On the Bible*, by Martin Buber, ed. Nahum N. Glatzer (Syracuse, NY: Syracuse University Press, 2000), xxx; Scholem, "Martin Buber's Conception of Judaism," in *On Jews and Judaism in Crisis*, 159.

3. See the introduction, notes 12 and 20.

4. *Two Types of Faith* is the great exception to the rule that Buber plays down the Second Commonwealth. Buber named chapter 10 of *Two Types of Faith* (a discussion of Jesus and Isaiah 53's image of the suffering servant) as containing additional material related to the planned third part of *Das Kommende*.

5. PF 216.

6. MRC has 300 footnotes; PF has 200 by my count. KG in its latest edition has 468. Nearly half (89) of the notes in PF appear in the first sixty pages.

7. Buber cites Deuteronomy 18:21 and Jeremiah 6:14, 14:13, 23:17, and 28:8–9.

8. PF 221.

9. Ibid., 219. Here Buber adapts his passage on idolatry from KG.

10. Buber's reading of Elijah, for example, interprets his defeat of the prophets of Baal through direct divine intervention as a kind of metaphorical representation of a popular memory that the historical Elijah was successful in his polemics against those prophets.

11. Ibid., 220–223.

12. Ibid., 204–205.

13. Buber's special regard for the Song of Deborah was discussed in chapter 3, especially note 85.

14. These "parts" correspond to a textual division concerned with the relationship of theological change to economic and political change: "According to the nature of things a change takes place here as in *the second part*: there through the formation of the state, and here, in the middle of *the third and last part*, through the . . . destruction of this state"; PF 3 (my italics). Since the final table of contents does not reflect a division into three parts, this language may survive from the original plan for part three of *Das Kommende*.

15. Dreyfus, "M. Buber: Messianic Mystery," *Da'at: A Journal of Jewish Philosophy and Kabbalah* 5 (Summer 1980): 117–133 [Hebrew]. Cf. Buber, "Das messianische Mysterium (Jesaja 53)," in SM 37–45.

16. "Ich habe keine Lehre" (I have no teaching) was Buber's refrain when he met with interested young kibbutznikim in his later years, a claim they found frustrating; Paul Mendes-Flohr, "Martin Buber's Reception among Jews," *Modern Judaism* 6.2 (May 1986): 124–126.

17. PF 3.

18. Ibid., 39.

19. Buber calls Abraham's journey a *hījra* several times; ibid., 41, 44. He is suggesting a parallel between Abraham and Muhammad as founders of theopolitical communities. Elsewhere he refers to collections of "Moses' Logia or Moses' Hadith," which may have assisted the first Deuteronomists in the composition of their book; ibid., 197. Although there were comparisons to early Islam in KG, these are more direct identifications between Jewish and Muslim traditions, perhaps reflecting composition in Palestine.

20. Ibid., 49.

21. Ibid., 24.

22. Ibid; WZB 257; *Torat* 18.

23. Ibid., 57–59.

24. Ibid., 62, 65–66, 64, 69.

25. Ibid., 67. Buber seems to expect his reader to know Alt's distinction between laws that are casuistic ("If someone . . . then you shall") and apodictic ("You shall/shall not"). The distinction was well known in biblical studies.

26. Ibid., 68.

27. KG 131.

28. PF 22–24.

29. Ibid., 23–24. This is in line with the discussion of "the Joshuanic reduction" in chapter 3.

30. Ibid., 72. Buber could have chosen many descriptors for this movement; the fact that he calls it "realist" is telling. When he uses "realist" negatively, he usually means self-described realist political theorists (enemies of utopianism).

31. Here we find the development of a theme dating back to the preface of the first edition of KG, namely the identity of the "eschatological tensions" mentioned there, which *Das Kommende* was to develop; KG 16. The preface to the second edition also refers to "great tensions" that "arose within Messianism." Ibid., 40. Only one of the three tensions enumerated in PF, however, corresponds to those enumerated earlier. The second and third tensions described in KG are dealt with in PF, but strangely not in the chapter "The Great Tensions"; whereas the second and third tensions found in PF are non-"eschatological" and simply provide dramatic occasion for narrative progress. This constitutes further support for my claim that PF lacks coherence thanks to its mixture of elements from *Das Kommende* with other material.

32. PF 84.

33. Ibid., 83.

34. Ibid., 100.

35. For this reading, in which David does not refer to himself but to a figure of the future, to work, one must not read *li davar tzur yisrael* as "The Rock of Israel said concerning me," as does the NJPS translation; instead, one reads "To me (the God of Israel speaks) is a ruler." Buber credits A. Klostermann with this interpretation, which in his view "has not been surpassed"; ibid., 85.

36. Ibid., 84.

37. Ibid., 102.

38. Buber calls Samuel's sacrifice at David's anointing "the last independent religio-political act of the prophet"; ibid., 100. David offers the sacrifice when the ark is brought back to Jerusalem (2 Samuel 6:17); Solomon at the dedication of the Temple (1 Kings 8:62f); Jeroboam I at the dedication of his rival northern sanctuary (1 Kings 12:32).

39. Ibid., 101.

40. PF 92.

41. Ibid., 93.

42. Buber accounts for the difference between the *baalim* of the fields and the references to "Baal" as a singular god by noting that "in the more developed Syrian culture," as revealed by the Ras Shamra discoveries, "the *baalim*, spirits lacking individuality, tend to unite into a personal god called Baal"; ibid., 89. Jezebel and her father (whose name is Et-baal) worship a *baal* of this type. This concentration of the numberless fertility powers in a single "lord of heaven and earth" is part of what makes the "frontal assault on baalism" and its slogan "YHVH vs. Baal" possible only in Elijah's time.

43. Ibid., 95.

44. Ibid., 95–96.

45. 1 Kings 18:36: "O Lord, the God of Abraham, of Isaac, and *of Israel*, let it be known this day that you are God *in Israel*." Presumably Buber highlights the twelve stones to forestall the interpretation that Elijah is speaking only of the northern kingdom.

46. Ibid., 97. Buber excuses Elijah from the massacre of the priests of Baal attributed to him by 1 Kings 18:40, reading it as symbolic of the persecution of the priests and prophets of Baal carried out by the rebel Jehu, whom Elijah anointed (I Kings 19:16, which Buber considers older than the contradictory tradition at 2 Kings 9:1–10 that one of Elisha's servants anointed Jehu).

47. Ibid., 98.

48. Ibid. Buber considers Jeremiah 35:6, where the Rekhavites (descendants of Yehonadav) claim to have received this tradition from their ancestor, a "precious communication" about the earlier period.

49. There are obvious parallels here to Buber's general politics. In modern terms, this might amount to a critique of "anarcho-primitivist" rejection of technical civilization and "spiritual" withdrawal from politics per se.

50. Ibid., 101. Buber faults Elisha's followers for settling in common, like the court prophets: "With Elishah and his 'sons of the prophets' . . . the spirit of Elijah had become the possession of a closed sect"; ibid., 117. The fact that even the noncourt prophets had formed a guild later prompts the prophet Amos to deny his own prophethood (Amos 7:14).

51. Ibid., 103.

52. Ibid., 128.

53. Ibid., 117–118. Buber dates significant portions of the Torah to the reign of Solomon and the kings immediately following him, in protest of the usurpation of YHVH's sovereignty. These include the Deuteronomic "kingship ordinance" (Deuteronomy 17:14–17), as well as much of the first part of Genesis (through the sacrifice of Isaac). In the remainder of the "Great Tensions" chapter, Buber analyzes how each episode of the primeval history provides the theological claim of YHVH's sovereignty with a narrative history. His interpretation of Genesis, which reads it as "the great historical document of the struggle for the revelation in the days before the writing prophets," whose main lesson is that "man must know that he cannot establish in earthly life his own regime, man's regime, and satisfy the power above by cult," provides yet another indicator of the primacy of theopolitics as his interpretive lens; ibid., 116.

54. Ibid., 100.

55. Ibid., 155. Buber's controversial Zionist circle was called "A Covenant of Peace" (*Brit Shalom*).

56. Ibid., 151.

57. Ibid., 119–120.

58. Ibid., 122–123.

59. The concept of ethical monotheism represents "a long tradition of German-Jewish thought that concluded that Judaism's particularity represents something of universal significance for all of humanity"; Leora Batnitzky, *Idolatry and Representation: The Philosophy*

of Franz Rosenzweig Reconsidered (Princeton, NJ: Princeton University Press, 2000), 32. Buber straddles this tradition; he believes Judaism's particularity to have universal ethical significance but prefers not to speak of "monotheism."

60. The statement of Amos 5:25—"Did you bring unto Me sacrifices and offerings in the wilderness forty years, O House of Israel?"—is a strong indicator to biblical criticism that the Pentateuchal descriptions of a full priestly system in the desert are late additions. The rhetorical question presumes the answer no, and would not make sense if directed to an audience with a well-developed historical memory that such sacrifices did in fact occur. Buber reads 5:26 ("Did you [at that time] carry [these idols] as your king?)" as a reminder of the ark.

61. Ibid., 126–127.

62. Ibid., 130.

63. Thus for Buber, Amos 7:7 comes before 4:4–13, which comes before 8:2, which comes before 5:2. Only after 8:2, God's announcement "The end is come upon my people Israel and I will pardon them no more" is the "prophecy of doom" uttered at 5:2. The terrible final vision of 9:1 follows this and leads Amos to make a speech that Buber finds split up and scattered in the verses 6:1–7, 6:11–14, and 5:27. This speech provokes the royal repression described at 7:10–13.

64. At Hosea 1:9 the prophet is instructed to name his youngest son *Lo-ammi*, "for you are not my people." Buber reads the concluding clause as "and I am not *Ehyeh* to you," meaning "I will not be present as I was before, in the meaning of my Name."

65. Thus Jonah, a "short story," represents the true sense of prophecy, despite not describing a historical prophet. Jonah announces an immutable decree, with no salvation whatsoever. Nonetheless, the Ninevites repent, saying, "Who knows, God may turn and repent, and turn from his fierce anger" (Jonah 3:9). "Human and divine turning correspond the one to the other; not as if it were in the power of the first to bring about the second, such ethical magic being far removed from biblical thought, but—'Who knows'"; PF 129–130.

66. Ibid., 153.

67. Ibid., 141.

68. Ibid., 152.

69. Ibid.

70. Ibid., 155.

71. Ibid., 163.

72. See note 3 earlier in this chapter.

73. Ibid., 156.

74. Ibid., 167–168.

75. Ibid., 160.

76. Ibid., 159, 169 (italics in original); WZB 379; *Torat* 126.

77. Ibid., 169. "'Keeping still' is holiness in regard to the political attitude of God and His people." / "Das »Stillehalten« ist die Heiligkeit als die »politische« Haltung Gottes und seines Volkes"; WZB 379. / מדת "השקט" היא הקדושה בחינת העמדה הפוליטית של אלהים ושל עמו; *Torat* 126.

78. Ibid., 169.

79. Buber regards this fragment, though earlier in the book, as dated later, to the moment of the abortive Assyrian assault on Jerusalem.

80. Buber designates 32:15–17 as a "messianic prophecy not to be denied Isaiah," but he does not go into any detailed argumentation with scholars who would ascribe the passage to a later writer.

81. Ibid., 168.

82. PU 149.

83. PF 170.

84. PF 174–5. Buber interprets *pele*, "wonder," as an adjective applied to the *name* ("His wonder-name will be"), thus avoiding the common Christian series "Wonderful, Counsellor, Mighty God" as epithets for a human king.

85. Ibid., 174 (original italics).

86. Ibid., 177.

87. Ibid., 178–179 (my italics).

88. The word used by the verse is *chasidav*, which is often rendered 'His holy ones.' Buber retains *chasidim* at first before offering the translation "his faithful tenants," both intending anachronism and not intending it.

89. PF 180.

90. Ibid., 184.

91. Ibid., 187–188.

92. Ibid., 162–163.

93. Ibid., 172.

94. Ibid., 163.

95. Ibid., 175.

96. Ibid., 183. The enigmatic exegesis suggests further parallels with Buber's contemporary situation, writing in the midst of destruction and unable to communicate his message, surrounded by political opponents who take instruction primarily from (their idea of) the memory and spirits of the dead. Following the reasoning of Buber's political opponents in the Zionist movement: we must honor our dead, we do it by living, to live we must do whatever is required, that is, military supremacy and demographic domination, this is the lesson the dead teach us.

97. Isaiah 8:19 ends with the words הלוא-עם אל-אלהיו ידרש בעד החיים אל-המתים. This can be read as a single continuous monologue attributed to the people ("Shall not a people seek unto its God, unto the dead on behalf of the living?") Buber reads it as a dialogue: the people ask, "Shall not a people seek unto its god," meaning the deceased ancestors, and the prophet's disciples respond "What? On behalf of the living, the dead?"

98. See notes 14 and 15 earlier in this chapter.

99. PF 194.

100. Ibid., 198. Buber offers a detailed account of the contents of the Hezekianic core of Deuteronomy, but engages no scholarship on the question. This core is said to include Deuteronomy 4:37; 6:5; 7:6–8, 10, 12, 15; 10:12–13, 15, 18, 20–21; 11:1, 13, 22; 13:4–5; 14:2; 19:9; 26:16, 18.

101. Ibid., 201.

102. Ibid., 197 (original italics).

103. Ibid., 209.

104. The Bible does not emphasize a special social reform connected with Josiah. Buber relies on Jeremiah 22:15–16, in which the prophet upbraids Josiah's son, Jehoiakim: "Did not thy father eat and drink, and do justice and righteousness? Then it was well with him. He judged the cause of the poor and needy; then it was well. Is this not to know me? says YHVH." Ibid., 197, 201.

105. Ibid., 212.

106. Ibid., 214.

107. Ibid., 216.

108. Ibid., 223.

109. Ibid., 217.

110. Ibid., 227.

111. Ibid., 218.

112. Ibid., 230.

113. Ibid., 231.

114. Ibid., 232 (original italics).

115. The sections on Job and Psalm 73 are placed here because Buber holds them to have been composed around the beginning of the exile, but they also stand alone, and somewhat interrupt the narrative.

116. For Buber the material that eventually became the book of Deutero-Isaiah encompasses Isaiah 40–55 (with the exceptions of 47, 49:14–26, and 50:1–3), as well as the fragments of 29:17–23 and 57:14–19 and 61:1. He does not believe in a "Trito-Isaiah"; the remainder of our book of Isaiah simply contains additions and accretions accumulated over time.

117. PF 260–261.

118. Later, Buber sketches the further steps that transform DI's vision into apocalyptic. DI speaks of a figure who ascends to his task, rather than descending from heaven; the book of Daniel then introduces "one like a son of man" who comes "with the clouds of heaven," and Enoch imagines the heavenly preexistence of this messianic figure. From here, Paul and especially John begin the process of deification. Buber, *Two Types of Faith*, trans. Norman P. Goldhawk (Syracuse, NY: Syracuse University Press, 2003), 102–113.

119. PF 262.

120. Ibid., 259.

121. Here there is finally an Israelite figure apparently concerned with the elaboration of a "monotheist theology," denying the existence of other gods and proclaiming them mere creations.

122. Here Buber dissents from a position taken by Hermann Cohen, whose interpretation cast the collective Israel as under a stark obligation to suffer, rejecting the Zionist attempt to create a privileged zone of Jewish safety and happiness; Hermann Cohen, *Religion of Reason out of the Sources of Judaism*, trans. Simon Kaplan (Atlanta: Scholars Press, 1993), 229.

123. The "suffering servant" song is usually said to begin at Isaiah 52:13 and continue until chapter 54, but there are many other references in Deutero-Isaiah to a servant of YHVH, and Buber uses one of these, at 49:5, to argue that the servant cannot be Israel, since it is the role of the servant "to bring back Jacob to Himself, that Israel may be restored to Him"; PF 270.

124. Ibid., 276.

125. Ibid., 274.

126. Ibid., 277.

127. Ibid., 284.

128. Ibid., 286.

129. Ibid., 287.

130. Ibid., 289.

131. Ibid., 290–291.

PART III

THEOPOLITICS AND ZION

Our period is marked by the phony realization of great dreams. What the blissful dreamers have dreamt materializes before our very eyes as a caricature.

 —Martin Buber

You don't know what order with freedom means! You only know what revolt against oppression is!

 —Gustav Landauer

7 Palestinian Rain
Zionism as Applied Theopolitics

Let the dreamers pass from one sky to another.
—Mahmoud Darwish

They speak about rebirth and mean enterprise.
—Martin Buber

Introduction: Buber's Zionism as Theopolitics in Action

For all the changes in Martin Buber's philosophy over the years, one constant is his inclination to the concrete and the everyday. In 1913, he proclaimed that "genuine religiosity . . . has nothing in common with the fancies of romantic hearts, or with the self-pleasure of aestheticizing souls, or with the clever mental exercises of a practiced intellectuality. Genuine religiosity is *doing*."[1] Fifty years later, this had not changed: "I don't believe in theories but in human example. . . . Not the truth as an ideal nor the truth as image, but the truth as action is what Judaism is all about. Judaism's goal is not philosophic theory or artistic creation but Torah as truth."[2] By Buber's own lights, then, his action should be the most important place we look to determine his teaching—and Zionism was the primary arena of his political action.[3] After a brief period at the turn of the century when he seemed to act as a representative of "official" Zionism, he adopted an oppositional position, which he held for the rest of his life, even as the content of this position and the vocabulary he used to describe it evolved. This shifting of vocabularies, the nuance with which Buber expressed his position, and Buber's idiosyncratic intellectual inheritance together make it difficult to pinpoint his Zionism in a single description.

The evolution of Buber's Zionism is best understood as a manifestation of his anarcho-theocratic understanding of Judaism, influenced by his collaborations with Gustav Landauer in politics and Franz Rosenzweig in biblical studies, along with his awareness of the growing cooperative-settlement movement in Palestine and the intensification of the Zionist-Arab conflict. No single book-length work represents this synthesis. However, *Ben 'am le-artzo* (Between a People and Its

Land, 1945), read in concert with Buber's occasional writings on Zionism, comes very close.[4] Despite his insistent refrain "I have no teaching," Buber's Zionism takes a consistent direction. The primary understanding of this Zionism has read it through *I and Thou* and the philosophy of dialogue. This strategy is not fruitless, since Buber's thoughts on the nature of human relationship can be readily applied to any situation of conflict. However, the strategy also has drawbacks. Buber's "ontology of the between," according to Mendes-Flohr, stresses the one-on-one encounter but never quite offers "a systematic explication of the transition from the *Zwie* to the *Vielgemeinschaft* (a *Gemeinschaft* of many); we are thus obliged to rely on inference."[5] Moreover, Buber never explicitly clarifies how the achievement of true community in one place can play an exemplary role for others to imitate.

If we start, though, from a presumption that Buber's Zionism is rooted in his theopolitics, we can link his intense interest in biblical history with his contemporary politics. We can approach his Zionism with his general politics in mind, such as the belief that "the creation of a genuine and just community on a voluntary basis . . . will show the world the possibility of basing social justice on voluntary action."[6] Like Landauer before him, Buber articulated this doctrine in both materialist and religious vocabularies, sometimes simultaneously but often in alternation, depending on his audience. Buber believed himself consonant with the deepest forces of reality when he imagined the fulfillment of Isaiah's prophecy that one day the word of the Lord would go forth from Zion and the Torah from Jerusalem. A sense of this prophecy as the fulfillment of the covenant between God and Israel underlies his oft-repeated conviction: "If Israel desires less than it is intended to fulfill then it will even fail to achieve the lesser goal."[7] The materialist version of the realization of this prophecy would be the world's respect for and eventual imitation of the achievement of the people of Israel, the rise of Jerusalem as the anarcho-theocratic center of the world between Washington and Moscow.

Zionism and Zionisms: Placing Buber on the Spectrum of Zionist Thought

Buber's Zionism is variously referred to as "cultural," "spiritual," "religious," and "binationalist." It is never called "political," since Buber's polemics are primarily directed against "political" Zionism. All these descriptors fail. Buber himself used the term *Wirklichkeitzionismus*, "Zionism of reality," which scholars have not adopted, perhaps because it would require immediate explanation, whereas other terms are familiar. I argue that "theopolitical Zionism" is perhaps the only way to capture the nuances of Buber's position.

Buber is frequently referred to as a "cultural" Zionist. Still, while he participated in the Democratic Fraction and sided with Ahad Ha'am, the founder of cultural Zionism, against Herzl and Nordau (the leaders of political Zionism), and while he passionately attempted to convince the World Zionist Organization to invest in such projects as a Jewish publishing house, he differed significantly from Ahad Ha'am on the matter of religion. As Martina Urban has written, "Whereas Ahad Ha'am and his largely Russian Jewish associates advocated renewal as the recasting of formal aspects of Jewish tradition—its literature, customs, language as well as select values into secular modalities—Buber understood Jewry's cultural heritage as a fount of abiding religious sensibilities . . . independent of the objective expressions of culture."[8] Furthermore, in his defense of Ahad Ha'am in *Die Welt*, Buber praised him as the man who helped create "spiritual" Zionism.[9]

Spiritual Zionism, then, might seem like a more appropriate designation than "religious" Zionism, given the non-Orthodox, non-halakhic nature of Buber's Judaism, despite the fact that he and Judah Magnes are grouped together with Rabbi Samuel Mohilever and Rabbi Abraham Isaac Kook in Arthur Hertzberg's *The Zionist Idea*, the standard textbook on the subject.[10] Moreover, there is a yawning gap between the *dati le'umi* (national religious), to whom the label "religious Zionism" is usually applied, and the "professors of Mount Scopus," among whom Buber is usually numbered.[11] This gap dates back to the period between the two world wars, when "Religious-Zionism . . . tended to adopt a distinctive 'right-wing' orientation."[12]

These divisions emerged in stages. Ernst Simon, who moved to Palestine in 1928, was one of the first board members of the Bnei Akiva (Children of Akiva) youth movement founded a year later in Jerusalem, which took as its motto "Purify your life through work and sanctify it through Torah."[13] Bnei Akiva, an offshoot of *Ha-Po'el ha-Mizrahi* (Mizrahi Worker), the labor wing of the religious-Zionist political party Mizrahi, promoted kibbutzim that combined religion and socialism through the idea of *Torah va-Avodah* (Torah and labor).[14] This effort was opposed by the Zionist executive, which favored secular settlements; it was not until the *chomah u-migdal* (tower and stockade) strategy of settling in clusters, in response to the Arab Revolt of 1936–1939, that permission was granted to establish the first religious kibbutzim, thus shaping their militaristic cast.[15] Bnei Akiva was the same organization that would one day graduate the members of the Gahelet (Embers) group from its yeshiva at Kfar Ha'roeh—men who would go on to form the core of the Gush Emunim (Bloc of the Faithful) settler movement after they took R. Zvi Yehuda Kook as their teacher.[16] From Ernst Simon to Zvi Yehuda Kook is a long way ideologically, but it was traversed in only a few decades.

This historical connection between one of Buber's most outstanding disciples and religious Zionism may seem tenuous, and happenstance should not obscure the fact that Buber stood on the opposite end of the political and religious spectrum. And yet Rabbi Aharon Lichtenstein, the head of Yeshivat Har Etzion in Alon Shvut (a settlement in the Gush Etzion bloc near Jerusalem), recently distinguished a true religious Zionist from "an individual who is committed to both *Yahadut* [Judaism] and Zionism." In a true religious Zionist, Lichtenstein argued, "the two are thoroughly intertwined."[17] By that criterion, Buber is more of a religious Zionist than the founder of the Mizrahi, R. Isaac Jacob Reines. For Reines, Zionism was primarily a matter of political expediency, separate from Judaism; for this reason he was one of the staunchest allies of Herzl, even supporting the plan to settle Jews in Uganda instead of Palestine if necessary.[18] Buber, in contrast, devoted a sympathetic section of *On Zion* to Reines's great rival, Rabbi A. I. Kook; with Buber the Gush Emunim slogan "There is no Zionism without Judaism and no Judaism without Zionism" is more fully endorsed than with Reines.[19] After all, it was Buber who said, in his analysis of the Song of Deborah, "No one can declare himself for Israel without declaring himself for YHVH."[20]

I admit to some intentional provocation here. There is no escaping the stark differences between Buber and the political movement that goes under the name of "religious Zionism," differences that date back to the Mizrahi World Conference in Krakow in 1933, which anticipated the Biltmore Program by nearly a decade in its proclamation that the final goal of Zionism is the establishment of a Jewish state.[21] The ultimate symbol of these differences is encapsulated in the last common term for Buber's Zionism: "binationalist." The groups with which Buber was associated from the 1920s through the 1940s sought to achieve binational solutions to the conflict between Zionism and the Palestinian Arabs: Brit Shalom (Covenant of Peace), the League for Jewish-Arab Rapprochement, and the Ichud (Unity).[22] In the Peel Commission's partition plan for Palestine in 1937, "religious-Zionist" leaders already saw a "renunciation" of areas that would be under Arab control, despite the large Arab majorities then living there. Meir Bar-Ilan, the head of the Mizrahi at the time, accused Chaim Weizmann, who supported partition, of endorsing the worldview of Brit Shalom.[23] The fact that Bar-Ilan assumed that this was an insult, and that Weizmann would see it as one, testifies to the negative perception of Brit Shalom in Zionist discourse. A further irony: Brit Shalom sought binationalist solutions partially to prevent partition of the land. But such ironies and misunderstandings are common in dealing with this movement.

Susan Lee Hattis has written that the name of Brit Shalom "came to be regarded amongst many Zionists as a synonym for 'traitors.'"[24] The group was founded in 1925 in Jerusalem as a study circle, focusing on Arab-Jewish relations, initially intending to place its conclusions at the service of the Zionist Executive. It published a newspaper, *She'ifoteinu* (Our Aspirations), and engaged in a few overt "political" activities, such as binational union organization, as well as "cultural" ones, such as Arabic classes for Jews.[25] It was notable primarily for the high-profile figures involved, including Buber, Gershom Scholem, Henrietta Szold, and Arthur Ruppin. Ruppin was director of the Palestine Land Development Company, and his involvement gave Brit Shalom a stamp of authority, although he eventually left the group, which disbanded completely in 1933.[26] Its membership never exceeded two hundred, and according to Hattis, neither Brit Shalom nor its somewhat similar "successor" movements were able to find "until 1946 a single serious Arab who was willing to accept their thesis."[27]

Brit Shalom was not a homogeneous group. According to one account, it was internally divided between moderates and radicals; according to another, even the radicals were sharply divided among themselves.[28] Tension revolved around the question whether agreement with the Arabs was merely a practical idea for Zionism or whether it was a sine qua non for the moral justification of Zionism. The name "Brit Shalom" eventually came to be identified more with the position taken by the radicals than with the historical group itself. As Adi Gordon writes: "Although generations have come and gone and political reality has changed utterly, Brith Shalom remains somehow very much present in Israeli consciousness—reflecting the association's transformation into a symbol of considerable mythological import."[29] Here, I adopt this "symbolic" usage, so that in retrospect Ruppin, who was a Brit Shalom member, was not really a "Brit Shalomnik," while Judah Magnes, who was not in Brit Shalom, represents its stance.[30] Buber, despite living in Germany for the duration of the movement's existence, was the spiritual father of this stance, which is generally seen as destined for marginality and failure. As the Israeli historian Tom Segev puts it, the tragedy of men like Magnes is that "there was no demand for their goodwill."[31] In accordance with this perception of insignificance, histories of Zionism and the State of Israel tend to devote little space to Brit Shalom. Yoram Hazony says that it "rarely receives more than a mention in books dealing with Israel's founding."[32] Howard Sachar's 1,020-page *A History of Israel* devotes but one sentence to Buber's impact on the young German Zionists who were to form the core of Brit Shalom, and only one paragraph to the group itself, since "it made hardly a dent on the leadership of Jewish Palestine. Neither did it evoke even the faintest response from the Arabs."[33] Conor Cruise O'Brien allots three paragraphs to Brit Shalom, and never mentions Buber, in his *Saga of Israel and Zionism*.[34] Martin Gilbert gives the movement equally short shrift.[35] Brit Shalom fares slightly better in Walter Laqueur's *History of Zionism*: it ranks a five-page discussion in the chapter on Jewish-Arab relations, along with five other mentions in this six-hundred-page work. Laqueur describes the group as "highly unpopular" and estimates its size and impact even less generously than Sachar: "The association had at no time more than a hundred members," who "had no mass basis" and whose "political impact was negligible."[36] The best summary of this consensus can perhaps be found in Michael Brenner's *Zionism: A Brief History*:

> Buber supported the idea of a bi-national state, which the Brit Shalom . . . was attempting to achieve. This organization existed for only a brief period (1925–33). The groups that succeeded it were few in number. Their members

were respected intellectuals who typically came from Central Europe. However, they lacked counterparts on the Arab side who recognized a Jewish right to a home in Palestine.[37]

One might expect a different treatment from "revisionist" Israeli histories, reputed to reconsider the Zionist past in ways more favorable to previously ignored or silenced voices. Yet Benny Morris's *Righteous Victims* mentions Brit Shalom only once in 694 pages, referring to it as "a significant but ultimately marginal development . . . repudiated [by the *Yishuv*] . . . as naïve and unrealistic."[38] Segev's *One Palestine, Complete*, which focuses on the Mandate period (1922–1948), during which Brit Shalom was active, nonetheless mentions the group on only two of its 519 pages.[39] The most recent general work, Anita Shapira's *Israel: A History*, continues the trend, with mentions on three of 475 pages.[40]

This collective emphasis on failure and marginality is sometimes coupled with an acknowledgment of Brit Shalom's ideological uniqueness.[41] This group took the problem of Jewish-Arab relations to be morally and practically primary at a time when other Zionist factions were still denying that a problem existed.[42] The association of Brit Shalom with binationalism, however, has contributed to seeing it as an idea irrevocably of the past. Binationalism apparently became impossible after the 1947 UN partition plan and the 1948 war, and it came to be viewed as a mere curiosity. History had decided in favor of the nation-state. But the term "binationalism," applied too broadly, is reductionist and misleading, obscuring more than revealing the history and content of Brit Shalom thought. Binationalism is a policy recommendation, offered in response to a particular set of options. It emerged, however, from a complex matrix of ideas. As Buber himself put it in 1947:

> This program [binationalism] is only a temporary adaptation of our path to the concrete, historical situation—it is not necessarily the path itself. The road to be pursued is that of an agreement between the two nations—naturally also taking into account the productive participation of smaller national groups— an agreement which, in our opinion, would lead to Jewish-Arab cooperation in the revival of the Middle East, with the Jewish partner concentrated in a strong settlement in Palestine. This cooperation, though necessarily starting out from economic premises, will allow development in accordance with an all-embracing cultural perspective and on the basis of a feeling of at-oneness, tending to result in a new form of society.[43]

Here Buber explains that binationalism is the contingent and temporary adaptation of "our path" to certain historical circumstances. To call Buber and his groups binationalist may be a helpful shortcut, but it is also a misleading exercise in political metonymy, calling an intellectual stance not by its most appropriate name but by the name of something with which it is closely associated. We have already seen the vast range of connotations that Buber can pack into a short phrase such as "a new form of society."

Buber's Zionism after 1916 was built on the foundation of the mystical, post-Nietzschean anarchism of Landauer and developed through an in-depth study of biblical theopolitics. Somewhat confusingly, however, Buber calls this complex and idiosyncratic mixture "Zionism" and continues to insist that this is what "true" Zionism must mean, no matter how many others with radically different ideas claim the term Zionism for themselves. Consequently, it has been difficult to properly contextualize his activity. Buber joins a strong sense of election, covenant, and command to a will to the immediate realization of socialism, yet he remains isolated both from socialist Labor Zionism and from religious Zionism.[44] The term "binationalist" points to the cause of this isolation, yet Buber's binationalism is merely a manifestation of his broader theopolitics. Only from this standpoint can we properly judge Buber's successes or failures, fifty years, four Israeli-Arab wars, and two Palestinian intifadas after his death.

In the Fray: Public Intellectual as Theopolitician

Bringing Landauer to Zionism, or Trying, 1919–1925

It is important to remember the connection between Buber's Zionist evolution and two other lines of development: the cooperative settlement movement, and the Zionist-Arab conflict. The turn of the century, the time of Buber's earliest Zionist activity, was also the close of the First Aliyah, and the moshav system of private, plantation-style settlement under professional managers on the payroll of the Baron de Rothschild. Only in 1910 was the first *kvutza*, Degania, established on collectivist principles, with its workers keeping a common treasury and exercising control over their own work through direct-democratic processes. By 1914, the end of the Second Aliyah, Degania had become a model for twenty-eight new *kvutzot* (totaling about 380 people).[45] The war interrupted the flow of Jewish immigration to Palestine, but by the time of the Third Aliyah in 1919, Buber, newly reinvested in Landauerian principles, began to take note of the increasingly central role that collective settlement was coming to play in the life of the new Yishuv. As Grete Schaeder has noted, the Zionist pioneers did not face the kind of obstacles that Landauer had known: "The Jewish commonwealth that was developing [in Palestine] would not be hampered by previously existing institutions and constitutional forms. Because that commonwealth was being founded by like-minded people creating afresh out of the primitive forms of community life, there was the possibility of charting new territories of creative socialism."[46]

There was no single model kibbutz, but certain broad principles dominated the movement. As stated by the Degania group in a letter to Ruppin, these aimed at "a cooperative community without exploiters or exploited."[47] This objective would be realized through the collective ownership of property, including the means of production; free distribution of consumer goods, according to need; the abolition of wage labor; decisions to be made by a general assembly of all the kibbutz members, with each member having an equal vote; the integration of manual and intellectual labor; a rotation of roles and duties with the equal dis-tribution of routine, monotonous tasks; the abolition of hierarchy in workplace management, with no "bosses" with power to inspect worker output or restrict worker movement; and health care for the sick and elderly.[48] Kibbutzim were oc-casionally, though not always, explicit about the sources of this form of com-munal organization in anarchism.[49] Members were untroubled by political theo-rists who worried that their ideas were impossible or contrary to human nature. When a Degania member was asked what would happen when a worker refused to pull his share, or took too much from the collective treasury, the response was "we would not love him."[50]

During the November Revolution, Landauer had issued a pamphlet enti-tled *Die vereinigten Republiken Deutschlands und ihre Verfassung* (The United Republics of Germany and Their Constitution), in which he laid out his vision for what would replace the Second Reich, which had just "collapsed in shame."[51] Lashing out against the demand for a central, elected German government to ne-gotiate postwar terms, Landauer wrote: "No longer shall there be atomized voters abdicating their power. Instead, there shall be municipalities, cooperatives, and associations determining their own destiny in big assemblies and through del-egates; delegates who are in constant exchange with their constituencies, who can be recalled and replaced at any time. . . . A republic is a public affair, a common body."[52] Landauer expressed the hope that the workers', soldiers', and peasants' councils, despite their ad hoc, spontaneous nature and their frequent conser-vatism, represented the core of an emerging democracy, a federative structure forming from the bottom up. Landauer hoped that Bavaria could lead Germany in this regard, and that Germany could in turn lead erring Russia, and perhaps inspire the countries of the Entente to have their own revolutions as well. Lan-dauer reminds us of Buber's concept of Zion:

> Even in its first undifferentiated form a tendency towards federation was in-nate in the Kvuza, to merge the Kvuzoth in some higher social unit; and a very important tendency it was, since it showed that the Kvuza implicitly under-stood that it was the cell of a newly structured society . . . the fundamental assumption was that the local groups would combine on the same principle of solidarity and mutual help as reigned within the individual group.[53]

That is, the anarchistic structure of each individual kibbutz would be replicated on a wide scale through the federation of the kibbutzim into regional and na-tional networks, as democratic in operation as the units composing them. If per-vasive enough, these networks would obviate the need for a state.

Landauer was never a Zionist, but neither did he express disapproval of Bu-ber's Zionist ideas. As early as 1901, he had criticized the imperialistic universal-ism of some comrades on the far left: "We have to realize that different cultures exist next to each other and that the dream that all should be the same cannot be sustained—in fact, it is not even a beautiful dream."[54] In 1913, he contributed an article to the volume *Vom Judentum*, published by Buber's disciples in the Prague Bar Kochba Society, in which he asked, "What is *Nation* other than a union of those who, brought together by unifying *Geist*, feel in themselves a particular duty toward humanity? To be a nation means to have a function."[55] On this basis he condemned the chauvinism of political Zionism, and regularly spoke to Zionist youth groups.[56] In declining to join in Buber's Zionist projects he vacillated between indifference and generous neutrality. "The more Germany and Turkey on the one side, England, America, and the political Zionists on the other, take an interest in Palestine," he wrote to Buber in 1918, "the more my attitude cools toward this region, to which my heart has never drawn me and which for me is not necessarily the site for a Jewish community."[57] A few months later he wrote: "Don't take it amiss, Buber, if I cannot participate in one or the other of your undertakings; everyone needs his own forms and springboards. That doesn't affect our harmony and community, which has grown much deeper in the course of these years."[58] Buber did not cease attempting to involve him, however. As late as March 1919 he persuaded Nahum Goldmann (1895–1982) to ask Landauer to speak at a conference in Berlin for German socialist Zionists. Goldmann also convinced Landauer to take part in a small preliminary convention in Munich, planned by Buber for April 1919; he specifically asked him to draft statements on decentralized society, nationalization of land, and worker control of industry.[59] The Bavarian Council Republic interrupted these plans and neither conference ever took place, but the correspondence shows that Landauer's "utopian" ideas were taken seriously by socialist Zionists at the time, who saw potential to apply them immediately in building nonhierarchical socialist settlements in Palestine.[60] After Landauer's death, Buber lamented that Zionism had never met its true, hidden leader: "Landauer's idea was our idea . . . and in accordance with this idea, Landauer was to have participated in the building of a new land and a new society as guide and mentor."[61]

These words were addressed to the Founders Conference of the German branch of Ha'poel Ha'tzair (The Young Worker), which took place in 1920 in Prague. Ha'poel Ha'tzair was a non-Marxist socialist Zionist group, led in Palestine by the farmer-philosopher A. D. Gordon (1856–1922). It was pacifist leaning, and a close, if not exact, fit for Buber ideologically. The conference was an early indication of Buber's success in bringing Landauer's ideas to the non-Marxist socialist Zionists.[62] Chaim Arlosoroff (1899–1933), a young leader of Ha'poel Ha'tzair who would later be instrumental in the founding of the Mapai, declared to the conference, "In our views as to building up our economy in Palestine and in the Exile the Weltanschauung of Gustav Landauer has served us as a foundation."[63] At the conference, Buber's group merged with another one to form the *Hitachdut Ha'poel Ha'tzair v'Tzeirei Tzion*, and it was as a delegate of this organization that Buber attended the Twelfth Zionist Congress in Karlsbad in 1921.

This was the first Zionist Congress to follow three momentous events: World War I, the Balfour Declaration, and the San Remo Conference, at which Britain assumed the Palestine Mandate. After the collapse of the Ottoman Empire, Great Britain and France were splitting the Middle East between them. The Balfour Declaration, issued by Britain in 1917, seemed to signify that Herzl's dream that a Great Power would grant the Jews a charter for Palestine had finally been realized. Buber, however, dissented from the common view that this was a boon to Zionism. In 1919, Buber had warned that "we must . . . make it clear that we have nothing to do with [the League of Nations'] present system of values, with imperialism masquerading as humanitarianism. We must therefore abstain from all 'foreign policy' except for those steps and actions which are necessary for the achievement of a lasting and amicable agreement with the Arabs."[64] In 1920, the first major outbreak of Arab violence against Jews in Palestine took place after a Nebi Musa march. Whereas many Zionists compared this to Cossack pogroms in Russia, viewing the Arab rioters as a mob incited by hateful antisemites, Buber perceived its political motive: "We . . . must not appear before the East, which is awakening from its dull slumber, as agents of a West which is doomed to destruction, lest justified suspicion fall on us . . . it depends on us."[65] At the Twelfth Congress, Buber repeated these warnings, proposing a resolution that would express solidarity with the Arab national movement and disavow imperialism:

> Our return to the Land of Israel, which will come about through increasing immigration and constant growth, will not be achieved at the expense of other people's rights. By establishing a just alliance with the Arab peoples, we wish to turn our common dwelling-place into a community that will flourish economically and culturally, and whose progress would bring each of these peoples unhampered independent development.
>
> Our settlement [in the Land of Israel], which is exclusively devoted to the rescue of our people and their renewal, is not aimed at the capitalistic exploitation of the region, nor does it serve any imperialistic aim whatsoever. Its significance is the productive work of free individuals upon a commonly owned soil. This, the socialist nature of our national ideal, is a powerful warrant for our confidence that between us and the working Arab nation a deep and enduring solidarity of true common interests will develop and which in the end must overcome all the conflicts to which the present mad hour has given birth.[66]

The resolution that was finally adopted, however, was so watered down that Buber viewed it as a mere "tactical gesture" meant to defend against the accusation that Zionism was hostile to the Arabs. In Buber's view, it lacked the courage of its convictions; it eliminated his rejections of domination, imperialism, and capitalistic exploitation, replacing them with expressions of indignation at the 1920 violence and a reaffirmation of the Balfour Declaration. Instead of calling for an "alliance" with the Arabs, it desired a mere "entente." Buber was so dismayed by this turn of events that he once again turned his back on the politics of Zionist Congresses, in which he felt it was impossible to participate "without compromising truth."[67] The Zionist movement appeared unwilling to heed his call to replace the Balfour Declaration, perceived as a guarantee of success, by uncertain negotiations with the Arabs of Palestine. For Buber, however, this was a new theopolitical hour, and the risk was religiously mandated: "God does not sign promissory notes. But blessed be the man who lends himself to God without any bill of exchange!"[68]

Brit Shalom: Ideology and Career, 1925–1933

In the autumn of 1925, Brit Shalom was founded in Palestine, and Buber, though still in Germany, became a member. Its founding charter, published in English, Arabic, and Hebrew, proclaimed that "the object of the Association is to arrive at an understanding between Jews and Arabs as to the form of their mutual social relations in Palestine on the basis of absolute political equality of two culturally autonomous peoples, and to determine the lines of their co-operation for the development of the country."[69] Its ideological uniqueness among Zionists is best explained by focusing on several major concrete and practical issues, issues that coincided with the major Arab grievances against Zionism: land acquisition, the rate and scale of immigration, and the policy known as *kibbush avodah*, the "conquest of labor."[70] On all these matters, Brit Shalom's stance (i.e., that of its "radical coterie") was undergirded by its opposition to sovereignty as a Zionist goal and its conviction that honoring Arab rights was a necessity for the fulfillment of Zionism, and not an obstacle to its achievements.

Most Zionists saw their methods of land purchase, like their general intentions, as morally innocent; they viewed sporadic and sometimes violent peasant resistance to it as nonpolitical in nature, or at least not nationalistically motivated. This was especially the case prior to 1900, when Jewish purchases seemed little different, from the perspective of the average fellah, from purchases by wealthy Arab landlords.[71] These purchases were few, at any rate: "By the [nineteenth] century's end, merely 21 Jewish settlements with about 4,500 Jewish inhabitants— two-thirds working in agriculture—had been established. These numbers were hardly large enough to have any serious impact on Arab agriculture."[72] Benny Morris notes that conflicts between early *moshavot* and evicted Arab peasants did occur, at Petach Tikva, Gadera, and Rehovot; in most of these cases, however, "once the initial disputes over land were settled, and the Arabs resigned themselves to their loss, hostility abated."[73] Neville Mandel agrees, noting that although the fellahin were generally surprised to learn that their land had been sold, first to wealthy landowners and then to Zionists, and although from their perspective this abstract transfer of title had nothing to do with their continuing rights to live and work on the land, they accommodated themselves to new conditions if they could secure work at the settlements.[74]

After 1900, however, the founding of the Jewish National Fund and the Palestine Land Development Company, both intended to coordinate Jewish purchases, changed things. These new agencies assumed that land purchase included the right to determine who lived on it and worked it; they also sought to prevent future resale of the land, now considered the perpetual and collective property of the Jewish people.[75] Moreover, the immigrants of the Second Aliyah developed an ideology, *kibbush avodah*, which made them more likely to employ exclusively Jewish workers. As a result, purchases after 1900 often involved the eviction of the Arab tenants and their replacement with Jewish settlers.[76] In 1905, Yitzhak Epstein, a Russian-born Jew who settled in the Upper Galilee in 1886 and would later become a member of Brit Shalom, gave a controversial speech at a conference of the cultural Zionist organization Ivriya. This speech was published two years later as an essay called "A Hidden Question;" in it he raised grave doubts about the Zionist method of land acquisition:

> We buy the lands, for the most part, from the owners of large estates; these owners, or their predecessors, acquired their land by deceit and exploitation and lease it to the *fellahin*. . . . [I]t is customary in Eretz Israel for the estate to pass from one owner to another while the tenants remain in their place. But when we buy such a property, we evict the former tillers from it. . . . [C]an we really rely on this way of acquiring land? Will it succeed, and does it suit our purpose? One hundred times no. . . . Will they not in the end rise up to take back with their fists what was taken from them by the power of gold? When we come to buy lands in Eretz Israel, we must thoroughly check whose land it is, who works it, and what the rights of the latter are, and we must not complete the purchase until we are certain that no one will be worse off.[77]

Epstein's plea evoked angry responses from Zionists. Moshe Smilansky responded in *Ha'poel Ha'tzair* that if Epstein was right, Zionists "have no place" in Israel: "The land of our fathers is lost to us. [Or] if the Land of Israel belongs to us, to the Jewish people, then our national interests come before all else. . . . It is not possible for one country to serve as the homeland of two peoples."[78] Smilansky's view that Zionists should consider their own interests paramount, and get to know Arabs only the better to fend them off, was more widespread than Epstein's moral anguish. As Berl Katznelson put it: "The quest for peaceful co-existence with the Arabs is not new. . . . To those who preach morality [to the Yishuv], we have only one thing to say: Come to Eretz Israel and prove that you could establish more amicable relations with the Arabs than we have."[79] Katznelson accused Brit Shalom of being "alienated."[80] His view was widely shared among Labor Zionists, who heard calls like Epstein's (if they heard them at all) as injunctions to do more than the Zionist movement could while also accomplishing its goals; they weighed the evils in a balance, and usually concluded that Zionist interests were paramount. Arthur Ruppin is a good example: while a member of Brit Shalom, he wrote that he was worried about the Zionist practice of purchasing land from "large landowners or creditors," often absentee, and hardly ever from "those who actually cultivate it."[81] Yet Ruppin himself personally spearheaded many of the early purchases that sounded the alarm about Zionism in the Arab world.[82]

The issue of land acquisition was tightly intertwined with the question of employment and gave rise to the fascinating problematic of *kibbush avodah*. A common account of this ideology emphasizes the socialist ideals of the Second Aliyah settlers; they were horrified by the structure of the *moshavot*, which to them looked distressingly similar to the European colonial societies of Algeria and Kenya. As Leslie Stein writes, the farmers of the First Aliyah "had come to terms with an economic structure in which farm plantations were based on the exploitation of cheap, casual labor. . . . [O]n average, each farmer employed the services of three Arab families, which meant that literally thousands of Arabs worked in the settlements."[83] This practice contradicted both their socialist sensibilities and their hope for a renewal of Jewish life through their own contact with the soil, and so the Second Aliyah settlers wanted to employ Jewish labor exclusively. Gershon Shafir, however, has emphasized the need to employ poor Jewish immigrants as the primary factor behind the widespread embrace of *kibbush avodah*; he argues that this policy constituted "the *critical* step in Israeli state-building and nation formation," since it "indicated a desire for the exclusion of Palestinian workers from the new society in the making."[84] Just as the Jewish National Fund had taken Jewish land off the market, the *Histadrut*, the Jewish labor movement's trade union founded in 1920, took Jewish labor off the market. Notably, the Revisionists hardly differed from the Labor Zionists on this issue, despite their general tendency to espouse right-wing, free-market economic views. Some Zionists foresaw that depriving Arabs of employment would be even more injurious than the mere purchase of land but nonetheless allowed their nationalism to overcome their socialism.

Brit Shalom's position was again distinctive. In 1930, Brit Shalom members broke with *kibbush avodah* and attempted to organize a binational union, by which the joint struggle between workers of both nations could break down cultural divisions.[85] This was not unique, as other binational unions did exist among workers more committed to communism than to nationalism.[86] However, Zionists who advocated such unions were accused of "spending too much time on the Arab question"; this contention was supported by the fact that while a few protests against *kibbush avodah* were mounted by leaders of Jaffa's Arab community, and a number of Arab leaders complained about the policy, the issue did not truly arouse the Arab community until the mid-1930s, when an economic crisis precipitated serious confrontations.[87] Despite this, Brit Shalom tried to avoid the exploitation of Arabs while simultaneously eschewing the economic segregation of *kibbush avodah*. A difference between the moderate and radical wings of Brit

Shalom emerged here. Ruppin wrote, "Our principle, which requires that all the work in our colonies be done by Jews only, does indeed suit our national interests, but robs the Arabs of the wages which they had been earning in our colonies."[88] Buber, however, contended that economic segregation was only *apparently* in the Jewish "national interest." In 1939, after the *thawra* [the Arab Revolt] had been under way for three years, and a strict Arab policy of economic segregation had been enacted, Buber lamented the Zionist movement's failure "to form a serious partnership with that people, to involve them earnestly in our building of the land, and to give them a share in our labor and in the fruits of our labor."[89]

Immigration was one question on which all Zionist factions seemed to agree. In Judah Magnes's view of the essentials of Zionism, he cited only three things: "Immigration. Settlement on the land. Hebrew life and culture."[90] To be sure, the urgency of immigration increased over time. Nothing united the Yishuv more than the British White Paper of 1939, which placed a blanket restriction on Jewish immigration at a time when Jews desperately needed to flee Europe. In 1935, more than sixty thousand Jewish immigrants entered Palestine, a rate that if sustained would have made Jews a majority by 1947.[91] However, even before the *thawra* (by which time Brit Shalom had already dissolved), various Zionist factions had different conceptions of what immigration meant, depending on their interpretation of Zionism itself. For Labor and for the Revisionists, immigration was a means to independence, conceived as sovereignty and a Jewish majority. This precisely is why the Arabs opposed it. For Brit Shalom, on the other hand, such a conception of immigration threatened the goal of a democratic society, as Ernst Simon warned the Jewish Agency in London in 1930:

> If the Jews renounce the plan of developing a majority they no longer need to oppose democratic institutions in the country. Such a peace conclusion would restore [the] confidence of progressive world opinion including the League of Nations. . . . If such a perfect peace is not arrived at . . . the Palestinian contingent of the Jewish people will have to fall in for hire with the imperialistic and reactionary forces and must develop all the virtues and all the vices of a warlike nation.[92]

In the face of Arab hostility to the idea of becoming a minority in their homeland, a Jewish majority could be achieved only by the use of force. David Werner Senator complained to Weizmann:

> If it is not assumed that the Great Powers are prepared to transfer the Arabs of Palestine from this country to other Arab countries, the [program of a Jewish commonwealth] can only mean partition. But here again, a workable partition seems to be possible only if at least a partial transfer [of the Palestinians from their homes to areas outside the Jewish state] is effected.[93]

Unlike either Labor or the Revisionists, Brit Shalom maintained that if Zionist goals could be achieved only through large-scale force, they not only did not deserve to be achieved but also in the long run would in fact fail to be achieved. Brit Shalom understood that under its program Zionism would have to dissent from the prevailing system of nation-states. As Hugo Bergmann put it in December 1929:

> [We demand that] in Palestine such a regime be constructed which *a priori* shall take all *national questions* out of the sphere of majority versus minority decisions so as to eliminate in advance any possibility of the majority ruling over the minority in its national affairs. In Palestine there is no room for "the people of the state" or for any "national sovereignty."[94]

Bergmann believed that the goal of Zionism was to draw on the experience of the Jews as "a classical minority people" and to "break up that majority spirit in the life of the nations, to set up a new national and political morality in the world."[95] This was the basis of Brit Shalom's willingness to compromise on the rate and scale of Jewish immigration. Other Zionists, however, saw this position as not only a forfeiture of the goals of Zionism but also naïve, as the Arabs would never consent to share power.[96]

These positions on land acquisition, economic segregation, and immigration were accompanied by a unique attitude toward the British role in Palestine. While Labor Zionists looked to Britain to protect Jewish interests, and Revisionists accused Britain of failing to meet its obligations to Zionism, Brit Shalom saw the alliance with Britain as a moral blemish on Jewish renewal. As Aharon Kedar puts it:

> Brit Shalom demanded that the Zionist movement disassociate itself completely from the Balfour Declaration, and replace it with an Arab declaration recognizing Zionist rights. The Balfour Declaration should be rejected even before any Arab declaration was made. . . . [It] was nothing but part of an imperialist transaction of dividing the spoils of World War I.[97]

Judah Magnes agreed that "the mandate has no sanction but that of the last war."[98] For Labor and Revisionist Zionists, however, the Balfour Declaration was that Great Power guarantee of Jewish success that Herzl had long sought from the sultans and czars. The idea of rejecting the Balfour Declaration dismayed even the Brit Shalom moderates, who saw it as insurance in the absence of an Arab agreement. Thus there was once again a gap between those who saw an Arab agreement merely as a practical goal and those for whom it was a moral necessity.

Brit Shalom faced a severe test four years after its founding. The mufti of Jerusalem, Hajj Amin al-Husseini, head of the Supreme Muslim Council (SMC), spent much of the 1920s promoting the importance of the *haram ash-Sharif* as a symbol of Islam (the Noble Sanctuary to Muslims; to Jews, *har habayit*, the Temple Mount; site of the Dome of the Rock and the al-Aqsa Mosque).[99] In 1928, the question of Jewish worship at the Western Wall sparked fears that the Zionists desired to conquer the Temple Mount. These fears were not speculation: Zionist figures had tried to purchase the land around the site, and in the context of Zionism's general aims, the idea of a design on the Noble Sanctuary was not far-fetched.[100] The mufti and the SMC tried to hold the British to their promise to maintain the status quo from the Ottoman period at the Western Wall. In November 1928, the SMC convened a General Muslim Conference in Jerusalem (attended for the most part by Levantine Muslims), which claimed the disputed site for Islam. During the first half of 1929, the mufti initiated an intense campaign calling for the defense of al-Masjid al-Aqsa. Jews were angered by Muslim building operations there, and Muslims by Revisionist demonstrations, during which the Zionist flag was raised and the Zionist anthem sung; there were also rumors that Arab residents of the neighborhood were beaten. A week later, crowds of Muslim worshippers gathered at the al-Aqsa mosque and attacked nearby Jewish communities. Jews retaliated, and over the following few days Arabs murdered Jews in Hebron and Safed, while Jews reportedly took vengeance in Jerusalem, Haifa, and Jaffa.[101] The British moved to suppress the violence, at the end of which 133 Jews and 116 Arabs had been killed, and 339 Jews and 232 Arabs wounded.[102]

These riots set the tone for the Zionist-Arab conflict in the 1930s. After 1929, the leadership on both sides faced internal challenges from more militant voices, and calls for moderation went unheeded. The mufti faced the new, secular pan-Arabist party Istiqlal (Independence), as well as the followers of Sheikh Izz al-Din al-Qassam, a Syrian-born *alim* (Muslim legal scholar) who came to Palestine fleeing the French invasion. Both factions advocated open struggle against both Zionism and the British; by contrast, the mufti's policy seemed overly accommodating.[103] Brit Shalom soon faced a parallel situation. Zionists were shocked at the violence in Hebron and Safed, where Jewish victims included a large number of unarmed, non-Zionist ultra-Orthodox, many Palestinian born.[104] Many Jews, embarrassed that the religious non-Zionists had failed to defend themselves, used their deaths to argue for armed Zionist strength.[105] Now that Zionists focused publicly on the Arab Question, Brit Shalom seized the opportunity to air its views. It saw the riots as fulfilling its fears and vindicating its predictions, and called for major policy changes on immigration and rejection of the Balfour Declaration.[106] As a result, it was accused of treason and insensitivity to the suffering Jews. The Labor newspaper *Davar* began to inveigh against Brit Shalom on a regular basis, refusing to publish its statement on the riots, while the majority of the public regarded Brit Shalom's proposals as a cowardly surrender to bullying. This was what Anita Shapira calls Brit Shalom's "finest hour."[107] Aharon Kedar, however, faults Brit Shalom for its response to 1929: "While the Jewish population of Palestine was still licking its wounds, Brit Shalom launched one of its most biting attacks on the policies of the Zionist movement.... [T]he association erred in the manner in which it appealed to the Jewish public."[108]

The negative reaction to Brit Shalom's positions split its radicals from its moderates. The latter included Ruppin and Jacob Thon, colleagues at the Zionist

Executive and the Palestine Land Development Company, the writer and activist "Rabbi" Benjamin, and the agronomist and director of the Jewish Colonization Agency, Haim Kalvarisky. Ruppin expressed his difference of opinion with Brit Shalom's "radical coterie":

> What we can obtain from the Arabs we do not need, and what we need we shall not be able to obtain. What the Arabs are willing to give us is at most minority rights for the Jews in an Arab state, according to the pattern of minority rights in Eastern Europe. . . . Zionism which is willing to give its hand to such a compromise with the Arabs will not gain the support of the Jews of Eastern Europe and would soon become Zionism without Zionists.[109]

However, Ruppin's ultimate resignation from Brit Shalom took place not because of its stance after the riots but because of the radical wing's support of Britain's policy in favor of the Legislative Council for Palestine. All "majority" Zionists opposed this concept, as the Jews would be outnumbered in any parliament. As Ruppin put it, "one should not regard democracy and the good of the people as identical concepts."[110]

Brit Shalom suffered another setback when one of its radicals, Hans Kohn, resigned from the Zionist movement. Kohn, a former member of the Prague Bar Kochba Society, moved to Palestine in 1925, became a director of the Keren Hayesod (the Palestine Foundation Fund, financial arm of the World Zionist Organization), and helped found Brit Shalom. Kohn published a biography of Buber in 1929, on which he worked very closely with his subject.[111] The close relationship between the two men added pathos to Kohn's admission to Berthold Feiwel, another Keren Hayesod director, that he had "become increasingly aware that the official policy of the Zionist Organization and the opinion of the vast majority of Zionists are quite incompatible with my own convictions."[112] Copying this letter to Buber, Kohn wrote:

> We are seeking a victorious peace . . . a peace whereby the opponent does what we want. . . . [I]t will be possible for us to hold Palestine and continue to grow for a long time. This will be done first with British aid and then later with the help of our own bayonets. . . . [T]he means will have determined the goal. Jewish Palestine will no longer have anything of that Zion for which I once put myself on the line. . . . What we support we cannot vouch for. . . . [E]ither Zionism will be pacific or it will be without me. *Zionism* is not *Judaism*.[113]

For Buber, Kohn's resignation represented a challenge to his own struggle to reshape Zionist policy and strategy. In response, he disagreed, not with Kohn's diagnosis of contemporary Zionist troubles, but with his decision to withdraw from the movement.[114] Buber was convinced that "if work is to be done in public life, it must be accomplished not above the fray, but in it."[115] Although this may seem like the kind of realpolitik that Buber normally opposed, he meant that idealists should not drop out of politics when it disappoints, or trade their ideals for some alternative set of putatively "realistic" principles, determined by the "laws" of politics. Rather, when reality resists, they should strive harder to mold it according to their ideals.[116] An idealistically informed politics is not simply a matter of applying principles: "There is no firmly established law, formulated once and for all, but only the Word of God and our current situation which we have to learn by listening. We do not have codified principles that we can consult. But we must understand the situation and the moment."[117] Buber would have preferred that Kohn remain in the movement and attempt to drive it rather than abandon it to the unscrupulous, the chauvinists, and the believers in realpolitik. To refuse to fight for the ideal is to betray it. Buber may have perceived that each new outbreak of violence empowered the Revisionists and strained efforts to establish Jewish-Arab joint groups.

Theopolitics in Action: Election, Covenant, and Reality

Buber integrated these struggles and setbacks into his general view of applied theopolitics. In his 1932 lecture "And If Not Now, When?" Buber states: "No matter how brilliant it may be, the human intellect which wishes to keep to a plane above the events of the day is not really alive. It can become fruitful, beget life, and live only when it enters into the events of the day without denying, but rather proving, its superior origin. Be true to the spirit, my friends, but be true to it on the plane of reality."[118] In this context, Buber repeated his analysis of ancient Israelite secularization, but as a contemporary warning, a prophecy, by his own definition: "We shall accomplish nothing at all if we divide our world and our life into two domains: one in which God's command is paramount, and the other governed exclusively by the laws of economics, politics, and the 'simple self-assertion' of the group." A person who accepts such a division "is not merely moving away from God. . . . [H]e is standing up directly against him. The atheist does not know God, but the adherent of a form of ethics which ends where politics begin has the temerity to describe to God, whom he professes to know, how far his power may extend." Such behavior is not merely wrong in a moral or ideological sense. It will also result, inevitably, in failure:

> Judaism is the teaching that there is really only One Power which, while at times it may permit the sham powers of the world to accomplish something in opposition to it, never permits such accomplishment to stand. . . . I am speaking of the *reality of history*. In historical reality we do not set ourselves a righteous goal, choose whatever way to it an auspicious hour offers, and, following that way, reach the set goal. If the goal to be reached is like the goal that was set, then the nature of the way must be like the goal. A wrong way, i.e., a way in contradiction to the goal, must lead to a wrong goal.[119]

In other words, it is not "more realistic" to abandon the commandment in the service of "success," because said success will not in fact be forthcoming.

Framed this way, as directly related to the accomplishment of one's goal, "this is not a so-called 'moral' claim, but rather a political argument."[120] Faith that God is the Lord of history means faith that success will follow the keeping of the commandment. With respect to Zionist politics, this means that "it may be characteristic of Zion that it *cannot* be built with 'every possible means,' but only *bemishpat* (Isaiah 1:27), only 'with justice.'"[121] Buber's stress here on "historical reality" is meant to indicate that even those who do not speak the "language of religion" should recognize the necessity of consonant means and ends.

The point was reiterated with more substance, in what is perhaps his most "traditional" use of religious language, Buber's letter to Mahatma Gandhi. Written in 1939, one year after his emigration to Palestine, and in the midst of the *thawra*, this letter has been described as "a serious cry for sympathy and help."[122] We do not know if Gandhi ever saw it. The letter was written in response to an editorial in which Gandhi argued that although his "sympathies were all with the Jews," the "untouchables of Christianity," whose persecution in Germany "seems to have no parallel in history," he could not condone the aspirations of Zionism as he understood them: "Palestine belongs to the Arabs in the same sense that England belongs to the English or France to the French. It is wrong and inhuman to impose the Jews on the Arabs. . . . [I]f they must look to the Palestine of geography [rather than the Palestine in their hearts] as their national home, it is wrong to enter it under the shadow of the British gun."[123] He urged Jews of Germany to pursue the strategy of nonviolence, or *satyagraha* (truth-force), which he had used in South Africa on behalf of the Indian community there, a "truly religious resistance offered against the godless fury of dehumanized man."[124] Buber bemoaned the fact that Gandhi's argument, "containing though it does elements of a noble and most praiseworthy conception such as he expects from this speaker—is yet barren of all application to his peculiar circumstances."[125] Buber pointed out: "We began to settle in the land anew 35 years before the 'shadow of the British gun' was cast upon it. We did not seek out this shadow; it appeared and remained here to guard British interests and *not ours*."[126] He rejected Gandhi's equation of South Africa with Germany, which he would not have made if he knew "what a concentration camp is like and what goes on there."[127] Moreover, Buber had witnessed many instances of nonviolent resistance in Germany, and none of them had the transformative effect Gandhi claimed for *satyagraha*. Finally, the South African Indians could invoke the existence of a mother country; the Jews of Germany could do no such thing. If the Indians were to be expelled from India, Buber asked, would Gandhi teach them that "the India of the Vedic conception is not a geographical tract but that it is in your hearts?" The land is not a mere symbol. But that is not to say, as Gandhi thought, that sanction for Zionism is sought in the Bible. It is not the promise of the land, Buber wrote, that is decisive, but rather the command:

The fulfillment of which is bound up with the land, with the existence of a free Jewish community in this country . . . communal ownership of the land (Lev. 25:23), regularly recurrent leveling of social distinctions (25:13), guarantee of the independence of each individual (Ex. 21:2), mutual help (Ex. 23:4ff), a common Sabbath embracing serf and beast as beings with equal claim (Ex. 23:12), a Sabbatical year whereby, letting the soil rest, everybody is admitted to the free enjoyment of its fruits (Lev. 25:5–7). . . . These are not practical laws thought out by wise men; they are measures which the leaders of the nation, apparently themselves taken by surprise and overpowered, have found to be the set task and condition for taking possession of the land. . . . We went into exile with our task unperformed. . . . We are not covetous, Mahatma: our one desire is that at last we may obey.[128]

Here, in the language of covenant and command, Buber states the view that he would restate years later, in secular language, in *Paths in Utopia*, when he wrote that "the kibbutz owes its existence not to a doctrine, but to a situation, to the needs, the stress, and the demands of the situation."[129] James Horrox has argued that this position has led the historiography of the kibbutz largely to underestimate the role of ideology in collective settlement in Palestine.[130] Horrox might have noted further that this is a familiar trope of Buberian praise, used to designate something that is socially alive rather than rigidified, and also, that this seemingly "nonideological" formulation is actually deeply ideological. By downplaying preexisting ideologies in the early kibbutzim, just as in his description of what the Israelites faced when they first entered the Land, Buber suggests that collective, nonhierarchical organization is just what happens when free people first meet problems that confront them as a group. The Bible presents one record of this truth; the story of the first kibbutzim presents us with another. But this happening-to-be-true takes the form of a command—the necessity that must be recognized and that in the end will be recognized.

In 1942, mainstream Zionism adopted the Biltmore Program and declared its intention to establish a nation-state with a Jewish majority. That same year, Buber and Magnes founded the *Ichud*, a splinter group in the League for Jewish-Arab Rapprochement. As the league absorbed Hashomer Ha'tzair and other, smaller parties, Buber and Magnes felt the need for a separate organization to represent their own views. The Ichud platform called for "Government in Palestine based on equal political rights for the two peoples," a "Federative Union of Palestine and neighboring countries," and a "Covenant between this Federative Union and an Anglo-American Union which is to be part of the future Union of the free peoples."[131] This quintessentially "binationalist" organization was an ad hoc response to war conditions and part of an international framework. This "official" binationalism was one element in Buber's response to British commissions, UN hearings, and requests for grand proposals. But it was only part of his effort to force Zionism to live together with the Palestinian Arabs. After 1948, when the

State of Israel was a fait accompli, he focused on the problems of Palestinian refugees, both external (in Lebanon, Jordan, and elsewhere) and internal (displaced families within Israel's borders). Buber had not decided, suddenly, that a nation-state founded on the principle of ethnic majority was an excellent form of social organization. Rather, like Samuel hearkening to the people's voice, he adapted to new circumstances the same basic theopolitical orientation, one that received paradigmatic expression for its time in the 1944 lectures collected in *Ben Am Le-Artzo* (hereafter *On Zion*).

The Third Commonwealth: *On Zion*

On Zion justifies reading Buber's biblical studies as expressions of his own theopolitical views. This may not seem to require demonstration—we have already seen Buber adopt the prophetic stance articulated in these writings in his own voice, in texts like "And If Not Now, When?" and the letter to Gandhi. However, two factors complicate matters. First is the "scientific" form of his biblical studies, repeated even in the section of *On Zion* dealing with the Bible, which contains ten times as many footnotes as the rest of the book. Second is Buber's tendency, found in all his intellectual-historical surveys, to write sympathetically about whatever he reads. Frequently, Buber will passionately present a subject's point of view, and then move to another, different point of view just as passionately, so that one has to derive his own position either from the argument's teleological structure (assuming that he presents the "most correct" position last) or from implicit subtext.

The first factor may be mitigated by some general considerations. Buber's lack of interest in *Wissenschaft* for its own sake and his consistent philosophical preference for the original and primordial over the secondary and belated both suggest that his biblical-critical writing may serve his own theopolitical convictions. *On Zion*, however, makes the connections explicit. The second factor remains problematic, for it must be decided on a case-by-case basis whether and how Buber adopts the positions of the classical sources he discusses. For example, when Buber discusses a rabbinic source that seeks to account for drought by pointing the finger at "the robbers, the slanderers, the insolent, those who support alms-giving in public but do not contribute themselves, [and] those who do not want to study the Torah," we may assume that Buber does not straightforwardly adopt the view that rainfall in fact depends on Torah students outnumbering the robbers.[132] Buber rarely bothers to disavow such ideas, although he may reject their explanatory value, as when he discusses Isaiah's reference to an earth-devouring curse: "An interpretation based merely on the punishment of a people by the reduction in the yield of its land or something of that kind is quite inadequate to explain such utterances."[133] The best guide to Buber's position on the individual views he discusses is their larger context. In a preface to the 1950 edition of *On*

Zion, Buber writes that the proclamation of the State of Israel required no change to his work, which "is intended to shed light not on the history of a political enterprise but on that of a religious idea or rather on the spiritual history of a faith. How much of the latter the political enterprise and its consequences will be able to realize will naturally be revealed only over the course of several generations. But it is only right that, as long as such a spiritual reality lives, history should be responsible to it rather than that it should be responsible to history."[134]

The introduction to *On Zion* notes that the national concept of the Jews is named after a place, not a people. It is not even named after the entire land, but only one site within it: "Zion is 'the city of the great King' (Psalms 48:3), that is of God as the King of Israel." This age-old concept was not born, like other nationalisms, with modernity and the French Revolution.[135] The concept of Zion denotes the marriage of a chosen people with a chosen land. This land can no more be exchanged for another than can its people. But the idea of election contained in the concept of Zion cannot be understood as a conferral of a benefit or as a sign of preexisting merit:

> In the tribes which united to form "Israel" this concept developed and became transformed in a special way: holiness is no longer a sign of power, a magic fluid that can dwell in places and regions as well as in people and groups of people, but a quality bestowed on this particular people and this particular land because God 'elects' both in order to lead His chosen people into His chosen land and to join them to each other. It is His election that sanctifies the chosen people as His immediate attendance and the land as His royal throne and which makes them dependent on each other. This is more a political, a theopolitical than a strictly religious concept of holiness: the outward form of worship is merely a concentrated expression of the sovereignty of God.[136]

To regard the land as the eternal property of the people, as a God-given deed, ignores the mission to make of it what God intended. Such an understanding pretends to piety but is actually rebellion. The people's relationship to the land is characterized partially by futurity, because the people have not yet fulfilled their mission. But because the land is a partner in the relationship, it is rooted in nature. "The holy matrimony of land and people was intended to bring about the matrimony of the two separated spheres of Being," nature and history.[137]

Thus the Jews are only a people, like any people, and the land is just a land like any other. Only the elected mission is special; Jews deserve special consideration only in their performance of this mission. To return the people to the land but ignore the mission is to attack the idea of Zion: "The secularizing trend in Zionism was directed against the mystery of Zion too." By insisting on Jewish engagement with the idea of Zion, Buber seeks not to *hekhsher* the Jewish state, like court priests of old, but the opposite: to save Zion from Zionism. This task, too, is age old. Buber writes: "With every encounter of this people with this land the task is set afresh, but every time it is rooted in the historical situation and its problems. If it is not mastered, what has already been achieved will fall into ruin. Once it is really mastered this may be the beginning of a new kind of human society."[138] But the level of difficulty seems to rise with each encounter. After the Exodus, the Israelites were relatively free to create their own way of life; they failed because of weakness and fear, internal corruption rendering them unable to deal with external military threats. Returning from the Babylonian Exile, they faced the obstacle of rule by a foreign power. With the return from the two-thousand-year exile, they face an even greater challenge: "One has to reckon with the coexistence of another people in the same country, of cognate origin and language but mainly foreign in tradition, structure, and outlook, and . . . this vital fact has to be regarded as an essential part of the problem."

The Arab "question" in Palestine follows and diverges from the "Jewish question" in Europe. Europe asked the Jews: "What are you going to do to become like us, to prove that you belong here, to prove that we should accept you, that you should have equal rights with us, the true people of these lands?" Similarly, for many Zionists the Palestinian Arabs were a question because they obstructed the way toward a Jewish state with a Jewish majority. Discussions of the Arab question focused on neutralizing their threat, achieving the "victorious peace" that Kohn described. The Jewish question, however, was also an internal Christian question, a theological problem in the self-definition of Christianity and its relationship to Judaism. Does Christianity require anti-Judaism, or is it in fact antithetical to Christianity? In retrospect, Christendom apparently failed the test posed to it by the Jews of Europe.[139] In this sense, Buber regards "the coexistence of another people in the same country . . . as an essential part of the problem"; at stake is the internal self-definition of Judaism. This challenge to Judaism must be met with urgency, for what happens in a small, rugged part of the earth to an insignificant, despised people can have cardinal importance for the future of humanity.

On Zion's four parts cover thousands of years of Jewish history in fewer than two hundred pages. The first part discusses the Bible, the second rabbinic literature, the third "the voice of the Exile," and the last modern Zionist thinkers. The first two sections stand out in Buber's oeuvre in that the section on rabbinic literature segues seamlessly from the section on the Bible, without the usual suggestion that the rabbis represent decline and rupture. Buber had come to believe that "as long as a nucleus of the people lives in the land" there is value in the "authoritative" sources and not only in the "underground" ones.[140] He even speaks, uncharacteristically, of the wisdom of the "later Babylonian masters of the Talmud," of the "intimate connection between Halakha and Haggada, between those passages which discuss the 'course,' the right course of life, the right fulfillment of the demands of life, and those which, whether they link up directly or only indirectly with the former, bring in life itself, in stories, descriptions and discussions."[141] What brings Buber to this positive characterization of rabbis and halakha is the prayer for rain, discussed in the tractate *Ta'anit*:

> The rain beats down through this treatise on fasting, not the ordinary familiar rain, but the long-yearned-for rain that is now at last descending whose sound testifies that it is the rain of God. At the same time it is not rain that might fall anywhere, but definitely and incomparably Palestinian rain, autumn rain and spring rain, which, like no other rain, is regarded not as the end of an assured sequence of climatic events but as the eternal renewal of God's mercy. Not only what has come down to us here of what was said in the land itself but also of what was said in Babylon, is concerned with *Palestinian* rain.[142]

This statement seems strange. Surely, we think, this is an occasion on which Buber does not mean to agree with his sources; he cannot possibly really believe that rain in Palestine is different from rain anywhere else. In a sense, however, he does. As he says of the prayer on the first fruits of the harvest (Deuteronomy 26:1–11), themselves symbolic of Israel's role as the first fruits in God's harvest of the whole of humanity: "One must not completely spiritualize such a conception and deprive it of the bodily substance without which the spiritual content would have no real stability. No symbol has authentic existence in the spirit if it has no authentic existence in the body."[143] Palestinian rain is the symbol, but not *merely* the symbol, of the connection between nature and history that is an essential part of God's revelation to the Israelites. It is to end a drought that Rabbi Akiva, the legendary second-century teacher and martyr, invents one of the most influential prayers in Jewish liturgy by addressing God both as *avinu*, "our father," and as *malkeinu*, "our king." The first term is rooted in nature, the second in history; the former expresses the individual's relationship to God, and the latter the relationship of the whole people.

In the first part of *On Zion*, "The Testimony of the Bible," Buber says that the importance of the prayer for the first fruits lies in its stress on renewal. One thanks God for the renewal of the seasons and the recurrence of the harvest, beginning with the words "I report this day unto the Lord thy God that I am come into the country which the Lord swore unto our fathers to give us" (Deuteronomy 26:3). Thus, every individual, every year, reports as if they themselves had just come into the country and received the gift of the land; the first fruits are brought in acknowledgment of this ever-renewed gift: "The uniformly recurring seasons with their blessings are bound to that unique historical act in which God led the people with whom He had made the covenant into the promised land. The creation itself bears witness to the revelation. . . . [T]he report of the Mishnah (*Bikkurim* III) [tells] of the living unity—from the small peasant and the artisan right up to the king—of a people experiencing and glorifying the blessings of Nature as the blessings of History."[144] This is reiterated in the various ways the Bible describes the relationship of humanity to the earth: from the linguistic connection of man, *adam*, to earth, *adama*, to the "cosmically ethical" conception of the way the land itself suffers for the sins of the people.[145] The sinful people cause the land to experience a certain inner decay, which Buber identifies by the Hebrew verb *chanaf*. This verb is often rendered "pollute" (as both the New Revised Standard Version and the New Jewish Publication Society translations have it), but Buber prefers the sense "to be out of joint," which he derives from the Arabic cognate *chanifa*, "to suffer from a sprained foot." Blood puts the land out of joint, says Numbers (35:33); sexual sins put the land out of joint, according to Jeremiah (3:1). Especially grievous are sins having to do with the soil itself: profiteering in the sale of the harvest, illicit acquisition of land, and failure to observe the Sabbatical year. The land's Sabbatical is equivalent to the people's Sabbath: "Just as all living beings in the community are liberated from the authority of all except the one Lord on the Sabbath . . . the idea is that the earth is for a time to be free, so as not to be subjected to the will of man, but left to its own nature, to be like no-man's-land. . . . [T]he repose of the field signifies a divine repose and its freedom a divine freedom."[146] The land is owed its Sabbatical; the failure to observe it (and there is no sign that it was ever observed) leads to the people being vomited out, so that the land will have its due in their absence: "The land is to become free at last by being emptied of human beings." This exile, however, is followed by the promise of return. The land rests in the people's absence, and if the people also repent of their sins, then both they and the land can turn back to God together. This is the meaning of the promise: not that God will always favor his people, but that he will never abandon them completely; there will always be another chance to create the Kingdom. The promise is easily misunderstood because one can err on the side of either absolutism, which breeds pride and overconfidence, or contingency, which leads to fear. The truth of the promise lies in between:

> Absoluteness and historicity seem to be mutually exclusive; where they are fused in a people's faith, a reality of the spirit arises, which, as we know from the message of the Bible, carries the breath of the Absolute far into the future history of the human race. . . . The Promise means that within history an absolute relationship between a people and a land has been taken into the covenant between God and the people.[147]

This historical action and reaction, which in *Kingship of God* Buber had called the *Reichsdialektik*, has its parallel within the land in the falling of the rain.

The biblical perspective that God does not distinguish between natural and supernatural continues into the Mishnaic period. Buber cites several rabbinic texts that compare rainfall to birth and resurrection:[148] "All at once we find ourselves in a world of faith in which rainfall and resurrection belong together . . . the rain is no more natural than the resurrection and the resurrection is no more miraculous than the rain."[149] Thus, some sages rank any day of rain greater than the day on which the Torah was given at Mount Sinai, because the care of Palestine is central to God's salvation of the whole world. But as always, this ever-renewed mercy depends on a movement toward God on the part of the people. The inter-action between the people's turning to God and God's turning toward the people is hidden; it is neither a matter of merit being rewarded nor of arbitrary grace being dispensed. Rather "the grace of God tries . . . to find some human merit to which it can relate itself, not necessarily a display of lifelong virtue but some-times the spontaneous sacrificial action of someone otherwise very much bound up with the lower things of this world, some action by which the doer himself is more surprised than anyone else."[150] God rewards this kind of action because he loves it and for no other reason; he loves Israel and sends rain on it because he loves it; he loves the whole earth and demonstrates this love through the medium of Israel. "Just as there is valid Halakha in spite of all the Halakhian controver-sies," writes Buber, "so there is also an authoritative Haggada."[151]

Here Buber raises a biblical contrast between Israel and Egypt that went un-mentioned in *Moses*: Egypt is nourished by its great river, the Nile, while Israel is dependent on God's mercy. "The land is insecure, 'it drinketh water of the rain of heaven'" (Deuteronomy 11:11).[152] This does not mean that God abandons other countries to causal nature, like the Deist God who winds the stopwatch once and lets it run down, but it does mean that the Israelites are especially conscious of their constant dependence on Heaven: "The Israelite praying for rain for his thirsty land is the man who will be praying later on for redemption. . . . [T]he great prophets . . . establish a close relationship between the thirst for water and the thirst for the Word of God, between the outpouring of the water and the out-pouring of God's spirit."[153] Buber suggests that this contrast may stem from an actual Egyptian belief in the special independence of their land from the whims of Providence; he cites a passage of Herodotus in which Egyptian priests extol the security of Egypt in comparison with Greece, which is subject to the arbitrariness of Zeus. Yet this arbitrariness also hints at the difference between YHVH and Zeus, or any other rain god: his direct leadership of his people, his faithfulness to his promise. Again, Israel lies between two extremes, the false security of Egypt and the arbitrary terror of Greece. This distinct theological security, manifested in the constant renewal of divine mercy through rain, manifests theopolitically in the prophecy of Isaiah (19:24–25): "In that day shall Israel be the third with Egypt and Assyria, a blessing in the midst of the earth, for YHVH has blessed him, saying, 'Blessed be Egypt my people and Assyria the work of my hands, and Israel my inheritance.'"

Buber interprets this prophecy as referring to Israel's elevation as a third great power in the midst of the two warring ones, a power whose unique mode of polity ends the war and blesses all three. Deutero-Isaiah expands the importance of Isaiah's theopolitical event even further by placing it at the center of a cosmic redemption, one that heals the ills of nature itself. There is a hint here of Buber's own hopes for his time: Israel would rise as a third between the two Cold War powers. But a line must again be drawn between the Isaianic and the Deutero-Isaianic versions of the prophecy. The former can be reformulated as a materialist wager: that the achievement of a nonhierarchical and voluntary religious social-ism in Israel will provoke imitation and interest around the world, and lead in turn to widespread abandonment of the failed ideologies of the West. The latter, however, is an eschatological conviction that is kin to the kind of messianism that Buber rejects in *Kingship of God* and elsewhere. It cannot be reformulated mate-rialistically, unless with anachronistic reference to the ecological crisis and the means necessary to avert it. The difference between Isaiah and Deutero-Isaiah suggests a tension in Buber's thinking about Zionism as a theopolitical project, which in turn suggests a tension in the idea of theopolitics itself. Does Zionism have an end, as political projects do, one that can be measured by success or fail-ure? Or does it have only a goal, as religious ways of life do, one that cannot be said to have ever been reached? Can we ever really arrive at Zion? The answers to these questions have great importance for how we evaluate Buber's life's work, especially in light of his consistent failure to have the kind of impact he wished for on the Zionist movement.

Conclusion: The Thing's Name

On the occasion of the sixty-fifth Israeli Independence Day, the left-leaning web magazine +972 published a commemoration of the holiday as it might take place in the fantasy alternate-universe state of "Librael."[154] In this imaginary country, refugees from around the world have enriched the meaning of the three weeks leading up to Independence Day, which begin with Passover and include Holo-caust Remembrance Day and Memorial Day. African Hebrews of Dimona tell their stories on Passover, adding the memory of the Middle Passage to the memo-ry of the Exodus from Egypt. Filipino Israelis and Darfuri Israelis share their his-tories and experiences of occupation and genocide on Holocaust Remembrance Day. Memorial Day has become a time to recall the struggles of one's ancestors, both Israeli and Palestinian, for their causes, the wars that thankfully no lon-ger need be waged. And on Interdependence Day (as many call it), everyone cel-ebrates their shared life and freedom. Of course, Librael does not exist. In the real State of Israel, these three weeks are a time of "hyper-nationalist consensus-building, of sharpening the supposed differences between us and them with a race razor." Enslaved migrant workers, jailed African refugees, Palestinians seek-ing to commemorate the Nakba, the "catastrophe" of their exile in 1948—these are excluded from the holidays. "Liberal Zionists," the piece concludes, "have had plenty of time to prove that it is possible for an ethnocracy to simultaneously be a liberal democracy. In this, they have failed miserably. . . . [I]sn't it high time that liberal Zionism retired?"

Liberal Zionists, defined as those who believe that the State of Israel can exist simultaneously as "a Jewish State" and as a thriving democracy with equal rights for all, might protest that this article blames them for a political climate largely created by the extreme political right. The argument accuses liberal Zionists of providing cover for such tendencies. Persisting in their own impractical vision, they refuse to ally themselves with the struggles of those to their left, who seek a greater transformation of Israeli society and thus aid and abet those to their right, whose blatant nationalism and chauvinism they presumably abhor.[155]

Is Martin Buber subject to this critique too? It would be hard to classify him as a liberal Zionist. Judith Butler has noted that Buber's "version of Zionism has become so anathematic in light of contemporary framings of Zionism that it now reads as 'post-Zionist' or simply anti-Zionist." In the same breath she castigates Buber's failure "to criticize Israel as a form of settler colonialism. . . . [T]he most consequential blindness in his position . . . was that he could not see the impossibility of trying to cultivate certain ideals of cooperation on conditions established by settler colonialism."[156] Referring presumably to Buber's statement to Gandhi that one should ask the soil itself who has the right to work it, she writes that he imported a "neo-Lockean rationale for land appropriation into his thought," failing to understand that "no 'common' projects could set aside the land seizures that had already taken place and that the basis on which he claimed Jewish right to the land installed an aggressive nationalism at the heart of his notion of cooperation."[157] Similarly, Atalia Omer has argued that "the binational proposal articulated by Brit Shalom and Ihud was and remains problematic in that it did not respond to intracommunal human rights dilemmas and it essentialized or fossilized the two cultures in their autonomous settings. It neglected to address the rights and status of individuals who do not affiliate with either community. . . . Buber et al. were not in a position to recognize the pervasiveness of the Ashkenazi orientalist discourse." She further alleges that "the binational plans devised by Brit Shalom and Ihud enabled bypassing internal questioning of the entitlement to settle Palestine and cultivate a Jewish/Hebraic culture therein. . . . The presumption of equality . . . normalizes the core narrative, which is one of injustice. . . . Buber's cohort's visions of binationalism are erroneously retrieved as an 'alternative' to the Israeli political project."[158]

These are serious charges. The final chapter of this book explores the extent to which they are justified. For now, we should remember how Buber himself (in an essay to which Butler refers, written not two weeks before the proclamation of the State of Israel) describes the evolution of the goals of the Zionist mainstream:

> That demand [for sovereignty] was expressed and presented in two different forms, one beside the other. The first form crystallized around the 'democratic' concept of the majority: we must endeavor to create a Jewish majority in a state that will include the whole land of Israel. It was evident that the meaning

of that program was war—real war—with our neighbors, and also with the whole Arab nation: for what nation will allow itself to be demoted from the position of majority to that of minority without a fight?

When that program was revealed to be illusory, a program of tearing off took its place. That is to say, tearing one part of the land away from the rest, and in the torn off portion—once again, a majority, and the thing's name would be a Jewish State.[159]

Neither conquest nor partition, for Buber, have much to do with Zion. The way of thinking that prioritizes sovereignty and majority is fundamentally corrupt. If an "aggressive nationalism" is to be found hidden somewhere in Buber's thought, it is not on the level of macropolitics. The purported ill effects of Buber's idea of land appropriation must be sought elsewhere.[160]

I have referred to Buber's proximity to religious Zionism, despite the fact that the majority of those who call themselves religious Zionists today do in fact valorize sovereignty and majority. This tendency was not a powerful one in Buber's own time, so his polemics are usually directed against the secular mainstream. Indeed, Buber accuses both Herzl and Ben-Gurion of "secularization."[161] With respect to Ben-Gurion, the first prime minister of the State of Israel, Buber adds: "This [secularization], which is supreme in the whole world at present, has very old roots. Even some kings in Israel are said to have gone so far as to employ false prophets whose prophesying was merely a function of State policy."[162] The juxtaposition of Ben-Gurion to the ancient kings of Israel tells us something about Buber's attitude to the state. It is not merely that Buber's day-to-day involvement in politics was characterized by pragmatism, which he saw as dictated by his idealism, although this is certainly true. It is also the case that his pragmatic idealism is mirrored in his vision of Israelite history, in which the banner of the kingship of God was first raised by those like Gideon, who sought God's justice in an anarcho-theocracy, and then passed on to the prophets, who sought to inspirit a popular monarchy. Buber may have wanted originally to realize Zion in a commonwealth of internally anarcho-socialist kibbutzim, federated in a system similar to the one Landauer had proposed for Germany, with tight economic and social cooperation between Jews and Arabs. But an unpredictable combination of external threats and internal corruption favored the trend toward a "State with a Jewish majority," a trend that easily won the day. Buber's "acceptance" of the State of Israel, then, can be read as a neo-prophetic gesture, bent on maximizing God's justice in the new situation.

Buber could have opposed the state's proclamation by founding a sect. Perhaps this is what his younger self, who praised the Essenes for their righteous separation from the community at large, would have done. But he was seventy years old in 1948, and his foremost disciples were not much younger. Perhaps he could have played the role of a Zvi Yehuda Kook to a kind of left-wing, religious-anarchist Gahelet, but no such group existed and the aftermath of the Holocaust and the state's creation would have been an inauspicious time for one to form. Nonetheless, the new circumstances did not deter Buber from his basic stance, even if he could no longer advance binationalist proposals. "I doubt if there is anything more important today," Buber wrote in 1956, "than the choice between two types of socialism." The opposition of these two types is a familiar one. Buber may have viewed the Labor Party, which dominated Israeli politics until 1977, as the Israeli equivalent of the German Social-Democratic Party:

> One is a so-called socialism that is imposed from above . . . the other is a socialism from below, a socialism of spontaneity arising out of the real life of society . . . the coming stage of humanity that will emerge from this great crisis of man depends in great measure on just this decision. It depends on whether it will be possible to set up over against Moscow another, spontaneous type of socialism, and I venture even today to call it Jerusalem.[163]

The privatization of Israeli industry, the transformation of Israel into a free-market society, and the occupation of the West Bank and Gaza did not loom large on Buber's horizon. Already in 1956 there were those who claimed, as Buber noted, that "the socialist impetus and the faith in the *kibbutzim* are largely exhausted." But he saw such claims as "a boundless exaggeration of a crisis that really exists and that must be recognized and overcome as such. Such crises are part of the life of man and the life of society." The direction and the path remain the same, even if one is pushed ever further back upon it. It is a matter of command: to push forward again on the path, however littered it may be with incorrect predictions, failed projects, and outdated formulas.

Notes

1. Buber, "Jewish Religiosity," in *On Judaism*, ed. Nahum N. Glatzer (New York: Schocken, 1995), 93.

2. Buber, "Zionism True and False," in *Unease in Zion*, ed. Ehud Ben-Ezer (New York: Quadrangle, 1974), 104.

3. Two exceptions to Buber's valorization of "Doing" are his consideration of Chinese "Non-Doing" and his interpretation of Isaiah's prophecy in the "theopolitical hour." In both cases the decision to "Not Do" takes on some of the positive qualities of Doing itself.

4. Buber, בין עם לארצו [*Ben 'am le'artzo*] (Jerusalem: Schocken, 1945). Cf. Buber, *Israel und Palästina: Zur Geschichte einer Idee* (Zürich: Artemis-Verlag, 1950); and Buber, *On Zion: The History of an Idea*, trans. Stanley Godman (Syracuse: Syracuse University Press, 1997). The first English edition (1952) was titled *Israel and Palestine: The History of an Idea*. The language of composition is uncertain.

5. FMD 120.

6. Buber, Judah Magnes, and Moshe Smilansky, *Palestine, a Bi-National State* (New York: Ihud, 1946), 32–36.

7. Buber, *On Zion*, xxi.

8. Martina Urban, *Aesthetics of Renewal: Martin Buber's Early Representation of Hasidism as Kulturkritik* (Chicago: University of Chicago Press, 2008), 71.

9. Steven J. Zipperstein, *Elusive Prophet: Ahad Ha'am and the Origins of Zionism* (Berkeley: University of California Press, 1993), 197.

10. "Religious Nationalists, Old and New," in Arthur Hertzberg, ed., *The Zionist Idea: A Historical Analysis and Reader* (New York: Atheneum, 1986), 440–465.

11. In its anti-intellectual overtones, this gap is analogous to the one invoked by politicians in the United States when they refer to "coastal elites."

12. Dov Schwartz, *Religious-Zionism: History and Ideology* (Boston: Academic Studies Press, 2009), 60.

13. Ibid., 68.

14. Aryei Fishman, *Judaism and Modernization on the Religious Kibbutz* (New York: Cambridge University Press, 1992); cf. Aryei Fishman, "The Religious Kibbutz Movement: The Pursuit of a Complete Life within an Orthodox Framework," in *Studies in Contemporary Jewry II* (New York: Oxford University Press, 1986), 97–115. N.B. The Hebrew *avodah* also means "service," in the sense of prayer and the ancient temple sacrifices. The religious kibbutzniks no doubt intended this sense as well.

15. Yossi Katz, *The Religious Kibbutz Movement in the Land of Israel, 1930–1948*, trans. Joseph Shadur (Ramat-Gan: Bar-Ilan University Press, 1996).

16. Aran, "From Religious Zionism to Zionist Religion: The Roots of Gush Emunim," in *Studies in Contemporary Jewry II*, 116–143.

17. Aharon Lichtenstein, "Diaspora Religious Zionism: Some Current Reflections," in *Religious Zionism Post-Disengagement: Future Directions*, edited by Chaim I. Waxman (New York: Yeshiva University Press, 2008), 3–30.

18. The early Mizrahi favored collaboration with political Zionism because it found cultural and spiritual Zionism threatening; Aran, "Religious Zionism to Zionist Religion," 125. A walkout of the Democratic Fraction at the Fifth Zionist Congress in 1901 took place when Herzl followed Buber and Weizmann by giving the floor to Reines, who railed against "Jewish culture" as a threat to Judaism; Ehud Luz, *Parallels Meet: Religion and Nationalism in the Early Zionist Movement (1882–1904)*, trans. Lenn J. Schramm (Philadelphia: Jewish Publication Society, 1988), 235–238.

19. Aran, "Religious Zionism to Zionist Religion," 120.

20. PF 24.

21. Schwartz, *Religious-Zionism*, 52.

22. Following the usage of the period, I refer to the Arabs of Palestine as "Palestinian Arabs" up through the British Mandate, since Jews born in Palestine then also referred to themselves as "Palestinians" and were so called by others, whereas Arabs rarely called themselves "Palestinians" with no additional specifications. After 1948, "Palestinian" refers to the Arab populations of the West Bank, Gaza Strip, the refugee camps, and the Palestinian diaspora, and to those Arabs with Israeli citizenship who identify as Palestinian.

23. Schwartz, *Religious-Zionism*, 59.

24. Susan Lee Hattis, *The Bi-National Idea in Palestine during Mandatory Times* (Haifa: Shikmona, 1974), 38.

25. Shalom Ratzabi, *Between Zionism and Judaism: The Radical Circle in Brith Shalom, 1925–1933* (Leiden: Brill, 2002); Aharon Kedar, "Brith Shalom," *Jerusalem Quarterly* 18 (Winter 1981): 55–85. Cf. Hagit Lavsky, *Before Catastrophe: The Distinctive Path of German Zionism* (Detroit: Wayne State University Press, 1996), 162–180; Kedar, "German Zionism and the Emergence of 'Brit Shalom,' In *Essential Papers on Zionism*, ed. Jehuda Reinharz and Anita Shapira (New York: New York University Press, 1996), 648–670; Adi Gordon, *Brit Shalom and Bi-National Zionism: The "Arab Question" as a Jewish Question* (Jerusalem: Carmel, 2008) [Hebrew]; Dietmar Wiechmann, *Der Traum vom Frieden: das bi-nationale Konzept des Brith-Schalom zur Lösung des jüdisch-arabische Konfliktes in der Zeit von 1925–1933* (Schwalbach: Wochenschau-Verlag, 1998).

26. Ruppin's involvement also discouraged Rabbi Judah Magnes, the first president of the Hebrew University, who was sympathetic to Brit Shalom, from becoming involved; he suspected that Ruppin "would be ready, if the possibility and the means were present, to get rid of the Arabs in a non-peaceful way." Arthur A. Goren, *Dissenter in Zion: From the Writings of Judah L. Magnes* (Cambridge, MA: Harvard University Press, 1982), 272. Magnes did, however, join the "successor" groups to Brit Shalom. He proved correct about Ruppin, who said in 1938: "I do not believe in the transfer of an individual. I believe in the transfer of entire villages"; Tom Segev, *One Palestine, Complete: Jews and Arabs under the British Mandate* (New York: Henry Holt & Co., 2000), 405.

27. Hattis, *Bi-National Idea*, 64.

28. Ratzabi, *Between Zionism and Judaism*, 22; Hagit Lavsky, "Nationalism in Theory and Praxis: Hans Kohn and Zionism," *Zion* 67.2 (2002): 189–212 [Hebrew].

29. Adi Gordon, "Review of *Between Zionism and Judaism* by Shalom Ratzabi," *Jewish Quarterly Review* 94.2 (Spring 2004): 422–427.

30. Here we refer not to the group itself, but to the "Brit Shalom school of thought," like Gideon Shimoni, *The Zionist Ideology* (Hanover, NH: Brandeis University Press, 1995), 368.

31. Segev, *One Palestine, Complete*, 411.

32. Yoram Hazony, *The Jewish State: The Struggle for Israel's Soul* (New York: Basic, 2001), xxix.

33. Howard Sachar, *A History of Israel: From the Rise of Zionism to Our Time* (New York: Knopf, 1986), 66, 180.

34. Conor Cruise O'Brien, *The Siege: The Saga of Israel and Zionism* (New York: Simon & Schuster, 1986), 174, 186.

35. Martin Gilbert, *Israel: A History* (New York: Doubleday, 1998), 62, 256.

36. Walter Laqueur, *A History of Zionism* (New York: MJF Books, 1972), 218, 251–255, 260, 264–266.

37. Michael Brenner, *Zionism: A Brief History*, trans. Shelley L. Frisch (Princeton, NJ: Markus Wiener, 2003), 115.

38. Benny Morris, *Righteous Victims: A History of the Zionist-Arab Conflict, 1881–2001* (New York: Vintage Books, 2001), 108.

39. Segev, *One Palestine, Complete*, 408–409.

40. Anita Shapira, *Israel: A History* (Waltham, MA: Brandeis University Press, 2014), 82, 142–143.

41. This is presumably the meaning of Morris's strange locution "significant but ultimately marginal," in *Righteous Victims*, 108.

42. Yehoyada Haim, *Abandonment of Illusions: Zionist Political Attitudes toward Palestinian Arab Nationalism, 1936–1939* (Boulder, CO: Westview Press, 1983), 3.

43. Buber, "The Bi-National Approach to Zionism," in *Towards Union in Palestine: Essays on Zionism and Jewish-Arab Cooperation*, ed. Martin Buber, Judah Magnes, and Ernst Simon (Westport, CT: Greenwood Press, 1972), 10.

44. Theopolitics distinguishes Buber not only from secular socialist Zionism and religious nonsocialist Zionism but also from the religious socialism of Kibbutz Dati, as described by Katz and Fishman. In Buber's time, the labor and kibbutz movements were largely secular; that ratio still holds today; James Horrox, *A Living Revolution: Anarchism in the Kibbutz Movement* (Oakland, CA: AK Press, 2009), 140n19.

45. Christopher Warhurst, *Between Market, State, & Kibbutz: The Management and Transformation of Socialist Industry* (London: Mansell, 1999), 57.

46. Grete Schaeder, "A Biographical Sketch," in LMB 28. See, however, Edward Said's comment on Marx: "As human material the Orient is less important than as an element in a Romantic redemptive project"; Said, *Orientalism* (New York: Vintage, 1994), 154.

47. Cited in Horrox, *A Living Revolution*, 18.

48. Viteles, *A History of the Co-operative Movement in Israel, Book One: The Evolution of the Co-operative Movement* (London: Vallentine, Mitchell & Co., 1966); Henry Near, *The Kibbutz Movement: A History*, vol. 1, *Origins and Growth, 1909–1939* (Oxford: Oxford University Press, 1992).

49. Joseph Trumpeldor: "Like Kropotkin, I believe that only a very large, territorially extensive commune leads to anarchy"; Meir Yaari: "[In the movement's early years] we were what is known as anarchists. . . . We believed in a prototype of future society in which the individual's life would be free of coercion, while being autonomous"; Manes Sperber: "[we were interested] in the anarcho-communist theory of Kropotkin, the revolutionary prince, far more than in Marxism"—all cited in Horrox, *A Living Revolution*, 35, 45.

50. Ibid., 71.

51. Gustav Landauer, "The United Republics of Germany and their Constitution," in *All Power to the Councils! A Documentary History of the German Revolution of 1918–19*, ed. and trans. Gabriel Kuhn (Oakland, CA: PM Press, 2012), 199–204.

52. Ibid., 201.

53. PU 146.

54. Landauer, "Anarchic Thoughts on Anarchism," in *Revolution and Other Writings: A Political Reader*, ed. and trans. Gabriel Kuhn (Oakland, CA: PM Press, 2010), 90.

55. Cited in Charles Maurer, *Call to Revolution: The Mystical Anarchism of Gustav Landauer* (Detroit: Wayne State University Press, 1971), 83; Landauer, "Sind das Ketzergedanken?" in *Philosophie und Judentum: Ausgewählte Schriften, Band 5*, ed. Siegbert Wolf (Hessen: AV Verlag, 2012), 362–368.

56. Gershom Scholem, *From Berlin to Jerusalem: Memoirs of My Youth*, trans. Harry Zohn (New York: Schocken, 1980), 53.

57. Landauer to Buber, February 5, 1918, LMB 230.

58. Landauer to Buber, May 10, 1918, LMB 231.

59. "Appendix II: Exchange of Letters: Goldmann-Landauer," in Horrox, *A Living Revolution*, 133–137.

60. A point stressed in GLPU 52–53.

61. Horrox, *A Living Revolution*, 43–44. This speech was published as "Der heimliche Führer." This was a special issue of Ha'poel Ha'tzair's journal dedicated to Landauer.

62. Gordon himself reportedly returned to Palestine from the conference claiming to have "found his ideas" in Landauer's writings; Michael Tyldesley, *No Heavenly Delusion? A Comparative Study of Three Communal Movements* (Liverpool, UK: Liverpool University Press, 2003), 48.

63. Ratzabi, *Between Zionism and Judaism*, 413; cf. GLPU 73; Horrox, *A Living Revolution*, 51. However, Arlosoroff later opposed Brit Shalom on economic segregation, immigration, and the Jewish-majority question; Zachary Lockman, *Comrades and Enemies: Arab and Jewish Workers in Palestine, 1906–1948* (Berkeley: University of California Press, 1996), 100–101.

64. Buber, "Toward the Decision," LTP 41.

65. Buber, "At This Late Hour (April 1920)," LTP 46. The perception of these riots as pogroms was reinforced by the prominent involvement of Christian Palestinians; Morris, *Righteous Victims*, 95.

66. Buber, "A Proposed Resolution on the Arab Question (September 1921)," LTP 61.

67. Twenty-six years later, Buber wrote that while this editing process was "an utterly simple and routine matter" for politicians, it "appalled [him] to such an extent that [he] still [hadn't] recovered from the shock." Buber, "Resolution on the Arab Question of the Twelfth Zionist Congress," LTP 65.

68. Buber, "Responsa on Zionist Policy," LTP 72.

69. "Brith Shalom," LTP 74.

70. For early Arab complaints about immigration and land sales, see Muhammad Y. Muslih, *The Origins of Palestinian Nationalism* (New York: Columbia University Press, 1988), 79. The British cited these two concerns as primary in the Shaw Commission Report, the Hope-Simpson Commission Report, and the Passfield White Paper; Philip Mattar, *The Mufti of Jerusalem: Al-Hajj Amin al-Husayni and the Palestinian National Movement* (New York: Columbia University Press, 1988), 53. The concern for economic segregation was noticed more in retrospect than at the time, but the newspaper *Mirat al-Sharq* wrote in 1934 that "the real struggle which now exists in the country is between Arab and Jewish labor," and with the 1936 Arab Revolt, the Arabs enforced retaliatory economic segregation; Yehoshua Porath, *The Palestinian-Arab National Movement, 1929–1939: From Riots to Rebellion* (London: Frank Cass, 1977), 130; Baruch Kimmerling and Joel Migdal, *The Palestinian People: A History* (Cambridge, MA: Harvard University Press, 2003), 62, 140.

71. Rashid Khalidi, *Palestinian Identity: The Construction of Modern National Consciousness* (New York: Columbia University Press, 1997), 103. The Ottoman Land Law of 1858, part of the Tanzimat (a broader attempt by the Ottoman authorities to Westernize and become competitive with Europe), replaced traditional communal usufruct with *tapu* (title deeds); Kimmerling and Migdal, *The Palestinian People*, 16. *Tapu* changed little for fellahin in the short term; however, peasants largely failed to register land in their own names, out of fear of conscription by the state, opening the door for the rising *ayan* class of urban notables to purchase huge tracts of land; Khalidi, *Palestinian Identity*, 37; Muslih, *Origins of Palestinian Nationalism*, 22.

72. Kimmerling and Migdal, *The Palestinian People*, 23.

73. Morris, *Righteous Victims*, 54.

74. Neville J. Mandel, *The Arabs and Zionism Before World War I* (Berkeley: University of California Press, 1976), 36.

75. As Menachem Ussishkin, head of the Jewish National Fund from 1923 to 1941, is reported to have said, "Once we have acquired a place, we will never leave." The "we" here indicates the attitude of the JNF, that it was purchasing land as a national body for the exclusive national use of Jews. This, combined with increasing strategic coordination with regard to exactly where purchases were made, gave land purchases a political significance that they lacked during the early years of Zionism. Cited in Baruch Kimmerling, *Zionism and Territory: The Socio-Territorial Dimensions of Zionist Politics* (Berkeley: Institute of International Studies, 1983), 85, 41.

76. Khalidi, *Palestinian Identity*, 103.

77. Yehuda Epstein, "A Hidden Question (1907)," trans. Alan Dowty, in *Prophets Outcast: A Century of Dissident Jewish Writing about Zionism and Israel*, ed. Adam Shatz (New York: Nation Books, 2004), 36–52.

78. Cited in Morris, *Righteous Victims*, 58.

79. Cited in LTP 8.

80. Akiva Ernst Simon, "The Arab Question as a Jewish Question," in *Unease in Zion*, 297.

81. Ruppin to Hans Kohn, May 30, 1928, in Kedar, "Brith Shalom," 70. For Ruppin on damages paid to evicted fellahin, see Kimmerling, *Zionism and Territory*, 115.

82. Gershon Shafir, *Land, Labor and the Origins of the Israeli-Palestinian Conflict, 1882–1914* (Cambridge: Cambridge University Press, 1989), 41–42.

83. Leslie Stein, *The Hope Fulfilled: The Rise of Modern Israel* (Westport, CT: Praeger, 2003), 93.

84. Gershon Shafir, "Zionism and Colonialism: A Comparative Approach," in *The Israel/Palestine Question: Rewriting Histories*, ed. Ilan Pappe (New York: Routledge, 1999), 88.

85. Hattis, *Bi-National Idea in Palestine*, 56–57. The British turned down the application for official registration on the grounds that Brit Shalom's collaborators in the effort, the Poalei Zion Smol (Left Workers of Zion) party, were suspected communists. Brit Shalom lacked the resources to pursue the union program alone.

86. Musa Budeiri, *The Palestine Communist Party, 1919–1948: Arab and Jew in the Struggle for Internationalism* (Chicago: Haymarket, 2010); Lockman, *Comrades and Enemies*.

87. Shafir, *Land, Labor and the Origins*, 89.

88. Ruppin to Kohn, May 30, 1928, in Kedar, "Brith Shalom," 71.

89. Buber, "Our Pseudo-Samsons," LTP 132.

90. Magnes, "Like All the Nations?" in *The Zionist Idea*, 443.

91. Haim, *Abandonment of Illusions*, 13.

92. Cited in Hattis, *Bi-National Idea*, 54.

93. David Werner Senator, "Letter of Resignation to Dr. Weizmann," in Buber, Magnes, Simon, *Towards Union in Palestine*, 54.

94. Cited in Kedar, "Brith Shalom," 74.

95. Bergmann, like Buber himself, is not simply recalling the multiethnic coexistence he experienced in the Hapsburg Empire. He is envisioning the possibility of a "new" thing entering the world, through the agency of Zionist theopolitics. Cf. Dimitry Shumsky, "Historiography, Nationalism and Dual Nationalism: Czech-German Jewry, Prague Zionists, and Sources of Hugo Bergmann's Dual-National Approach," *Zion* 69.1 (2004): 45–80 [Hebrew].

96. LTP 15.

97. Kedar, "Brith Shalom," 60.

98. Shimoni, *Zionist Ideology*, 375.

99. The SMC was created in 1922 by the British to promote Muslim solidarity rather than Arab solidarity as a force in Palestinian politics (Christian Arabs had played a central role in the development of Arab nationalism and anti-Zionist activity in Palestine). Kimmerling and Migdal, *The Palestinian People*, 85.

100. Yehoshua Porath, *The Emergence of the Palestinian-Arab National Movement, 1918–1929* (London: Frank Cass, 1974), 258.

101. A Jewish Agency investigation in 1929 concluded that "in isolated cases," some Jews "shamefully went beyond the limits of self-defense," but specifics are lacking. Segev, *One Palestine, Complete*, 327.

102. Mattar, *Mufti of Jerusalem*, 48; Morris, *Righteous Victims*, 116.

103. On the Istiqlal, see Porath, *The Palestinian-Arab National Movement*, 126; Mattar, *Mufti of Jerusalem*, 66; Kimmerling and Migdal, *The Palestinian People*, 97, 110. On al-Qassam, see Abdullah Schleifer, "Izz al-Din al-Qassam: Preacher and *Mujahid*," in *Struggle and Survival in the Modern Middle East*, ed. Edmund Burke III and David N. Yaghoubian (Berkeley: University of California Press, 1993), 137–151.

104. Morris, *Righteous Victims*, 114.

105. Anita Shapira, *Land and Power: The Zionist Resort to Force, 1881–1948* (New York: Oxford University Press, 1992), 186.

106. These are characterized as "concessions," but this is incorrect. With the exception of immigration restrictions in the late 1930s, Brit Shalom was not calling for concessions but for mainstream Zionism to adopt its policies.

107. Shapira, *Land and Power*, 186.

108. Kedar, "Brith Shalom," 62.

109. Ruppin to Dr. Victor Jacobson, December 3, 1931, in Hattis, *The Bi-National Idea in Palestine*, 58.

110. Goren, *Dissenter in Zion*, 315.

111. Hans Kohn, *Martin Buber: Sein Werk und Seine Zeit. Ein Versuch über Religion und Politik* (Hellerau: Jakob Hegner, 1930).

112. LTP 96–100.

113. Ibid.

114. The first edition of LTP was published in 1983, when Kohn's archives were still closed. Any letter Buber wrote to Kohn in response to his resignation was inaccessible to Mendes-Flohr at the time of his compilation; he constructed Buber's response from allusions and comments in letters and lectures from the period immediately following Kohn's letter. The archives have since been opened, but neither the New York nor Cincinnati archives contain a letter from Buber to Kohn on this matter.

115. Buber, "Gandhi, Politics, and Us (1930)," in PW 137.

116. LTP 32n48.

117. Buber, "Politics Born of Faith (1933)," in *A Believing Humanism: My Testament, 1902–1965*, trans. Maurice Friedman (New York: Simon & Schuster, 1967), 178.

118. Buber, "And If Not Now, When?" LTP 103.

119. Ibid., 105.

120. Buber, "Soul-Searching," LTP 77.

121. Buber, "And If Not Now, When?" LTP 104–105.

122. Glatzer, foreword to *On Zion*, xii.

123. Mohandas K. Gandhi, "The Jews," in LTP 106–111.

124. Ibid.

125. Martin Buber to M. K. Gandhi, February 24, 1939, in LTP 111–126, 113.

126. Ibid., 124.

127. Ibid., 115.

128. Ibid., 118–119. Buber admitted that he was not speaking for the whole Zionist movement.

129. PU 142.

130. Horrox, *A Living Revolution*, 23.

131. Buber, "The Ichud," LTP 148–149.

132. Buber, *On Zion*, 42.

133. Ibid., 13.

134. Ibid., xv.

135. Ibid., xvii. One thinks here however of Landauer's treatment of revolution itself as age old, not an Enlightenment product.

136. Ibid., xviii.

137. Ibid., xx.

138. Ibid., xxi. *N.B.*: again here as with Bergmann, the "new" kind of society that Buber associates with Zion.

139. European "Christendom" here being conceived as one project of a certain Christianity but not necessarily the defining feature of any possible Christianity (let alone the "true" one).

140. Buber, *On Zion*, 39. The third part represents this as well, though to a far lesser extent—Yehuda Halevi's *Kuzari* being a Zionist favorite in addition to a classic of Jewish apologetics.

141. The word translated here as "course" is given as "Gang" in *Israel und Palästina*, 56; and as הליכות (*halikhot*) in *Ben 'am le-artzo*, 42, which literally means "walkings" and colloquially means "manners," from the same root as *halakha*.

142. Buber, *On Zion*, 40.

143. Ibid., 8.

144. Ibid., 9.

145. Ibid., 13.

146. Ibid., 15.

147. Ibid., 18.

148. Babylonian Talmud, *Taanit* 2a: "Three keys are in the hand of the Holy One, blessed be He, that have not been delivered into the hands of an emissary. And they are the key of rain, the key of birth and the key of the resurrection of the dead." Cited by Buber (though only as "the Gemara") in *On Zion*, 41.

149. Ibid., 40.

150. Ibid., 43.

151. Ibid., 46.

152. Ibid., 24.

153. Ibid., 26.

154. David Sheen, "Liberal Zionism at 65: Fantasy and Reality," +972, April 11, 2013, http://972mag.com/liberal-zionism-at-65-fantasy-and-reality/69008.

155. See Yitzhak Laor, *The Myths of Liberal Zionism* (New York: Verso, 2009).

156. Judith Butler, *Parting Ways: Jewishness and the Critique of Zionism* (New York: Columbia University Press, 2012), 36.

157. Ibid., 37.

158. Atalia Omer, *When Peace Is Not Enough: How the Israeli Peace Camp Thinks about Religion, Nationalism, and Justice* (Chicago: University of Chicago Press, 2013), 30–31, 42, 169.

159. Buber, "Zionism and 'Zionism,'" LTP 223.

160. The question of the necessary conditions for "certain ideals of cooperation" to be cultivated is a thorny one, as Butler has acknowledged in a more recent and deeper consideration of Buber; Butler, "Versions of Binationalism in Said and Buber," in *Conflicting Humanities*, ed. Rosi Braidotti and Paul Gilroy (New York: Bloomsbury Academic, 2016), 185–210.

161. Buber, *On Zion*, 125.

162. "[Ben-Gurion] is one of the proponents of that kind of secularization which . . . keeps men from hearing the voice of the living God. This secularization takes the form of an exaggerated politization. This politization of life here strikes at the very spirit itself. The spirit with all its thoughts and visions descends and becomes a function of politics." Buber, "Zionism True and False," *Unease in Zion*, 117.

163. Buber, "Socialism and Peace," LTP 277.

8 This Pathless Hour
Theopolitics in the Present

We know absolutely no details about our immediate way; it may lead over Russia, it may lead over India. The only thing we know is that our way does not lead through the movements and struggles of the day, but over things unknown, deeply buried, and sudden.

—Gustav Landauer

Even those communities which call the spirit their master and salvation their Promised Land, the "religious" communities, are community only if they serve their lord and master in the midst of simple, unexalted, unselected reality, a reality not so much chosen by them as sent to them just as it is; they are community only if they prepare the way to the Promised Land through the thickets of this pathless hour.

—Martin Buber

Introduction: Community Still Coming

We have traced the roots of Buber's theopolitics in his friendship with Gustav Landauer, its development in his biblical writings, and its application in his Zionism. In this final chapter we connect it with urgent themes of contemporary thought.

Buber wrote at a time when the world seemed to be a battlefield between ideological titans. Political conflicts were consistently and plausibly portrayed as clashes between alternative ways of life, even alternative conceptions of the human. In the decades following his death, no doubt in reaction to the perception that these ideological battles had endangered human life on an unprecedented scale, theorists began to suspect such "grand narratives" and sought to keep "comprehensive conceptions of the good" out of politics.[1] Francis Fukuyama's notorious proclamation of "the end of history," however, was soon belied by the global resurgence of religiously identified conflicts, dubbed the "clash of civilizations" by Samuel Huntington.[2] And after 9/11, neoconservatives portrayed the War on Terror as successor to World War II and the Cold War, in scale and ideological freight.[3] The spectacular violence in the media drew popular attention to the fact that the secularization thesis was being discredited in academia, and this led to the reconsideration of the very category of the secular.[4] This reconsideration explains why irreligious philosophers and theorists have taken a renewed interest in religion, speaking of a "return of religion" and a "post-secular" turn in the humanities. Postcolonial studies have also contributed to this shift, highlighting the meaning and effect of concepts like secularism when forcibly applied to colonized peoples.

A long historiographical tradition treats modern ideologies as secular versions of religious and messianic ideas.[5] For example, the absolute sovereignty of the modern state may be seen as a secularization of the sovereignty of God (as in Schmitt), or the revolution sought by the radical left as a secularized version of the messianic redemption (as in Löwith). Some in this tradition view secularization as having successfully detached itself from its religious origins. Others view secularization as moving beyond religion, even if it must still question its origins to better separate from them.[6] Still others see secularization as thoroughly "religious," despite its own claims to the contrary. The contemporary turn to the postsecular draws on these traditions while also modifying them in important respects. I focus here on the secularization of one particular theological theme: messianism. Buber himself, in *Paths in Utopia*, compared Marxist and utopian socialism according to the type of eschatological stance embodied in each. His view provides a position from which to engage contemporary postsecular theory that seeks to deploy the messianism of Saint Paul in the service of revolution.[7] These works occasionally reference Buber's own work on Paul, *Two Types of Faith* (which contains the last fragment of the unfinished work on *Das Kommende*). The argument will begin, perhaps counterintuitively, by recontextualizing the Buber-Scholem debate over Hasidism, revealing theopolitical implications of Scholem's apparently objective and scholarly application of methodological rigor to Buber's alleged deployment of Hasidism for neo-romantic ends.

The collapse of the Soviet Union in the early 1990s led to proclamations of the end of history and the beginning of a postideological age. Since then, a variety of poststructuralist micropolitics have prevailed over efforts to assert a single dominant leftist paradigm. While some have attempted to revive a kind of academic Leninism, these efforts have been sclerotic and superficial, as they lack connection to actual social movements.[8] Anarchism, however, has been observed in several recent social movements: in 1994, the Zapatista rebellion in Chiapas, Mexico; in 1999, the so-called battle in Seattle and the subsequent global justice movement; in 2011, the *indignados* in Spain and Occupy Wall Street in the United States, and in 2016, in the autonomous canton of Rojava in northern Syria. The evolution of anarchism from its "classical" form in the 1930s to today's range of "postanarchist," "postleftist," and other movements owes much to the intellectual legacy of Gustav Landauer. The relationship between the academic postsecular turn and contemporary social activism seems unclear; anarchism today remains largely loyal to its Enlightenment origins. However, academic theory is often quasi-anarchistic in interests, if not goals, analyzing what Eric Santner has called "the political theological (or perhaps better, the *biocratic* constitution of modern life)" in terms of both "the foundation and constitution of political authority" and "the patterns and procedures whereby human beings come to be vested with the authority of the various 'offices' they occupy and the ways in which such procedures of investiture, such transferences of symbolic authority, are ultimately legitimated."[9] Resemblances between classical anarchism and contemporary academic theory can likely be accounted for by attention to successive waves of Nietzsche interpretation. The question of whether there can be a liberatory Nietzsche, or any political Nietzsche at all, is linked to the question of whether politics as the subject matter of political science departments has more than a heuristic existence—this is a question anarchism has brought to the fore from its inception, and for which it has been declared "unpolitical."

Finally, we turn again to Zionism. The romance between Zionism and the international left ended long ago, and in Israel the hegemony of Labor has steadily eroded since the 1977 victory of Menachem Begin and the Likud party, descendants of Jabotinsky's Revisionists. Furthermore, from a perspective attuned to settler colonialism, the problems with the Israeli state go deeper than whether the "left" or the "right" runs the government; the tragedy is not that a dream was betrayed but that anyone ever dreamed it at all. Here we assess what is living and what is dead in the applied theopolitics to which Buber gave the name "Zionism." It may be, in the end, that theopolitical Zionism and secular radicalism still converge in the coming community. Or, as Buber once said: "Today appearance is currently opposed to appearance. But within the hidden sphere of the future the meeting has begun to take place."[10]

Messianism

> *The Lord shall reign for Ever and Ever (Ex. 15:18).* R. Jose the Galilean says: Had the Israelites at the Sea said: "The Lord *is* king forever and ever," no nation or kingdom would ever have ruled over them. But they said, "The Lord *shall* reign."
>
> —Mekhilta Shirata

Gnosticism and the Thorn of Apocalypse: The Buber/Scholem Debate Revisited

Both Buber and Scholem were radicals, Zionists, and Brit Shalom members; both were instrumental in the revival of interest in Jewish mysticism and myth. Nonetheless, as Martina Urban puts it, "starting in the 1960s, the Scholem-Buber controversy, which was a debate both on scholarly method and on Jewish identity, became one of the fundamental controversies in Jewish studies."[11] In 1961, the same year that eighty-three-year-old Buber was elected the first president of the newly founded Israel Academy of Sciences and Humanities, Scholem claimed that although Buber was largely responsible for introducing Hasidism to the West, and thus that in some sense "we are all his disciples," nonetheless "the spiritual message he has read into these writings is far too closely tied to assumptions that derive from his own philosophy of religious anarchism and existentialism and have no roots in the texts themselves."[12] Buber had known for some time of Scholem's private, unpublished reservations about his approach.[13] In 1943 he had heard Scholem explain some of his reservations in person. In Scholem's recollection of this encounter twenty years later, Buber had responded: "If what you are now saying were right, my dear Scholem, then I would have worked on Hasidism for forty years absolutely in vain, because in that case, Hasidism does not *interest* me at all."[14] Scholem's student, Rivka Schatz-Uffenheimer, had voiced a critique of Buber's conception of Hasidism clearly reflecting the views of her teacher, but the article of 1961 was the first time they appeared under Scholem's name.[15] Buber replied briefly, but ill health prevented a fuller response. Between Buber's death in 1965 and his own passing in 1982, Scholem's position came to dominate the field.[16] Since then, scholars have continued the controversy, reexamining the claim of Scholem and his students to a more accurate, historical picture of Hasidism over Buber's forcing the movement into his preconceived world picture.[17] The persistence of the controversy indicates the centrality of its basic themes to the study of Jewish thought.[18]

The debate takes place on two levels: methodology and content. Methodologically, Scholem accuses Buber of failing to be a historian; Buber responds that his presentation is not intended to be history. On the level of content, the debate concerns the nature of the Hasidic attitude toward the world. Buber contends that Hasidism affirms the world through hallowing and sanctification, whereas Scholem argues that Buber overlooks the connections between Hasidism and previous, otherworldly forms of Jewish mysticism: "The Hasidic authors obviously did not believe that they had in any way broken with the gnostic tradition of the Kabbalah and, little as Buber wants to admit it, they wrote clearly and plainly as Gnostics."[19] Scholem's use of the term "gnostic" here is central to the debate. As Benjamin Lazier has observed, the terms "gnostic" and "Gnosticism" had special connotations in European thought of the interwar period: "Alienation is wildly overdetermined in gnostic theology: man is alienated from himself, from an absent, transcendent God, and above all from the material, sensuous universe in which he lives, created as it was by an evil, malicious demiurge."[20] This understanding of Gnosticism, which Buber and Scholem shared, stemmed from certain religious movements of antiquity, anathematized by the Church Fathers as "knowledge [*gnosis*] falsely so-called" and categorized variously by modern scholars as a sect of Christianity, as a Christian or Jewish heresy, as a proto-Christian religion, or as an independent syncretic tradition drawing on Persian and Hellenistic sources. It is ironic that this conception of Gnosticism was actually a construction of interwar European thought, in its own struggle with whether to denigrate the corporal and exalt the spiritual, whether to affirm or deny the existing world.[21] Nonetheless, this understanding grounded the debate: if a spiritual movement is influenced by Gnosticism, as Scholem argued Hasidism was, then its emphasis on the holiness present in the here and now could only serve the eventual annihilation of the here and now, either by diverting the soul from the concrete toward transcendent reality or by seeking out the transcendent hidden by the concrete. Scholem accuses Buber of confusing the Hasidic attitude toward the reality of created existence with the hidden sparks that the Hasid seeks to extract *from* that reality.

According to Scholem, Buber wrongly denies the Gnosticism present in Hasidism because of his "religious existentialism" and "religious anarchism." These are used synonymously, as Scholem understands them: "To put it bluntly, Buber is a religious anarchist and his teaching is religious anarchism. By that I mean the following: Buber's philosophy demands of man that he set himself a direction and reach a decision, but it says nothing about which direction and which decision. . . . Whether right or wrong, Hasidism could not share this essentially anarchical view since it remained obligated to Jewish tradition."[22] Whether or not this is an accurate description of Buber's philosophy, of interest here is Scholem's characterization of anarchism.[23] In the version of the article republished in Scholem's *Messianic Idea in Judaism*, the following gloss on "religious anarchist" is omitted: "[It is] a term that is not meant to disparage him; I am an anarchist myself, though not one of Buber's persuasion."[24] Scholem does not specify which sort of anarchist he is himself, but he does make clear that he thinks Buber is a "religious" anarchist. This vague term could designate someone like Tolstoy, whose anarchism has a religious basis, but Scholem clearly has a more restricted definition in mind: a person whose anarchism manifests itself *with respect to* the sphere "religion."

A slight detour is in order. Scholem professed a far warmer attitude toward Buber's Bible scholarship than to his work on Hasidism.[25] In 1932, upon the publication of *Kingship of God*, he wrote to Buber, "The principles you apply concretely here result in nothing less than a completely new line of biblical scholarship . . . despite the conciliatory nature of your polemic, no one can have any doubt about the murderous consequences for a hitherto widely held attitude which result from an acceptance or success of the attitude demanded by you." Scholem is unclear about this "hitherto widely held attitude," except to connect it to a "front" forming against Buber "among the Protestants." Later in the letter, however, he introduces a new topic:

> As for your presentation of, and formulations about, theocracy and anarchy, I have read them with the utmost interest, since I have come to the same conclusion in my own studies (you must have found it expressed in my critique

of [Rosenzweig's] *Star of Redemption*). The significance of this connection for *every* stratum of Jewish reality is incalculable, and I deem myself fortunate to have found confirmation of your testimony of this in such a prominent place.[26]

Scholem directs us to his analysis of the *Star of Redemption* for an understanding of his views on Buber's presentation of theocracy and anarchy. This assessment says that "few works have been as provocative since the appearance of the *Guide of the Perplexed* or the *Zohar* . . . in the long run this work will need ever increasing critical attention."[27] He admits that the ten years since the first edition is a short period in the life of such a work as the *Star*, which would only reveal its full significance to a future generation. In his letter, however, Scholem refers to a "critique" of Rosenzweig. There is only one point in the review that could be called critical, and it does indeed involve the words "theocracy" and "anarchy."

Scholem sees Rosenzweig's project as an "attempt to deduce the two possibilities for theocratic modes of life in Judaism and Christianity from the dialectics of the concept of redemption." Since Rosenzweig's descriptions of religious realities derive from liturgical calendars, Scholem's "theocratic modes of life" seem to refer to Jewish and Christian ritual, congregational lives. To call such life, however devoted, "theocracy" suggests a radically different sense of the term from the one in the sixth chapter of Buber's *Kingship of God*. There Buber speaks of "the kingship of God as such" as a historical tendency toward actualization "which can be no other than a political one," since YHVH "is not content to be 'God' in the religious sense . . . not constitution of cult and custom only, also of economy and society."[28] Scholem seems to acknowledge this when he speaks of the "strangely church-like aspect which Judaism unexpectedly sometimes takes on" in Rosenzweig's work. However, a closer look reveals that it is by no means an anarchic "constitution of economy and society" that Scholem finds lacking in Rozenzweig's conception of theocracy:

> To be sure, by his use of the doctrine of the anticipation of redemption in Jewish life . . . Rosenzweig took a decided and hostile stand against the one open door in the otherwise very neatly ordered house of Judaism. He opposed the theory of catastrophes contained in Messianic apocalypticism which might be considered the point at which even today theocratic and bourgeois modes of life stand irreconcilably opposed. The deep-seated tendency to remove the apocalyptic thorn from the organism of Judaism makes Rosenzweig the last and certainly one of the most vigorous exponents of a very old and very powerful movement in Judaism, which crystallized in a variety of forms. . . . Apocalypticism, as a doubtlessly anarchic element, provided some fresh air in the house of Judaism; it provided a recognition of the catastrophic potential of all historical order in an unredeemed world. Here, in a mode of thought deeply concerned for order, it underwent metamorphosis. The power of redemption seems to be built into the clockwork of life lived in the light of revelation, though more as restlessness than as potential destructiveness.[29]

Anarchy here equates to apocalypticism, chaos, and catastrophe. It is the part of theocracy that disrupts, rather than embodies, theocratic order. Opposition to apocalypticism stems from the kind of will to order and regularity that Rosenzweig displays in his carefully planned system of philosophy. Scholem's conception of anarchy, then, like his conception of theocracy, applies to "religion" rather than to life as a whole; anarchy is the chaos within "religion"—the "fresh air" that blows through an "ordered house." It is thus quite distant from any conception of anarchy, including Landauer's, that descended from Proudhon's claim that "anarchy is order." The sentence of Scholem's that comes closest to Buber's idea of lived theocracy is his recognition that "theocratic and bourgeois modes of life stand most irreconcilably opposed" where anarchy is lived out. However, for Scholem, this anarchy takes the form of "the theory of catastrophes contained in Messianic apocalypticism," whereas for Buber, this anarchy takes the form of the noncatastrophic attempt to realize God's sovereignty in ordinary life—not only in "religion."

This is perhaps what Scholem meant when he said "I am an anarchist myself"—that he was a partisan of the apocalyptic. The double role of anarchy in Scholem's work supports this contention. Scholem sees the demonic and destructive forces in Judaism as vital forces for change; the movements to neutralize apocalyptic messianism lead to quietism, which leads to stagnation. This attitude to history, influenced perhaps by the young Buber's speeches on Judaism, might be described as a "dialectical spiritualism." It sees a struggle across the centuries between different visions of Jewish revelation, in which destruction can, as Bakunin had it, beget new creation. The idea that Judaism is a struggle over time between competing conceptions led to Scholem's objection, "scientific" at first glance, to Buber's claim to have located the essence of Judaism in just some expressions of the Bible and Hasidism. The idea of Scholem as objective scholar, embracing a historicist approach to Judaism as a variegated phenomenon throughout time, must be reexamined in view of the fact that Scholem also came to maintain, as David Biale writes, "that Jewish theology, encompassing both rationalism and demonic irrationalism, is *anarchistic:* it yields no one authoritative formula or dogma."[30] Anarchism thus functions simultaneously as the description of Scholem's entire dialectic and of one of its poles. Despite Scholem's ostensible antipathy to apocalyptic messianism, his campaign to restore it to its proper place in Jewish history was no mere manifestation of scholarly rectitude; it reflects the idea that apocalypticism represented something vital and important, if dangerous, whose value had to be stressed in the face of Buber's denigration of it.[31]

If Scholem's anarchism takes the form of an indirect identification with the apocalyptic, then Buber's anarchism (that "persuasion" with which Scholem did *not* identify) takes a form that opposes the apocalyptic. This confrontation between two types of anarchism is also a conflict between two types of eschatology. The vagueness of the term "religious anarchism," which Scholem applied both to Buber and to himself, has worked to veil the theopolitical nature of these oppositions.[32] Buber's name for that which opposes the apocalyptic was the "prophetic." He articulated this perspective, developed throughout his biblical writings, most clearly in a 1954 essay entitled "Prophecy, Apocalyptic, and the Historical Hour." The central attribute of prophecy for Buber, exemplified by Jeremiah, is its recognition that "the unique being, man, is created to be a centre of surprise in creation. Because and so long as man exists, factual change of direction can take place towards salvation as well as towards disaster, starting from the world in each hour, no matter how late."[33] Apocalyptic, exemplified by the Revelation to John and by 4 Ezra, forecloses such natality: "Everything here is predetermined, all human decisions are only sham struggles. The future does not come to pass; the future is already present in heaven, as it were, present from the beginning."[34] Scholem mentions that Buber sees Marx as a modern secular version of an apocalyptic writer; Marx is "indifferent to the inner change of human beings which precedes the change of the world, being only concerned with the unalterable course of events that will swallow up previous history in a revolutionary way—and who thinks that the coming catastrophe of these events ought, if anything, to be hastened."[35] Scholem links this position to the Barthian school of theology as well; he notes that in his effort to combat this modern Gnosticism in both its religious and its secular forms, Buber tended not only to play down its significance in the history of Judaism but also to relax his strict opposition to the Law, whose antiapocalyptic qualities now seem more positive. However, Scholem ignores the fact that Buber elsewhere constructs a modern prophetic counterpart to Marx. This occurs in *Paths in Utopia*, a work ignored in Scholem's forty-four-page essay on Buber.[36] "In the socialist secularization of eschatology," Buber writes, the two forms of eschatology correspond to two rival streams of socialism: "The prophetic form in some of the systems of the so-called Utopians, the apocalyptic one above all in Marxism."[37] He elaborates: "All suffering under a social order that is senseless prepares the soul for vision, and what the soul receives in this vision strengthens and deepens its insight into the perversity of what is perverted."[38] This vision of a better life, which Buber notes is "experienced as revelation or idea," religiously or philosophically, emerges from the existing conditions of humanity and resolves in ideas of a perfect time (the messianic vision) or a perfect place (the utopian order of the Ideal). Both create images that seem impossible, but "what may seem impossible as a concept arouses, as an image, the whole might of faith, ordains purpose and plan. It does this because it is in league with powers latent in the depths of reality. Eschatology, *in so far as it is prophetic*, Utopia, in so far as it is philosophical, both have the character of realism." Contra Scholem, there is another eschatology beyond the messianic, a vision of what is *not* impossible.

Scholem was a leftist, secular Zionist, not a political anarchist. He once wrote that "the social and moral thought of anarchists like Tolstoy and Landauer has had an influence on the building of a new life in Eretz Yisrael that should not be underestimated"; but, he added, while "my own development moved markedly in this direction . . . the chances of establishing an anarchistic society became ever more dubious to me. The optimistic assumptions about the nature of man on which all anarchist doctrines are based were subject to serious philosophical and historical doubts—unfortunately, I would say."[39] This tone of sorrow and regret that human beings are incapable of living without domination often prefigures an apocalyptic turn, as illustrated by Buber's theopolitical history of Israel.[40] To be sure, Scholem insisted that Zionism be seen as a secular movement. However, as Moshe Idel has written, "Scholem . . . attempted to preach that Zionism was not a messianic movement. . . . [H]e believed that the latter invoked apocalyptic elements, while the former is a voluntaristic enterprise based upon what he called a process of 'entering history,' that is, taking political responsibility for the fate of the Jews."[41] Scholem emphasized apocalypticism as a scholar, because of its persistence and importance, but he repudiated it as a citizen, owing to its danger. He ignored, however, the possibility created by Buber's rejection of apocalypse and gnosis: the mundane, nonapocalyptic achievement of anarchism or utopian socialism as a form of political responsibility for the fate of the Jews.[42] The effects of Scholem's dividing "religious" anarchism from anarchism is evident in the works of those influenced by his conception of apocalyptic.

Gnosis and Time: Taubes, Agamben, and the World's Passing Away

Hans Jonas is the chief exponent, in his work *Gnosis und spätantiker Geist* (Gnosis and the Spirit of Late Antiquity, 1934), of the idea that "gnosis" was not merely the goal of a loose grouping of late-antique sects but a permanently available *Daseinshaltung* (stance of being).[43] In a 1929 letter to his teacher, the Protestant theologian Rudolf Bultmann, Jonas identified Paul's Epistle to the Romans as the high point and locus classicus of the gnostic stance, which had recently been revived (in Jonas's eyes) by Karl Barth. Paul's description of helplessness before the commands of the Law and the desperate need for grace, in which Jonas saw the outlines of a general philosophical anthropology, marked the ultimate in world denial. Moreover, Jonas felt that Paul's critique of Judaism went far deeper than that of Jesus himself: "As a Jew, I feel myself attacked by Jesus' critique not essentially, but only in a particular expression of Jewish piety. By Paul, however, I feel myself essentially and basically struck."[44] Buber, who shared Jonas's negative attitude toward gnostic world denial, also shared his negative view of Paul.[45] Scholem, who might have been expected to oppose Buber on this, declined to devote a study to Paul.[46] However, a onetime student of his, Jacob Taubes, took up Scholem's position on the question and radicalized it, first by claiming Paul as a

Jewish heretic ("an apostle *from the Jews* to the nations"), and second by explicitly identifying with the Pauline position in a way that Scholem would not.[47]

In a 1963 essay, Taubes portrayed Buber's anti-Hegelian conception of history—particularly his refusal to accept the "verdicts" issued by historical events—as fundamentally anti-Pauline.[48] Taubes sees Paul as the source of such Hegelian tropes as the cunning of history (when human efforts unwittingly produce the opposite of desired outcomes) and the revelation, at history's end, of the predetermined meaning of all past events (the way that the end of any story gives shape to what has gone before). Paul's God uses ruses: the Law is given to Israel for its redemption, but in the meantime it multiplies transgression, only to allow grace to abound later; the messiah is crucified, but then resurrected. To be sure, Hegel replaces God with Reason as Spirit, but the dialectic remains, by which evil secretly births good, and good unexpectedly transforms into evil, and all this adds up to a grand story of providential salvation.[49] Pauline gnosis also underlies the philosophy of Hegel's rebellious disciple, Karl Marx, for whom the despised class, the proletariat, takes on the messianic function of universal redeemer.[50]

Taubes, however, thinks that Buber fails to completely sever this gnostic-apocalyptic constellation from the prophetic stance he supports. Taubes focuses on the tension in *The Prophetic Faith* between the continuity of the prophetic alternative even amid increasing despair, culminating in Jeremiah, and the dissolution of that alternative in the prophets of the Exile: "But what crucial exception does Deutero-Isaiah present! What use is a typology concerning the prophetic and apocalyptic experience of history if Deutero-Isaiah, whom Buber rightly calls 'the originator of a theology of world history,' has to be exempt from the rule?"[51] Paul, in contrast, makes great use of Deutero-Isaiah's notion of atonement through the suffering of God's servant. If Buber had been willing, Taubes says, to hold fast to his dichotomy, clearly placing Deutero-Isaiah among the apocalyptics, then perhaps his interpretation "could have . . . struck at the heart of Paul's theology of history, thus meeting his great antagonist face to face." Instead, Buber puts Deutero-Isaiah in a liminal category, where he may retain his "open" messianic interpretation of the suffering servant who appears repeatedly through time.[52] For Taubes, Buber displays "a messianic inspiration without employing in general the form of eschatological actuality. Paradoxically expressed: it is a messianism of continuity." Quoting Hegel's passage from *Phenomenology of Spirit* on the "beautiful soul," so pure that he refuses to act in the world, Taubes criticizes Buber's messianism as incapable of self-actualization. Buber's "romantic nostalgia" for the moments of immediate encounter in history, whether the direct rule of YHVH, the early Christian community, or the early Hasidim, does not recognize the necessity of being embodied in institutions.[53] Moreover, Taubes argues, Buber ignores the alternative that is present within apocalypticism: "The apocalyptic seer confronts us with the alternative whether we perceive the change, the new beginning in history, or whether we are blind to the new day that is actually dawning. This new alternative is of such dramatic tension that it divides believers and unbelievers into children of light and children of darkness."[54] Far from sapping the will to action, Taubes points out that apocalyptic determinism has provided an intense motivating force.[55]

Taubes's criticisms of Buber are rooted in Scholem's understanding of apocalyptic messianism, which Taubes holds in highest regard: "[Whoever] understands what Scholem presents in the eighth chapter of *Major Trends in Jewish Mysticism* can penetrate more deeply into Paul's messianic logic than by reading the entire exegetical literature."[56] The reference is to Scholem's discussion of "Sabbatianism and Mystical Heresy."[57] Taubes criticizes the treatment of Paul in Jewish studies in language reminiscent of Scholem's earlier critique of *Wissenschaft des Judentums*:

> Now it happens that the Jewish study of Paul is in a very sad state. There is a literary corpus about Jesus, a nice guy, about the rabbi in Galilee, and about the Sermon on the Mount; it's all in the Talmud and so on . . . there is a consensus in Liberal Judaism (not in Orthodox Judaism, which hasn't moved an inch), that is, a sort of pride in this son of Israel. But when it comes to Paul, that's a borderline that's hard to cross.[58]

After dismissing most Jewish books on Paul with contempt, Taubes admits one exception:

> The most important Jewish book on Paul, written deeply from the heart and as an attack, is Martin Buber's *Two Types of Faith*. This book deserves to be taken seriously; it's based on a thesis that I think is highly dubious but from which I have learned a great deal. . . . Buber of course wants Jesus . . . on the positive side (which is very hard to do, since he was more of an apocalyptic than a prophet), and Paul belongs on the other.[59]

However, it is not merely Buber's prophetic-apocalyptic dichotomy per se to which Taubes objects. He focuses, as most readers of *Two Types of Faith* have done, on its eponymous thesis: there is a Jewish faith, *emunah*, a relationship of trust in the God one happens to encounter, and a Greek faith, *pistis*, which one adopts upon the recognition that some proposition or other is true. Buber holds that Paul's *pistis* is a philosophical faith whose Greek origin requires no discussion. Taubes dissents: "Buber here misses the whole point of the thing, which is that 'faith in' is by no means only Greek but is *the center of a messianic logic*."[60] For proof of this, however, Taubes does not philologically investigate the term *pistis*; rather, he adduces a series of anecdotes about Sabbatianism.[61] These are meant to show that "the internal logic of events demanded a faith that is paradoxical, that is contradicted by the evidence."[62] Shabbetai Zvi converted to Islam, Jesus died on the cross; to believe in them *anyway* becomes an equivalent, in apocalyptic faith, for all the commandments of the Law ("works"): "Now you understand my corrective to Buber. . . . That Buber is a sensitive and a great figure—we don't need to talk about that. But regarding this point, which to me is all important, he misses completely, and with such sureness that we can only be amazed. This is what we can learn from Gershom Scholem, implicitly, in this eighth chapter on Sabbatianism."

Taubes's polemic against Buber envisions a Paul who was a revolutionary in his own time and can be appropriated in ours. Contending against both the Roman Empire and the Jewish establishment that tolerated it (which Taubes anachronistically condemns as "liberal"), Paul indicts the whole ideology of *nomos* (law) that ruled the Hellenistic world. Paul's apocalyptics turns this ideology on its head, proclaiming the one crucified in the name of *nomos* as the true emperor. Taubes presents two parallel theses with respect to this revolutionary Paul. First, that Paul sees himself as "outbidding Moses," justifying the founding of a new people of God from within the perspective of the original people: "The apostle takes the election of Israel seriously. This is embarrassing for modern Christianity, but that's the way it is. . . . Better to live with embarrassments than to transfigure the text."[63] His second thesis is that Paul's gnostic-apocalyptic stand finds parallels in modernity, especially in interwar Germany. Rosenzweig, Barth, Buber, Schmitt, and Benjamin are all cited as participants in a modern Pauline mood to some degree and in their respective fields: Barth in theology, Schmitt in law, and so on. Not all of these, of course, are revolutionary figures. Barth, for example, holds that theology can legitimate neither the political order nor the revolution against it, and Schmitt responds to the apocalyptic mood by taking on the role of *katechon*, the one who seeks to hold back the messianic culmination by maintaining the status quo.[64] But for Taubes it is Walter Benjamin who most directly represents the Pauline position.[65] He describes Benjamin's "Theological-Political Fragment" as "dialectical theology outside the church," a lay version of Barth.[66]

Taubes's Paul is a Zealot, but unlike the Jerusalem Zealots in Josephus's account of the Jewish rebellion against Rome, Paul does not counsel armed uprising: "Under this time pressure, if tomorrow the whole palaver, the entire swindle were going to be over—in that case there's no point in any revolution!"[67] In Taubes's view, the opening paragraph of Benjamin's "Theological-Political Fragment" recapitulates this position:

> Only the Messiah himself completes all history, in the sense that he alone redeems, completes, creates its relation to the messianic. For this reason, nothing that is historical can relate itself, from its own ground, to anything messianic. Therefore, the Kingdom of God is not the telos of the historical dynamic; it cannot be established as a goal. From the standpoint of history, it is not the goal but the terminus. Therefore, the secular order cannot be built on the idea of the Divine Kingdom, and theocracy has no political but only a religious meaning.[68]

Benjamin's fragment impresses Taubes by its straightforward reference to "the Messiah," rather than any of the modern euphemisms. But Taubes hastens to clarify Benjamin: "But it mustn't be misread! It doesn't mean that concepts of theocracy aren't political."[69] Here Taubes simply seems engaged in flagrant misreading; doesn't Benjamin really, as clearly as anything in this fragment, say the opposite? Taubes's claim is rooted in the concluding part of the fragment:

> The secular order should be erected on the idea of happiness. The relation of this order to the messianic is one of the essential teachings of the philosophy of history. . . . [J]ust as a force, by virtue of the path it is moving along, can augment another force on the opposite path, so the secular order—because of its nature as secular—promotes the coming of the Messianic Kingdom. The secular, therefore, though not itself a category of this kingdom, is a decisive category of its most unobtrusive approach. For in happiness all that is earthly seeks its downfall, and only in happiness is its downfall destined to find it. . . . For nature is messianic by reason of its eternal and total passing away.
>
> To strive for such a passing away . . . is the task of world politics, whose method must be called nihilism.

In Taubes's view, the notion of nihilistic secular politics causing the world to pass away is a combined allusion to 1 Corinthians 7:31 and Romans 13, while the rhythm of nature passing away is an exegesis of Romans 8:18–25. The profane world has no significance; it cannot be sanctified. There is no divine immanence here; there is nothing to be done on one's own behalf; salvation is transcendent: "The drawbridge comes from the other side."[70] According to Taubes, both Benjamin and Barth share this gnostic sense of an abandoned world that awaits salvation.

This Pauline Benjamin, together with Taubes's criticism of Buber's *Two Types of Faith*, live on today in the work of the contemporary Italian philosopher Giorgio Agamben. Agamben agrees that Benjamin's philosophy of history is Pauline, but he disagrees that Paul is apocalyptic: "What interests the apostle is not the last day, it is not the instant in which time ends, but the time that contracts itself and begins to end . . . the time that remains between time and its end."[71] The apostolic vocation also differs from the prophet's: "The prophet is essentially defined through his relation to the future. . . . This is what marks the difference between the prophet and the apostle. The apostle speaks forth from the arrival of the Messiah. At this point prophecy must keep silent, for now prophecy is truly fulfilled."[72] The position of the apostle between prophecy and apocalyptic is crucial for Agamben, since "According to Scholem—who holds a view fairly widespread in Judaism—the messianic antinomy is defined as 'a life lived in deferment' . . . in which nothing can be achieved: 'So-called Jewish existence,' he writes, 'possesses a tension that never finds true release.'"[73] Apostleship, however, announces that messianic time has already arrived, and "the time that remains" is not simply additional chronological time, as the end is indefinitely postponed; rather, it is a different *experience* of time itself, one that happens *now*: "the *pleroma* of *kairoi* is understood as the relation of each instant to the Messiah—each *kairos* is *unmittelbar zu Gott* [immediate to God], and is not just the final result of a process (as is the case with the model Marxism inherited from Hegel."[74] Such a faith cannot be described as a "holding something to be true," as Buber had it; on the contrary, it is identical with the qualities Buber had ascribed to the Hebrew *emunah*.[75]

Agamben's Paul is a revolutionary too, seeking "to create a space that escaped the grasp of power and its laws, without entering into conflict with them yet rendering them inoperative" through his *euanggelion* (good message) of the crucified Messiah, which is "power for he who believes" (Romans 1:16).[76] Contained in this message is the concept of messianic *klesis* (calling), as defined in 1 Corinthians 7:17–22. For Agamben, *klesis* "indicates the particular transformation that every juridical status and worldly condition undergoes because of, and only because of, its relation to the messianic event. . . . For Paul, the *ekklesia*, the messianic community, is literally all *kleseis*, all messianic vocations. The messianic vocation does not, however, have any specific content; it is nothing but the repetition of those same factical or juridical conditions *in which* or *as which* we are called."[77] Yet these conditions are now lived, as Paul urges, through the modality of "as not": "that even those having wives may be as not having, and those weeping as not weeping, and those rejoicing as not rejoicing, and those buying as not possessing, and those using the world as not using it up. For passing away is the figure of this world. But I wish you to be without care" (1 Corinthians 7:29–32). Agamben describes this messianic "as not" as "*the revocation of every vocation* . . . the vocation calls the vocation itself, as though it were an urgency that works it from within and hollows it out, nullifying it in the very gesture of maintaining and dwelling in it."[78]

A strange revolution, indeed. At one point Agamben even compares the law under messianic *katargesis* with the law under the Schmittian state of exception, explicitly mentioning the Nazi decree of February 1933. While exception is eventually itself superseded in Paul's figure of love, it is unclear exactly how this overcoming differs from the original messianic suspension. Agamben's reading of Paul is best understood within the framework of his own larger philosophical project, including his argument that Paul is the hidden hunchback theologian pulling the strings of historical materialism in Benjamin's first thesis "On the Concept of History."[79] There is no immediate textual reason or cue requiring us to assume that Benjamin has a particular theology or theologian in mind when he writes of "theology" here, yet Agamben insists on it.[80] This claim is placed at the end of *The Time That Remains*, titled "Threshold or *Tornada*," suggesting that it relates to the previous six days of his seminar in the same way that the tornada relates to the six verses of a sestina, and the Sabbath to the six days of Creation.[81] Agamben views Benjamin's idea of a "*weak* messianic force" both as derived from Paul and as the primary resource for contemporary revolutionary thinking. Like

Buber, Agamben rejects apocalyptic eschatology; however, he distinguishes the messianic vocation of apostleship from the prophetic alternative, because he sees the prophetic as unmistakably oriented toward the future. Agamben sees the "weak messianic force" as capable of rendering contemporary *nomos* inoperative; it is "the one thing needful," to use Jesus' words.[82]

Yet Buber's vision of the prophetic was also directed toward the present, the moment in which the people decide whether to return to God. True, the prophets failed; they are "ineffective" in the same sense that Buber himself was ineffective. But they are no *more* ineffective than Agamben's Paul himself, whose revolutionary doctrine apparently stands in need of rescue from the traditional view that he taught obedience to worldly authority, or at most "a sort of mental reserve, or, in the best of cases . . . a kind of Marranism *ante litteram*."[83] We may not be able to evaluate the prophets and Paul by the standard employed by politics, such as the "successful" enactment of a plan. Agamben writes elsewhere, "One day humanity will play with law just as children play with disused objects, not in order to restore them to their canonical use but to free them from it for good."[84] Yet Agamben's Benjaminian-Pauline Gnosticism faces the challenge of articulating its own power of action, which has been muted in an effort to distinguish it from the apocalyptic type of Gnosticism. In meeting this challenge, it must avoid the opposite extreme, the valorization of action and decision for their own sake.

The Blizzard of the World

The chorus in Leonard Cohen's "The Future" (1992) warns of imminent chaos: "Things are going to slide, slide in all directions / Won't be nothing / Nothing you can measure any more / The blizzard, the blizzard of the world has crossed the threshold / and it's overturned the order of the soul."[85] The protagonist of this song seeks escape from relativist hell, yearning for a place to stand—leading to an interesting juxtaposition: "Give me back the Berlin Wall / Give me Stalin and Saint Paul / I've seen the future, brother / it is murder." By comparing Stalin and Paul, Cohen's protagonist here anticipates the career of Alain Badiou, who in 1992 had already written his major philosophical work, *L'être et l'événement* (*Being and Event*), but who was still five years away from publishing *Saint Paul: La fondation de l'universalisme* (*Saint Paul: The Foundation of Universalism*). A member of the 1968 generation in France, but a longtime opponent of "postmodern" thought, Badiou has sought to enact what the Slovenian philosopher Slavoj Žižek has called a repetition of the Platonic gesture, shattering the poststructuralist hall of mirrors by founding a new universalism. Explaining his attraction to Paul, Badiou writes:

> For me, Paul is a poet-thinker of the event, as well as one who practices and states the invariant traits of what can be called the militant figure. . . . [T]here is currently a widespread search for a new militant figure . . . called upon to

succeed the one installed by Lenin and the Bolsheviks at the beginning of the century, which can be said to have been that of the party militant.[86]

For Badiou, contemporary cultural and historical relativism too easily accommodates the false universality of global capitalism, and it can be challenged only by another universalism. The necessary militancy of that universalism is Badiou's insistent theme.

Like Agamben, Badiou sees Paul as opposing two dominant discourses. But whereas Agamben sees apostleship as a new attitude to messianic time, situated between the prophetic and the apocalyptic, for Badiou apostleship is an attitude to dominance, situated between the Jewish prophet (constructed, as in Agamben, as a figure who speaks of the future) and the Greek philosopher. "If one demands signs," Badiou writes, "he who performs them in abundance becomes a master for him who demands them. If one questions philosophically, he who can reply becomes a master for the perplexed subject. But he who declares without prophetic or miraculous guarantees, without arguments or proof, does not enter into the logic of the master."[87] Paul is the spokesperson of weakness, claiming no validity for his message other than the message itself. Badiou notes that in contrast to much later Christian tradition, Paul "firmly holds to the militant discourse of weakness," refraining from either miraculous demonstration or philosophical proof. Paul's fidelity to the crucified messiah has a lesson for anyone who "is the subject of a truth (of love, of art, or science, or politics)."[88] Attempts to convince others through *logos*, or signs, or mystical testimony, seem pious but in reality they claim power for one's self. The faithful subject knows that only the event and the fidelity to it ensure subjecthood.

Badiou's insistence on militancy, however, risks being untrue to his insights into fidelity:

> The lengthy years of communist dictatorship will have had the merit of showing that financial globalization, the absolute sovereignty of capital's empty universality, had as its only genuine enemy another universal project, albeit a corrupt and bloodstained one: that only Lenin and Mao truly *frightened* those who proposed to boast unreservedly about the merits of liberalism and the general equivalent, or the democratic virtues of commercial communication.[89]

Badiou takes the ability to generate fear, the historical "success" of state communism, as an index of its effectiveness. Since this fear, according to Badiou, arises for those in power (little is said here of the fear of communism felt by the powerless), this indexing is one more way in which Badiou belongs to those who, despite refuting the state, as Agamben suggests, "are often unable to liberate themselves from a point of view of the state."[90] If the function of the militant in Badiou's text is only "the *public declaration* of the event by its name," then why the need to measure?[91] The temptation to measure the effectiveness of militancy through its ability to generate fear among the enemies of the event may be understood as an infidelity. The possibility of such an infidelity, even after the "subjectivation" Badiou refers to in this text as "resurrection," raises once again the problem of sin, which was supposedly overcome through the grace of the event. This brings us back to prophetic *teshuva*, and to Leonard Cohen's protagonist in "The Future," who hears voices telling him to repent, and wonders what they mean.

I do not mean to suggest that Buber's theopolitical vision of the prophetic is the one, true way, and that apocalyptic, gnostic, or materialist deviations are false. Agamben denies Paul's apocalypticism only to declare him a revolutionary without arms; Badiou denies Paul's relationship to dialectics, only to affirm that "Grace . . . is affirmation without preliminary negation; it is what comes upon us in caesura of the law. It is pure *encounter*."[92] Each thinker describes his "new" Paul as having some qualities that Buber prized but simply didn't see in Paul. Nor was Buber himself always consistent in his own theopolitical understanding, which harbored a tension between the element of free choice essential to the prophetic alternative and the confidence of redemption. Occasionally, in denigrating historical success, Buber makes it seem as though one can discern the signs of the eventual victory of the prophetic in the details of previous failures. In doing so, he inappropriately conflates the political and religious realms, betraying theopolitics for political theology. He is truer to his own theopolitics when he insists, like Badiou's militant Paul, both that the prophetic is in league with reality and that obedience to the prophetic call carries no guarantee of success.[93] Only then does he elaborate those theopolitical alternatives to Gnosticism, nihilism, and statist forms of communism and Zionism that were so attractive even to Scholem, who wrote, "To engage Buber intellectually meant to be tossed hither and yon between admiration and rejection, between readiness to listen to his message and disappointment with that message and the impossibility of realizing it."[94] This "impossibility" is questionable. Impossibility is one of the oldest categories problematized by anarchism.

Anarchism

> Can serious questions regarding power be asked?
> —Pierre Clastres, "Copernicus and the Savages"[95]

Anarchy and Order

Scholem and Buber's disagreement on anarchism is about order and chaos. Scholem associates anarchism with the chaos of apocalyptic messianism while neglecting the centrality of order and worldliness in the anarchic vision. However, now a step back must be taken. In Žižekian fashion, we might note that if every discussion of anarchism begins with the disclaimer that anarchism is not really about chaos and violence, but rather a sophisticated political tradition grappling with the problematics of order in freedom, we should be suspicious. Perhaps something important about anarchism is lost in these denials. Because anarchism is an ideology of freedom, must not even ordered freedom contain a strong element of the unpredictable?

Consider the CrimethInc. Ex-Workers' Collective, a "centerless, amoebic, invisible" social phenomenon that refuses to define itself as an organization and sometimes publishes books.[96] It defines "crimethink" as "the stirrings of a new world, smuggled across every border in the heads and hearts of a dissident nation of millions, thrown through plate glass windows on notes tied to bricks."[97] It makes outrageous gnostic/neo-situationist claims on its own behalf: the claim, for example, to be "a force that exists beneath the currents of history, outside the chain of events . . . the first stirrings of a revolt that will take us all *out* of history. . . . [W]e have come to be the ones to fire the first shots of the third and final world war, the war which will be fought for total liberation." It combines unreconstructed Enlightenment opposition to religion ("Everything that glorifies 'God' and the afterworld slanders humanity and the real world") with criticisms of everything from gender roles to the exploitation of animals and the marketing of deodorant. It calls for readers to "stop thinking of anarchism as just another 'world order,' just another social system," and to conceive of anarchism instead "as an individual orientation to yourself and others, as a personal approach to life."[98] Murray Bookchin (1921–2006), the founder of social ecology, who decried the individualism of American anarchism, its preference to express revolutionary commitments through style rather than the grind of social organizing, would probably have described CrimethInc. as "lifestyle anarchists."[99] To which CrimethInc. might have replied: *Your Politics are Boring as Fuck.*[100] They insist that politics should be as joyous as one wants life in general to be. Rejecting the charge that miniature interventions and resistances are an ineffective praxis, CrimethInc. sardonically notes that "staying alive is reformist: you keep trying the same basic approach, hoping for a different outcome. Suicide, on the other hand—guaranteed results. If you want to solve a problem, *solve it.*"[101]

The more orderly vision of anarchism, meanwhile, lives on in Michael Albert and his idea of participatory economics, or Parecon.[102] Albert found himself faced constantly with the question of what he and his fellow activists proposed to put in capitalism's place, if not a Soviet-style command economy. Participatory economics is his attempt at an answer. It is not a blueprint to follow, but an effort to show how humans create economies rooted in values and priorities, so that one can imagine how alternative values and priorities—solidarity, equity, and diversity—would generate an alternative to capitalism. While it may not yet be a practical or widespread economic model, Parecon nonetheless contrasts sharply with the stylistic romanticism of CrimethInc. Parallel tendencies can be found on a local level, in the focus of anarchist activists on issues of process and decision making, often involving continuous tinkering with varying models of consensus versus majority vote.

These tendencies of thought and action diverge wildly, yet social movements around the world draw on them without discrimination.[103] The uprising of the Ejército Zapatista de Liberación National (EZLN) in Chiapas, Mexico, on New Year's Day 1994, which prevented the Mexican government from privatizing land belonging to indigenous Indians, speaks primarily in an indigenous vocabulary and rejects political classification; it has nonetheless spurred discussion of its parallels to anarchism.[104] The global justice movement (also called the alter-globalization movement) of the late 1990s and early 2000s, which challenged the pro-corporate financial policies of the World Trade Organization, the International Monetary Fund, and the World Bank, was influenced by anarchist ideas.[105] In 2011, on the heels of riots in Greece and the protests of the Spanish *indignados*, the Occupy Wall Street movement birthed encampments in nearly every American city and demanded that the United States reckon with the growing economic inequality threatening its democracy. Most recently, amid the chaos of the Syrian civil war and the rise of the Islamic State, a Kurdish-led multiethnic movement has been attempting to run its own autonomous canton, Rojava (in northern Syria near the Turkish border), according to the principles of "democratic confederalism," an ideology of local, decentralized organization inspired by Bookchin.[106] One can certainly debate the wisdom or efficacy of these movements, but they are clearly a contemporary political phenomenon of some moment.[107] This is perhaps why Jeffrey Stout, a prominent theorist of "radical democracy," treats anarchism as a relevant interlocutor despite his strong philosophical and strategic disagreements with it.[108]

Although CrimethInc. might consider a preoccupation with anarchist theory a useless bore, the drive to preserve the element of surprise is nonetheless precisely what lies behind Landauer's criticism of state-directed economies and Buber's refusal to prescribe blueprints and programs to the young kibbutzniks. This brings us, however, to one of the tensions in theopolitics. On the one hand, theopolitics eliminates the possibility of theological justification for any political order. This is in line with Barthian thinking, in which transcendence cannot justify immanence. On the other hand, a reader could be forgiven for thinking that Buber treats anarchism precisely as the form of political order that theopolitics justifies. The solution to this subtle quandary is the move to emphasize the spontaneity and freedom of a future anarchist society. In *Paths in Utopia*, Buber approvingly cites the reluctance of Proudhon, the first thinker to self-describe as an anarchist, to contribute another "system" to the pile constructed by Saint-Simon, Fourier, and their like: "I have no system, I will have none, and I expressly repudiate the suggestion. . . . My business is to find out the way humanity is going and, if I can, prepare it."[109] Buber admires Proudhon's refusal to declare allegiance to materialism or idealism:

Proudhon believes neither in blind providence from below, which contrives the salvation of mankind out of technical and material changes, nor in a free-ranging human intellect, which contrives systems of absolute validity and enjoins them on mankind. He sees humanity's real way in the deliverance from false faiths in absolutism, from the dominion of fatality.[110]

This position led Proudhon to oppose centralist communism, as well as social planning: "[Proudhon] refuses to equate a new ordering of society with uniformity; order means, for him, the just ordering of multiformity."[111] We cannot foresee the shape of a decent society, because we cannot anticipate the problems that will emerge and the solutions that will be devised for them. What matters is room for spontaneity and innovation now, during the struggle to create it: "We may not 'know' what Socialism will look like, but we can know what we want it to look like, and this knowing and willing, this conscious willing itself influences what is to be—and if one is a centralist one's centralism influences what is to be."[112] Buber berates Kropotkin for simplifying Proudhon, "by setting up in the place of the manifold 'social antinomies' the simple antithesis between the principles of the struggle for existence and mutual help," but he praises him for his claim that "we conceive the structure of society to be something that is never finally constituted."[113] By contrast, Marx and Lenin were politicians and planners who subordinated their utopian ends to a simplistic analysis of social problems in which everything reduces to struggle for control of the means of production; as a result, "the political act of revolution remained the one thing worth striving for; the political preparation for it—at first the direct preparation, afterwards the parliamentary and trades unionist preparation—the one task worth doing, and thus the political principle became the supreme determinant."[114] Lenin failed to recognize that "a bureaucracy does not change when its names are changed"; as a result, he ushered in a society that eliminated spontaneity and free association.[115] Reordering government without first reordering society, Lenin failed to grasp that "changed power-relations do not of themselves create a new society capable of overcoming the power-principle."[116]

This criticism of Lenin echoes the standard anarchist critiques of state communism dating back to Bakunin. It is significant, however, that Buber places Landauer as the last in the line of theorists he considers in *Paths in Utopia*. For Landauer, the state is neither an institution nor a structure, but rather "a condition, a certain relationship between human beings, a mode of human behavior; we destroy it by contracting other relationships, by behaving differently. . . . State is status—a state, in fact."[117] This attitude is widespread in contemporary anarchism, found in everything from pamphlets to punk rock lyrics; for example, this is arguably what the punk band Against Me!, in their song "Those Anarcho-Punks Are Mysterious . . .," means when they proclaim, "We're all presidents, we're all congressmen, we're all cops in waiting."[118] No pure, ideal people can overthrow the state because the people are the state; they inhabit and embody the state when they relate to each other in authoritarian and hierarchical ways. Social revolution seeks to identify and transform these ways; political revolution results from such a process, rather than catalyzing it. In Landauer's voluntarist formula: "Socialism is possible and impossible at all times; it is possible when the right people are there to will and to do it; it is impossible when people either don't will it or only supposedly will it, but are not capable of doing it."[119] Willing does not guarantee immediate, total success; Buber and Landauer do not forecast the end of all coercion. There are ways we coerce one another unknowingly. "Revolution" to usher in a wholly new society is therefore not the essential task; rather, this new society must be constantly prefigured:

> To test day by day what the maximum of freedom is that can be realized to-day; to test how much "State" is still necessary to-day, and always to draw the practical conclusions. In all probability there will never—so long as man is what he is—be "freedom" pure and simple, and there will be "State," i.e. compulsion, for just so long; the important thing, however, is the day to day question: no more State than is indispensable, no less freedom than is allowable. And freedom, socially speaking, means above all freedom for community, a community free and independent of State compulsion.[120]

Such a struggle may not be assumed to be an invisible, "quietist" one. If the gap between the maximum of realizable freedom and the existing state of affairs is great enough, then the effort to close it will appear in the form of a "radical" activism. Such an activism should not automatically be considered unrealistic or utopian, and it certainly should not be treated as a chiliastic effort to immanentize the eschaton. This is what was at issue between Buber and Scholem, which is why it was so significant that Scholem left political anarchism out of his definition of anarchism. Political anarchism claims that while there may still be undiscovered coercion in a decentralized, nonhierarchical society, the achievement of such a society is for this precise reason not "utopian." If society operates at an extreme of indecency, then even the pragmatic effort to achieve a decent society, with no aim at final perfection, has a radical cast. Yet this effort nonetheless falls under the shadow of the Kingdom.

Resentment and Power: Nietzsche, Anarchism, and Theory

Landauer's anarchism was part of the first great wave of the Nietzsche craze in Germany, an attempt to reconcile Nietzsche's emphasis on individualism and will with the struggle for a just community. This was to ignore Nietzsche's disdain for the anarchists and socialists of his time, whom he considered overly hospitable to secularized Christian resentment. It also meant developing a positive anarchism, an anarchism without resentment and unsatisfied with "critique," that adopted Nietzsche's drive to affirmation and sought to actualize itself in real projects. Landauer's murder prematurely ended this effort. The era of "classical" anarchism continued for several decades, culminating in the struggle of the Spanish anarchists against Franco's fascists from 1936 to 1939, before declining after the defeat of the Confederación Nacional de Trabajo-Federación Anarquista Ibérica.[121] In the 1960s, however, the rise of the counterculture and situationism, especially in France, saw a renewed effort at a libertarian interpretation of Nietzsche. Meanwhile, the failings of the Soviet Union became as clear to the international left, including Western Marxists, as they once had been to anarchists alone. Buber had stated in *Paths in Utopia* that man "has come to realize that in spite of everything he likes to call 'progress' he is not traveling along the highroad at all, but is picking his precarious way along a narrow ledge between two abysses."[122] But Jean-François Lyotard went further: "The purposiveness that the twentieth century has witnessed has not consisted, as Kant had hoped, in securing fragile passages above abysses. Rather, it has consisted of filling up those abysses at the cost of the destruction of whole worlds of names. . . . Capital is that which wants a single language and a single network, and it never stops trying to present them."[123] Michel Foucault, meanwhile, declared, "One can say to many socialisms, real or dreamt: Between the analysis of power in the bourgeois state and the idea of its future withering away, there is a missing term—the analysis, criticism, destruction, and overthrow of the power mechanism itself."[124]

In its political moments, poststructuralism followed the suggestion of Adorno and Horkheimer that the joint failure of capitalism and communism, as well as the rise of fascism, resulted from their common ancestry in the Enlightenment.[125] Just as Lyotard singles out Kant, the French theorists faulted the notion of the free and rational Cartesian-Kantian subject for containing implicit oppressions. The universal horizon of the liberation sought by the Enlightenment came to be considered imperialist in itself, responsible for "the destruction of whole worlds of names"; the desire for "a single language and a single network" is condemned in favor of the valorization of difference and particularity.[126] This attack led to defenses: Badiou's demand for a true universalism in opposition to capitalism's false one, and Jürgen Habermas's defense of the Enlightenment as unfinished.[127] The debate was about the role of reason: whether it was the sleep or the dream of reason that produces monsters.

The poststructuralists do not generally consider the various attempts to create cooperative societies as a particularly important site of struggle. Instead, they take the critique of rationalist planning as an invitation to think on an even smaller scale, hoping to avoid Enlightenment imperialism by delving into relationships and practices, including writing, to locate oppressive patterns that require deconstruction and alternatives. This is the basis for Foucault's studies of the clinic, the prison, the classification of sexualities, and so on. The result is the creation of a micropolitics quite different from the traditional ideas of Enlightenment radicals, who reacted to the domination of history by states and their wars by making war on their states. This micropolitics has been criticized in "modernist" leftist and anarchist circles, as really being a kind of conservatism and quietism in disguise, since its proponents seem unwilling to prescribe any concrete actions, let alone to promise far-reaching change.[128] Despite, or perhaps in response to, these charges, some writers have emphasized continuities between poststructuralism and classical anarchism.[129] Todd May argues that even though some may deny poststructuralism the status of a political theory, "by grafting poststructuralism onto a tradition in whose light it has not been grasped—the anarchist tradition—it is possible to articulate a poststructuralist framework without betraying its fundamental micropolitical commitments."[130] May argues that such thinkers as Foucault, Lyotard, and Deleuze share anarchism's rejection of a vanguard party, its vision of numerous and intersecting sites of oppression, and its recognition that "changes of power at the top do not bring social transformation."[131] Similarly, Saul Newman writes that "anarchism and poststructuralism, as different as they are, can be brought together on the common ground of the unmasking and critique of power."[132] Both May and Newman recognize that the critique of Enlightenment humanism prevents poststructuralism from finding its own precedents in the classical anarchist thinkers; the French thinkers cannot share the early anarchists' view of power as purely oppressive or of a unitary, basically good human nature. However, as Richard Day has recognized, Landauer had already questioned these assumptions:

> Through his contact with Nietzsche's work, Landauer anticipated poststructuralist theory in analyzing capitalism and the state form not as "things" (structures), but as *sets of relations between subjects* (discourses). Based on this analysis, he was able to understand how small-scale experiments in the construction of alternative modes of social, political, and economic organization offered a way to avoid both waiting forever for the Revolution to come *and* perpetuating existing structures through reformist demands.[133]

Thus there is a real structural homology between Landauer's anarchism and an influential field of contemporary theory.

Many of these shared concerns persist even when theorists like Badiou or Žižek, under the influence of Lacan, have taken exception to the postmodern consensus, perceiving it as debilitating or obscurantist.[134] Here various intellectual inheritances, including a concern with ideology (characteristic of Louis Althusser), a concern with the figure of the father and with individual relationships to authority (characteristic of psychoanalysis), and the idea of biopolitics (characteristic of Foucault's late work) combine to question authority in all areas of life. For example, Eric Santner, comparing Rosenzweig's *Star of Redemption* and Benjamin's "Critique of Violence," notes that coercive law displays not merely strength and affirmation of legal order but also "something rotten":

> What manifests itself as the law's inner decay is the fact that rule of law is, in the final analysis, without ultimate justification or legitimation, that the very

space of juridical reason within which the rule of law obtains is established and sustained by a dimension of force and violence that, as it were, holds the place of those missing foundations. At its foundation, the rule of law is sustained not by reason alone but also by the force/violence of a tautological enunciation—"The law is the law!"[135]

Santner also suggests that Freud failed to see "that if indeed the Jewish God is a kind of Master, he is one that, paradoxically, suspends the sovereign relation."[136] Much of Santner's work on *Star of Redemption* is concerned with showing how Rosenzweig presented Judaism and Christianity as alternative ways of "detaching" or "unplugging" from the "hegemonic succession of empires, rulers, regimes, and ideologies."[137]

More recently, questions of the location and nature of power and authority have been reconnected to larger narratives of secularization and historical transformation. The work of Ernst Kantorowicz on the medieval idea of the king's two bodies, the mortal individual body and the "body politic" or "pompous body," which exceeds him and outlasts him, has provided a fertile ground for theorists like Santner:

> The crucial thought at the heart of the doctrine of the King's Two Bodies is that within the framework of the political theology of sovereignty, the signifiers that represent the subject for other signifiers are, so to speak, "backed" or "underwritten" by the sublime flesh, the sacral soma, of the monarch. With the demise of the political theology of kingship, this "personal" source of libidinal credit disappears. Postmonarchical societies are then faced with the problem of *securing the flesh* of the new bearer of the principle of sovereignty, the People. Biopolitics—and its near relative disciplinary power—can be grasped as the strategies deployed by modern societies to secure this new underwriting arrangement.[138]

Santner's account can be read as a secularization narrative that focuses on continuities between the Middle Ages and modernity. It stresses the paradigmatic moment of the end of monarchy following both the progressive Renaissance and Enlightenment narrative (emergence from medieval darkness to the dawn of a better day) and the Marxist story (the transition from feudalism to capitalism as a movement from one form of economic exploitation to another, but no less revolutionary for all that). Here we transition from one form of investment in a system of signifiers to another, with emphasis on what persists through the transition: not exploitation, but a need for security in one's identity and place in the world.

The political anthropologist Pierre Clastres asked this question: "What explains the transition from non-coercive political power to coercive political power, and how does the transition come about?"[139] For Clastres, the contortions of Western political theory around power, utopia, and human nature seem ridiculous in the light of anthropological fieldwork: "One is confronted ... by a vast constellation of societies in which the holders of what elsewhere would be called power are actually without power; where the political is determined as a domain beyond coercion and violence, beyond hierarchical subordination; where . . . no relationship of command-obedience is in force."[140] Clastres criticizes Western ethnography for its question-begging treatment of "archaic" societies as "without power"; this presupposes political power as already identified with the relation of command and obedience and the attendant violence of that relation. In Clastres's wider perspective, political power is universal and can take forms other than domination. The question then becomes, "What causes domination?" We might even ask why anyone ever believed in divine-right monarchy at all. This is a question that theopolitics claims to answer.

Buber's theopolitical history of Israel enfolds into it an explanation of the transition from noncoercive to coercive power. Buber is closer to classical Western political theory than to Clastres's anthropology, since he conceives of anarchic freedom as a difficult struggle rather than presupposing it as an ordinary state in which many societies persist in a relatively untroubled way.[141] Nonetheless, Buber provides a clear account of the rise of systematic coercion and violence in Israelite society, which shares elements with Landauer's *Revolution* and Oppenheimer's *The State*. The tribes fail to overcome a military threat through uniting as in the past. Meanwhile, corruption of the nondynastic principle opens a door for the institution of a human dynasty. The warrior capable of repelling the enemy is offered the kingship. Previous victorious generals refused such a position, but years of oppression under foreign powers have weakened the understanding of freedom in divine sovereignty that made those refusals possible. Initially, the human king is a mere viceroy of YHVH, the true king; his power is checked by the prophets who speak in the divine name. But the kings soon bring about a secularization that precludes the involvement of YHVH in politics except through the king's mediation, authorized by the new political theology of sovereignty. The de facto secularization is covered up through the royally sponsored Temple cult. The prophets denounce the kings and the Temple, foretelling the appearance of a good king who will carry out his function, but they achieve only minimal concessions, frequently being ignored or harassed unto death. Eventually, the monarchy fails to achieve even the very purpose for which it was instituted, the defense of Israel, and collapses in ignominy. At this point, some recall that Israel once had the wisdom to avoid the monarchical adventure completely, but others indulge in a nostalgic vision of past sovereign glory. A future king is imagined who will restore this glory to defeated Israel: the Messiah.

The Bible records this sorry tale, and the kingship psalms and exaltation of the Davidic line cannot completely erase the fact that the monarchy was born of fear and weakness and died in disgrace and dishonor. Following the dismal career of the Second Commonwealth, and the failed revolt against Rome, it was primarily Christians and Muslims who felt the need to legitimize sovereign power through political theology, and ultimately bury the human origins of the system of divine monarchy.[142] The canonical sites of a "modern" attitude to sovereignty, beginning perhaps in the Monarchomach treatises and continuing in Hobbes and Locke, often reinterpret 1 Samuel 8 and can be read as an effort to remember the human origins of monarchy so as to hold the king to his contractual commitments to the people.[143] But the public's recollection that it created the sovereign itself is traumatic, as Santner and other readers of Kantorowicz have shown, because it undermines the perception of a secure natural order of which the king was the linchpin, bringing to mind once again the fundamental groundlessness of all human orders. The specter of this groundlessness must be immediately abolished through the reestablishment of the natural order, this time in natural rights, the idea of the nation, and the invisible hand of the market. However, in modernity the human origins of the polity are not easily forgotten, thus the explosion of ideas and ideologies purporting to locate the ultimate ground or meaning of political life. The era of liberatory politics, wherein each new movement tries to outdo the previous one in terms of what it liberates, exemplifies this phenomenon: socialism denounces liberal rights as merely formal; classical anarchism views state socialism as a sham equality; poststructuralism declares the entire Western philosophical heritage, including the very concept of the subject, to be a stricture on our every thought and action. Even the attempts to acknowledge the groundlessness of political order seem to partake in this type of outflanking, through implicit claims that it is only through such acknowledgment that oppression can be defeated.

Theopolitics, by reminding us of the sovereignty of God, also reminds us of the groundlessness, which we would prefer to forget, of all human order. It does not provide a new foundation, but neither does it enjoin paralysis until we can discover the logical way out of the deadlock of outflanking. It absorbs the positivity of Nietzsche's stance along with his critique. Landauer once proclaimed, "Someone who understands and pronounces the ills of his times further increases them."[144] This Dionysian insight can also be found in a more pragmatic register, in the contemporary Jewish theologian Steven Kepnes:

> Modernity was and continues to be, in its transformed postmodern stage, an age of revolutions with promised utopias. . . . [A]ll these revolutions failed precisely because they were built on a rejection of that which came before them. And so we see the dialectic of rejection or repression of the past followed by the return of the repressed, in which the revolution is denied and the past reinstated. . . . The lesson of the political and philosophical revolutions of modernity and postmodernity is that it is impossible to move forward without taking the past with you. Taking the past into the future for the sake of the future, however, requires creative strategies—strategies of repetition, interpretation, and mediation—that sublimate and re-present the past as a usable past.[145]

This was the goal of Buber's theopolitical project: to repeat, interpret, and re-present the Jewish past as usable for the great Jewish awakening in which he saw himself involved. Buber absented himself from the debate between revolution and reform, speaking instead of "renewal." Renewal intervenes between break and continuity, between revolution and reform. By problematizing the parallels between religious and secular messianisms, it decouples apocalyptic messianism from social-prophetic commitment and distinguishes the redemptive vision of the wolf lying down with the lamb from the achievement of a society in which conflicts between individuals and groups no longer manifest on a macro level as an unjust political order. The question remains whether and how the failure of theopolitics in Buber's context, like the failures of so many other anarchisms, should be seen in light of its "successful" rival movements.

Zionism

> Everything, so he had taught, depends on living what one believes in; was he living what he believed in?
>
> —Martin Buber

> Rabbi Yitzhak Ze'ev ("Velvl") ha-Levi Soloveitchik of Brisk, who lived in Jerusalem, once heard a member of the Neturei Karta curse the State of Israel, to which he responded, "This man is a Zionist."
>
> —Aviezer Ravitzky

A Dream Betrayed versus the Telos of Settler Colonialism

Despite the dramatic changes, literal and political, in the Israeli-Palestinian landscape over the past half century, the issues pertaining to the essential nature of the conflict are still framed in ways that recall the debates of the 1920s and 1930s. This is because the logic of the conflict has never changed. Zionists still think of their situation in terms of physical security: their "right to exist" as a community in their ancestral land. Palestinians continue to see themselves as resisting Zionist encroachment on their ancestral land, and continue to face a whole apparatus of processes that prevent them from moving freely, accessing essential public goods, and exercising collective power. Even though the borders of the State of Israel have been uncertain for decades, every new conflict seems to result in shrinking the land claimed by the Palestinians. The rhetoric in each community, too, still reflects the old divides: the Jewish factions debate which actions are most likely to preserve their Jewish polity; the Palestinians, which methods of resistance will succeed in salvaging Palestinian land and gaining Palestinian independence. The narrowness of contemporary discourse about Zionism is a commonplace of that discourse itself; one bloc continues to treat Zionism as a morally obligatory position, and the other treats it as morally proscribed.

Buber is ritually invoked by Jewish activists seeking to buttress their positions, but there is no true heir to his distinct position among today's social movements. Judith Butler provides evidence for this claim when she simultaneously observes that Buber's politics read as "anti-Zionist" today and that he was deluded from the beginning about the nature of Zionism, since his ideals of cooperation simply could not be achieved under conditions of settler colonialism. He is thus too radical for the liberal Zionists and too Zionist for the anti-Zionists. This polarization of discourse might be a logical outcome of historical events. Because most Zionists wanted Jews to dominate the land, to own it as property, to achieve an ethnic majority in it, to establish a sovereign government over it, we should define Zionism according to their goals rather than those of Buber and his comrades in the "radical coterie" of Brit Shalom, a tiny minority within a tiny minority in the movement. This conclusion poses serious problems, however, since we cannot understand Buber without describing his thought as a form of Zionism, nor can we easily define his thought in other terms.[146] Thus, it seems that it must remain a Zionism. But was it deluded?

James Horrox sees the kibbutzim as examples of successful anarcho-socialist organization, at least internally, that could potentially have formed the lasting infrastructure of the new Yishuv as a whole. "The fact that this vision would ultimately not come to fruition . . . is attributable to a series of larger-scale betrayals that occurred during the British Mandate period, as the dream pursued by the early communards was systematically manipulated and hijacked by the emerging Zionist institutions of the state-to-be."[147] From Gershon Shafir's perspective, however, this is naïve. The kibbutzim were never more than a means to what the World Zionist Organization called "national colonization," or "pure settlement." The kibbutzim solved the dual problem of providing land and labor for unpropertied Jewish immigrants, thus serving the economic and demographic needs of the movement. The *moshavot*, the plantation-based system of the First Aliyah, were modeled on Arab agricultural methods: field-crop rotation, mostly grains, intended for local consumption, but the yields of the methods were too low to sustain the settlers' desired "European standard of living," and they appealed to sponsors for subsidies. These subsidies came with strings attached in the form of agricultural reforms; under Rothschild the *moshavot* switched to cash crops, international market orientation, and monoculture. This situation necessitated a more intense level of labor and a "large, seasonal, and low-priced labor force," composed either of Arabs or Jews. Despite these strategies, the returns of the *moshavot* did not satisfy their investors, and they were ultimately judged failures. Against this background, the kibbutz alternative was not necessarily an ideological reaction on the part of idealistic Second Aliyah immigrants to the exploitative nature of *moshavi* labor. The kibbutz and the "conquest of labor" allowed for the profits of Jewish colonies to remain in Jewish hands:

The political questions would find their solution once most of the land in Palestine was in Jewish hands, most of the population was Jewish, the Jews dominated the economy, especially agriculture, and the Jewish residents demanded autonomy. Demography and agricultural work were interconnected in assuring control of land. These were the operative conclusions of Arthur Ruppin's 1907 plan, upon the submission of which he was appointed to head the Palestine Office, in 1908.[148]

Franz Oppenheimer's *moshav* at Merhavia, from which the first *kvutza*, Degania, split off a year later (citing objections to wage labor and hierarchical management), was founded under the auspices of this plan, and as such the kibbutz must be seen as a colonial enterprise from the outset. Horrox awkwardly concedes the point that the kibbutz movement was betrayed not only by the forces of state socialism but also "by the underlying reality that Zionism was, from the outset, in the service of colonialism."[149] A nexus of economic and demographic interests accounts both for the militarization of the settlements and for the eventual agreement of the Zionist labor movement to territorial partition, maximizing Jewish population density by reducing the land area of the new state: "It was precisely the acknowledgment of the conflict of real interests that led the Jewish immigrants to transform their position as combatants in a clash of forces into one of champions of a socially, psychologically, and ultimately a morally coherent and legitimating vision."[150] Liberal Zionists like to distinguish themselves from more radical (and thus illegitimate) critics of the State of Israel by saying that the problem is 1967 (the date of the Six-Day War and the beginning of the occupation of the West Bank and Gaza), whereas for these other critics, the problem is 1948 (the existence of the State of Israel itself). If we were to extend this practice of using individual dates to stand in for ways of conceptualizing when things went wrong, we might initially say that for Buber, as for Horrox, the problem is 1917, the date that imperial and statist forces initiated a long-term program of control over the Zionist project. For Shafir, however, and for others like him, the problem is 1882: settlement in colonies.

A teleological conception of Zionist development, as emerging necessarily from the socioeconomic conditions on the ground, strikes at the heart of Brit Shalom ideology, more deeply than the contingent fact that they failed to find interlocutors. In its thoroughgoing materialism, this idea contrasts more starkly with Buber's perspective than does the usual leftist claim that Zionism, only superficially socialist and secular, was in reality indebted to romantic, *völkisch* nationalism.[151] Here we have a flat denial of the relevance of ideology to the course of events. However, such an attitude is just as inappropriate in the Zionist context as in the so-called German *Sonderweg* (special path), a term used to designate a controversy about the distinct historical trajectory of Germany among European nations, or in the classic "Whig interpretation of history," which imagines all historical events as building inevitably toward greater freedom and enlightenment. At the start of World War I, Zionism was in a precarious position. The majority of the thirty-five thousand Second Aliyah settlers (themselves only a tiny fraction of the overall emigration of millions of Jews from Eastern Europe to points west, primarily the United States, during the same period) had given up, leaving the movement with more emigrants than immigrants.[152] It was not inevitable that the Ottoman Empire would collapse, that Britain would issue the Balfour Declaration and receive the Mandate for Palestine, that the Palestinian Arab politicians would be so ineffectual, or that Hitler would come to power in Germany.

Shalom Ratzabi has written that "the political and social worldview of the members of the radical coterie in Brit Shalom was shaped and formed at the end of the First World War. The ingredients of this worldview can be understood as a coherent doctrine based on their connection to religious socialism, rather than on the basis of reality in Palestine from the time of their *Aliyah* until the establishment of the State."[153] This is certainly true. But Buber and Brit Shalom addressed themselves not to the Arab movement, which they understood no better than did their Zionist contemporaries, but to their own movement, which they understood well enough. Regarding Brit Shalom's much-discussed failure to find Arab interlocutors, a better question might be whether it could have convinced the Zionist movement of its claims. There is reason to doubt this, given the different experiences of the Central European Zionists, who hailed from a multiethnic urban milieu, and the Russian Zionists, who had borne the brunt of ethnic powerlessness before 1917. But even if the discursive environment was unfavorable to Brit Shalom's aims, this does not require a teleological interpretation of Zionist history.

From a historical point of view, anarchism was a negligible force in Palestine, where it was outmaneuvered, just as in Germany, not by fascism but by social democracy. Ben-Gurion and the Histadrut, the eventual power base of the Mapai party, co-opted the kibbutzim and transformed them into state-building institutions. That this was so easily done should deeply concern the partisans of the anarchist version of the kibbutz vision. That it had to be done is something that should give pause to those who see the kibbutz movement as nothing but a tool for settler colonialism.[154] And it raises a question for Butler's contention that "the most consequential blindness in Buber's position . . . was that he could not see the impossibility of trying to cultivate certain ideals of cooperation on conditions established by settler colonialism."[155] That question is: If certain ideals of cooperation cannot be cultivated under settler colonialism, are other ideals of cooperation possible? If so, what distinguishes these separate sets of ideals? If not, is this a counsel of despair to any contemporary efforts at decolonization, which must surely take cooperative forms?[156]

Religious Zionism versus Post-Zionism

Buber rarely discusses religious Zionism. His polemics were usually directed against Labor and Revisionism, the primary Zionist camps in his lifetime. However, he devotes a few extraordinary pages to the praise of Rabbi Abraham Isaac Kook. Buber did not fully endorse Kook's position, which he saw as necessary but one sided:

> The significance of the regaining of the land of Israel by the people of Israel is to be understood on three levels, each of which, however, only reveals its full meaning in connection with the other two. On the first level it is acknowledged that the people can only in the land achieve its own existence again; on the second, that it is only there that it will rediscover its own work, the free creative function of its spirit; on the third, that it needs the land in order to regain its holiness. The first stage, taken by itself, results in a narrow political view, the second by itself in a narrow intellectual view and the third by itself in a narrow religious view. All three must be taken together if we are to understand what is meant by the rebirth of the Jewish people.[157]

Buber associates Rav Kook with the third stage. This earns him the honor of being the man "in whose person, as in that of no other contemporary, the holy substance of Israel has been incorporated." Rav Kook also acknowledges the "claims of holiness in the national movement to a greater extent than anyone else in the Zionist thought of our time, without making it the object of a constricting religious requirement." Rav Kook recognizes that "the mysteries always teach us to combine the holy with the profane."[158] This leads him to understand the importance of reasserting the holiness of nature and the body, and to denounce both the spirituality that stands aloof from the material as well as the secular rebellion against that spirituality. In the future, these contending parties will realize that they both need and complement each other.

Rav Kook impresses Buber by his understanding that the secular rebellion needs to be radical, since it was caused by the prior repression of "pure" spirituality. For Rav Kook, this rebellion indicates the birth pangs of the Messiah. Buber presents Rav Kook's messianism as similar to his own; Rav Kook's "I see with my own eyes the light of the life of Elijah rising" echoes his own confidence that the seeds of the future redemption are contained in the present. However, Rav Kook's messianism carries within it a strong sense of "the irony of history," which functions in a way similar to Hegel's "cunning of reason."[159] Individual intentions are detached from their consequences, and they can contribute, unbeknownst to themselves, to a larger process. It is unclear whether Buber intentionally played down this feature of Rav Kook's thought. Buber's own position seems much closer to that of the Gurer Rebbe, who said of Rav Kook that "his love of Zion is so excessive that he deems pure what is impure and treats it favorably [BT Eruvin 136,] . . . and this is the source of the strange things he says in his writings."[160] Little in Buber's work on Zionism suggests that one can contribute to a "messianic process" in spite of oneself, but we do find a commitment to what is valuable in the thoughts and actions of contending parties.

Buber did not live to see Gush Emunim (Bloc of the Faithful) become an important player in Israeli-Palestinian affairs. It is well known that in the hands of Zvi Yehuda Kook, the thought of Rav Kook the elder was transformed as it was translated into political action. Aviezer Ravitzky has described this transformation as "overcoming tensions and avoiding questions that Kook left open."[161] We will never know what Rav Kook, the man who said that "it is not for Jacob to engage in political life as long as statehood requires bloody ruthlessness and demands a talent for evil," and who perceived the reemergence of the Jewish polity as necessarily coextensive with the eschaton itself, would have thought of his son's contention that "a land under the dominion and sovereignty of a people— this is a state. The Torah commands us to have a State, and if there is a need for conquest and war to fulfill this, then we are compelled to do so. This is one of the 613 precepts of the Torah."[162] Had Buber witnessed the growth of militant religious Zionism, he might have sharpened his theopolitics to combat this new political theology.

From the theopolitical standpoint, Gush Emunim only seems to oppose secularization. To be sure, it benefits from the secular state's indulgence of whatever claims to support Jewish interests while also furthering its own. Here I would recall Buber's claim that one can worship YHVH as an idol, either as Baal or as Molech. Baalism pays lip service to YHVH but tries to stand simultaneously on two branches, granting the reign over some realms of life to Baal. Molechism strives to outdo everyone else in the worship of YHVH, but in the process it makes YHVH into an idol, along with the land, the people, and the Torah. If Buber's religious Zionism seems close at times to that of the right, it is the closeness of theopolitics and political theology, of *melekh* and *molekh*. It is a closeness separated by an unbridgeable gap, as if an ouroboros could not quite bite its own tail.

This does not bring Buber any closer to the post-Zionist or anti-Zionist enemies of religious Zionism, however, as long as they also subscribe to the binary that pits the religious and particular on one side against the secular and universal on the other. The liberal refrain that religion is the problem in the Israel-Palestine conflict, and that religion must be "kept out of it," stems from the success of religious Zionism in claiming the territory that secular Zionism abandoned. The checkered relationship between Judaism and Zionism, which for years was led by antireligious radicals and opposed by religious Jews, has been covered over by a new normality in which Judaism and Zionism become virtually identical. Interested observers with superficial knowledge of the history of the conflict make similar claims about the supposedly detrimental role of Islam while ignoring the relative novelty and innovation embodied in the claims of Hamas that Palestine is an Islamic *waqf* (endowment) and more holy than other lands.[163] Public conversation today is generally hospitable to claims that the more religious one is, the more maximalist and uncompromising one must be. Buber's Zionism attempts to transcend this binary. As Marc Ellis has written, Buber's view of renewal and regeneration "occurs in relation to history, to the land, and to the people who inherited the land"; he does not seek to overcome all three by abolishing history in an immanent eschaton. Regeneration "represents the rebirth of Jewish witness and values: survival without witness can only be seen as failure."[164] But this "witness" that Buber can provide cannot mean insisting on coexistence while also allowing every possibility for coexistence to be attacked and destroyed:

> Addressing conciliatory words to others and occupying oneself with humane projects is not the way to make peace. We make peace ... wherever we are destined and summoned to do so: in the active life of our own community and in that aspect of it which can actively help determine its relationship to another community. The prophecy of peace addressed to Israel is not valid only for the days of the coming of the Messiah. It holds for the day when the people will again be summoned to take part in shaping the destiny of its earliest home; it holds for today. "And if not now, when?" (Ethics of the Fathers, 1:14). Fulfillment in a Then is inextricably bound up with fulfillment in the Now.[165]

Conclusion: On Being Late Born

In the introduction to *Legend of the Baal-Shem*, Buber said that he interpreted Hasidic stories as one *Nachgeborenen*, or late born. Despite his active role in Zionism from its beginning, however, a sense of too-lateness attends his Zionist career as well. Gustav Landauer's criticism induced his profound philosophical and political about-face in 1916, when Buber was already famous for his Hasidic tales and his Prague lectures. The Balfour Declaration was issued just a year later, and one year after that Buber wrote that the argument "we must create by all means a majority [of Jews in Palestine] as soon as possible" caused his heart to "stand still." In 1919, while Buber was attempting to interest Landauer in the potential of cooperative settlement in Palestine, David Ben-Gurion and Berl Katznelson were founding the Achdut Haavoda (United Labor), the core of what would soon become the Histadrut; meanwhile, the newly formed Muslim-Christian Association was voicing Arab demands for sovereignty, the unity of Palestine with Syria, and the rejection of the Balfour Declaration. The third text in Mendes-Flohr's collection of Buber's writings on Jews and Arabs was already entitled "At this Late Hour."[166] In 1925, when Brit Shalom was formed, mainstream Zionists had already given up on dialogue with Arabs; the British Mandate was in full swing, and the left wing of the Gedud Haavoda (Labor Battalion) had already lost out to the Achdut-dominated Histadrut in its effort to hold its kibbutzim to the values of decentralization and Arab solidarity.[167] By the time Buber arrived in Palestine, in 1938, the hour truly was late. The countryside was in the throes of the Arab Revolt; the battle lines were drawn and his own message had less traction than ever. Without absolving Buber of all responsibility for the failure of his politics, one may ask how he could have pursued his own goals in a way that was more Buberian—a more interesting approach, perhaps, than simply enumerating the historical obstacles he faced.

The most common criticism of Buber's Zionism among those who were sympathetic to it was that he did not live up to his own creed. He did not move to Palestine until forced to flee Germany. This criticism was repeated many times by Scholem, once in 1961 at a celebration on the occasion of the completion of Buber's German translation of the Bible. At the event, Scholem remarked that the translation served also as a commentary: "Time and again when we have encountered difficult sections of the Bible many of us have asked ourselves: What does Buber have to say about this? Not so very different from our asking ourselves: What does Rashi say?"[168] Of course, Scholem's praise was not without a word of criticism on its place in its historical context. The language of Buber's translation was not merely the German of the 1920s but a kind of utopian German, a German "present potentially in the language." The collaboration with Rosenzweig made the translation a *Gastgeschenk*, a guest offering to the German people from the Jews, represented by a Zionist and a non-Zionist. Yet Scholem felt compelled to ask: "For whom is this translation now intended and whom will it influence? Seen historically, it is no longer a *Gastgeschenk* of the Jews to the Germans but rather—and it is not easy for me to say this—the tombstone of a relationship that was extinguished in unspeakable horror. The Jews for whom you translated are no more. Their children, who have escaped from this horror, will no longer read German."[169] There is a criticism implicit in this question: Buber was too deeply invested in Germany to honor his own Zionist convictions by coming to Palestine and treating Palestine as the future center of Jewry. Instead, he gave the Germans a utopian Bible—a gift they had not requested and now could not accept.

Scholem has a point. Most of Buber's Prague disciples preceded him to Palestine by many years. Hugo Bergmann arrived in 1920; Hans Kohn in 1925 (although he left again in 1934); Ernst Simon in 1928. Only Robert Weltsch waited as long as Buber, before moving to London in 1945, and only Max Brod arrived later, in 1939. What kept Buber in Germany? Perhaps simply his personality: he was a Central European intellectual, not a Levantine activist. Or he may have felt called on to engage the political-theological problematics of Germany, through his translation work with Rosenzweig, his editorship of *Die Kreatur*, and the "spiritual resistance" of Jewish adult education in the Nazi period. One could also accuse his Zionism of failing to meet his own standards. He allowed himself to indulge in certain Labor Zionist illusions about imaginary differences in attitudes between the Arab fellahin and the rich effendis supposedly inciting them to anti-Zionism, and occasionally succumbed to the romantic notion of "making the desert bloom." But all these criticisms touch upon his personal failings only as a politician. There is a bittersweet irony when one advocates practicing what one preaches and fails oneself to follow this precept. But if hypocrisy can be praised as the lip service vice pays to virtue, then mere failure should be treated more generously.

Zionism may have been a largely secular movement, but except in its most extreme Revisionist forms, it always tried to point beyond itself. Herzl himself expressed this in his liberal universalist way; he too saw Zionism as aiming at more than national survival. The Jewish state was meant to "redound mightily and beneficially to the good of all mankind."[170] In his utopian novel *Old-New Land* he has a character tell the farmers of a small settlement that without "tolerance," "your cultivation is worthless and your fields will revert to barrenness."[171] For both the Labor Zionists and the Brit Shalom circle, Zionism was about not merely saving Jewish bodies but also altering the Jewish soul. Both stressed immigration and settlement, but the commitment to an overarching moral imperative meant different things to Brit Shalom and to the Labor Zionists. Here is the criterion by which to distinguish liberal-socialist Zionism from Buber's position: where a conflict of interest was unavoidable, the former defended recourse to violence and the assertion of Zionist interests as tragic but necessary. Buber was not a pacifist, but he did hold that if recourse to violence seemed necessary, then the path that led to that decision was morally faulty in some way. Immediate correction was required to foreclose similar "tragically necessary" choices in the future. It seems to me that this is the test that Buber never failed; this is the difference tested in the theopolitical hour.

Notes

1. Jean-François Lyotard, *The Postmodern Condition: A Report on Knowledge*, trans. Geoff Bennington and Brian Massumi (Minneapolis: University of Minnesota Press, 1984); John Rawls, *Political Liberalism: Expanded Edition* (New York: Columbia University Press, 2005).

2. Francis Fukuyama, *The End of History and the Last Man* (New York: Free Press, 1992); Samuel Huntington, *The Clash of Civilizations and the Remaking of World Order* (New York: Simon & Schuster, 1996).

3. David Frum and Richard Perle, *An End to Evil: How to Win the War on Terror* (New York: Ballantine, 2004), 35.

4. The secularization thesis has been defined as the idea that "modernization necessarily leads to a decline of religion, both in society and in the minds of individuals"; Peter L. Berger, ed., *The Desecularization of the World: Resurgent Religion and World Politics* (Grand Rapids, MI: William B. Eerdmans, 1999), 2. Cf. Talal Asad, *Formations of the Secular: Christianity, Islam, Modernity* (Stanford, CA: Stanford University Press, 2003).

5. Karl Mannheim, *Ideology and Utopia: An Introduction to the Sociology of Knowledge*, trans. Louis Wirth and Edward Shils (New York: Harvest, 1936); Karl Löwith, *Meaning in History: The Theological Implications of the Philosophy of History* (Chicago: University of Chicago Press, 1957).

6. Hans Blumenberg, *The Legitimacy of the Modern Age*, trans. Robert M. Wallace (Cambridge, MA: MIT Press, 1985).

7. Eric L. Santner, *The Royal Remains: The People's Two Bodies and the Endgames of Sovereignty* (Chicago: University of Chicago Press, 2011), 31. David Nirenberg has urged caution

toward Pauline discourse, given the centrality of "Judaism" as a figure of error in Paul; Niren-berg, *Anti-Judaism: The Western Tradition* (New York: W. W. Norton & Co., 2013), 60, 490n21.

8. Jeffrey Stout raises this point in a discussion of the term "democracy," which is seen by some as an unrealized goal, by others as a system that must be destroyed, and by "the ideo-logues of capital and empire" as the name of the best possible form of political organization. Stout, *Blessed Are the Organized: Grassroots Democracy in America* (Princeton, NJ: Princeton University Press, 2010), 248–250.

9. Santner, *The Royal Remains*, xii.

10. Buber, "Three Theses of a Religious Socialism," in PW 113.

11. Martina Urban, *Aesthetics of Renewal: Martin Buber's Early Representation of Hasidism as* Kulturkritik (Chicago: University of Chicago Press, 2008), 1.

12. Gershom Scholem, "Martin Buber's Interpretation of Hasidism," in *The Messianic Idea in Judaism and Other Essays on Jewish Spirituality* (New York: Schocken Books, 1995), 229, 247.

13. MBLY 284.

14. Scholem, "Martin Buber's Conception of Judaism," in *On Jews and Judaism in Crisis*, ed. Werner J. Dannhauser (New York: Schocken Books, 1976), 167.

15. Rivka Schatz-Uffenheimer, "Man's Relation to God and World in Buber's Rendering of the Hasidic Teaching," in *The Philosophy of Martin Buber*, ed. Paul Arthur Schilpp and Mau-rice Friedman (La Salle, IL: Open Court Press, 1967), 403–434.

16. While Scholem expanded his criticism after Buber's death to cover the latter's broader conception of Judaism, references to the "Buber-Scholem controversy" tend to restrict them-selves to the Hasidism debate. Scholem, "Martin Buber's Conception of Judaism," 126–171.

17. David Biale, *Gershom Scholem: Kabbalah and Counter-History* (Cambridge, MA: Har-vard University Press, 1979), 165–170.

18. K. E. Grözinger, "The Buber-Scholem Controversy about Hasidic Tale and Hasidism— Is There a Solution?" in *Gershom Scholem's "Major Trends in Jewish Mysticism" 50 Years After: Proceedings of the Sixth International Conference on the History of Jewish Mysticism*, ed. Peter Schäfer and Joseph Dan (Tübingen: J. C. B. Mohr, 1993), 327–336.

19. Scholem, "Martin Buber's Interpretation of Hasidism," 231, 235.

20. Benjamin Lazier, *God Interrupted: Heresy and the European Imagination Between the World Wars* (Princeton, NJ: Princeton University Press, 2008), 21–22.

21. With the discovery of the Nag Hammadi library in 1945, scholars had direct access to "gnostic" texts, unmediated by the descriptions of the church fathers. However, as Karen King has written, modern historiography has often shared the heresiological assumptions of the Church Fathers themselves; King, *What Is Gnosticism?* (Cambridge, MA: Harvard University Press, 2003), 2, 200.

22. Scholem, "Martin Buber's Interpretation of Hasidism," 245.

23. Perhaps Scholem is describing the Buber of 1915, whose exaltation of kinesis enabled him to endorse war as a transcendental *Erlebnis*. This was the Buber against whom Scholem first rebelled, and he may never have believed that Buber changed. Regardless, it is significant that Scholem permits himself to refer to this view as an anarchism.

24. Scholem, "Martin Buber's Hasidism, a Critique," *Commentary* 32 (1961): 315.

25. This may be due to its generally "scientific" presentation, which impressed Scholem even as he saw through it, calling it "pneumatic exegesis with learned notes." Scholem, "Martin Buber's Conception of Judaism," 165.

26. Scholem to Buber, June 29, 1932, in LMB 385–387.

27. Scholem, "On the 1930 Edition of Rosenzweig's *Star of Redemption*," in *The Messianic Idea in Judaism*, 320–324.

28. KG 118–119.

29. Scholem, "On the 1930 Edition of Rosenzweig's *Star of Redemption*," 323.

30. Biale, *Gershom Scholem*, 7. Contrast to Scholem's portrayal of Zionism and messianism, for both of which he employed the singular; Moshe Idel, "Messianic Scholars: On Early Israeli Scholarship, Politics and Messianism," *Modern Judaism* 32.1 (February 2012): 32.

31. Myers, "The Scholem-Kurzweil Debate and Modern Jewish Historiography," *Modern Judaism* 6.3 (October 1986): 261–286.

32. Scholem's article appeared in response to a solicitation by *Commentary* editor Norman Podhoretz for criticism of what he called "the Buber cult."

33. Buber, "Prophecy, Apocalyptic, and the Historical Hour," in PW 198.

34. Ibid., 201. Cf. Hannah Arendt, *The Human Condition* (Chicago: University of Chicago Press, 1998), 9, 247.

35. Scholem, "Martin Buber's Conception of Judaism," 163–164.

36. Scholem's neglect of PU may reflect his reluctance to discuss his differences with Buber on politics generally and Zionism in particular.

37. PU 10.

38. Ibid., 7–8.

39. Scholem, *From Berlin to Jerusalem: Memoirs of My Youth*, trans. Harry Zohn (New York: Schocken, 1980), 53–54.

40. Recall Buber's sneering summation of the pro-monarchical refrain in Judges: "One sees the shrugging of shoulders, hears the superior, regretful tone: 'At that time they simply didn't have a king in Israel!'" KG 82.

41. Idel, "Messianic Scholars," 22.

42. Ibid., 40.

43. Lazier, *God Interrupted*, 33.

44. Ibid., 44–45.

45. Buber, *Two Types of Faith*, trans. Norman Goldhawk (Syracuse, NY: Syracuse University Press, 2003)

46. He did write that *Two Types of Faith* was Buber's "weakest book." Scholem, "Martin Buber's Conception of Judaism," 164.

47. Jacob Taubes, *The Political Theology of Paul*, trans. Dana Hollander, ed. Aleida Assmann and Jan Assmann, in conjunction with Horst Folkers, Wolf-Daniel Hartwich, and Christoph Schulte (Stanford, CA: Stanford University Press, 2004), 48.

48. Jacob Taubes, "Buber and Philosophy of History," in *Philosophy of Martin Buber*, 451–468.

49. By the 1980s, however, Taubes had come to see Hegel's concept of world-spirit as advanced against Paul; *Political Theology of Paul*, 43.

50. Taubes points out that already in the generation of the Young Hegelians, Moses Hess, whom Buber singles out in *On Zion* as his own forerunner, had criticized Hegel and Marx for their historical determinism. "Buber and Philosophy of History," 458.

51. Ibid., 460.

52. Ibid., 462.

53. Ibid., 467.

54. Ibid., 460.

55. Buber might respond that the energy and motivation imparted by apocalyptic conviction are related to despair and the yearning for success: apocalypticism promises imminent victory in a way that the prophetic cannot. Thus it creates an energy, which savvy politicians can harness, but it cannot create the new world it desires.

56. Taubes, *Political Theology of Paul*, 50.

57. Scholem, *Major Trends in Jewish Mysticism* (New York: Schocken, 1995), 287–324.

58. Taubes, *Political Theology of Paul*, 5.

59. Ibid., 6–7.

60. Ibid., 7 (original italics).

61. Such a philological investigation was later undertaken by David Flusser, who concluded that while Buber's etymological distinction between *pistis* and *emunah* was invalid, his "basic position" is correct if considered to describe an internal Christian problem (the problem of the faith of Jesus versus the faith in Jesus). Flusser, afterword to *Two Types of Faith*, 175–235.

62. Taubes, *Political Theology of Paul*, 10.

63. Ibid., 39, 47.

64. Taubes understands that Schmitt recognizes the same problematic as he does but responds in the opposite manner; ibid., 103.

65. Excepting Freud for the moment, a "direct descendant of Paul" through his grappling with guilt; ibid., 89.

66. Ibid., 75.

67. Ibid., 54.

68. Walter Benjamin, "Theological-Political Fragment," in *Walter Benjamin: Selected Writings*, vol. 3, *1935–1938*, trans. Edmund Jephcott et al., ed. Howard Eiland and Michael W. Jennings (Cambridge, MA: Harvard University Press, 2006), 305–306.

69. Taubes, *Political Theology of Paul*, 71.

70. Ibid., 76.

71. Giorgio Agamben, *The Time That Remains: A Commentary on the Letter to the Romans*, trans. Patricia Dailey (Stanford, CA: Stanford University Press, 2005), 62.

72. Ibid., 61.

73. Ibid., 69. Agamben's vague reference to "a view fairly widespread in Judaism" depends problematically on Scholem's "Toward an Understanding of the Messianic Idea."

74. Ibid., 76. *Pleroma* of *kairoi* means something like "the fullness of times."

75. Agamben refers to Flusser's recontextualization of Buber's distinction as a problem in Christianity; ibid., 125–126.

76. Ibid., 27.

77. Ibid., 23.

78. Ibid., 23–24.

79. Walter Benjamin, "On the Concept of History," in *Walter Benjamin: Selected Writings*, vol. 4, *1938–1940*, trans. Edmund Jephcott et al., eds. Howard Eiland and Michael W. Jennings (Cambridge, MA: Belknap Press of Harvard University Press, 2006), 389.

80. Walter Benjamin, *Über den Begriff der Geschichte*, Walter Benjamin Werke und Nachlaß Kritische Gesamtausgabe 19, ed. Gérard Raulet (Berlin: Suhrkamp, 2010), 16, 59.

81. Agamben, *Time That Remains*, 33.

82. But see Brian Britt, "The Schmittian Messiah in Agamben's *The Time That Remains*," *Critical Inquiry* 36 (Winter 2010): 262–287.

83. Agamben, *Time That Remains*, 33.

84. Giorgio Agamben, *State of Exception*, trans. Kevin Attell (Chicago: University of Chicago Press, 2005), 64; Britt, "The Schmittian Messiah," 268; cf. Agamben, *Time That Remains*, 69–70, 145.

85. Leonard Cohen, *The Future*. © 1992 by Columbia Records, CK 53226. MP3.

86. Alain Badiou, *Saint Paul: The Foundation of Universalism*, trans. Ray Brassier (Stanford, CA: Stanford University Press, 2003), 2. Cf. Slavoj Žižek, *The Puppet and the Dwarf: The Perverse Core of Christianity* (Boston: MIT Press, 2003), 130.

87. Ibid., 59; cf. 1 Corinthians 1:22–24.

88. Ibid., 53–54.

89. Ibid., 7.

90. Agamben, *Time That Remains*, 52.

91. Badiou, *Saint Paul*, 88.

92. Ibid., 66.

93. KG 109.

94. Scholem, "Martin Buber's Conception of Judaism," 127.

95. Pierre Clastres, *Society against the State: Essays in Political Anthropology*, trans. Robert Hurley and Abe Stein (New York: Zone Books, 1987), 7.

96. CrimethInc. Ex-Workers' Collective, *Days of War, Nights of Love: Crimethink for Beginners* (Canada: CrimethInc. Free Press, 2001), 9.

97. CrimethInc. Ex-Workers' Collective, *Expect Resistance: A Field Manual* (Canada: 2008), 4.

98. CrimethInc. Ex-Workers' Collective, *Days of War, Nights of Love*, 34.

99. Murray Bookchin, *Social Anarchism or Lifestyle Anarchism: An Unbridgeable Chasm* (Oakland, CA: AK Press,1995). Bookchin's charges were answered bitterly by Bob Black, *Anarchy after Leftism* (Birmingham, UK: CAL Press, 1997), in what became known as the "lifestylist controversy." Bookchin was also answered by NietzsChe Guevara in *Lifestyle Monarchism*, a book that may or may not exist; *Days of War, Nights of Love*, 281.

100. Nadia C., "Face It, Your Politics Are Boring as Fuck," in *Days of War, Nights of Love*, 188–192.

101. Ibid., 244.

102. Michael Albert, *Parecon: Life after Capitalism* (London: Verso, 2003).

103. Richard J. F. Day, *Gramsci Is Dead: Anarchist Currents in the Newest Social Movements* (London: Pluto Press, 2005).

104. Subcomandante Marcos, *Our Word Is Our Weapon*, ed. Juan Ponce de León (New York: Seven Stories Press, 2001); cf. Staughton Lynd and Andrej Grubacic, *Wobblies & Zapatistas: Conversations on Anarchism, Marxism, and Radical History* (Oakland, CA: PM Press, 2008).

105. David Graeber, *Direct Action: An Ethnography* (Oakland, CA: AK Press, 2009).

106. Wes Enzinna, "A Dream of Secular Utopia in ISIS' Backyard," *New York Times Magazine*, November 24, 2015.

107. Nathan Schneider, "Occupation for Dummies: How It Came About, What It Means, How It Works and Everything," *Occupied Wall Street Journal*, Fall 2011; Kate Khatib, Margaret Killjoy, and Mike McGuire, eds., *We Are Many: Reflections on Movement Strategy from Occupation to Liberation* (Oakland, CA: AK Press, 2012).

108. Stout, *Blessed Are the Organized*, 19, 258, 303, 307, 311n72.

109. PU 24.

110. Ibid., 26.

111. Ibid., 36.

112. Ibid., 115.

113. Ibid., 38, 43.

114. Ibid., 96.

115. Ibid., 117.

116. Ibid., 81.

117. Ibid., 47.

118. Against Me! *Those Anarcho Punks Are Mysterious* . . . © 2002 by No Idea Records, NO IDEA 129. MP3.

119. PU 47.

120. Ibid., 104.

121. See the classic account of anarchist Barcelona in George Orwell, *Homage to Catalonia* (San Diego: Harcourt, Brace & Co., 1980); Sam Dolgoff, ed., *The Anarchist Collectives: Work-

ers' *Self-Management in the Spanish Revolution* (New York: Black Rose, 1990); Chris Ealham, *Anarchism and the City: Revolution and Counter-Revolution in Barcelona, 1898–1937* (Oakland, CA: AK Press, 2010); Frank Mintz, *Anarchism and Workers' Self-Management in Revolutionary Spain*, trans. Paul Sharkey (Oakland, CA: AK Press, 2013).

122. PU 129.

123. Jean-François Lyotard, "Judiciousness in Dispute, or Kant after Marx," trans. Cecile Lindsay, in *The Aims of Representation*, ed. Murray Krieger (New York: Columbia University Press, 1987), 64.

124. Michel Foucault, "The Politics of Soviet Crime (1976)," in *Foucault Live*, ed. Sylvere Lotringer, trans. Mollie Horwitz (New York: Semiotext[e], 1989), 130. Foucault is usually viewed as shifting away from a purely negative view of power. This quote thus illuminates the potential overlap between a fundamental affirmation of "power" and the traditional anarchist vocabulary of the destruction of its major manifestations, often described as the distinction between power and domination.

125. An oversimplified version of the thesis of Max Horkheimer and Theodor W. Adorno, in *Dialectic of Enlightenment*, ed. Gunzelin Schmid Noerr, trans. Edmund Jephcott (Stanford, CA: Stanford University Press, 2002).

126. On the reception of "French theory" as a consistent "ideology," see François Cusset, *French Theory: How Foucault, Derrida, Deleuze, & Co. Transformed the Intellectual Life of the United States*, trans. Jeff Fort (Minneapolis: University of Minnesota Press, 2008).

127. Stephen Eric Bronner, *Reclaiming the Enlightenment: Toward a Politics of Radical Engagement* (New York: Columbia University Press, 2004).

128. Michel Foucault, "On the Genealogy of Ethics," in *The Foucault Reader*, ed. Paul Rabinow (New York: Pantheon Books, 1984), 343; Noam Chomsky and Michel Foucault, *The Chomsky-Foucault Debate* (New York: New Press, 2006), 36–59.

129. Gabriel Kuhn, "Anarchism, Postmodernity, and Poststructuralism," in *Contemporary Anarchist Studies: An Introductory Anthology of Anarchy in the Academy*, eds. Randall Amster, Abraham DeLeon, Luis A. Fernandez, Anthony J. Nocella II, and Deric Shannon (New York: Routledge, 2009), 18–25.

130. Todd May, *The Political Philosophy of Poststructuralist Anarchism*, (University Park, PA: Penn State University Press, 1994) 3–4; May, "Anarchism from Foucault to Rancière," in *Contemporary Anarchist Studies*, 11–17.

131. May, *Poststructuralist Anarchism*, 14.

132. Saul Newman, *From Bakunin to Lacan: Anti-Authoritarianism and the Dislocation of Power* (New York: Lexington Books, 2001), 7; Saul Newman, *The Politics of Postanarchism* (Edinburgh: Edinburgh University Press, 2010).

133. Day, *Gramsci Is Dead*, 16.

134. Badiou, *Saint Paul*, 76.

135. Eric L. Santner, *On the Psychotheology of Everyday Life: Reflections on Freud and Rosenzweig* (Chicago: University of Chicago Press, 2001), 57.

136. Ibid., 27.

137. Ibid., 63.

138. Santner, *The Royal Remains*, xv. The reference is to Ernst H. Kantorowicz, *The King's Two Bodies: A Study in Medieval Political Theology* (Princeton, NJ: Princeton University Press, 2007).

139. Clastres, *Society against the State*, 24.

140. Ibid., 11–12.

141. Buber's criticisms of biblical scholars parallel Clastres's critique of ethnology. Buber argues that contemporary biblical scholars cannot recognize power in premonarchical Israel,

because "Israel," a name that applies to the confederation of tribes only when it comes together to perform a task for YHVH, is more like the Iroquois League than the Germany of the kaiser.

142. On Muslim political theology, see Aziz al-Azmeh, *Muslim Kingship: Power and the Sacred in Muslim, Christian and Pagan Polities* (London: I. B. Tauris, 2001); cf. Wael B. Hallaq, *The Impossible State: Islam, Politics, and Modernity's Moral Predicament* (New York: Columbia University Press, 2012).

143. Eric Nelson, *The Hebrew Republic: Jewish Sources and the Transformation of European Political Thought* (Cambridge, MA: Harvard University Press, 2011). Premodern literature on kingship is rich with accounts of the king's duties to his people and to principles of justice. Theopolitics would see such literature primarily within the sphere defined by political theology. Hence the fierce reaction against Machiavelli's perceived corruption of mirror-for-princes literature, and against the Ottoman leadership when it appeared to abandon the classical Islamic Circle of Justice for European liberalism. Cf. Quentin Skinner, *The Foundations of Modern Political Thought*, Vols. 1–2 (Cambridge: Cambridge University Press, 1978), 128–138; Elizabeth F. Thompson, *Justice Interrupted: The Struggle for Constitutional Government in the Middle East* (Cambridge, MA: Harvard University Press, 2013), 17–19, 30–36; Wael B. Hallaq, *An Introduction to Islamic Law* (New York: Cambridge University Press, 2009), 72–75. Only with the modern period, symbolized by the French Revolution, does the delineation of kingly duties serve as a rationale for critique from a standpoint conceived as outside the political-theological order. As Michael Walzer has noted, kings were killed for centuries, without this ever amounting to an attack on the *arcana imperii*; Walzer, *Regicide and Revolution: Speeches at the Trial of Louis XVI*, trans. Marian Rothstein (New York: Columbia University Press, 1992), 5.

144. Gustav Landauer, *Revolution*, in *Revolution and Other Writings: A Political Reader*, ed. and trans. Gabriel Kuhn (Oakland, CA: PM Press, 2010), 138.

145. Steven Kepnes, *Jewish Liturgical Reasoning* (New York: Oxford University Press, 2007), 9.

146. Seeing "theopolitics" as a category central to Buber's political thinking should not obscure the fact that a certain form of Zionism was the major expression of this thinking.

147. James Horrox, *A Living Revolution: Anarchism in the Kibbutz Movement* (Oakland, CA: AK Press, 2009), 88.

148. Gershon Shafir, *Land, Labor and the Origins of the Israeli-Palestinian Conflict, 1882–1914* (Cambridge: Cambridge University Press, 1989), 154.

149. Horrox, *A Living Revolution*, 90.

150. Shafir, *Land, Labor, and the Origins*, 209.

151. Ze'ev Sternhell, *The Founding Myths of Israel: Nationalism, Socialism, and the Making of the Jewish State*, trans. David Maisel (Princeton, NJ: Princeton University Press, 1998).

152. Anita Shapira, *Land and Power: The Zionist Resort to Force, 1881–1948* (New York: Oxford University Press, 1992), 62.

153. Shalom Ratzabi, *Between Zionism and Judaism: The Radical Circle in Brith Shalom, 1925–1933* (Leiden: Brill, 2002), 424.

154. This question is separate from the fate of the movement's Marxists, who prioritized communism over nationalism.

155. Judith Butler, *Parting Ways: Jewishness and the Critique of Zionism* (New York: Columbia University Press, 2012), 36.

156. Butler's more recent work on Buber seeks to avoid such despair, arguing that "the political task is precisely to forfeit neither self-determination nor cohabitation." Butler, "Versions of Binationalism in Said and Buber," in *Conflicting Humanities*, ed. Rosi Braidotti and Paul Gilroy (New York: Bloomsbury Academic, 2016), 204. Or as Juliano Mer-Khamis put it, "There

is one and one thing only that really upsets and disbalances the Zionist regime[:] . . . Palestinians and Jews working shoulder to shoulder, and nothing else." Cited in Marcelo Svirsky, *Arab-Jewish Activism in Israel-Palestine* (Burlington, VT: Ashgate, 2012), ix. Mer-Khamis was a filmmaker, actor, and activist of mixed Jewish and Palestinian Christian descent; he was assassinated in Jenin in 2011. No group claimed responsibility.

157. Buber, *On Zion: The History of an Idea*, trans. Stanley Godman (Syracuse, NY: Syracuse University Press, 1997), 147–154.

158. According to Nahum Glatzer, Buber had manuscript notes of Rav Kook available to him in the preparation of this section; ibid., vii. If so, he had sources beyond *Orot*, which was criticized by Orthodox writers for lending aid and comfort to Zionist secularism by seeming to detach the holiness of the Zionist effort from obligations to halakha. Glatzer, introduction to *Orot*, by Abraham Isaac Kook, ed. and trans. Bezalel Naor (Northvale, NJ: Jason Aronson, 1993), 37.

159. Aviezer Ravitzky, *Messianism, Zionism, and Jewish Religious Radicalism*, trans. Michael Swirsky and Jonathan Chipman (Chicago: University of Chicago Press, 1996), 111.

160. Ibid., 110. This is the difference between Buber's prophetic eschatology and Scholem's disavowed apocalyptic messianism; cf. Amnon Raz-Krakotzkin, "The Golem of Scholem," in *Politik und Religion im Judentum*, ed. Christoph Miething (Tübingen: De Gruyter, 1999), 223–238.

161. Ravitzky, *Messianism, Zionism, and Jewish Religious Radicalism*, 123.

162. A. I. Kook, "The War," in Hertzberg, *The Zionist Idea: A Historical Analysis and Reader*, ed. Arthur Hertzberg (Philadelphia: Jewish Publication Society, 1997), 422; Z. Y. Kook, *Torat Eretz Yisrael: The Teachings of HaRav Tzvi Yehuda HaCohen Kook*, ed. and trans. Tzvi Fishman (Jerusalem: Torat Eretz Yisrael Publications, 1991), 287.

163. Andrea Nüsse, *Muslim Palestine: The Ideology of Hamas* (Amsterdam: Harwood Academic Publishers, 1998), 48.

164. Marc Ellis, *Towards a Jewish Theology of Liberation: The Challenge of the 21st Century*, 3rd ed. (Waco, TX: Baylor University Press, 2004), 189.

165. Buber, "And If Not Now, When?" in LTP 106.

166. The text, from April 1920, responds to the first major outbreak of Jewish-Arab violence in Palestine by warning that only by living up to its true socialist principles, adhering to nonviolence, and forming a joint front with the Arabs can Zionism avoid "the constant spiritual pogrom that threatens us in the Land of Israel." Buber, "At this Late Hour," LTP 41–46.

167. Viteles, *A History of the Co-operative Movement in Israel, Book One: The Evolution of the Co-operative Movement* (London: Vallentine, Mitchell & Co., 1966), 78; Henry Near, *The Kibbutz Movement: A History*, vol. 1, *Origins and Growth, 1909–1939* (Oxford: Oxford University Press, 1992), 63, 78.

168. Gershom Scholem, "At the Completion of Buber's Bible Translation," in *The Messianic Idea in Judaism and Other Essays on Jewish Spirituality* (New York: Schocken Books, 1995), 316.

169. Ibid., 318.

170. Herzl, *The Jewish State*, in Hertzberg, *The Zionist Idea*, 226.

171. Herzl, *Old-New Land*, in Hertzberg, *The Zionist Idea*, 153.

Conclusion
The Narrow Ridge, the Razor's Edge

We made certain declarations but no attention was paid to them. In politics one is judged by one's successes.

—Martin Buber

Dimensions of Theopolitics

Conclusions typically contain balance sheets, assessments of what is living and what is dead in an object of historical study, and other such summarizing efforts. But for now these judgments may be left to readers. Instead of issuing such verdicts, I consider a few directions in which future thinking on Buber and theopolitics might turn. Some of these represent issues I intend to address in future work. All represent problems that I hope others will take up and grapple with.

First, Buber's thought was intensely concerned with *Gemeinschaft*, with "true community," in the sense that romanticisms both left and right gave to that term. Buber's *Gemeinschaft* has often been thought of in terms of his I-Thou relationship; here we considered it in terms of the theopolitical demand to embody an anarchist kingdom of priests and a holy nation. Either way, though, the ideal of political community has historically made liberals very nervous. Liberalism, after all, can be said to begin with a denial of this ideal, and disputes between various forms of liberalism and communitarianism continued to animate political theory through recent decades. Liberalism thinks of itself as being about recognizing and acknowledging the conflicts that persist—and should persist—in society, under conditions of reasonable pluralism. In response to these perennial conflicts, which stem from basic human differences that cannot be wished away or suppressed by nontotalitarian means, liberalism offers structures and frameworks through which these differences may be mediated. It reserves its idealizations for these frameworks themselves, which are represented as flawed, but decent and potentially perfectible, mechanisms to allow members of society to nonviolently exercise their freedoms, to exchange reasons and elaborate norms while being protected from the excesses of their own neighbors.[1] Yet despite what anti-liberals like Schmitt might say about liberalism's denigration of the political, the state retains its monopoly on violence in this picture, both for the purposes of police and for the national defense. Liberal thinkers, however, prefer to focus on freedom of discourse and on reason giving, with the underlying framework of violence postulated as a necessary condition of this freedom insofar as it protects the rights of minorities. From such a perspective, Buberian theopolitics may seem to lack a realistic account of how disagreements are mediated, leaping straight to an imagined communal oneness that seems neither possible nor desirable.

There is a rich recent literature on religion and democracy. The students of liberals of the previous generation, such as John Rawls, Jürgen Habermas, and Richard Rorty, have drawn on the philosophies of their teachers and responded to religionist and communitarian critiques of liberalism (from Charles Taylor, Stanley Hauerwas, and others), making the case that contemporary liberalism can allow a wider latitude for public arguments based in religion than was previously thought.[2] It is therefore not the religiosity of Buber's theopolitical ideas per se that would primarily concern these thinkers, or even his anarchism (although anarchism is subject to a line of liberal criticism), but rather his emphasis on prophecy and charisma, his apparent Judeo-centrism, and his seeming lack of interest in rational argumentation. As Randi Rashkover has argued, Buber's account of the prophetic is "insufficiently reflective."[3] If true, this charge has implications that are not merely a matter of philosophical taste—existentialism versus neo-pragmatism as flavors of contemporary thought. A theopolitics that is insufficiently reflective must also necessarily lack the ability to respond to suffering and protect the weak. It therefore holds little promise for contributing usefully to ordinary democratic life, let alone for healing the world-historical wound in Palestine.

It would take a whole article, or perhaps even a book, to respond fully to this concern, and at any rate (as I hope my discussion of his Zionism has shown) I am not interested in assuming the role of Buber advocate, defending him against all comers. Nonetheless, I emphasize two points as an initial reflection on what Buber might have said about this question, had he discussed it with liberals. First I would stress Buber's claim, made in Der Gesalbte, that "the gift of the spirit is not separated from human categories."[4] Although primarily concerned in his biblical writings to bring out what he sees as the faith of the biblical writers and editors, he frequently offers notes on how this faith might manifest in contemporary times. The category of the prophetic is frequently used today to designate religiously inspired social critique, and biblical charisma is not necessarily far from the authority earned by gifted individuals in activist settings.[5] Second, one might focus, as Cathleen Kaveny has recently done, on the place of prophetic indictment as a rhetoric existing alongside deliberative reason-exchange in our societies. Even as we note the potential dangers of this rhetoric, we can draw lessons from the paradigms of excellence in its performance, from Isaiah to Martin Luther King, to guide and inform its contemporary practice.[6]

Another potential direction for fruitful thinking on Buber and theopolitics involves comparative, collaborative work within and between the Abrahamic traditions (Judaism, Christianity, and Islam), as well as between those traditions and the secular public sphere.[7] A prominent trend in Anabaptist theology, and other Christian streams, has long singled out the conversion of the Emperor Constantine as the beginning of "Caesaropapism," a project of "Christendom" that pursued domination and forgot the teaching of Jesus that the church should be separate from the world. Contemporary efforts to make Christianity into a civil religion, united with patriotism and nationalism, are descended from Caesaropapism in this view, and thus err theologically as expressions of Christianity. Meanwhile, the contemporary scene presents us with a wide variety of states purporting to be Islamic, from Iran to Saudi Arabia, which Buber would no doubt encourage us to think of as hierocracies rather than theocracies (although, since Muslim ulama are not "priests," alternative terminology might be appropriate). These tight links between state and clergy, though often presented as typical of some timeless and monolithic paradigm of Islamic governance, have certainly also been questioned on Islamic grounds.[8] What might it mean, for thinkers compelled by these traditions, to think together with Buber and his Jewish conception of how God's own sovereignty relates to human institutions? Does depicting God as a king necessarily eventuate in oppression on earth? Or can this image, paradoxically, liberate human beings from bondage to other human beings?

One of the most important and insightful Jewish thinkers on political-theological questions today is David Novak, who typically takes a positive attitude toward liberal democracies.[9] For Novak, it is plain that this type of government has done the least harm to Jewish bodies and souls. Moreover, for Novak, the liberal-democratic state is much less likely than the monarchy, the empire, the fascist state, or the communist state to make itself into the object of idolatrous worship. Thus, although Novak worries about the potential of such a state to enact discriminatory policies if its majorities are misguided, he advocates that Jews be active and proud citizens of liberal democracies, and in this sense his views are broadly characteristic of the Jewish mainstream. Buber's theopolitics offers a challenge to this view.[10] According to Buber, there is an original covenantal model with which any Jewish theopolitics must reckon, which excludes the institutions of sovereign state, standing army, and private property (beyond a few generations) on which liberal democracies in their current forms rely. One could reply to Buber from a liberal standpoint that such institutions are desirable and necessary, but he would insist that such a response forsakes something Jewishly pivotal.[11] Keeping that core, then, may require a rethinking of the liberal concerns with pluralism and diversity from a standpoint that does not depend on the armed state to set and enforce the conditions under which that conversation takes place. What exactly that rethinking might look like is for the future to tell.

Finally, there is the question of reintegrating Buber's theopolitics with his philosophical anthropology. Having bracketed the philosophy of dialogue for the purposes of elaborating the theopolitics, it remains to be seen what might result from a thorough and conscientious remelding of the two. Such a remelding might admit that Buber's general thinking about the human being and about the nature of relationship per se plays an important role in his thinking about the lives people live together in community, without using this insight to convert the specificities of Buber's theopolitical exegeses into mere "applications" of the principle of dialogue. Creative thought on Buber and politics continues to be done through the prism of his dialogical philosophy; bringing that together with his theopolitics will certainly bear fruit for the future.[12]

The Constitution and the Jubilee

Gustav Landauer echoed and amplified Thomas Jefferson's call for a rebellion every twenty years: he called for revolution as the cornerstone of a constitution. Under the influence of his friend Martin Buber, he invoked the biblical institutions of the Sabbatical and the Jubilee:

> Let him who has ears, hear. You shall sound the trumpet through all your land! The voice of the spirit is the trumpet that will sound again and again and again, as long as men are together. Injustice will always seek to perpetuate itself; and always as long as men are truly alive, revolt against it will break out. Revolt as constitution; transformation and revolution as a rule established once and for all; order through the spirit as intention; that was the great and sacred heart of the Mosaic social order. We need that again: a new rule and transformation by the spirit, which will not establish things and institutions in a final form, but will declare itself as permanently at work in them. Revolution must be a part of our social order, must become the basic rule of our constitution.[13]

This is the underlying impulse of Buber's theopolitics, both in his interpretation of the biblical history of Israel and in his Zionism. For many years, barriers between the left and religion, communism and anarchism, postcolonialism and Zionism, and apocalyptic messianism and prophetic eschatology have prevented Buber's theopolitics from coming into clear view.

Now that Buber's theopolitics has been elucidated, what can we expect from it? It may be that theopolitics will be completely ignored. That would not be surprising. Or perhaps it will be seen as an antipolitics. The defenders of the traditional conception of politics as necessarily dependent on statehood and violence may consider theopolitics irrelevant. Or it may happen that contemporary apocalyptists, confronted by the renewed possibility of severing the Kingdom of God from the eschaton, will realize that they are political "realists" after all.

It is true that theopolitics does not promise security. Like Israel itself, both land and people, it is dependent on mercy from elsewhere. It may not be seized on by those grasping for a way out of chaos, since it offers only the narrow ridge between abysses. And even that narrow ridge is itself perilous to walk on; the narrow ridge is also the razor's edge. "Failures" are therefore inevitable. Nonetheless, even these failures may compare well with what today is usually called "success" in politics and economics.

While this book was being written, the Occupy Wall Street movement flared up, dominated the headlines, and then disappeared. In the short period of its prominence it confused many by refusing to "make demands" on the political system. Now that it seems to have died down, many shake their heads and marvel, as Max Weber did at his poor, *Weltfremde* friend, Ernst Toller, at the "idealism" of those who pursue social change outside the pragmatic path of reform through the major political parties. Without concrete goals, after all, how is one to measure one's progress or success? The question is not unreasonable.

Theopolitics severs the Final Judgment and the Last Day from the Kingdom of God. It proposes that a decent society is within the realm of possibility, and that even if the contours of such a society are hard to imagine, it should not be consigned to the far side of the messianic advent. The liberation of the human being and the redemptive healing of Creation are two different matters, and only the deepest despair could have given rise to their conflation. This after all is the lesson of the Exodus, which freed the Israelites and instituted the kingship of God, without thereby transforming the human being into something other than human. The demand for setting and achieving certain political goals is fair, which is why Buber set one political goal after another. The fact that none of these goals was met may suggest his failings as a politician, but not that the goals were inherently impossible. In this spirit, the anarchist anthropologist David Graeber, at the end of a book found in many Occupy encampment libraries, makes the following statement:

> I have largely avoided making concrete proposals, but let me end with one. It seems to me that we are long overdue for some kind of Biblical-style Jubilee: one that would affect both international debt and consumer debt. It would be salutary not just because it would relieve so much genuine human suffering, but also because it would be our way of reminding ourselves that money is not ineffable, that paying one's debts is not the essence of morality, that all these things are human arrangements and that if democracy is to mean anything, it is the ability to all agree to arrange things in a different way.[14]

What Graeber says about debt holds just as true for the seemingly intractable Israeli-Palestinian Hundred Years' War. Buber, who had once compared himself to Cassandra in the context of the Bavarian Revolution, did so again in 1947, speaking now of the *Ichud*:

Does this Cassandra act? She, too, only speaks. She does not act because she is not authorized to do so and because at this juncture action without authorization would be madness. But her speeches are as many deeds—because they point to the path. The history of the present and the coming generations will prove that her speech was action and the road indicated, the only one leading to Jewish renewal in Palestine.[15]

In nonapocalyptic politics it is possible to conduct experiments and to test their results. Before "redemption" implied the healing of creation, it meant the ransoming of captives. Thus it does not contradict Buber's basic prophetic stance when he argues that an attuned understanding of history will eventually, and not only at the End, reveal what condemns and what redeems.

Notes

1. See, e.g., Judith Shklar, "The Liberalism of Fear," in *Political Thought and Political Thinkers*, ed. Stanley Hoffmann, 3–20 (Chicago: University of Chicago Press, 1998).

2. Jeffrey Stout, *Democracy and Tradition* (Princeton, NJ: Princeton University Press, 2004); Christopher Eberle, *Religious Conviction in Liberal Politics* (New York: Cambridge University Press, 2002). Habermas has engaged intensely in these conversations himself; Jürgen Habermas, *Between Naturalism and Religion*, trans. Ciaran Cronin (Malden, MA: Polity Press, 2008); cf. Judith Butler, Jürgen Habermas, Charles Taylor, and Cornel West, *The Power of Religion in the Public Sphere*, ed. Eduardo Mendieta and Jonathan Vanantwerpen (New York: Columbia University Press, 2011).

3. Rashkover, untitled paper presented at "Martin Buber: Philosopher of Dialogue," a conference held at the Spertus Institute and University of Chicago, October 18–19, 2015. Rashkover's primary reference for Buberian theopolitics, however, is his essay "Symbolic and Sacramental Existence," from *On the Origin and Meaning of Hasidism*, ed. and trans. Maurice Friedman (New York: Horizon Press, 1960), 152–181—a text I do not address in this book.

4. SM 313.

5. Jeffrey Stout, *Blessed are the Organized: Grassroots Democracy in America* (Princeton, NJ: Princeton University Press, 2010), 94, 134, 289.

6. Cathleen Kaveny, *Prophecy without Contempt: Religious Discourse in the Public Square* (Cambridge, MA: Harvard University Press, 2016).

7. Buber also opens doors to engagements between Judaism and Chinese traditions, though not with the consistency and determination he devotes to Christianity or Islam. See Irene Eber, "Martin Buber and Taoism," *Monumenta Serica* 42 (1994): 445–464.

8. Patricia Crone, "Ninth-Century Muslim Anarchists," *Past and Present*, no. 167 (May 2000): 3–28.

9. David Novak, *Covenantal Rights: A Study in Jewish Political Theory* (Princeton, NJ: Princeton University Press, 2000); David Novak, *The Jewish Social Contract: An Essay in Political Theology* (Princeton, NJ: Princeton University Press, 2005).

10. Novak embraces many social policies that are small-*c* conservative; nonetheless, it seems fair to characterize his overall stance as small-*l* liberal insofar as it justifies and supports the institutions of liberal democracy on Jewish theological grounds.

11. He would say the same thing, of course, to any misguided advocates of a revived Jewish monarchy. And one does not have to be a monarchist to think that Buber undervalues the role of the king and the Temple in biblical religion; Jon D. Levenson, "Introduction to the 2016 Edition," in PF xxi.

12. See, e.g., Akiba J. Lerner, *Redemptive Hope: From the Age of Enlightenment to the Age of Obama* (New York: Fordham University Press, 2015), which ranges Buber alongside Richard Rorty to ask about the possibilities and limits of hope itself; and William M. Plevan, "Encounter and Embodiment: Martin Buber's Philosophical Anthropology Reconsidered," PhD diss., Princeton University, 2017.

13. Gustav Landauer, *For Socialism*, trans. David J. Parent (St. Louis, MO: Telos Press, 1978), 130.

14. David Graeber, *Debt: The First 5,000 Years* (Brooklyn, NY: Melville House, 2011), 390.

15. Buber, "The Bi-Nationalist Approach to Zionism," in *Towards Union in Palestine: Essays on Zionism and Jewish-Arab Cooperation*, by Martin Buber, Judah Magnes, and Ernst Simon (Westport, CT: Greenwood Press, 1972), 10.

Appendix
Martin Buber to Hans Kohn, October 4, 1939

Talbiyeh, Jerusalem,
Oct 4, 1939

Dear Professor Kohn,

As you surely know, the publication of longer books in German is now as well as impossible for me. So I have been thinking for some time, whether I could translate in collaboration with Palestinian friends some new works of mine into English, both manuscripts that are already finished and books not yet completed and also such that as yet are only drafted, and whether I could in the future publish as far as possible my books in English, not as translations, but as original works. Now the war compels me to make haste, as—beside the reduction of my regular income and beside the increasing expense in living—there is not any more possibility of getting allowances from my Polish estate, which has been occupied by the Russians. For this reason I should like to ask you, if you could help me to find the necessary connexions.

I have not ceased to write, but I have not published any ~~long~~ book for some years. Therefore it is now a matter of no less than 5 or 6 longer books and some short ones. All or nearly all of them are in my opinion of interest for the English and American public.

The longer works are:

1. The Problem of Man. It ~~contained~~ consists of two parts: a historical account of the question, "What is Man?" and a critical inquiry into some attempts of our time (especially Heidegger and Scheler) to answer it. This is a philosophical treatise, already finished, of about 150 pages, containing some conceptions of importance, and not very difficult to understand.
2. The Faith of Israel (outline of a history of Hebrew religion till the end of Babylonian exile; it is what I call "Glaubensgeschichte"). This book of about 250 pages I have finished some days ago. Although it is based on independent research and contains many new things as well in exegesis as in history of religion, it is written in rather popular style. I was induced to write it by a

request of Prof. Van der Leeuw, the known Dutch historian of religion, to write the section on the religion of the Old Testament for a general history of religion composed by Christian Dutch scholars only—I am the only Jew between them. In the fury of writing it became double the size agreed upon, and I am obliged to condense, but I would publish the whole unabridged in another language. The authorisation of the Dutch editor will be available.

3. A Hasidic novel, dealing with the wars of Napoleon, as seen with the eyes of Polish Jewry. I wrote it some years ago and was not wholly satisfied with it. I think it necessary to rewrite it, but I have the impression it will be read more than all my other books. Of course it is now a most actual subject.

4. I am also thinking of composing a collection of Hasidic stories and anecdotes and a fellow-book on Hasidism and its function in the history of religion out of published and unpublished matter of mine.

5. Judaism and Christianity. Till now there is only a rough draft of this book (that will contain about 300 pages) and stenograms of my three Frankfort courses on the subject. The book consists of 3 parts: 1. The God, 2. Sin and redemption. 3. The Messiah. This book too can be understood by a wide public.

6. Religion and Politics. For this book there is only a pile of schemes and sketches. It shall contain 3 parts: a history of the relation between religion and politics, from ancient China up to our time; a systematic disquisition with examples; and practical conclusions for the main problems of actual society, state and civilization. I cannot yet say anything about the volume of the book, but certainly this will be the most voluminous of all my books— and perhaps the most important too.

The little manuscripts are:

a. On Education (about 100 pages), consisting of the already published "Rede uber das Erzieherische" (revised), a lecture on character education and one on national education (of course antinationalist). The second and the third lecture were delivered before a Jewish public (at Jerusalem) and treat some Jewish problems beside the general theme.

b. Power and Powerlessness of the Spirit, two Jerusalem lectures of actual interest (about 50 pages).

c. Abraham, an exegetical paper, rather easy to understand (about 60 pages).

As you see, ~~two~~ some of the longer books have not yet received their final form, and one of them has to be elaborated altogether. To be able to perform this big piece of work beside my university courses, I must free myself of all the petty cares of the next future. You will understand me better, if you will realize, that not only Raphael's daughters are receiving their education in our house, but also Eva and her family (that are now provided at Ben Shemen most scantily and for an undetermined time) are needing our help and perhaps will need it yet much more. What I must therefore strive to find, is an institution, who will grant me for some time an adequate allowance, in return for which I should deliver now my finished manuscripts and in a space of time to be agreed upon the [illegible] other books mentioned. The settling of accounts would have to be made in some way on the basis of the returns from the sale of the books.

~~This is an appeal to your friendship. I am sure, we have are still bound to each other and we have still a common cause, which will be supported by your help to me.~~ [These lines are covered by a single pencil line in four strokes—possibly in Kohn's hand, to indicate his intention to omit this text in the version of the letter forwarded to Adolph Oko. —Ed.]

Please communicate with the men that could take part in promoting the scheme. As yet I have not written about it to anyone, but I think of writing to Dr. Oko.

I shall be very grateful for an early reply, if only temporary.

With kind regards,   Yours faithfully,   Martin Buber

If the circumstances will permit, I should like to undertake a lecture tour to America in the autumn of 1940. [Added along the left side of page 3. —Ed.]

Selected Bibliography

Avnon, Dan. *Martin Buber: The Hidden Dialogue*. 20th Century Political Thinkers. New York: Rowman & Littlefield Publishers, 1998.

Barton, Natalie. "The Jewish Expectation of the Kingdom According to Martin Buber." PhD diss., Ludwig-Maximilians Universität, 1967.

Ben-Ezer, Ehud. *Unease in Zion*. New York: Quadrangle Books, 1974.

Brody, Samuel Hayim. "Is Theopolitics an Antipolitics? Martin Buber, Anarchism, and the Idea of the Political." In *Dialogue as a Trans-Disciplinary Concept: Martin Buber's Philosophy of Dialogue and its Contemporary Reception*, edited by Paul Mendes-Flohr, 61–88. Studia Judaica Band 83. Berlin: Walter de Gruyter, 2015.

Buber, Martin. *A Believing Humanism: My Testament, 1902–1965*. Translated by Maurice Friedman. New York: Simon & Schuster, 1967.

———. *Ben Am Le-Artzo*. Jerusalem: Schocken Press, 1945 [Hebrew].

———. *Briefwechsel aus sieben Jahrzehnten, Band I: 1897–1918*. Heidelberg: Lambert Schneider Verlag, 1972.

———. *Briefwechsel aus sieben Jahrzehnten, Band III: 1938–1965*. Heidelberg: Lambert Schneider, 1975.

———. *Darkho shel Miqra*. Jerusalem: Mossad Bialik, 1997 [Hebrew].

———. *The First Buber: Youthful Zionist Writings of Martin Buber*. Edited and translated by Gilya G. Schmidt. Syracuse, NY: Syracuse University Press, 1999.

———. *Israel und Palästina: Zur Geschichte einer Idee*. Zurich: Artemis-Verlag, 1950.

———. *Königtum Gottes*. Berlin: Schocken Verlag, 1932.

———. "Landauer und die Revolution." *Masken: Halbmonatschrift des Düsseldorfer Schauspielhauses* 14.18–19 (1919): 282–291.

———. *The Martin Buber Reader: Essential Writings*. Edited by Asher Biemann. New York: Palgrave Macmillan, 2002.

———. *Martin Buber Werkausgabe. Band 2.1: Mythos und Mystik. Frühe religionswissenschaftliche Schriften*. Edited by David Groiser. Gütersloh: Gütersloher Verlaghaus, 2013.

———. *Martin Buber Werkausgabe. Band 3: Frühe jüdische Schriften, 1900–1922*. Edited by Barbara Schäfer. Gütersloh: Gütersloher Verlaghaus, 2007.

———. *Martin Buber Werkausgabe. Band 14: Schriften zur Bibelübersetzung*. Edited by Ran HaCohen. Gütersloh: Gütersloher Verlaghaus, 2012.

———. *Moshe*. Tel Aviv: Schocken Press, 1945 [Hebrew].

———. *On Judaism*. Edited by Nahum N. Glatzer. New York: Schocken Books, 1995.

———. *On the Bible: Eighteen Studies*. Edited by Nahum N. Glatzer. Syracuse, NY: Syracuse University Press, 2000.

———. "On the History of the Problem of Individuation: Nicholas of Cusa and Jakob Böhme." Translated by Sarah Scott. *Graduate Philosophy Journal* 33.2 (2012): 371–401.

———. *On Zion: The History of an Idea*. Translated by Stanley Godman. Syracuse, NY: Syracuse University Press, 1997.

———. *Netivot Be'utopia*. Tel Aviv: Am Oved, 1947.

———. "Die Revolution und Wir." *Der Jude* 3.8–9 (November–December 1918): 345–347.

———. *Torat Hanevi'im*. Tel Aviv: Mossad Bialik, 1950 [Hebrew].

———. *Two Types of Faith*. Translated by Norman P. Goldhawk. Syracuse, NY: Syracuse University Press, 2003.

———. "Warum muss der Aufbau Palästinas ein sozialistischer sein?" In Martin Buber, *Kampf um Israel: Reden und Schriften (1921–1932)*, 283–302. Berlin: Schocken Verlag, 1933.

Buber, Martin, and Franz Rosenzweig. *Scripture and Translation*. Translated by Lawrence Rosenwald and Everett Fox. Bloomington: Indiana University Press, 1994.

Buber, Martin, Judah Magnes, and Ernst Simon, eds. *Towards Union in Palestine: Essays on Zionism and Jewish-Arab Cooperation*. Westport, CT: Greenwood Press, 1972.

Cohn, Margot, and Rafael Buber, eds. *Martin Buber: A Bibliography of His Writings, 1897–1978*. Jerusalem: Magnes Press, 1980.

Di Cesare, Donatella Ester. "Martin Buber and the Anarchic Utopia of Community." Unpublished manuscript.

Gordon, Adi. "Nothing but a Disillusioned Love: Hans Kohn's Break from the Zionist Movement." In *Against the Grain: Jewish Intellectuals in Hard Times*, edited by Ezra Mendelsohn, Stefani Hoffman, and Richard I. Cohen, 117–142. New York: Berghahn Books, 2013.

Gordon, Peter E., and John P. McCormick. *Weimar Thought: A Contested Legacy*. Princeton, NJ: Princeton University Press, 2013.

Graeber, David. *Debt: The First 5,000 Years*. Brooklyn, NY: Melville House, 2011.

Harvey, Warren Zev. "Kingdom of God." In *20th Century Jewish Religious Thought*, edited by Arthur A. Cohen and Paul Mendes-Flohr, 521–525. Philadelphia: Jewish Publication Society, 2009.

Hattis, Susan Lee. *The Bi-National Idea in Palestine during Mandatory Times*. Haifa: Shikmona, 1974.

Kant, Immanuel. *Anthropology, History, and Education*. Edited by Günter Zöller and Robert B. Louden. Translated by Mary Gregor, Paul Guyer, Robert B. Louden, Holly Wilson, Allen W. Wood, Günter Zöller, and Arnulf Zweig. Cambridge: Cambridge University Press, 2007.

Kaplan, Leonard, and Rudy Koshar, eds. *The Weimar Moment: Liberalism, Political Theology, and Law*. Lanham, MD: Lexington Books, 2012.

Kedar, Aharon. "Brith Shalom." *Jerusalem Quarterly* 18 (Winter 1981): 55–85.

Kepnes, Steven. *The Text as Thou: Martin Buber's Dialogical Hermeneutics and Narrative Theology*. Bloomington: Indiana University Press, 1992.

Kohn, Hans. *Martin Buber: Sein Werk und seine Zeit. Ein Versuch über Religion und Politik*. Hellerau: Jakob Hegner Verlag, 1930.

Kuhn, Gabriel, ed. *All Power to the Councils! A Documentary History of the German Revolution, 1918–1919*. Oakland, CA: PM Press, 2012.

Landauer, Gustav. *Anarchism in Germany and other Essays*. Translated by Stephen Bender and Gabriel Kuhn. San Francisco: Barbary Coast Publishing Collective, 2005.

———. *Anarchismus. Ausgewählte Schriften, Band 2*. Edited by Siegbert Wolf. Hessen: Verlag AV, 2008.

———. *Antipolitik. Ausgewählte Schriften, Band 3.1.* Edited by Siegbert Wolf. Hessen: AV Verlag, 2010.

———. *Beginnen: Aufsätze über Sozialismus.* Edited by Martin Buber. Köln: Marcan-Block Verlag, 1924.

———. "Ein Leumundszeugnis für Herrn John Henry Mackay." *Der Sozialist*, October 10, 1898.

———. *Nation, Krieg, und Revolution. Ausgewählte Schriften, Band 4.* Edited by Siegbert Wolf. Hessen: Verlag Edition AV, 2011.

———. *Philosophie und Judentum: Ausgewählte Schriften, Band 5.* Edited by Siegbert Wolf. Hessen: AV Verlag, 2012.

———. *Revolution.* Berlin: Karin Kramer Verlag, 1974. Originally published as *Die Revolution.* Frankfurt: Rütten and Loening, 1907.

———. *Revolution and Other Writings: A Political Reader.* Edited and translated by Gabriel Kuhn. Oakland, CA: PM Press, 2010.

———. *Sein Lebensgang in Briefen.* 2 vols. Edited by Martin Buber. Frankfurt: Rütten & Loening, 1929.

———. *Skepsis und Mystik: Ausgewählte Schriften, Band 7.* Edited by Siegbert Wolf. Hessen: Verlag Edition AV, 2010.

———. *Der Werdende Mensch: Aufsätze über Leben und Schrifttum.* Edited by Martin Buber. Potsdam: Kiepenheuer, 1921.

Lebovic, Nitzan. "The Jerusalem School: The Theopolitical Hour." *New German Critique* 105, 35.3 (Fall 2008): 97–120.

Maurer, Charles B. *Call to Revolution: The Mystical Anarchism of Gustav Landauer.* Detroit: Wayne State University Press, 1971.

Mendes-Flohr, Paul. "Martin Buber's Reception Among Jews." *Modern Judaism* 6.2 (May 1986): 111–126.

Mendes-Flohr, Paul, and Anya Mali, eds., with Hanna Delf von Wolzogen. *Gustav Landauer: Anarchist and Jew.* Berlin: Walter de Gruyter, 2014.

Mendes-Flohr, Paul, and Jehuda Reinharz, eds. *The Jew in the Modern World: A Documentary History.* 3rd ed. New York: Oxford University Press, 2011.

Moonan, Willard. *Martin Buber and His Critics: An Annotated Bibliography of Writings in English Through 1978.* London: Routledge, 1981.

Moore, Alan, and David Lloyd. *V for Vendetta.* New York: Vertigo, 1995.

Mühsam, Erich. *Liberating Society from the State and other Writings: A Political Reader.* Edited and translated by Gabriel Kuhn. Oakland, CA: PM Press, 2011.

Oppenheimer, Franz. *The State.* Montreal: Black Rose Books, 2007.

Rashkover, Randi, and Martin Kavka, eds. *Judaism, Liberalism, and Political Theology.* Bloomington: Indiana University Press, 2014.

Ratzabi, Shalom. *Anarchism in "Zion": Between Martin Buber and Aharon David Gordon.* Tel Aviv: Am Oved, 2011 [Hebrew].

———. *Between Zionism and Judaism: The Radical Circle in Brith Shalom, 1925–1933.* Leiden: Brill, 2002.

Rosenzweig, Franz. *On Jewish Learning.* Edited by Nahum N. Glatzer. Madison: University of Wisconsin Press, 2002.

———. *Philosophical and Theological Writings.* Edited and translated by Paul W. Franks and Michael L. Morgan. Indianapolis: Hackett, 2000.

Schaeder, Grete. *The Hebrew Humanism of Martin Buber*. Translated by Noah J. Jacobs. Detroit: Wayne State University Press, 1973.

Schilpp, Paul Arthur, and Maurice Friedman, eds. *The Philosophy of Martin Buber*. Library of Living Philosophers 12. La Salle, IL: Open Court, 1991.

Schmitt, Carl. *The Concept of the Political, Expanded Edition*. Translated by George Schwab. Chicago: University of Chicago Press, 2007.

———. *The Crisis of Parliamentary Democracy*. Translated by Ellen Kennedy. Cambridge, MA: MIT Press, 1988.

———. *Dictatorship*. Translated by Michael Hoelzl and Graham Ward. Malden, MA: Polity Press, 2014.

———. *The Leviathan in the State Theory of Thomas Hobbes*. Chicago: University of Chicago Press, 2008.

———. *Political Theology: Four Chapters on the Concept of Sovereignty*. Translated by George Schwab. Chicago: University of Chicago Press, 2005.

———. *Political Theology II: The Myth of the Closure of Any Political Theology*. Translated by Michael Hoelzl and Graham Ward. Malden, MA: Polity Press, 2008.

———. *Roman Catholicism and Political Form*. Translated by G. L. Ulmen. Westport, CT: Greenwood Press, 1996.

Scholem, Gershom. "Martin Buber's Hasidism, A Critique." *Commentary* 32 (1961): 305–316.

———. *The Messianic Idea in Judaism and Other Essays on Jewish Spirituality*. New York: Schocken Books, 1995.

———. *On Jews and Judaism in Crisis*. Edited by Werner J. Dannhauser. New York: Schocken Books, 1976.

———. *On the Possibility of Jewish Mysticism in Our Time & Other Essays*. Edited by Avraham Shapira and translated by Jonathan Chipman. Philadelphia: Jewish Publication Society, 1997.

Schwarzschild, Steven. "Buber and His Biographer." *Judaism* 34.3 (Fall 1985): 433–443.

Shafir, Gershon. *Land, Labor and the Origins of the Israeli-Palestinian Conflict, 1882–1914*. Cambridge: Cambridge University Press, 1989.

Silberstein, Laurence J. *Martin Buber's Social and Religious Thought: Alienation and the Quest for Meaning*. New York: New York University Press, 1990.

Simon, Ernst Akiva. "Jewish Adult Education in Nazi Germany as Spiritual Resistance." *Leo Baeck Institute Yearbook I*, edited by Robert Weltsch, 68–104. London: East and West Library, 1956.

Taubes, Jacob. *The Political Theology of Paul*. Translated by Dana Hollander. Edited by Aleida Assmann and Jan Assmann, with Horst Folkers, Wolf-Daniel Hartwich, and Christoph Schute. Stanford, CA: Stanford University Press, 2004.

Urban, Martina. *Aesthetics of Renewal: Martin Buber's Early Representation of Hasidism as Kulturkritik*. Chicago: University of Chicago Press, 2008.

Weber, Max. *Political Writings*. Edited by Peter Lassmann and Ronald Speirs. New York: Cambridge University Press, 1994.

———. *The Vocation Lectures*. Edited by David Owen and Tracy B. Strong. Translated by Rodney Livingstone. Indianapolis: Hackett, 2004.

Index

SAMUEL HAYIM BRODY is Assistant Professor of Religious Studies at the
University of Kansas.